American
Political
Parties

Social Change and Political Response

AMERICAN POLITICAL PARTIES

Social Change and Political Response

Everett Carll Ladd, Jr.
University of Connecticut

W · W · NORTON & COMPANY · INC · New York

For
Carll, Corina, and Melissa

Contents

PREFACE   ix

INTRODUCTION: SOCIETY, POLITICAL AGENDA, CHANGE, AND
THE PARTY RESPONSE   1

  Environment: The Political Agenda as an Organizing Principle   1
  The Concept of Sociopolitical Periods   2
  Periods and Parties   3
  Party Position and the Meaning of *Party*   7
  Change, Yes; Development, No   9
  The Plan of the Book   10

Part I
THE AMERICAN SETTING
FOR POLITICAL PARTIES

1. THE ADVENT OF PARTY   15

  The Nature of Aristocracy   16
  The Collapse of Aristocracy   18
  The Meaning of Egalitarianism   20

2. CONFLICT, CONSTITUTION, AND PARTY   28

  Conflict Situations   34
  Constitutional Setting   45
  Change within the Bounds of Continuity   53

Part II
PARTIES IN THE SWEEP OF
AMERICAN SOCIETAL EXPERIENCE

3. THE PARTIES IN THE RURAL REPUBLIC   57

The Society and Its Political Agenda   57
The Party System, 1790–1860: A Structural Overview   79
The Parties: Positions in the Agenda   85
The Parties in Electoral Competition   93
Race, Conflict and the Party System   103

4. THE PARTIES IN THE INDUSTRIALIZING NATION   109

The Society and Its Political Agenda   109
The Party System, 1865–1925: A Structural Overview   147
The Parties: Positions in the Agenda   150
The Parties in Electoral Competition   166
The Parties in the Industrializing Nation   177

5. THE PARTIES IN THE INDUSTRIAL STATE   180

The Society and Its Political Agenda   180
Social, Economic, and Political Power:
    Ascensions and Displacements   187
The Party System, 1926–1970: A Structural Overview   205
The Parties: Positions in the Agenda   207
The Parties in Electoral Competition   228
The Parties in the Industrial State   240

6. ON THE FUTURE OF AMERICAN POLITICS: THE
    EMERGENT SOCIETY AND THE PARTY SYSTEM   243

The Condition and Meaning of Mass Affluence   243
The Technological Society   256
Class and Status: Changes in the Cutting Edge of Conflict   267
The New "Political Class": Style, Power, and Public Philosophy 275
The Parties and the Emergent Society   281

BIBLIOGRAPHICAL COMMENTARY   313

Index   317

Preface

Histories of political institutions have been written from any number of perspectives, so I should state at the outset the concerns and premises which guided this history of the party system in the United States. The two centuries of America's existence as an independent nation have been the most dynamic in world history, and furnish an immense body of information on how changes in the larger society require changes in political life. Students of comparative politics have long described the differences among political systems found in different sorts of social systems as the latter are territorially distributed; they have given less attention to political variations resulting from differences in social setting in a single country *over time*. This history of the American party system is a work in comparative politics along a *temporal* rather than a *territorial* dimension. I think that political parties offer an especially good focus for such comparative political investigations because they are so sensitive to many of the principal political reflections of change in the society: new political demands; transformations of interests, interest groups and coalitions; the alteration of the basic structure of conflict.

Examinations of the relationship of changes in the party system to other changes in the social system often raise the matter of causal priority. Which should be seen as the dependent variable? While there is obviously a process of continuous interaction, it seems that the burden of the flow is toward the parties. Attention will be directed to the response of the party system to social change because that appears to be the principal direction of response in the interrelationship. Put differently, I see the parties as creatures of American society, and argue that changes in the party system can be understood only in the context of social change.

Looking back over the two years this study was in progress, I am keenly aware of how heavy my debts to others are. This book was a collective endeavor, and I want to express my deep appreciation to those who have worked with or otherwise assisted me.

The efforts of three persons deserve special recognition. Charles D. Hadley, now on the faculty of Louisiana State University, assisted in all phases of data gathering and analysis. Mrs. Eleanor Wilcox was the principal typist of the several drafts of the manuscript, and she helped me meet the schedule I had set, often, I know, at the cost of considerable inconvenience to herself. Mrs. Anne-Marie Mercure typed portions of the manuscript, assisted in the production of the tables and figures, supervised the work of student associates, and was a valuable source of editorial advice.

Many of my students at the University of Connecticut were employed in data collection and organization. Mitchell Cohen was a valued associate throughout the project. Others who assisted are Robert Atwell, Thomas Breen, Richard Giampa, Mary Turner Hadley, Lauriston King, Burt Roffman, and John Wadsworth.

This study benefited from several research facilities. I drew heavily upon the survey holdings of the Connecticut Social Science Data Center. Most of these data were made available to the Connecticut Center by the Inter-University Consortium for Political Research and the Roper Center for Public Opinion Research. Computer analysis was done on the University's IBM 360-65 facility, which is supported in part by grant GJ-9 from the National Science Foundation.

I wish to thank, for their thoughtful criticism and encouragement, Professors Walter Dean Burnham of Washington University, Theodore J. Lowi of the University of Chicago, and Seymour Martin Lipset of Harvard University, three colleagues and friends who read an earlier draft. It is hard to imagine an author's being privileged to receive more expert advice than they provided.

American Political Parties profited greatly from the careful attention of Donald S. Lamm of W. W. Norton. I would be quite remiss if I did not here acknowledge his assistance in the revision of the manuscript, as well as his consideration for my peace of mind throughout the endeavor.

Finally, I want to thank my wife, Cynthia, and my children Carll,

Corina, and Melissa. This expression is not dictated simply by affection.
Each gave up things he or she would have preferred so that I would be
free to write the book, and each with unfailing good humor tolerated a
cantankerous author.

E. C. L.

Storrs, Connecticut
February 1970

Introduction:
Society, Political Agenda, Change,
and the Party Response

This is a history of the American political parties which focuses upon the response in the party system to substantial and continuing changes in American society. It seeks to describe the effective environment in which the parties have operated. The environment of any political institution, of course, is complex. There are the other political institutions and processes with which it interacts—the other components of the political system. And the environment extends to the entire social system of which the political system, is precisely, a subsystem. Given this extent and complexity, any treatment of the environment of the American party system must be highly selective; it must focus on those interactions which most affect the structure and operation of the parties. Political parties are in ordered relationships with other components of the social system, but the implications of these relationships vary enormously. Both the sun and a small man-made satellite exert gravitational pull on the earth. Yet is there any doubt which one an account of the gravitational system in which the earth is located would emphasize?

Environment: The Political Agenda as an Organizing Principle

In this volume we will discuss a number of ways in which the many dimensions of the American societal experience have shaped and constrained the party system. One emerges with special importance as an

1

organizing principle, and receives prominent treatment throughout our analysis. This is the concept of an *agenda of politics*. Every society generates its distinctive coalitions of political interests, and these in turn make demands on the public sector. The many relationships of contending groups and interests come together in a conflict situation, involving the scope and substance of disagreement over public policies and the relative strength of the several sides to these disagreements. The political agenda encompasses those things which the political system is concerned with and the manner, from symbolic representation to formal policy response, in which it deals with them.

The centrality of the concept of an agenda of politics in a study of political parties becomes apparent when one notes that parties live off disagreements in the society about what purposes government should serve. They are constantly at work ordering and arranging the agenda, seeking out positions on which to build majority support. They do not create the agenda, but more than any other political institution they are at all times involved with it. Just as the complex mix of societal relationships dictates the general content of the agenda of politics, so the agenda determines the boundaries of party competition and conflict.

The Concept of Sociopolitical Periods

As societies evolve, of course, agendas change. New policies and new controversies appear, and some things which were thought to be pressing problems cease to concern the body politic. This matter of the constantly changing agenda will occupy our attention. In a relatively static social order, the problem of keeping up with the political agenda is not difficult; once set, it persists. The items become familiar. But in a society as dynamic as the United States, items are added and deleted with extraordinary rapidity. Thus the agenda of the mid-1890s bears little resemblance to that of the 1840s, the one of 1936 has little in common with that of 1896, and the political agenda of the United States at the end of the 1960s is very different indeed from the agenda at the middle of the New Deal.

Clearly, every piece of social change the United States has experienced has not substantially altered the political agenda. But the *accumulation* of changes at certain points has. The components of a setting are never completely static, are subject to a wide array of changes which begin at different points and progress at different rates; finally, these merge to produce a new sociopolitical setting substantially different from the preceding one. This brings us to the concept of a *sociopolitical period* as a reference to the persistence of an underlying set of social and economic relationships and its accompanying political agenda over a bloc of time. In this volume we suggest the basis for ordering 180 years of American societal experience in four great sociopolitical periods, each defined not by the passing of years but by the changing of society. Chapters 3 through 6 develop the case for each as a reasonably coherent setting, and describe the fabric of partisan conflict and competition each sustained.

The four periods we identify are analytical abstractions. As useful as this periodization schema is as a device to help us distinguish the forest from the trees in a constantly changing social and political landscape, it presents us with some sticky problems as well. Just how much change must occur before we decide that one sociopolitical period has been replaced by another? We argue, for example, that the span of time from regime formation up to the Civil War should be considered a single period. Other analytical perspectives, however, could break (indeed have broken) these seven decades into at least two periods. Many analogies to this problem can be found. Picture a large tub of bright blue paint into which a tube is slowly releasing drops of yellow pigment. The original color is at once changed, but no eye would describe the changes as "significant" for a time. Then depending on the observer and the intended use, the point is reached where a new color is said to have emerged. Are blue and green the different colors, with all else but variations of these "true" colors? Or are the various intervening shades perceived as "distinctly different"?

In the present study, we stand rather far back from the object, a century and three-quarters of American political life. The four sociopolitical periods we identify and work with differ more on the order of blue and green than, say, bittersweet and burnt orange.

Periods and Parties

The Majority Party as "Sun"

Some states have had prolonged periods when the only competition was among factions of a dominant party, but nationally in the United States two-party competition has been the rule. The two national parties, however, have rarely been evenly matched. Most of the time, one has been clearly ascendant, in Samuel Lubell's words the "sun," with the other big party a "moon" in orbit about it.[1] The rising and setting of these majority party suns have been few and far between in American political history: the Jeffersonian Republican party was such a majority sun, so too the Jacksonian Democrats; after the Civil War the Republican sun rose slowly, then blazed brightly until it set in the night of the Great Depression, and the Democratic sun moved quickly up over the horizon.

Describing the majority-minority party relationship in terms of sun and moon, while a bit confused astronomically, is useful since it calls attention to the great continuities in the basic structure of American party competition. Just as social change has been continuous but fundamental transformations of the social setting few and far between, so party competition has varied in numerous ways from election to election but underlying patterns can be seen to endure over prolonged periods of time. Many observers have detected a close and powerful relationship between sociopolitical period and these "sun and moon" associations of the major parties. The way Lubell put it is insightful, if in one regard confused:

Each time one majority sun sets and new sun rises, the drama of American politics is transformed. Figuratively and literally a new political era begins. For each new majority party brings its own orbit of conflict, its own particular rhythm of ethnic antagonisms, its own economic equilibrium, its own sectional balance. . . . Each new majority party also brings its own opposition.[2]

There is a relationship between the rise of a new majority party and the beginning of a new political era, but it appears to be in the opposite direction from what Lubell suggests: it is not the new majority party which brings "its own orbit of conflict," but rather a new "orbit of conflict" which often requires a new majority party. Or, to put it a bit more precisely, a party holds majority status because in political style, social group support, and general policy orientations it speaks to the ascendant concerns and constituencies of a sociopolitical period.

In each period in American history, a loose collection of social groups can be identified whose political style, interests, values, and policy orientations were controlling for the society. These majority coalitions

1 Samuel Lubell, *The Future of American Politics* (Garden City, N.Y.: Doubleday, 1956), Chapters 10, 11.
2 *Ibid.*, p. 216.

have been highly variegated, but typically have been built around some social collectivity which by its numbers, other resources (especially economic), and/or strategic location has been especially influential. Such collectivities we call *political classes*. Independent, land-owning farmers were the political class in the United States from regime formation until the Civil War. There was nothing approaching unanimity of opinion among such agriculturalists on all matters of public policy in the period. Still, they were the political class. They had similar orientations to work, similar expectations about what government should and should not do, and they shared a general conception of what the good society looked like. Their vision of America guided the Republic, their positions on the items of the political agenda determined the broad outlines of public policy response. Around this political class, majoritarian electoral coalitions formed. And after the Civil War, a new political class of entrepreneurial businessmen gradually displaced the old, and around the "new class" new majority electoral coalitions gathered.

Majority parties in the United States have held their ascendant status for prolonged periods because they have served as electoral vehicles for coalitions of interests that were majoritarian; they have been the party "homes" for the preponderance of the elites of the majority coalitions. In style and policy, they have best met the interests and desires of those coalitions. We are making a fully compatible argument when we find the majority party holding its ascendant status because it is "the party of the agenda." The composition of a majority coalition and the content of a political agenda are both products of an underlying social setting. The majority party has succeeded in articulating those policy positions which the majority coalition has demanded.

In no instance in 180 years of American party life has a national minority party become the majority party other than through the movement from one basic sociopolitical setting to another. This is not to say, however, that movement from one setting or period to the next necessarily requires the establishment of a new majority party. It is possible for a majority party to be so transformed that it becomes the instrument of a new majority coalition as it was of the old; indeed, we will argue in Chapter 6 that this appears to have happened in the contemporary period. Nor must a majority party survive throughout the reign of a majority coalition. A party organization may disintegrate, leaving the majority coalition to look for a new home. This occurred in the first period after regime formation. The Jeffersonian Republicans became the "sun" as the party of agrarian America. So successful were they that—aided by the strategic errors of their Federalist opponents and the general fragility of political parties as new political organizations— they found themselves after 1817 the only national party. This situation could not last. Party organization atrophied without competition. Eventually, factional struggles deepened, and new party organizations took shape around the contending factions. In 1840, as in 1810, land-owning farmers were the political class; but they were no longer operating through the Republican party, a party killed by success.

One large qualification is in order. The relationship—societal setting ——→majority coalition + political agenda——→majority party—simply has not been so neat and clear in the real world as the above discussion suggests. Chapters 3 through 6 will demonstrate that the relationship holds, but it holds along the order of prevailing tendencies. One important factor muddying the picture has been the determined effort most of the time of both big parties in the national two-party system to find support throughout the society, and specifically within the political class. They have had ample opportunities. Big social collectivities in the United States have never been unified political forces pursuing carefully defined political interests. So it has never been the case that all or nearly all members of a political class/majority coalition have provided a coherent constituency for the majority party—which the latter in turn has serviced in some single-minded fashion. The relationship we have sketched here and which we develop in the chapters that follow is intended only to account in a general way for the long day of the American majority party suns, to explain that their ascendancy has not been some casual development but has been linked tightly to the larger course of American social experience.

The Minority Party as "Moon"

Calling the minority party the "moon" suggests not only that it has glowed less brightly than the majority "sun," but that it has been bound in some fixed way to the majority and that it has been forced to follow a course determined by the majority. This has indeed been the case, and the relationship can be seen primarily in terms of policy response. The majority party as the party of the agenda has staked out policy positions to which the minority continually has had to react. This has given it two basic courses of action. At times it has said, "Me too, only a bit differently." That is, it has accepted the policy orientations of the majority as basically sound, and has sought to persuade the electorate that it could accomplish the specified objectives a little better. It has directed its *primary* appeals to many of the same interests the majority party represents. Following this, the minority party has been able to win when it has nominated a decidedly more attractive candidate or when the majority has been plagued by division, scandal, and the like.

Often, in pursuit of this strategy, the minority party has resorted to nominating candidates able to generate strong nonpartisan appeals. For example, of the Whig party candidates between 1836 and 1852, only Henry Clay in 1844 was a man of Whig principles; William Henry Harrison in 1836 and 1840, Zachary Taylor in 1848, and Winfield Scott in 1852 were army generals, better known for feats upon the field of battle than for political activity. A century later, the Republicans chose this course in nominating General Dwight Eisenhower.

Some in the minority party, of course, do not court the majority coalition, for they are opposed to what it seeks. The minority party of a two-party system necessarily becomes the principal vehicle for all those social groups which resent and resist the prevailing responses to the political agenda of the period. The majority party cannot readily be captured by the dissenters of an agenda, for it is the primary instrument for the majoritarian position. It is the minority party which is vulnerable. To take a prominent example, in the presidential elections of 1896, 1900, and 1908, with William Jennings Bryan its candidate, the Democratic party was "captured" by agricultural dissenters from the course of American industrialization. The party rode in futile battle against the policy definitions of the then-majority Republicans. When the minority follows this course and lends its name to those interests fundamentally dissatisfied with prevailing public policy, it risks disastrous defeat— unless it is the point of transition from one social setting to another. The Democrats paid this price with Bryan. The Republican nomination of Senator Barry Goldwater in 1964 represents the same type of minority party response—a frontal assault—and had the same result.

There has been a constant tension in the weaker of the two big parties, then, between those who would make the party a slightly altered carbon copy of the majority and those who would direct it to some basic challenge of the majority.

Party Position and the Meaning of *Party*

In the chapters which follow, we examine the positions of the political parties in the policy struggles of the several sociopolitical periods in

American history. Just what is understood by *party* when we describe
party position? The question is important because three quite distinct
constructions of *party* are often encountered.

1. Party as Organization

There is the formal machinery of party ranging from local committees (precinct, ward, or town) up to state central committees, and
the people who man and direct these. The party is "the organization" or
"the machine."

2. Party as the Mass of Supporters

Millions of Americans think of themselves today as Republicans or
Democrats. For some, this identification is strong, and they consistently
back candidates running under the party label. For others, the attachment is relatively weak and casual. Here, party exists in the eyes of its
beholders; it is a bundle of electoral loyalties.

3. Party as a Body of Notables

Most political leaders in government and outside it are identified by
a party label. *Party* is sometimes used to refer to that collectivity of
notables who accept the party label, and party policy then becomes the
prevailing policy tendencies among this collectivity.

Obviously, these are not in fact three separate entities but rather
components of one broader structure: we agree with Sorauf's view of
party as a "tri-partite system of interactions."[3] But the components are
sufficiently distinct that we must be quite precise as to which we have
in mind. For example, if the question is asked, "Is the Democratic party
in South Carolina a strong party?" the answer can be either yes or no,
depending on the component. As an organization, the South Carolina
Democracy is extremely weak and ineffective; but the Democratic party
as a bundle of loyalties in the South Carolina electorate is still potent.

As we describe the policy positions of the parties, we are thinking of
the third component, party as a body of notables. At no time has there
been party organization—for example, a central committee—able to
issue authoritative and binding pronouncements in the name of party
elites. Party organization in the United States has never made policy.
As for the rank-and-file adherents of the respective parties, they have

[3] Frank Sorauf, *Party Politics in America* (Boston: Little, Brown, 1968), p. 10.

been on the whole far less involved in and conversant with policy matters than their party leaders, and, partly because of this, less distinct or differentiated programmatically.[4] The policy positions of the parties as we describe them below are the positions of party notables.

Change, Yes; Development, No

This volume is centrally concerned with *response and adaptation* in the political parties. It is *not* a book about the *development* of the American party system, for the simple yet basic reason that there has not been very much development.

Throughout the sweep of modern—post-seventeenth-century—history, there have been basic changes in technology and economic life which have precipitated far-reaching transformations of society. These techno-logical-economic changes, while occurring at different rates in different countries, have been largely unidirectional: capacity has steadily in-creased, capacity to harness or dominate the physical environment, capacity to produce goods and services. Our long exposure to unidirec-tional technological and economic change has given birth to a notion of development generally as *steady movement toward some increased capacity,* and this has been carried into our thinking about politics. But has there been development—thus understood—in political systems? And if so, precisely what type?

Political development is sometimes described as change in which the political system's capacity to maintain itself—its legitimacy—is in-creased. But by this standard it simply is not clear whether there has been any development of the American political system over the last 150 years. The French political system in 1700, with an aristocratic regime, apparently had a higher degree of legitimacy, a greater capacity to maintain itself than at any time in the nineteenth century. The shift from ascriptive class to egalitarian societies invariably has been ac-companied by a crisis of legitimacy of regime, of varying intensity and duration.

It seems clear that the steady growth of technological and economic capacity—properly described as economic development—has permitted,

[4] See the careful study by Herbert McClosky and his colleagues, "Issue Con-flict and Consensus Among Party Leaders and Followers," *American Political Science Review* (June, 1960), pp. 406–427; and Angus Campbell, *et al., The American Voter* (New York: John Wiley, 1960), especially Chapters 8 and 9.

even demanded, certain parallel political responses. Advances in communications and transportation have moved political systems away from localism and parochialism, toward larger and larger units of operation. The industrially advanced society requires enormously complex social organization, and large governmental bureaucracies as well as private bureaucratic structures are testimony to this; the more interdependent the society, the more complex the tasks of management. Such political responses to far-reaching technological and economic growth can properly be described as *political development*. But thus understood, it does not seem that development has been a prime component of the changes and adaptations in American parties in response to the many facets of a dynamic environment.

The Plan of the Book

In looking at the American party system, one must be impressed both by the large measure of change and by the massive continuities. These reflect change and continuity in the broadest dimensions of the American societal experience. It is hard to imagine a society which has changed so much and yet in a number of fundamental regards remained so much the same. *Beaucoup de choses changent, plus peut-être restent pareil.* What has changed and what has remained the same dictate the organization of this book.

Part I describes the partisan products of those social features which have not much changed. Three continuities stand out. (1) The United States was, at regime formation in 1789, an egalitarian society heavily suffused with an ideological tradition we refer to as *Liberal*. It is still that. Chapter 1 discusses this, and shows how these societal conditions made this country the birthplace of parties as durable and permanent features of the political landscape. (2) Although the issues have changed many times over the last 180 years, the *scope* and *depth* of conflict has remained remarkably constant. (3) Constitutional arrangements in the United States in most basic regards have endured. In Chapter 2, we describe how these continuities in conflict and constitution have resulted in a distinctive type of American party system. If a citizen of the 1970s were miraculously picked up and deposited back in the age of Andrew Jackson, he would find many things different and "old-fashioned," but the *type* of party system would be impressively similar.

Still, there have been changes aplenty. When the Constitution was ratified the United States was a rural and agricultural nation of 4 million. Today we are more than 200 million, and the society is urban, industrial, and complexly integrated. What kinds of responses in the party system have been required by such societal transformations? They are greatest, we find, in the related areas of policy position and constituency. Partisan disagreements are defined by the political agenda, and the agenda has continued to change. Parties are coalitions of interests, and the composition of these coalitions and their competitive relations have been greatly altered. In Chapters 3 through 6, we describe party conflict and competition in the context of four great sociopolitical periods in American history.

PART

I

THE AMERICAN SETTING FOR POLITICAL PARTIES

1

The Advent of Party

The gradual development of the principal of equality is, therefore, a Providential fact. It has all the chief characteristics of such a fact: it is universal, it is durable, it constantly eludes all human interference, and all events as well as all men contribute to its progress. . . . There is a country in the world where the great social revolution which I am speaking of seems to have nearly reached its natural limits. . . . The emigrants who colonized the shores of America in the beginning of the seventeenth century somehow separated the democratic [egalitarian] principle from all the principles which it had to contend with in the old communities of Europe, and transplanted it alone in the new world.

—ALEXIS DE TOCQUEVILLE, *Democracy in America*

The American party system is three-quarters through its second hundred years, and thus is the oldest in the world. When, in the 1790s, parties took shape in the United States and began a struggle for control of government in popular election contests, their architects really had no model on which to build, no blueprints to follow. A new political institution was being established. Today, political parties are found throughout the world. While it is not true that parties are a universal— present in all contemporary states—they are found in such widely disparate, sociopolitical settings as the United States, the Soviet Union, China, India, South Africa, and Venezuela.[1]

[1] We agree with the proposition that some institutions called political parties in developing countries really do not meet the criteria. ". . . [it seems] logical not to think that a small band of African oligarchs constitutes a political party. If we bear this caveat firmly in mind, we can better understand why and how it is possible in many post-colonial nations for so-called 'political parties' both to materialize and to disappear with rapidity" (Joseph LaPalombara and Myron

Political parties may be less than two centuries old and of Western origins, having first appeared fully defined in the United States. Politics, however, surely precedes party. So the question arises: Why did this structure, which now appears to be such an integral part of the political life of many nations, appear so late? What are the necessary social conditions for political parties? What has taken place in the last two centuries or so to require the performance of functions previously not performed, and thus to require the formation of a new political institution to perform them? Such an inquiry is necessarily large and involved, and we will have to ask the reader to permit us to engage in generalization so broad as to demand modification if more extended treatment were possible.

A set of social and economic transformations began in the seventeenth and eighteenth centuries in Western Europe, the various dimensions of which have received different names: *egalitarian,* if the focus is on participation or involvement in the making of decisions for the system; *industrial,* if we look at economic life; *scientific;* and *technological,* if attention is drawn to the explosion of knowledge. These egalitarian-industrial-technological changes can properly be described as a revolution; and from its beginnings in Europe in the seventeenth century, this revolution has progressed through a number of stages and has pushed out geographically to become global. The egalitarian revolution has produced important modifications in political institutions and processes, and the advent of parties is a part of this. Political parties are children of egalitarianism. They have no place in pre-egalitarian societies, and their presence in some form which denotes the basic commonality of function cannot be avoided in any egalitarian system.

The Nature of Aristocracy

We can begin to understand the egalitarian revolution and the manner in which it produced the social base for new political institutions like parties by noting its enemy—what it was directed against. It was an attack on *ascriptive class societies,* societies in which social position was

Weiner, *Political Parties and Political Development* [Princeton: Princeton University Press, 1966], p. 29). The problem of how *political party* is to be construed will occupy us below, and it is enough here to note that the label may get attached to rather traditional cliques or factions simply because political parties are such "natural"—i.e., frequently encountered—institutions in the middle of the twentieth century.

determined by birth.[2] These are commonly called *aristocratic* since *aristocracy* is a generic name for the hereditary ruling class of an ascriptive class society. The aristocracy, a small fraction of the population, typically possessed a monopoly of all or nearly all the components of high social position, such as wealth, prestige, and power, and occupied a position of legally defined privilege. Most people in aristocratic societies were blanks, having no say in the social, economic, and political decisions of the system, and were permanently fixed in a distinctly subordinate position.

The varieties of aristocratic ideology defended legal and social inequality, feudal privilege, and arbitrary government as being in the proper and unalterable nature of things. Societies were conceived of as organic, not atomistic. Each class had a fixed place in the society, and duties and obligations to it which had to be met for the well-being of the whole. In the corporal analogies so common to ideological defenses of aristocracy in Europe, the superordinate-subordinate relationship of nobles and peasants was likened to that of head and limb. What nonsense it would be to speak of the equality of the two. They are naturally different in their abilities, and each has its proper place and function. The one will never occupy the position of the other, nor should it. The head decides for the human body, and so does the aristocracy for the society.

There is much more, of course, and varieties of aristocratic defenses are as numerous as the varieties of aristocratic experience. But a primary component of political ideology in flourishing ascriptive societies has been the definition of permanent subordinate status for broad social groups and their complete exclusion from the decision-making processes as natural and proper.

The great nineteenth-century French social commentator Alexis de Tocqueville made his principal contribution in exploring the collapse of aristocratic and the birth of egalitarian societies. Tocqueville may have been more impressed by certain features of aristocracy than most cur-

---

[2] There presumably never was an ascriptive class society completely lacking in social mobility, in which position at birth and at death were everywhere the same. In England in 1600, for example, there was limited mobility for the handful of wealthy export merchants who bought estates and were absorbed into the landed gentry, and for hired laborers who became small leaseholders. But if English society of that time is viewed as a two-tiered system, as it legitimately can be, it is evident that movement between the upper class and the lower orders was so sharply limited as to be, in terms of the expectations of the bulk of the population, impossible. For extended treatment of this, see Lawrence Stone, *The Crisis of the Aristocracy* (Oxford: Oxford University Press, 1965).

rent observers, but allowing for this charitable evaluation of its potential, his analysis is penetrating:

The nobles, high as they were placed above the people, could not but take that calm and benevolent interest in their fate which the shepherd feels toward his flock; and without acknowledging the poor as their equals, they watch over the destiny of those whose welfare Providence had entrusted to their care. The people, never having conceived the idea of a social condition different from their own, and never expecting to become equal to their leaders, received benefits from them without discussing their rights. They became attached to them when they were clement and just, and submitted to their extractions without resistance or servility, as to the inevitable visitations of the Deity. . . . As the noble never suspected that anyone would attempt to deprive him of the privileges which he believed to be legitimate, and the serf looked upon his own inferiority as a consequence of the immutable order of nature, it is easy to imagine that some mutual exchange of goodwill took place between two classes so differently gifted by fate.[3]

The Collapse of Aristocracy

Ascriptive class societies have not been historical rarities; in their various forms, indeed, they represent the dominant variety of post-primitive society. Egalitarian societies are historically exceptional. The massive repudiation of aristocratic arrangements after the seventeenth-century in Western Europe and since then throughout the world thus is among that handful of fundamental political events. It is also an event requiring a far more elaborate and systematic analysis than we can give it here. But some threads in the explanation are evident enough.

In the first instance, with the transition from agricultural to industrial societies, there was an expansion of resources. Under what conditions is it possible that the millions will readily acquiesce to extensive privileges for the few from which they and their children are formally and permanently excluded? Only when there is in fact no possibility of most men living beyond bare subsistence, no matter what the manner of distribution. In societies of gross scarcity, if any culture is to flourish, it is only by arbitrarily granting privilege to a few. Aristocracy offers a morally tenable standard for parceling out values only in scarcity-bound societies. Let the pie dramatically expand—and that is what the economic-technological developments began to achieve in the

---

[3] Alexis de Tocqueville, *Democracy in America* (New York: Mentor, 1956), p. 31. Tocqueville was not unaware that aristocracy often did not meet its potential. His *L'Ancien Régime et la révolution* is a scathing indictment of the failure of the French aristocracy before 1789.

seventeenth and eighteenth centuries—and groups of men outside the hereditary privileged class will step forward to claim their share, will come to feel that life owes them something other than perpetual wretchedness. With the prospect of continuing growth in economic output, it became possible, not a cruel hoax, to say as Jefferson did in the American Declaration of Independence that *all men* have a birthright to the vigorous pursuit of earthly happiness.

There is a continuing interaction between physical and psychological processes, between events and ideas. The economic stirrings of industrialization created new expectations. Masses of men came to believe that they could change the way they lived. Society became more and more secularized, as energies were channeled into altering the here and now. It became possible to view man in a different light, as a sovereign being with rights, not merely duties. "Individualism," Tocqueville wrote in *Democracy in America,* "is a novel expression, to which a novel idea has given birth. Our fathers were only acquainted with *egoism* (selfishness)." Individualism is a luxury of societies which see the possibility of escaping the absolute domination of scarcity.

In the West during the seventeenth and eighteenth centuries, new ways of viewing man's psychological apparatus which provided the intellectual underpinnings of individualism were formulated. The brain came to be seen in the best scientific thought as a simple Newtonian machine. Ideas come from the senses. The job of the brain is organizing the sensations brought to it. If the inputs (the sensations drawn from the individual's environment) can be controlled, then the output (that is, the way a person thinks and perceives, indeed, the type of person he is) can be determined. This brain, this simple machine, is approximately the same for all men: the outputs are different (that is, men are different) only because the inputs vary. The brain, Locke wrote, is at birth an "empty cabinet," a "white paper," "void of all characters, without any ideas." What man becomes depends upon what his environment causes to be placed or written in it.[4]

4 See John Locke, *Essay Concerning Human Understanding,* 2 vols. (Oxford: Oxford University Press, 1894). Their mechanistic psychology and sensationalist epistemology gave many philosophers of the seventeenth and eighteenth centuries great confidence in the possibilities of social engineering. They were uncompromising environmentalists. The eighteenth-century French *philosophe* Claude Adrian Helvetius, for example, argued at length in his writings that it was possible through legislation to so structure the environment in which citizens live that all could be made virtuous: "If citizens could not procure their own private happiness without promoting that of the public, there would then be none vicious but fools" (*De l'esprit,* or *Essays on the Mind and Its Several Faculties* [London, 1759], Essay II, Chapter 22, p. 111). See my essay "Helvetius and

This is heady stuff. Men are approximately equal in natural capabilities; they differ in performance only because the environments of some are less good. How, then, is the permanent privilege of the aristocracy to be justified? They are simply men blessed with better environments. In sum, just as the economic expansion of the industrial revolution created the material output to offer promise to common men that life had something for them beyond gross deprivation, the intellectual basis of individualism was developed through a view of man's psychology that attributed performance to environment.

Still other events promoted popular involvement in the social, economic, and political life of nations. Developments in transportation and communications increased the flow of information and ideas among an ever-larger audience. The level of education increased enormously, and new groups were given the intellectual tools to participate in public life. With the growth of technology, scientific knowledge became an important resource in contests for power. "Gradually the diffusion of intelligence," Tocqueville observed, "caused learning and talent to become a means of government; mental ability led to social power, and the man of letters took a part in the affairs of the state. The value attached to high birth declined just as fast as new avenues to power were discovered."[5]

Society became more heterogeneous and differentiated as economic development produced new social groups. An entrepreneurial class can certainly be found prior to the seventeenth and eighteenth centuries, but there was a tremendous expansion of this "middle class" and a proliferation of specialized professional groups. Having arrived at positions of economic importance in the new order, operating from new centers of power which the economy had generated, confident in their ability to understand the world and to participate in it, told by the new ideologies that there was no tenable basis for the continued privilege of the hereditary ruling class, these middle classes launched their demands for change in the structure of participation, demands which we call egalitarian.

The Meaning of Egalitarianism

The egalitarian revolution was not made to produce a social situation in which everyone was in fact in a position equal to that of all others.

---

d'Holbach: 'La moralisation de la politique'," *Journal of the History of Ideas*, 22 (April–June, 1962), pp. 221–238.

[5] Tocqueville, *Democracy in America*, p. 27.

Rather, it insisted that achievement be substituted for birth as the determinant of status; that new social groups be involved in the vital decisions affecting social, economic, and political life; that politics cease to be a closed affair played out among members of an hereditary elite. Although its initial movers were the entrepreneurial classes so enormously strengthened in the early phases of industrial development, the appeals tended to be universalistic, and the economic-technological transformations which nourished them did not stop in 1800. Thus, the egalitarian revolution has gone through a number of stages, each extending the processes begun in the West in the seventeenth and eighteenth centuries. Each successive stage has required that new social groups be included among those whom elites must "take into account." Put somewhat differently, the egalitarian revolution in its various stages has changed the status of more and more social groups from *blanks* to *participants,* in the sense that they could no longer be ignored by those making social, economic and political decisions for the system.

It is hard to be sufficiently precise about the category *participants,* those who must be "taken into account," but the political implications of transforming masses of citizens from blanks to participants are evident enough. Compare, for example, dictatorial or authoritarian regimes in egalitarian and pre-egalitarian societies. In the latter, the ruler(s) could afford to attend to the masses in a casual or occasional manner. Referring to this casualness in the regimes of Louis XV and Louis XVI in France, Tocqueville wrote that "they only trampled on the people whom they did not see."[6] The absolute monarch could ignore most of the populace as blanks. But the citizenry of an egalitarian society cannot be ignored, and absolutist-inclined leaders must develop far more elaborate machinery for their supervision, manipulation, mobilization and control. We have a new word for absolute dictatorship in an age of *mass as participants:* totalitarianism.

The Soviet Union today is an egalitarian society. Its citizens are not "taken into account" through democratic processes, but neither are they ignored in decision-making like the peasantry of Tsarist Russia. There is an ideology, Communism, which posits the idea that the masses have a right to be considered. As a technologically advanced society, the Soviet Union requires much of its common men if the promise of technology—both for the people and for the power of the state—is to be realized. For the U.S.S.R. to grow to super-power status between 1918 and 1958, it was necessary that millions of Soviet citizens be pro-

[6] Tocqueville, *L'Ancien Régime et la révolution* (Oxford: Oxford University Press, 1933), p. 117.

foundly changed in value orientations and economic roles, and this could not have been accomplished by ignoring them. Besides, if the absolutist elite of an egalitarian society ever tried to ignore the mass of inhabitants as the old monarch could and did, it would almost certainly be overthrown by a counter-elite appealing to the many as an instrument in the power struggle. In sum, although the ways in which the massive number of participants of an egalitarian society are considered vary markedly from democratic to authoritarian regimes, the situation of mass involvement is readily distinguished from the complete exclusion practiced in ascriptive class societies.

The transition from an aristocratic to an egalitarian system can best be understood in terms of the expansion of the participant category. Aristocratic orders had their participants, but this group was not numerous. In England in 1600, for example, it can be said to have included the groups Stone identifies as (a) "great export merchants," and (b) "plain gentlemen, mostly small landed proprietors but also in part professional men, civil servants, lawyers, higher clergy, and university dons." The ruling elite would then be his "county elite," the upper gentry "who controlled county politics under the patronage of the local nobleman, who provided the M.P.s and Deputy Lieutenants, and who dominated the bench of Justices"; and, of course, the monarch and the titular peerage.[7] The elite thus defined numbered about 600 families, and the participants were no more than 2 percent of the population:

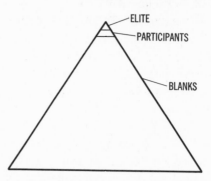

In contrast, in an egalitarian society such as the United States today, a large majority of the population are participants. No effort has been made to compute the numbers with any arithmetic precision, and severe problems in defining the categories are really not being confronted. But if the elite is thought of generally as those with significant direct in-

[7] Stone, pp. 51–52.

fluence over major decisions, and the participants as those who must be paid attention to in some regular and continuing fashion by the elite, then the following is probably a fair visual representation:

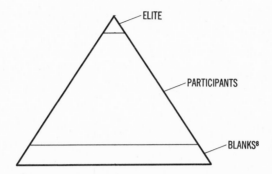

These immense changes in the structure of participation which we describe as egalitarian have occurred at different times and speeds in various nations. Great Britain was already launched into the egalitarian revolution in the 1600s, but its extension was gradual over the next two centuries. In France, this revolution began much later, and when it did begin, the movement was rapid and violent. The old aristocratic order in France, though mortally wounded in 1789, did not quickly or easily expire, and the middle classes continued to battle with aristocratic remnants throughout the 1800s. The egalitarian revolution began not in eighteenth- but in twentieth-century Russia, and followed a still different course. The United States, "the first new nation," presents yet another pattern: we were, in Louis Hartz's words, "born liberal," born egalitarian.[9] Settled at the very time that ascriptive class arrangements were coming under severe challenge in western Europe, and settled, moreover, predominantly by the lower and middle classes; the United States proved hostile to aristocratic transplants, and they never really took root.

The egalitarian revolution progressed farthest and fastest in the United States because as virgin territory there was little here in its way, and we were in the nineteenth century the country to which those seeking to assess the political implications of egalitarianism looked. So many of the modifications in political institutions and processes which have followed from egalitarianism first appeared in the United States. We

[8] Among the blanks in contemporary America would be such disparate groups as at least a portion of the "invisible poor," those who are grossly apolitical, and the mentally deficient. *Participant* is not, of course, an undifferentiated category.

[9] Louis Hartz, *The Liberal Tradition in America* (New York: Harcourt, Brace & World, 1955).

had universal manhood suffrage more than a half-century before the British. We had the first regularly functioning and broadly representative legislatures in the world. And we had the first party system.

The Variety of Party in Egalitarian Societies

This brings us directly to the question of what a political party is, or to put it differently, what basic functions party performs. We can begin by talking about the principal manifest function of party as *linkage,* the linkage of participants and the decision sectors. Certain structures in pre-egalitarian societies have performed limited linkage functions, of course. Cabals, cliques, factions are all names for more-or-less organized groups of leaders attempting to influence or control decision-making. But with egalitarianism, the segment of the population which must be considered becomes mass, and performance of the linkage function must be more formal, regularized, continuous, and organizationally elaborate. Political parties are brought into this in several ways. They set up some ongoing organization at the local level, and provide for regular relationships between local units and others in national decision sectors, such as a national party bureaucracy or a party organization in the legislature. They also offer their names, as symbol reference, to leaders and a mass citizenry; thus they are an important vehicle for promoting popular cohesion for—and against—leaders and their programs. They provide common political identities for elites and the rank and file: "You can't tell the players without a scorecard." Party as symbol is thus a link, a source of cues and direction. This elaborate linkage is designed to achieve the more effective governance or control of the polity.[10]

The genus *party* thus defined is found only in egalitarian political climates. But there are many species of party which show adaptation to the variety of egalitarian climes. We can consider some of these and the kinds of environments which produce them.

In the first place, the neatness of the analytic dichotomy egalitarian–pre-egalitarian has no empirical equivalent: societies go through a period in which they are becoming increasingly egalitarian. The United States was more egalitarian in 1836 than in 1800, Britain more egalitarian in

[10] Other political institutions, such as interest groups, are engaged in linkage in egalitarian societies. We agree with Sorauf that many organizations "serve as political intermediaries between the micro-politics of the individual and the macro-politics of political institutions and political systems." Linkage is a demanding activity in an egalitarian society, and parties are a prominent, but not exclusive, instrument for performing it. See Frank Sorauf, "Political Parties and Political Analysis," in William N. Chambers and W. Dean Burnham, eds., *The American Party Systems* (New York: Oxford University Press, 1967), pp. 34–36.

1884 than in 1832.[11] Political parties assume different forms when a country is near the beginning of its egalitarian transformations than when it is approaching the end. Compare, for example, the structure of the Liberal party in Great Britain in 1850 with that of the Labour party in 1925. It is generally agreed that the modern political party appeared in Britain with the organization of local registration societies by the Liberals after the 1832 Reform Act, which extended the suffrage. But mass participation was still relatively limited in 1850; witness the high degree of popular political deference, and the fact that less than 20 percent of the adult male population could vote. In this "halfway house" toward egalitarianism, the Liberal party of 1850 operated on informal caucuses and a weak and decentralized organization. Party "members" were not numerous, and were relatively notable people. In contrast, the Labour party in a far more egalitarian Britain in 1925 was a mass party. Party affairs were much more formalized, constituency organization more extensive and regular.[12] In general, linkage by parties becomes more elaborate and routinized as the society becomes increasingly egalitarian, that is, as the number of participants expands.

Parties bear the marks of the point in history in which the egalitarian transformations which summoned them occurred. In countries like the United States in which egalitarianism came early, the first parties typically evolved out of the activities of legislators. In the case of both the Federalists and the Jeffersonian Republicans, the legislative group first took shape, then local electoral organization appeared; finally, the two were permanently linked. The parties were formed as like-minded legislators became aware of and responded to the implications of a popular suffrage. Great Britain in the nineteenth century provides another example of parties of legislative origins becoming increasingly aware of the need for extra-parliamentary organization with the extension of the suffrage in the reforms of 1832, 1867, and 1884. But parties growing out of later egalitarian thrusts, or arising in countries affected later by egalitarianism, typically have had quite different births. Those formed in

---

[11] The historian Lee Benson (*The Concept of Jacksonian Democracy* [Princeton: Princeton University Press, 1961]), in arguing against the notion that the Whigs were merely an extension of the old Hamiltonian Federalists and the Democrats of Jefferson's Republicans, maintains that the American political system had become far more egalitarian in 1836 than it was in 1800. He suggests that the second quarter of the nineteenth century be described as the "Age of Egalitarianism."

[12] See Samuel H. Beer, "Great Britain: From Governing Elite to Organized Mass Parties," in Sigmund Neumann, ed., *Modern Political Parties* (Chicago: University of Chicago Press, 1956), pp. 9–57.

the late nineteenth century and since have been for the most part of extra-parliamentary or external origin, having grown out of existing groups, associations, or movements. Thus, socialist parties were often established by trade unions, as the Trade Union Congress in Britain created the Labour party to serve as its electoral-legislative arm early in this century. Another variation of the externally created party can be seen in developing countries where nationalist movements transformed themselves into political parties. In still another version, the political party took shape where there was neither a legislative system or colonial domination: the Communist party of the U.S.S.R. is this type of externally created party.

The more leisurely process of parties taking shape as legislative elites respond to the need for constituency organization before a growing electorate is largely a European-North American phenomenon, occurring at the beginning of the egalitarian revolution in the eighteenth and early nineteenth centuries. Since then, even in states with parliamentary systems, new parties have generally had their roots in extra-parliamentary movements. Why? After the early period, the models for political parties and other mass organizations were present; the egalitarian society was not something being groped toward, but had concrete form. Thus, the gradual process of a legislative elite slowly coping with more participants was no longer tenable.

The extra-parliamentary parties continue to bear the mark of the movement or association which created them, or from which they evolved. One commentator maintains that they remain more centralized than parties of legislative origins, are more disciplined, more ideologically coherent. Their legislative elites are less independent of extra-legislative organization, which possesses a greater motive force in the life of the party.[13]

Parties vary widely in structure and function from regime to regime. In a democracy, power tends to flow up over the links of party: party allows the rank and file to participate more effectively in the selection of leaders and in passing judgment on their performance. Parties are preoccupied with all phases of organizing and contesting elections. In a totalitarian state such as the Soviet Union under Stalin, in contrast, the

---

[13] Maurice Duverger develops at some length this distinction between internally and externally created parties (*Political Parties,* 2nd English ed., revised [New York: John Wiley, 1959] , xxiv–xxxvii). There is more than a little evidence, it should be noted, that under some conditions the influences of extra-legislative origins can be eroded. Witness the heightened prominence and influence of the legislative elites of such European socialist parties as the Labour party in Britain and the Social Democratic party in West Germany.

flow of power is almost uniformally downward. Party assumes a form by now familiar: the totalitarian mass party, the single party, superordinate to the state, brooking no dissent, "the all-powerful, infallible, protective, transcendent Party; the Party raised to the dignity of an end in itself. . . ."[14] The party exists to permit a ruling elite to shape, organize, and mobilize public opinion, to persuade and educate, to communicate decisions which it has taken, to keep tabs on the widespread enterprises of an enormously complex system, to achieve something approaching central direction over lower levels of administration involved in the implementation of policy and programs. "Democracy" and "totalitarianism," of course, do not exhaust the range of types of regimes; the mixes of democratic and authoritarian forms are many, and each places different requirements on the party system.

Because of these and many other environmental factors, parties and party systems have taken diverse shapes in egalitarian societies. Party systems can be classified by the number of parties, the structure of competition, the sources of conflict and the ideological configurations which conflict assumes, and the extent of the involvement of the parties in the policy processes or outputs of the political system. Parties can be described comparatively in terms of their organizational structure, the meaning of membership in them, how disciplined and centralized they are, what they see as their proper relationship to the state. But in all this it is important that genus and species not be confused. That basic commonality of function which makes it entirely proper analytically to refer to Communist in China and Republican in the United States as two species of the genus party is that both are organizations set up in egalitarian societies to link mass citizenry with decision sectors with the central objective of effectively governing the system.

The American party system took shape in the closing years of the eighteenth century as a principal early response in political institutions to egalitarianism. The *type* of party system then formed reflected the many features of the sociopolitical setting which was the United States of that time, and the *changes* and *adaptations* in the party system speak to the continuing transformations of American society.

14 Duverger, p. 122.

2

Conflict, Constitution, and Party

On March 4, 1841, Martin Van Buren, the "Little Magician," yielded to Benjamin Harrison, the "Hero of Tippecanoe," the presidency of a largely agricultural nation of 17 million. The America of Van Buren and Harrison seems in many ways far removed from the one we occupy, a technologically advanced, intensely interdependent, metropolitan nation of 200 million. Yet the party system in which they operated does not appear quaint or exotic. Indeed, in some very obvious ways it much resembles our own. When Democrats and Whigs grappled for power, the term "two-party system" conveyed the same mixture of truth and fiction that it does now. In *most* of the major election contests, and above all in that for the presidency, only candidates described as Whigs or Democrats won. If *party* is thought of as a bundle of loyalties in an electorate which surface around a name or symbol, and if *system* refers only to the totality of party conflict, then in the late 1830s, the 1960s, and indeed throughout most of our history we have had what Clinton Rossiter has described as a "persistent, obdurate, one might almost say *tyrannical* two-party system."[1] But if *party* instead suggests a *unified, integrated organization,* the U.S. had in Van Buren's day—and it still has—something very unlike a two-party system. There has never been any substantial national party bureaucracy, no equivalent of the central office of the parties of the European left. Our national parties have been, organizationally, only loose alliances of autonomous state parties. There were twenty-six state party systems in 1841 in just the sense that there are now fifty state party systems. Even this fails to do justice to the decentralization, for in many cases state parties too have been organizationally elusive, little more than coalitions of largely independent local

[1] Clinton Rossiter, *Parties and Politics in America* (Ithaca, N.Y.: Cornell University Press, 1960), p. 3.

units. The governmental parties, officeholders bearing the party label, have never functioned as coherent, disciplined policy instruments. Many of the key legislative enactments in the 1830s and 1840s, as in the 1960s, were made by informal bi-party alliances.[2]

The Whigs and Democrats resembled Maurice Duverger's "*cadre parties*": groupings of activists "for the preparation of elections, conducting campaigns and maintaining contact with the candidates."[3] They lacked a mass *membership* in the sense of persons formally enrolled, card-carrying and dues-paying. There were no "official formalities" in admission, and, as Duverger wrote of cadre parties generally, "no precise criteria of membership and only the adherent's activity within the party [could] determine the degree of participation."[4] Adherents or supporters the Whigs and Democrats had aplenty, but not members. This is still the case. A voter becomes a Republican or a Democrat simply by declaring himself that. There is no one to stop him, and he takes on no responsibilities when he makes the declaration. To participate in primary elections for selecting the party's candidates, a voter has at most to declare his affiliation at some specified time prior to the primary, and he may change this stated affiliation as *he* wishes. In six states, he may cast his vote in the selection of the Republican or Democratic candidates without ever disclosing which party he prefers: American parties, in short, have always offered their names promiscuously to any and all wishing them.[5]

[2] The *degree* of unity in the legislative parties has varied from one period to another. So have the bases of disunity. Sibley has shown, for example, that sectional divisions were not as influential in congressional voting in the 1840s.

[3] Maurice Duverger, *Political Parties,* 2nd English ed., revised (New York: John Wiley, 1959), p. 64.

[4] *Ibid.,* p. 71. Duverger distinguished between *cadre* and *mass* parties. In the latter he included the parties of the European Left which made membership an explicit act and which built party activity intimately upon the membership. Of the French Socialist party he wrote: "In its eyes the recruiting of members is a fundamental activity, both from the political and the financial standpoints. In the first place, the party aims at the political education of the working class. . . . Secondly, from the financial point of view, the party is essentially based upon the subscriptions paid by its members . . ." (p. 63). His prototype for the cadre party was that "party of notables," the old Radical Socialists of France. Duverger recognizes that parties often do not fit neatly into the cadre and mass types, and specifically that the fit is bad in the case of "heterogeneous" American parties (p. 65). But the core of his distinction is whether mass membership is formal and entails explicit responsibilities. Since it never has in the United States, the American parties are properly described as of the cadre variety.

[5] The six states are those with the "open primary": Alaska, Michigan, Minnesota, Montana, Utah and Wisconsin. The statement that the voter takes on no responsibilities when he declares party affiliation is qualified only slightly by the fact that some states permit observers at the polls in primary elections to challenge declarations by voters of their party attachments, and require those challenged to

The major parties in 1841 were not doctrinal or even programmatic, and neither are the major parties today. Tweedledum and Tweedledee, some have called them. This isn't true, of course. There have been substantial policy differences between the parties, but these have existed as "controlling tendencies" within each body of party leaders, not as neat doctrinal fissures. Parties in America have not been instruments for formulating and, if in power, implementing sharply differentiated program packages. The Whigs in the late 1830s and the 1840s were the most likely home of men of commerce and industry; they were the principal spokesmen for a newer, more integrated, money-based and commercial society. The Democrats in national conflict did stand as the main defenders of the "old republic," the more localized agricultural society.[6] But though there were significant policy differences between the primary thrusts of the Whig and Democratic leadership (as in our day between Democrats and Republicans), it would be far from correct to raise pictures of a party of tillers of the soil in unremitting and coherent policy conflict with a party of businessmen. That never occurred. *Business* and *agriculture* were loose categories, and there wasn't a sharply defined *business interest* or *agricultural interest*. Many developments like those in transportation were welcomed by some in agriculture and some in business, and were resisted by others in both camps. Both parties contained disparate groups, and interests were never neatly polarized.

The diversity of those marching behind Whig and Democratic banners was certainly substantial. The new Whig coalition, like its opponent, embraced (though not in equal numbers) protectionists and antiprotectionists, those who favored the bill to recharter the Second Bank of the United States and those who opposed it, states' rights advocates and strong nationalists, businessmen and farmers. Nothing about this, however, should surprise an American accustomed to a Republican party

take an oath of loyalty—to the principles of the party or to its candidates. Since ballots are secret, however, such pledges are unenforceable.

[6] There can be little doubt that a clear majority of prosperous businessmen had come, by the early 1840s, to support the Whigs. This touches a hot point in the argument among historians over the nature of Jacksonian democracy. But the increasing preference of men of business for the Whigs in the 1830s and 1840s is now rather well documented. Frank Gatell has examined the party affiliations of New Yorkers who in 1845 were worth $100,000 or more:

	WHIG	DEMOCRAT
(n = 642)	84.3%	15.7%

"New York money in 1845," Gatell concludes, "was decidedly Whig" (Frank Otto Gatell, "Money and Party in Jacksonian America: A Quantitative Look at New York City's Men of Quality," *Political Science Quarterly*, 82 [June, 1967], p. 243).

which houses men as far apart as John Lindsay and Strom Thurmond, or a Democractic party with Lester Maddox and L. Mendel Rivers as well as Eugene McCarthy and Carl Stokes. Presumably any political party has some internal ideological disagreements, but the big American parties in the days of Jackson and Van Buren as today have contained the *entire* spectrum of substantial ideological argument. In the major disagreements party leaders have found many behind their own banner with whom they disagree as strongly as with anyone following the opposition standard.

The distinctiveness of the American pattern perhaps becomes clearer if we look at three alternate models of conflict between two parties. None of these can be found in its pure form in the real world. In the first, every leader of Party *A* finds those of his own party with whom he has the greatest policy differences closer to him than *any* of those in Party *B*.

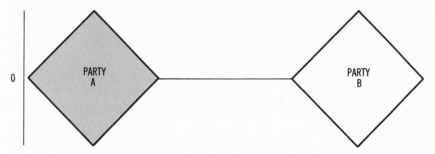

Spectrum of ideological argument[7]

In the second, some in Party *A* find themselves closer to some *Bs,* but those near the centers of the two parties are closer in policy terms to all their fellow partisans than to any in the opposition.

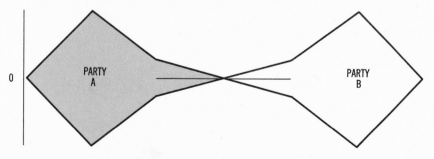

Spectrum of ideological argument

[7] The *spectrum* is intended as an illustrative device, *not a theoretical description.* We wish only to suggest that elites recognize *distance* between their policy preferences and those of others; some positions are very acceptable, i.e., very close to one's own, and others totally unacceptable.

In the third, even those leaders occupying the ideological center of *A* find as many in *B* close to their position as they do in their own party.

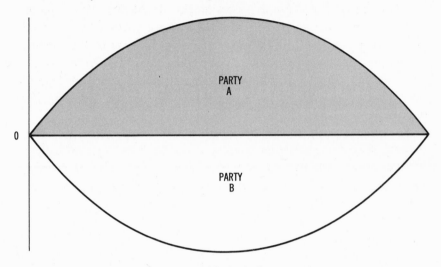

Spectrum of ideological argument

The United States throughout its history has been closer to the third than to either of the first two models. It has not been precisely the third; if it had, our parties would in fact have been Tweedledum and Tweedledee. Instead, the distribution of party leaders over the spectrum of ideological argument has tended to look like this:

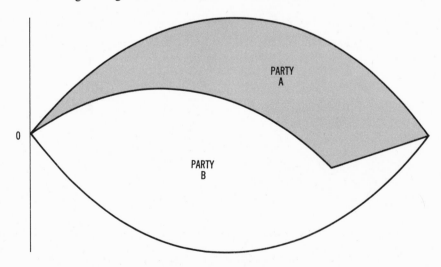

Spectrum of ideological argument

It is in this sense that our big coalitions have "stood for something" while harboring substantial differences.

The parties of the 1840s, like those of the 1960s, practiced a politics of accommodation. In Rossiter's happy description, American parties have been "creatures of compromise . . . vast, gaudy, friendly umbrellas under which all Americans, whoever and wherever and however minded they may be, are invited to stand for the sake of being counted in the next election."[8] In accommodation politics, the search goes on for appeals to win votes in most if not all major social groupings. This practice of talking as though support among all social collectivities was expected differs sharply from that in many European countries, where parties have often spoken as if it would be unnatural and indeed in a sense undesirable if some other groups of partisans found them attractive.

Reference to the historical existence of an *American party system* means not only that since 1800 there have been parties here, but that there has been a particular type of party going about its business in the governing process with a particular style. Some elements of continuity in our party system are to be expected: the United States has been a democracy, and all parties in democratic politics should share some characteristics which set them apart from the varieties of party in nondemocratic regimes, such as a preoccupation with the election process. But ours has been a distinctive type of democratic party system. The basic continuities can be summed up under the headings *Structure* and *Style:*

STRUCTURE

Two-party system
Party organization: weak; decentralized; independent state and local
   units
Supporters rather than members
Undisciplined, noncoherent governmental parties

POLITICAL STYLE

Lack of programmatic coherence or doctrinal purity
Internal ideological divisions extending over the entire spectrum of
   substantial ideological argument in the system

[8] Rossiter, p. 11. Some suggested amid the troubled politics of 1968 that the United States had seen "the last stand of accommodation politics." We think this unlikely. Describing our parties as "creatures of compromise" doesn't imply that compromise has always been easy, that conflict has been insubstantial. Even in 1968 the effort of the major parties was toward accommodation.

Appeals to all principal social groups
Accommodation politics

The "why" of these continuities must be found, of course, in continuities in the parties' sociopolitical environment. Two broad components of that environment seem to be the most influential: the *conflict situation* and the *constitutional setting*. The first of these is far more complex and important, and requires careful dissection.

Conflict Situations

Egalitarian without an Egalitarian Revolution

Party systems are directly involved in the processing of conflict. Conflict differs vastly, of course, in form and effect, and notably in the ease with which it can be resolved. One of the most difficult types of conflict which political systems have been asked to handle since the eighteenth century is that attendant upon the breakup of aristocratic societies and the establishment of some form of egalitarian or open-class order. The United States avoided transformation from aristocratic to egalitarian, and stood when the Constitution was adopted as a remarkably homogeneous society in class, political culture and political ideology.[9] Our party system has been what it has in part because of the battles it has *not* had to fight.

Aristocracy means, we know, much more than a political regime in which power rests with an hereditary elite. It includes as well an entire array of attendant social and economic institutions, a powerful intrenched class benefiting from the prevailing order and willing to fight to maintain it, an elaborate ideological structure justifying the closed-class or caste arrangements as legitimate and proper, and a broad range of political attitudes and values widely diffused through a political culture supportive of the aristocratic system. This superstructure of aristocracy, when fully elaborated, as throughout Europe in the eighteenth century, was not easily or quickly eradicated. Those who rode the crest of the egalitarian and industrial revolutions in Europe continued for a century-and-a-half after the transformations began to confront residues—in varying strength—of the old order. The middle class of

---

[9] *Political culture* refers to the system of beliefs about patterns of political interaction and political institutions, the orientations of the members of a political system to all aspects of politics.

France, to take a specific example, still had to deal *after* the French Revolution with a real flesh-and-blood aristocracy, still had to operate in a political culture fractured by competing liberal and aristocratic premises. Not so in the United States. The *middle class*—historically understood as the class between aristocracy and peasantry—was from the outset the *whole* here. We were settled when the egalitarian and industrial-technological revolutions were beginning to uproot aristocracy in Europe itself, and the aristocratic transplants were far feebler than if they had come from healthy stock. They clashed, moreover, with raw physical necessities of life in the Colonies, and foundered on the *petit bourgeois* impulses of the population. The owership of land was denied the European peasantry, but land was available in such abundance here that in place of a peasantry there developed a class of agrarian capitalists. The United States never had a revolution against aristocracy because it was never an aristocratic society.[10] This is what led Tocqueville to assert that we had the great advantage of having arrived at "a state of democracy without having to endure a democratic revolution; [having been] born equal, instead of becoming so."

It is hard to overemphasize the importance of American society's being established *de nouveau,* cut off from the social, economic, and political institutions—and the ideological defenses—of ascriptive class societies. There were political disagreements aplenty among those who put in operation the new constitutional regime in the late eighteenth century. But these were disagreements within a liberal tradition. American liberal society—capitalistic, achievement-oriented, egalitarian, individualistic, committed to secular progress—did not confront viable aristocratic institutions and ideology, and possessed a singular ideological unity.

"History had already accomplished the ending of the old European order in America. . . ."[11] That is it in a nutshell. There was one class in America, a middle class. There was one basic ideological system, liberalism. There was a remarkably homogeneous political culture through which the values and assumptions that go along with liberalism,

[10] There were, to be sure, feudal relics such as primogeniture in some of the colonies, but these were *only relics.* For thoughtful discussion of the absence of any viable aristocratic tradition in the United States, see Bernard Bailyn, *The Ideological Origins of the American Revolution* (Cambridge, Mass.: Harvard University Press, 1967); and Hartz, *The Liberal Tradition in America* (New York: Harcourt, Brace & World, 1955).

[11] Louis Hartz, *The Liberal Tradition in America* (New York: Harcourt, Brace & World, 1955), p. 71.

about man, and the role of government, and the arrangements of the society, were widely diffused. At times, Americans forgot that this was so and reached back to their European past for a nomenclature that did not fit. Thus Hamilton, spokesman for middle-class mercantile capitalists, was excoriated as an aristocrat. And for their part, the Hamiltonians branded Thomas Jefferson's acquisitive agrarian capitalists "the mob." But the importance of such rhetorical distortions can easily be overdrawn. Jeffersonians may have *called* their opponents aristocrats, but they didn't *act* as though they were at war with those seeking to establish an entirely different kind of—aristocratic—social order. They *acted* as though they were agrarian capitalists contending with mercantile capitalists who wanted the same *basic* arrangements they did.

What our having become egalitarian without having had to undergo an egalitarian revolution meant for the development of the American party system in the early period is clear. The parties were not preoccupied with doctrinal matters: Since nearly everyone adhered to the same doctrine or basic ideological system (liberalism) it could be taken for granted. "There has never been a 'liberal movement' or real 'liberal party' in America: We have had only the American Way of Life. . . ."[12] Since there were no sharp doctrinal divisions between the emerging parties, it is not surprising that party activists did not see their opponents as darkly as their European counterparts did, and that a political party became less a body of the faithful and more a group of men who happened to feel that their best interests were likely to be promoted by working together at a particular time. Differences tended to be blurred and fudged: clear and pronounced only on the extremes, detectable as prevailing tendencies at the respective centers, and often difficult indeed to locate among individual party activists. Nothing in this situation of homogeneity in class, culture, and ideology required a two-party system, and indeed for a time in the early nineteenth century there was a kind of one-party system—with factional struggles among those who rallied behind the broad Jeffersonian standard. But in a political system not fractured by deep doctrinal divisions, there may well be a natural dualism, in which those dissatisfied with the "ins" come to rally behind a common banner as the "outs." The formation of the Republican and Federalist parties in the 1790s and the Democratic and Whig parties in the 1830s appears to have taken place in just this way.

To summarize, the type of party which the United States has had—

[12] *Ibid.,* p. 11.

flexible, nondoctrinal, broadly inclusive, practicing political accommodation—requires a society without deep division in class, political culture,
and political ideology. Ours has been relatively homogeneous, and this
is *partly* because we entered the Age of Egalitarianism having completely escaped aristocracy.

The Avoidance of Sharp Discontinuities in Political Culture

Nothing assured that the American population would *remain* homogeneous in its basic political orientations. There are a number of ways
in which discontinuities might have developed, producing conflict so
deep and hard to handle as to require a quite different sort of party
system. What are some of these, and why did we avoid them?

One source, common to the so-called "developing nations," is *borrowing*. Countries lagging in the momentous process of economic and
political modernization have tended to borrow heavily from those further
along, but their populations have never absorbed these cultural infusions
uniformly. The process is familiar. A colonial power may start things
by setting up institutions modeled after its own. Later, students go to
a mere advanced country for their education, and return with large
helpings of a cultural tradition quite different from their homeland's.
While the description of political cultures as bifurcated into *traditional*
and *modern* is too simplistic, it is clear that portions of the elites of
countries behind in economic development—and hence in the various
sociopolitical transformations which it precipitates—have borrowed
heavily from their more advanced neighbors and in so doing have introduced an enormous divide into their nations' political cultures. The
United States has not borrowed in this way and hence has not suffered
the consequences in a fractured culture, basically because it has led
in economic development.

Deep cultural divisions can occur when pieces of territory are combined to form a new or an enlarged state. The unification of Italy
presents an interesting case. South of Rome the basic structures of society
are "traditional"; in the North they are much more "legal-rational."
"The division of Italy into major sub-cultures is a critical datum. Northern
Italy differs from the South on almost every significant variable. Culturally the North is European, the South is Mediterranean; the North
was exposed directly to 18th- and 19th-century European thought; these
ideas permeated the South later and very imperfectly. The North is
heavily industrialized . . . the South is still largely rural. . . . By com-

parison to the North, the South is desperately poor, and the data indicate that during recent years of rapid economic development the gap between the two regions has actually widened. . . . Thus the South is not unlike many of the so-called underdeveloped countries. It is deeply steeped in tradition; it is economically backward; it lays great stress on the importance of family, religious, and village primary structures."[13] Thus, LaPalombara concludes, "North and South are hostile toward each other, and this fact contributes considerably to the country's lack of political consensus and integration."[14] The United States absorbed large pieces of new territory after regime formation, but their political culture was largely shaped by settlers from the older sections of the country. Here again, the "virgin land" element looms large in the American experience.

Cultural discontinuities can occur when, for any of a variety of reasons, one portion of a country starts developing in a different way than the rest. It is here that the United States has found its most substantial culture dissimilarities, between North and South. These were modest at the time of regime formation, but widened as the nineteenth century went on. In part this resulted from the industrialization of the North while the South remained a rural-agricultural society. It was partly a product of the more rigid social stratification in the South, intimately linked, of course, to slavery, but not limited to the black-white caste separation. Upon this conflict between North and South the accommodationist two-party system broke up in the 1850s. And after the Civil War, the differences in political culture which set the South apart from the rest of the nation *helped* prop up a peculiar regional one-party system which provided many of the exceptions to the prevailing patterns of national political life.

The North-South division in political culture is not the only such division the United States has had. This country was built on massive waves of immigration—between 1860 and 1929 about 32.5 million persons emigrated here—and many of the immigrants came from substantially different political cultures. What is remarkable is the success of the system in keeping the resulting discontinuities in culture—and the conflict they produced—of relatively modest proportions.

For the most part the United States since regime formation has managed to avoid the introduction of "indigestible" cultural discontinui-

---

[13] Joseph LaPalombara, "Italy: Fragmentation, Isolation, Alienation," in Lucian Pye and Sidney Verba, eds., *Political Culture and Political Development* (Princeton: Princeton University Press, 1965), pp. 304–305.

[14] *Ibid.*, p. 306.

ties. And the party system thus processed conflict in which most of the contending groups conceived social and political life in roughly the same terms. The accommodationist two-party system could not have persisted were this not the case.

The Extent of System Confidence

Social systems vary in their success in meeting the demands placed upon them, and the American system has been unusually successful. The greater the success of any system in meeting demands, the less intense the conflict.

The demands which a citizenry make in a egalitarian society are many, but some of the most important and persistent are economic: that the system provide a *volume* of goods and services and a *distribution* of these sufficient to meet *perceived* needs.[15] The content of economic demands reflects an *irreducible core of needs*—for food, shelter and clothing—but also *expectations* that depart in varying degrees from that core.

Expectations are partially fixed, we know, by pictures of what others are doing, and Americans have never at any point in history had the example of another system surpassing their own economically. The importance of this for the conflict situation is hard to overemphasize. In 1799, in a world with far less productive capacity than our own, per capita income in the United States probably exceeded $400 (in 1968 dollars), more than in most of the developing world today.[16] Early in the nineteenth century, our per capita output, which has been close to that of Great Britain, clearly surpassed it, and continued to grow at a faster rate. And Britain is, of course, a wealthy country, compared with most of the rest of the world. Per capita income in the United States has been greater than in any other country for more than a century, and for the most part the gap has been widening, not diminishing. Being ahead in this way does not assure basic satisfaction with the economic system, but it does make it much less likely that expectations far in

15 Though we will refer analytically to such sub-systems as the *economic* and the *political*, the distinction is only analytic. Political institutions are, for example, "held responsible" or generally evaluated in terms of their association with economic satisfactions, even when economic developments are not really amenable to substantial control from the political institutions.

16 We say that per capita income in 1799 *probably* exceeded $400 because the estimates are highly tentative. Economic historians know very little about how much Americans produced or earned in the years before the Civil War; there are extremely few raw data to work with, findings differ, and their accuracy is clearly open to question.

excess of the system's capacity will generate extensive demands which cannot be met, with this sharp conflict manifesting itself in dissatisfaction with a wide range of social institutions.

Not only has the American economy produced more than its rivals, but—starting from a fairly high position—it has registered steady and impressive gains for well over a century. The valleys have been few and the peaks many as advances in technology and economic organization have pushed the system ahead. Since 1840, our economy has grown at a rate of about 1.6 percent per year in real terms, which means that holding prices constant, per capita income has gone up by this amount, doubling every forty-three years.

An economic system with this level of growth in capacity and this margin over its competitors has powerful resources for dealing with demands. The type of conflict which results when basic economic demands go persistently unmet has to a high degree been avoided. Economic success thus understood seems to have contributed mightily to an overall picture of system success, to a willingness of Americans to work within the boundaries of the established institutions, social and political as well as economic. There has been general confidence in the system's capacity.

When political institutions are able to persist they develop a type of legitimacy born of habituation. American political institutions have carried the same names, taken the same basic form for 180 years. They are old friends. They are natural. They are objects of national pride. They are *American*. A comparative study of the political cultures of the United States and four other countries by Gabriel Almond and Sidney Verba yielded some interesting data on the pride of citizens in their political institutions.[17] Respondents were asked: "Speaking generally, what are the things about this country that you are most proud of?" They were not directed in any way to select political characteristics, and the expression of political pride, when it occurred, was spontaneous.

Given this degree of support in the United States, it isn't surprising that those unhappy with policy developments have been reluctant to take the institutions on. And because of this reluctance, in a kind of snowball effect, confidence has grown further that, whatever the disagreements, they would be processed with a familiar, stable, and predictable institutional order.

Confidence in the system, support for the core political institutions

[17] Gabriel Almond and Sidney Verba, *The Civic Culture* (Princeton: Princeton University Press, 1963), p. 102.

TABLE 2.1

Expression of Pride in Political Institutions, by Nation

	UNITED STATES	GREAT BRITAIN	GERMANY	ITALY	MEXICO
Percent who say they are proud of governmental political institutions	85	46	7	3	30

and processes—these are ingredients in a markedly conservative culture. Robert Lane has provided a striking demonstration of this:

If the Eastport [the name Lane gave to the community in which he was interviewing] common man is a conservative, it is in a special sense. He is not opposed to change, does not take a dim view of human nature (for the most part), has no love of tradition and, although not egalitarian, does not stand for a social hierarchy, either; these are not the ingredients of his conservatism. But he is conservative in the sense that he has no program for structural changes in society, he is markedly loyal to the prevailing system of government, believes in private property and capitalism, holds that he is living in a moral order where people get pretty much the rewards and punishments they merit, and assumes the general responsibility for his own fate.[18]

Lane found that his working-class men had a high degree of confidence in the system, so much so that they were not at war with those who had succeeded better than they within it. Thus one responded:

Personally, I think taxes are too hard. I mean a man makes, let's say $150,000. Well my God he has to give up half of that to the government—which I don't think is right.[19]

You get what you deserve:

Well, I think it's hard because . . . not because of the class itself, or what the influence they have on you, but you just seem to reach a certain point, and if you don't have it, you just don't—you don't make the grade. I've found that to be true. I always seem to be one step away from a good spot. And it's no one's fault—it's my fault I just don't have the education—just don't—just don't have what it takes to take that step.[20]

[18] Robert Lane, *Political Ideology* (New York: Free Press, 1967), pp. 250–251. Lane interviewed at length fifteen working-class men living in the New Haven, Connecticut, area.
[19] *Ibid.*, p. 69.
[20] *Ibid.*, p. 70.

One expression of system confidence which is especially influential in the party system is the way opponents are viewed. Since they, too, share this confidence, they are not too dark or threatening. Almond and Verba asked a series of questions to measure how respondents viewed their own party and their partisan opponents, and the contrasts between the United States and Italy are illuminating.[22] One of the most interesting of these measures involved asking the respondent: "How would you feel if your son or daughter married a supporter of the——party? Would you be pleased, would you be displeased, or wouldn't it make any difference?" This was repeated for each of the big parties in the country. As the reader would expect, Americans were largely indifferent to the partisan affiliations of the future mates of their children.

TABLE 2.2

How Supporters of the Major Parties View the Marriage of a Son or Daughter within or across Party Lines in the United States*

PERCENTAGE WHO WOULD FEEL	REPUBLICAN TOWARD REPUBLICAN MARRIAGE	REPUBLICAN TOWARD DEMOCRATIC MARRIAGE	DEMOCRAT TOWARD DEMOCRATIC MARRIAGE	DEMOCRAT TOWARD REPUBLICAN MARRIAGE
PLEASED	16	3	11	3
DISPLEASED	0	4	0	4
INDIFFERENT	84	93	89	92
OTHER AND DON'T KNOW	0	0	0	1
TOTAL PERCENT	100	100	100	100
TOTAL NUMBER	309	309	464	464

* Source: Gabriel Almond and Sidney Verba, *The Civic Culture* (Princeton: Princeton University Press, 1963), p. 135.

But the reactions of Italians were very different. Here is how Italian Christian Democratic (DC) voters responded to the prospect of a son or daughter marrying a partisan of the Italian Communist party (PCI) or of the Left-Socialists (PSI)

Since the various social groups in the U.S. do not see themselves as too far apart, they can be appealed to by a single party. They are *combinable* as groups perceiving greater social distance among themselves are not. There is thus strong incentive for a party seeking national

[22] Almond and Verba, pp. 123–160.

TABLE 2.3

How Supporters of the Major Parties View Marriage of a Son or
Daughter within or across Party Lines in Italy*

PERCENTAGE WHO WOULD FEEL	DC TOWARD DC MARRIAGE	DC TOWARD PCI MARRIAGE	DC TOWARD PSI MARRIAGE
PLEASED	59	1	1
DISPLEASED	1	58	46
INDIFFERENT	29	28	39
OTHER AND DON'T KNOW	11	13	14
TOTAL PERCENT	100	100	100
TOTAL NUMBER	353	353	353

* Source: Almond and Verba, p. 137.

power to make the broadly inclusive appeal, because if it does not, its opponent will generally seize the opportunity. Accommodationist politics
means two big parties making inclusive appeals. Parties trying to be inclusive can hardly concern themselves with doctrinal purity, and to the extent
that they succeed in being inclusive they become umbrella parties containing the spectrum of contending positions (although not with the
same distribution of each contending position). The "natural" tendency
to duality—such as it is—obviously is facilitated when opposing groups
do not see each other too darkly, when the demands they are making
are not mutually destructive.

Two points may have been blurred and need a little retouching. System
success is a relative thing. Perfect or complete success—all groups finding all of their demands satisfactorily met—never occurs. There have
been times throughout American history when some groups have found
their demands so frustrated that they have rejected the parties trying
to be inclusive and have lashed out in third-party movements. In many
cases—as with the third parties of agricultural America like the Populists—the estrangement bred of substantial unmet demands faded as
the demands came to be met. In other cases, the failure has been long-
term, but the estranged group has been so small that it has despaired
of success in a politics where the two major parties were practicing
accommodationist politics, and has not sustained a persistent minor
party. Black Americans are the primary example.

Secondly, the conflict situation associated with relative system confidence shouldn't be understood as *consensus,* as the absence of conflict. There have always been important divisions, as various groups have pushed for government action or inaction on behalf of their interests. We have only suggested that political conflict has been more easily processed, not as deep, in large part because the contending groups have had enough confidence in the capacity of the system to meet their demands that they have been willing to operate within it. Since they haven't sustained substantial challenges, they haven't seen each other doing something which could not be tolerated. The fewer the demands of social groups that are met, the more likely it is that they will make anti-system demands; and the more they make anti-system demands, the more threatening they are perceived as by others in the system. System success is mother to manageable conflict in the egalitarian society, and the American system always has been successful. This has encouraged if not required nondoctrinal, accommodationist, umbrella parties.

Parties and Social Change

To realize the promise of the technological-economic developments of the last two centuries, societies have had to be transformed. It has been necessary, for example, that the population be relocated from the countryside to towns and cities, and that people adapt to the highly impersonal work situation of big corporate structures. The United States as a new liberal society has been culturally and structurally oriented to these social changes often referred to as *modernization.* Because they have occurred sooner and more easily here, governmental action in their behalf has not been required. Samuel Huntington contrasts this American experience with that of Asian, African, and Latin American countries, where modernization has run into all kinds of societal obstacles: "The gaps between rich and poor, between modern elite and traditional mass, between the powerful and the weak—gaps that are the common lot of 'old societies' trying to modernize today—contrast markedly with the 'pleasing uniformity' of the 'one estate' that existed in eighteenth-century America."[23] Most of the countries of the developing world are what Clifford Geertz has called "old societies and new states."[24] The modernization of a traditional society in a short span of time—whether the Soviet Union, China, or the United Arab Republic

[23] Samuel Huntington, "Political Modernization: America vs. Europe," *World Politics,* 18 (April, 1966), p. 410.
[24] Clifford Geertz, ed., *Old Societies and New States: The Quest for Modernity in Asia and Africa* (New York: Free Press, 1963).

—requires intervention by a powerful centralized authority in government, and the political party typically has played a big role. The "single, monolithic, hierarchical, but 'mass,' party"—with its model the Communist party of the Soviet Union—has been an important instrument in the "forced" modernization of traditional societies.

The American experience is not very relevant to most developing nations because modernization was able to occur here without concerted government intervention. The American party system was never asked to *effect* sweeping social change. Loosely disciplined, organizationally elusive, decentralized, internally divided, moderate, and nonprogrammatic parties are perfectly suited to a system in which the principal impetus for modernization comes from outside government, in which conflict over this social change is minimal.

Geographic Variations

Many important political arguments have been organized geographically in the United States, and North-South is only the most salient geographic locus. This is not surprising in a big, continent-spanning country where social composition and economic life historically have varied sharply from one region to another. Consider the differences in 1850 between the rural, slave-owning, plantation South; the free-soil, family-farm economy of the West; and the expanding mercantile and industrial northeastern seaboard. Thus quite distinct agenda of politics have existed in the several regions at the same point in time. The substance of political argument in South Carolina and New York—in 1850, 1900, 1950, and 1968—have been very different, and the "Democratic party" could not have been competitive in both with similar policy stances. The "notorious localism" of American politics which has expressed itself in the regularity with which voters have rewarded a congressman or senator who makes a practice of opposing the national leadership of his party has roots in these geographic differences in agenda. Since 1787 our national parties have been coalitions of state parties facing in somewhat different directions, in recognition of the geographic organization of conflict.

Constitutional Setting

The type of conflict the United States has had furnishes some powerful constraints for the party system. But another, perhaps more mundane, component of the influential environment—the constitutional order—

cannot be ignored. We understand the *constitutional order* to encompass not just the Constitution of the United States but all the principal institutions, procedures, and laws of American government. Several elements of the constitutional order have left a deep imprint on the party system.

One-Man Executives

Political executives in the United States—mayors, governors, the president—are one-man executives. The cabinet in a parliamentary regime is typically defined as *collectively* the executive. The prime minister is *primus inter pares,* but the *among equals* is taken seriously. In contrast to this is the formal constitutional superiority of the American president. His cabinet is composed not of equals but of administrative subordinates. The collective or cabinet executive of parliamentary regimes can be—and often is—divided among two or more parties, but the American presidency is an all-or-nothing affair. The need to pool resources to win it has been a powerful force keeping the disparate elements of its national Republican and Democratic parties together. Third-party movements can't avoid the challenge, "A vote for ———— is a wasted vote because he cannot win." While in a troubled year like 1968 a third-party candidate may garner a lot of votes, the staying power of such parties is sapped. They cannot, as in parliamentary regime, build up a legislative bloc which participates in electing the executive, bargaining for positions—cabinet offices—within it. If a minor party in the U.S. cannot raise *the serious possibility* of winning more votes than any challenger in states with at least 270 electoral votes, it is ever open to the "wasted vote" charge.[25] A one-man executive is hardly sufficient to assure a two-party system, but it stimulates the coalescing of diverse interests into blocs with some chance for a national majority. The coalescing of smaller parties into broader electoral coalitions in the contests for the presidency of the Fifth French Republic is an interesting example of how the introduction of a powerful presidential executive in a country with a parliamentary tradition can by itself help restructure the party system.

The Winner-Take-All Electoral System

Most elected officials in the United States are chosen on a winner-take-all basis: that is, the candidate with the most votes in the district

[25] The reader is aware that the Constitution of the United States provides for the selection of the president by an Electoral College in which each state has as many electors as it has United States senators and representatives. All fifty states provide—although they need not—that the slate of electors receiving the most votes in the popular quadrennial balloting shall constitute the state's electors.

is selected. This is more precisely described as a *single-member district, simple-majority, single-ballot* system: *single-member district,* because each electoral district has one representative only, for example, only one congressman from each congressional district; *simple-majority* because the candidate with the most votes wins whether or not he has 50 percent of the votes; *single-ballot* in that everything is settled in this one balloting, with no provision for runoffs.[26] The United States shares this winner-take-all electoral system with some other countries including Canada and Great Britain, but it is by no means the standard form throughout the world. Many countries have operated with various forms of *proportional representation.*

The varieties of proportional representation (PR) are numerous and involved.[27] But, in general, PR specifies multi-member rather than single-member districts; and in place of a winner-take-all arrangement in which the candidate with the most votes gets the seat, a system through which the seats from the multi-member districts are divided among the contending party slates in proportion to their shares of the popular vote. A concrete illustration might help clarify this. The first legislature of the Fourth French Republic was elected in 1946 under a form of PR referred to as the "highest average" system. The *department* was established as the basic constituency (although in some of the bigger *departments* two or even three constituencies were carved out).[28] The number of seats for each constituency was determined by the number of people residing in it, with approximately one seat for each 55,000 voters. Thus a *department* with 325,000 residents had six seats. The parties in each constituency were required to present lists of as many candidates as there were seats. The voter then cast his ballot for the *list* as a whole, voting for the party and the decision of the party leaders in setting up the list rather than for individuals. The voter was not permitted to substitute names or alter the order of the names as they appeared on the list. After the votes were counted, seats were distributed

[26] While general elections in the United States don't provide for runoffs, some states have established second ballots under some conditions in primary contests. This is common in the South, where from the late nineteenth century until recently the only substantial contests were in the Democratic primary, and where it was not unusual for as many as a dozen candidates to enter a primary contest. Since in so large a field a candidate with the most votes often had a distinct minority of the total votes cast, a provision was made for a runoff primary, typically between the two candidates with the highest vote totals in the first balloting.

[27] For an excellent description of proportional representation arrangements, see Duverger, pp. 206–280.

[28] The French *department* is a large political administrative unit. There are ninety-five of them.

to the parties in proportion to the votes they received in each constituency. Theoretically, if the French Communist party received 35 percent of the popular vote in a constituency with six seats, the first two candidates on its list of six would be elected. In fact, pure PR was not used, but instead a complicated system based on the principle of the "highest average vote per seat." This tended to give the parties with the larger number of votes in each *department* a somewhat bigger proportion of the seats than they would have gained under pure PR.[29]

PR thus encourages multi-partism. Under it, a party with a small minority of the popular vote in a big multi-member constituency can gain representation. In contrast, with the single-member district, simple-majority electoral mechanics used in the United States, a party with 15 or 20 percent of the vote in a constituency gets no representation at all. The only chance for a minor party to win seats is when its popular vote is unusually concentrated: a distinct minority nationally but a simple majority in certain constituencies.

One of the most prominent demonstrations of the influence of the single-member district, simple-majority mechanics in the maintenance of the two-party system took place in Britain in the early years of this century. In 1900, Great Britain had two great political parties, the Conservatives and the Liberals, but this traditional two-party system was broken up when organized labor decided to contest for power directly. By the end of World War I the new Labour party had become the second largest, relegating the Liberals to third place. The Liberals still were very strong in the popular vote, winning between 18 and 30 percent of the vote nationally between 1918 and 1930. But there were relatively few constituencies in which they could gather a simple majority, that is, more votes than either Labour or the Conservatives. Thus, a marked disparity appeared between the Liberal party's share of the popular vote and its share of the seats in Parliament. In every election after 1918, the Liberals got a smaller proportion of the seats than of the votes: in 1929, for example, with 23.4 percent of the popular vote, they won only fifty-eight seats (9.4 percent). The persistence of this phenomenon can only produce discouragement among the party's voters, culminating in a decision to "make your vote count" by supporting candidates of the more acceptable of the two major parties. The underrepresented Liberal voters deserted their party in droves in the 1930s,

[29] For a thorough description of proportional representation in the Fourth French Republic, see Philip Williams, *Politics in Postwar France,* revised ed. (London: Longmans Green, 1958).

and this great party of the nineteenth century, the party of Gladstone, was destroyed.[30]

A political party in third place in a winner-take-all system is very likely to be underrepresented in legislative seats (unless it has an extraordinary geographic concentration) and this underrepresentation must, if it persists, discourage the party's electors. In general, American electoral arrangements have worked against third parties, have helped preserve the great duality.

The Federal System

The decentralization and internal diversity of the major national party coalitions in the United States is partly the result of differences in the agenda of politics in the various sections of a big country. But it is furthered too by the fundamental institutional constraints of a federal system. Under American federalism, two layers of government—the state and national—have received formal constitutional recognition. A lot has happened since 1789 to change the practice of American federalism, blurring the distinction between *the national sphere* and *the state sphere*. Elaborate cooperative arrangements have been worked out in such basic areas of public policy as education. But one prime feature of American federalism has not changed: state governments remain centers of political power. A party which controls a state government controls a power base sufficient to sustain it. It is, in short, partly because state governments have substantial political powers, formally recognized, that state party systems organized around and sustained by them have a high degree of coherence and persistence.

The Constitutional Separation of Executive and Legislative

Nearly a century ago, Woodrow Wilson lamented the lack of coherence in our governmental parties, and many observers have since dwelled on this theme. Our parties, it is said, are not *responsible*. *Responsible party government* works this way: the competing parties develop programs and take them to the electorate; one wins a majority and then holds together and coherently enacts its program; at the next election, voters have the clear choice of continuing that party in office or of kicking it out in favor of a similarly coherent opposition. But what happens in the United States? One party may win a large majority in both houses of Congress and may at the same time control the

[30] For a careful treatment of the collapse of the Liberal party, see Trevor Wilson, *The Downfall of the Liberal Party, 1914–1935* (London: Collins, 1966).

presidency, and still be unable to enact the programs which its leaders—the president and the elected majority leaders of the Congress—support. Why is this the case? Because Democrats do not hesitate to vote with Republicans, and control frequently is in the hands of inter-party blocs and coalitions. Thus, since World War II, a *conservative coalition* drawing its strength from midwestern Republicans and southern Democrats has often held sway in the national legislature.[31]

The causes of this lack of discipline or coherence in the governmental parties can be found in the geographic organization of conflict and the impact of federalism, described above, but also in the formal structure of executive-legislative relations. The president and Congress are elected separately, and the tenure of office of each is entirely independent of what the other does. The president cannot dissolve Congress, and the latter cannot remove the executive (except in the extraordinary act of impeachment). Though Congress and the president are inseparably linked in the governing process (the president proposes legislation, Congress enacts it, the president may veto bills passed by Congress, and the departments of the executive branch must administer bills signed into law by the president) they are institutionally distinct.

In a parliamentary country like Britain, the chief executive is part of the legislature. The prime minister and his cabinet have seats in Parliament, and hold their executive positions as leaders of the legislative majority, which constitutionally can vote them out of office at any time. Since the executive requires a legislative majority, the failure of Labour (or Conservative) members of Parliament to support their government brings down their government. It is hardly surprising, then, that members of the majority party do not frivolously vote against the programs on which the executive—their party's leaders—stakes the government's life. But in the United States, what happens if Democratic senators and representatives vote against the program of the Democratic president? The program may be defeated, of course, but the Democratic president and his administration remain securely in office until the end of its four-year term. And it is possible—indeed it has happened in four of the eleven Congresses between 1946 and 1968—for one party to

[31] For the principal criticisms of American political parties as lacking responsibility, the reader should see E. E. Schattschneider, *Party Government* (New York: Holt, Rinehart & Winston, 1942); James MacGregor Burns, *Congress on Trial* (New York: Gordian, 1946); Burns, *The Deadlock of Democracy* (Englewood Cliffs, N.J.: Prentice Hall, 1963); and the report issued in 1950 by the Committee on Political Parties of the American Political Science Association, *Toward a More Responsible Two-Party System* (New York, 1950).

control the presidency and another one or both houses of the legislature. The institutional separation of the president and Congress, in short, encourages a lack of coherence in the legislative party; just as the parliamentary practice of making the executive part of and immediately responsible to the legislature places a premium on coherence in the legislative party which may persist even in the face of substantial private dissatisfactions.

The constitutional separation of president and Congress contributes to a lack of discipline and coherence in our political parties in another way. There is a pronounced division within each party nationally between the presidential and congressional wings, a division which one commentator has discussed in terms of "four-party politics." James McGregor Burns has argued that

to see the pattern of power at the national level only in terms of two parties is grossly misleading. The balance between one or two parties, on the one hand, and (at the national level) over a thousand personal parties (one for the President, one for each member of Congress, and at least one for each rival for the office, in both parties), on the other hand, has been struck not in a two-party power system, nor in a multi-party system, but in what is essentially a four-party system. The four national parties are the Presidential Democrats, the Presidential Republicans, the Congressional Democrats, and the Congressional Republicans. The groupings that have been described as "wings" of the two major parties in these pages are, in any meaningful sense, separate though overlapping parties.[32]

Burns was not suggesting that these "four parties" are separated by neat boundaries, but that each—presidential Republicans, congressional Republicans, presidential Democrats, congressional Democrats—has the base for an independent and distinct existence. First, the president and Congress are two major centers of power, and the avenues to control of each very different. The presidency is a great popular office, sensitive to national swings of opinion. The operations of the Electoral College— which give to the candidate receiving a plurality of the popular vote all of the state's electoral votes—provide a powerful incentive for nominating men with a good chance of winning that plurality in a high proportion of the big states, which means men able to appeal effectively to "swing" groups in these typically competitive states. But if success for the presidential party requires responsiveness to shifts in national opinion and to the interests of pivotal groups in big industrial states, majorities in

[32] Burns, *The Deadlock of Democracy*, p. 196.

Congress are built from one-party districts that are often the most insulated. Power in Congress belongs to those able to secure repeated re-election, thus accumulating seniority and, through seniority, control of the committee system. While some representatives do secure regular re-election from highly competitive districts, longevity comes far easier and more commonly to those in "safe" districts which by their relative homogeneity lack the social base for sustaining more regular competition.

Another factor differentiating the presidential and congressional parties can be expressed as a political contradiction of a geometric theorem, that the whole *is not* equal to the sum of its parts. That is, the competition for the presidency is not simply the sum of 435 congressional contests. Voting for president is heavily shaped by the pull of national issues and images, while the fabric of political argument in congressional races is more parochial, with voters appearing to apply quite different standards of judgment. Moreover, the highly publicized and visible presidential contests bring out a much larger portion of the voting-age population. Between 1932 and 1944, the average turnout in Presidential elections was 59.1 percent, while that in the off-year congressional elections was 41.0 percent, or a mean "drop-off" of 27.8. For the elections from 1948 through 1960, the average presidential turnout was 60.3 percent, the off-year congressional turnout 44.1, or a "drop-off" of 24.9.[33]

Recruitment into the presidential party—thought of as candidates for president and, when successful, the men appointed to high office in the Executive branch—and the congressional party is obviously different. Burns notes that

the Presidential Republicans for decades have been drawing internationalist-minded men out of the universities, law schools, and metropolitan law and banking firms of the East: men like Elihu Root, Henry Stimson, John Foster Dulles, Douglas Dillon. Such men rise up the ladders of administrative, usually corporate or governmental, life. The steps towards eminence in the Congressional party are typically quite different: small town lawyer in a heavily Republican area, district attorney (or its equivalent), state legislature, then National House or Senate. Their background is more parliamentary and less bureaucratic.[34]

[33] W. Dean Burnham, "The Changing Shape of The American Political Universe," *American Political Science Review,* 59 (March, 1965), p. 10. "Drop-off" is the reciprocal of the percentage of the presidential year total vote which is cast in the immediately following off-year congressional election.
[34] Burns, *The Deadlock of Democracy,* p. 200.

From different patterns of recruitment come men with different styles, different views of the world and its problems.

The argument, in short, is that Congress and the presidency are separate centers of power with substantial autonomy, with influence in each achieved through different routes, each "weighted" toward a different segment of the electorate, rewarding men of different career lines and political styles. And the result has been that these two wings of both the Republican and Democratic parties—or, if one prefers to use Burns's terminology, the congressional and presidential Republican parties and the congressional and presidential Democrats—have differed doctrinally. Specifically, the presidential wing of the Republican party was more receptive to the innovations of the New Deal, and later the Fair Deal, than the congressional Republicans; the former moved quickly to make its peace with the new agenda.

Change within the Bounds of Continuity

Through the nearly two centuries since regime formation, the American party system has been dominated by two big, amorphous national coalitions of state and local parties. The major parties have never possessed organizational or programmatic coherence. Each has contained within it virtually the entire spectrum of significant policy or ideological positions, aiming at inclusiveness in its group appeals. Each has asked nothing of its "members" except a vote. The American major parties have not governed, but have facilitated the organization of government; they have not initiated change, but have sought to manage, exploit (for electoral advantage), and otherwise respond to change.

This type of party system has persisted because the conditions necessary to it have persisted, and these conditions involve primarily conflict and constitution. It is essential that the changes in the substance of partisan argument and in the composition of the parties' electoral coalitions which the following chapters describe be seen to have occurred within the bounds of these continuities. For a history of response and adaptation in the party system is a matter much more of new music than new dancers.

PART

II

PARTIES IN THE SWEEP OF AMERICAN SOCIETAL EXPERIENCE

3

The Parties in the Rural Republic

The first great social and political period in post-independence America lasted from regime formation to the tumultuous years before the Civil War. Though the society was dynamic, changing throughout, this period did possess an internal unity. The United States was an egalitarian, pre-industrial society. A majority of the work force labored in unmechanized agriculture. A majority of the people lived on farms or in tiny villages. And the preponderance of political power rested with a class of land-owning agriculturalists.

The Society and Its Political Agenda

The Working Out of Egalitarianism

The United States occupies a unique position in the birth of modern politics since it entered the Age of Egalitarianism unburdened by a large aristocratic legacy. A continent-spanning territory sparsely inhabited by a native population much less advanced in technical and economic development received middle-class European immigrants who were "spun off" from the mother countries as aristocracy was coming under severe challenge in Europe itself. Yet while the United States at regime formation was already a liberal and egalitarian society, it was as well a society embarking upon something very new, following a path which had not previously been trod. The first period saw, then, a working out of egalitarianism, a moving in political institutions and political style to what the basic social relationships had ordained. It was a time of groping for a politics in harmony with the society.

American politics in 1790 was not in any sense aristocratic, but its style was still deferential—relative to what it was to become in the next decades. *Deferential* means that most people expected politics to be handled by the "better sort" of the society, expected the "common folk" pretty much to defer to their betters. This is not at all surprising. The entire experience of western politics in 1790 was aristocratic. From the outset, the United States had rejected core aristocratic arrangements, but it did not immediately dispense with all remnants of the aristocratic style. The American political style of the 1790s and the early years of the nineteenth century is sometimes called "oligarchic," but this is putting it too strongly. The "better sort" ran politics not through force but because few expected things to be otherwise in this more deferential political culture.

This situation didn't last long. It had, after all, no place in such a wide-open, individualistic, egalitarian society, but was a vestigial style from aristocratic days. Thus, in the 1820s and 1830s, American public life became increasingly less deferential, a development which the historian Lee Benson describes as a victory for "egalitarianism": "After 1815, not only in politics but in all spheres of American life, egalitarianism challenged elitism and, in most spheres and places, egalitarianism won."[1] But the victory of egalitarianism had long since been won; this was the victory of a political style compatible with egalitarianism. The Harrison–Van Buren presidential contest in 1840—with its silence on issues, a rough-and-ready flavor, its symbolism (such as the log cabin), and the stimulation of hard cider—is often cited as revealing a significant departure from the politics of 1796 or 1800; indeed it does, but the populistic "new politics" of the 1830s and 1840s was the natural style of an agricultural society of wide resource distribution, in which the majority of the white population were land-owning farmers.

The American setting at regime formation had been so without precedent that the actors in it were to a degree confused as to what would be its manner of operation. In Europe in 1800, the counterparts of Hamilton and Jefferson were allies—custodians of an embattled liberalism—still confronting powerful proponents of an aristocratic tradition in church and state, and still facing a peasantry which did not share their liberal cosmology. In America the traditional enemies of liberalism in aristocracy and peasantry were absent, and Jeffersonians and Hamiltonians did battle, each seeing the other more darkly than they

[1] Lee Benson, *The Concept of Jacksonian Democracy* (Princeton: Princeton University Press, 1961), p. 336.

should. The upper strata of the middle class, by failing to realize that here there was nothing threatening them and by railing against the people, fixed themselves as conservative elitists and for a time lost their chance to rule.[2]

This confusion in political dialogue ended as Americans came in the course of the first period to understand their society better. In the 1830s and 1840s, the philosophy of democratic capitalism replaced the old Hamiltonian fear of the people. Thus Daniel Webster came to insist that "the visible and broad distinction" between the many and the few of "the old countries of Europe" was not to be found in the United States. In a society where aristocracies, peasantries, and proletariats were missing and where virtually everyone had the mentality of an independent entrepreneur, capitalism was democratic and hardly threatened by the demos: by 1840 most American leaders understood this.

This process of the logical working out of egalitarianism affected the fabric of American political institutions and processes. Few of the founders believed that the United States should be a democracy. They did want it to be republican. This distinction, of which we hear echoes in contemporary pronouncements of conservative spokesmen, is fairly important. Liberalism did not posit a democratic polity, did not insist upon political institutions based around one man, one vote. It did reject heredity as a basis for selecting political leadership, and required that leaders should reflect popular wishes, both in their actions and in the manner of their selection. But the *populace* was seldom considered to mean even the adult white male population. Every one of the thirteen states in the 1790s imposed a property qualification for voting. But early in the nineteenth century, property requirements were dropped in state after state, until by 1828 universal (white male) suffrage had been achieved. Not only was the right to vote extended, but techniques and organization for popular electioneering were developed, which by the 1830s were mobilizing a mass electorate. The framers of the Constitution envisioned the president selected by an electoral college of wise and dispassionate men chosen by the several state legislatures; the electors, equal in number to the membership of Congress, would consider the needs of the Republic and exercise their independent judgment. The presidency was thus to be doubly insulated from the people. But one layer of intended insulation was ripped away after the election of

[2] For the most complete analysis of this confusion, see Louis Hartz's brilliant book *The Liberal Tradition in America* (New York: Harcourt, Brace & World, 1955).

just one president—Washington—with the *pledging of electors:* the majorities in the state legislatures began choosing electors pledged to a particular candidate for the presidency, thus transforming the electoral college from a body for independent judgment to a vehicle for carrying out the wishes of popularly elected state legislative majorities. Then in the 1820s another large step in democratizing the presidency was taken, as all the states except South Carolina shifted from legislative designation to popular election of the slates of electors. At this same time, the nomination process was opened to a measure of popular influence as presidential candidates came to be chosen by national delegate conventions in place of the original selection instrument, the congressional caucus. The National Republicans (later to be the Whigs) held the first presidential convention of sorts in Baltimore in 1831, at which Henry Clay was nominated, and in 1832 their opponents renominated Andrew Jackson at the first full-fledged convention.

Alexis de Tocqueville visited the United States in the Age of Jackson primarily to observe at close hand the product of egalitarianism: ". . . I have selected the nation . . . in which its [egalitarianism] development has been the most peaceful and the most complete, in order to discern its natural consequences. . . . I must confess that, in America, I saw more than America; I sought there the image of democracy itself, with its inclinations, its character, its prejudices, and its passions, in order to learn what we have to fear or to hope from its progress."[3]

The America of the first sociopolitical period *was* something special in the "family" of nations—the first egalitarian society, with immense new possibilities *and* new problems. Tocqueville was not alone in searching for the social and political meanings of egalitarianism. In their own and typically less intellectually conscious ways, a nation of Americans were engaged in this pursuit. The seven decades after regime formation thus assumed a distinctive flavor, as a pre-industrial society with an extremely equalitarian distribution of resources worked out appropriate political institutions and political style.

The Agricultural Society at the Beginning of the Industrial Revolution

Throughout its first seven decades, the United States was a farming nation. Most men earned their living in agriculture, and most of the productivity of the economy was agricultural. In 1800, more than four out of every five who worked were farmers; and although the non-agricultural work force grew faster, farmers were still about two-thirds

[3] Tocqueville, *Democracy in America* (New York: Mentor), p. 36.

of the total in 1850. In 1839, the earliest year for which reasonably accurate data have been obtained, agriculture accounted for nearly 70 percent of the value of the commodity output of the American economy. The total value added to the economy by all forms of manufacturing that year was, in current prices, a little less than a quarter of a billion dollars.[4] Figure 3.1 clearly shows the ascendancy of agriculture in American economic life up to 1860. Curiously, such data are often lost sight of in descriptions of conflict in this period. For example, Herbert Agar asserts in his fine book on the American party system that Jefferson through the Embargo Act of 1807 and the Non-Intercourse Act of 1809 did much to put "agrarianism . . . on the defensive and [make] capitalism . . . dominant."[5] Yet three decades after these embargoes, "dominant capitalism" was accounting for less than 30 percent of the productivity of the American economy! Those manufacturing enterprises which developed in this agricultural economy typically were small hand and neighborhood industry. American capitalism was mercantile, not industrial.

The dominant place of agriculture in the first half of the nineteenth century is revealed by other social characteristics. The astonishingly high birth rate—55 live births per 1,000 population in 1800, 52 in 1840—points to an economy where large families were an asset. Since most people worked in unmechanized agriculture, education beyond that required for literacy was unnecessary. Besides, this pre-industrial society could not afford to sustain any substantial portion of its productive-age population in "nonproductive" educational pursuits. The U.S. educational system was a primary school system. Of the 3.5 million pupils

[4] These data on the "value added" by different segments of the economy should be construed as only general approximations; economic data on the pre–Civil War period are fragmentary and often, due to the manner of their compilation from inadequate records, imprecise. The reader can have confidence in the general picture these data reveal. For an explanation of the distinction between "value added by selected industries"—the most reliable output series of comprehensive coverage for pre-1870 America—and "gross national product" (GNP), which is now commonly used, the reader is referred to *Historical Statistics of the United States, Colonial Times to 1957* (Washington, D.C.: U.S. Government Printing Office, 1960), pp. 133–134.

[5] Herbert Agar, *The Price of Union* (Boston: Houghton Mifflin, 1950), p. 165. The Embargo and Non-Intercourse Acts forbade commerce with foreign nations; the former with all countries, the latter with France and England and their dependencies only. These measures were intended as commercial retaliation against warring France and England, countries which had not respected American neutrality and were interfering massively with American shipping. Since American exports were largely agricultural commodities and our imports heavily of manufactured goods, the burden of the embargoes did fall on agriculture—denied markets—and did help domestic manufactures—freed from competition.

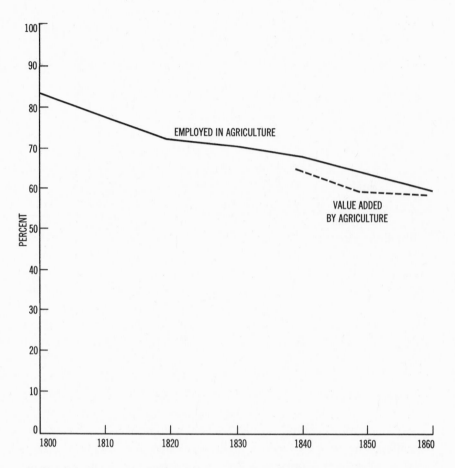

Figure 3.1. Percentage Employed in Agriculture, and Percentage of All Output Accounted For by Agriculture, Selected Years 1800–1860*

   * Source: U.S. Bureau of the Census, *Historical Statistics of the United States, Colonial Times to 1957* (Washington, D.C.: U.S. Government Printing Office, 1960), pp. 74, 139. *Value added* is defined as "the value of output, at producers' prices less the value of commodities consumed in production, at delivered prices" (p. 133). Figure for 1800 from Herman E. Krooss, *American Economic Development* (Englewood Cliffs, N.J.: Prentice-Hall, 1966), p. 27.

enrolled in 1850, only 20,000 were in grades nine and above; less than 1 percent of the population were high school graduates; and the degrees awarded by all institutions of higher education numbered fewer than 3,000.

The Boundaries of Economic Conflict

   To understand conflict in this pre-industrial society posed on the brink of massive industrialism we must recognize that the claims and attractions of an agricultural order were persuasive. Jefferson really did believe that a nation of self-sufficient, independent, land-owning farmers was vastly preferable to one in which bankers made profits manipulating commercial paper, and in which burgeoning manufactures produced, in turn, cities, an impoverished urban proletariat, and class conflict. Even Martin Van Buren, who made his reputation as a canny political technician, not as an ideologically inclined politician, often referred to the threat to the "good (agricultural) society" from the "money power." Late in his life, looking back on a long political career which spanned the latter four decades of the period we are discussing, Van Buren concluded that "a statement of the extent to which the business, as distinguished from the agricultural and other laboring classes, have been banded together in our political contests by a preference for Hamilton's principles and by the instrumentality of the money power, would be regarded as incredible if the facts were not indisputable and notorious."[6] He took satisfaction that the Hamiltonian or business position had been rebuffed because "it failed signally, as has been stated, with the most numerous and consequently the most powerful class of our citizens— those engaged in agriculture. . . . It not only failed to attract their sympathies in its favor, but excited their dissatisfaction. . . ."[7] In general, farmers saw themselves doing the real, the tangible work of the nation and yet were supporting, often handsomely it seemed, a category of men whose "work" was merely the shuffling of paper.

At the same time, the United States was an agricultural society in the West at the beginning of the Industrial Revolution, and the American farmer had the "mentality" not of a peasant but of an independent entrepreneur. The Rural Republic was a liberal society, and the intellectual components of liberalism—its rationalism, achievement orientation, commitment to secular progress—are prime cultural antecedents for capitalistic development. Many observers described this cultural congeniality of early America to machinery and practical science. Tocqueville found Americans a restless people, eager in pursuit of "physical gratification," always trying to increase their fortune. "To minds thus predisposed, every new method which leads by a shorter road to wealth, every machine which spares labor, every instrument which diminishes the cost of production, every discovery which facilitates

[6] Martin Van Buren, *Inquiry into the Origin and Course of Political Parties in the United States* (New York: Augustus M. Kelly, 1967; first printed, 1867), p. 224.
[7] *Ibid.*, p. 227.

pleasures or augments them, seems to be the grandest effort of the human intellect."[8] A number of commentators have contrasted the ease with which Americans accepted the introduction of machinery to the anti-machinery riots in England in the 1820s and 1830s.[9] The opposition in agricultural America to change in the direction of a money-based order was tempered, then, by a general receptivity to technology and enterprise.

Although most people earned their livelihood in agriculture, the pressures toward "enterprise," toward commercial, financial, and as the period progressed, manufacturing, activity—were incessant; and these occurred in an environment which—while resisting them at some points —was far from consistently hostile. A sharp polarization with all financial, mercantile, and manufacturing interests neatly aligned against all agriculturalists never occurred. The reaction of most American farmers to the emergent industrialism appears to have been highly ambivalent.

There *were* a series of quite concrete issues in which the interests of industry collided with those of the agricultural sector. The tariff was one of these. Americans whose political memories are bounded by the Depression of 1929 may find it hard to believe that tariff policy was once a major domestic issue. Tariff arguments in the first half of the nineteenth century (as subsequently) were often confused, as a welter of producers sought favorable tariff rates in the areas of their immediate interests and entered an involved assortment of mutual backscratching arrangements. But in this chaotic score, there was the recurring theme of high protective tariffs vs. free trade; and businessmen engaged in manufacturing came to provide the main support for the former, while opposition to high protection came from farmers-as-consumers of imported manufactured goods and from farmers-as-exporters of such cash crops as cotton, who thus were wedded to free trade among nations. In general, as manufacturing developed, the demands for protection gained strength; and as the Northeast became the center of incipient American industrialism, its political spokesmen came to be the principal proponents of high protection. Since the preponderance of political power remained with agriculturalists throughout the first period, tariffs remained relatively low (much higher after 1828 than free traders

[8] Tocqueville, p. 167.
[9] See, for example, Hugo Meier, "Technology and Democracy, 1800–1860," *Mississippi Valley Historical Review* 43 (March, 1957), pp. 629–631.

South and West desired, but lower than what they were to become after the Civil War, when the industrialists took control).

Policy with regard to banking, currency, and financial manipulations is another area in which the emergent money-based economy clashed repeatedly with the traditional agrarianism. Once again, it is hard for us, accustomed to a relatively stable and well-managed banking and currency system, to appreciate the problems posed in the first half of the nineteenth century. State banks, without regulation, often issued credit far in excess of what was justified by their reserves; paper money —which circulated largely as the notes of state-chartered banks—was supposedly redeemable in specie (gold and silver) but often was highly unstable, of fluctuating value. There was no coherent plan for meeting the currency and credit needs of the nation.

Farmers were chronically in need of credit to purchase land or to finance their operations while waiting for the sale of a cash crop, and in the monetary setting of the first half of the nineteenth century this meant that they often had cause for unhappiness. For example, settlers rapidly pushed west after the War of 1812, faster even than roads or markets could follow them, and borrowed money from local banks which were in turn in debt to the Bank of the United States.[10] The latter did nothing to discourage excessive loans by local western banks until the end of 1818, when it ordered its branches to present all state bank notes for payment and to renew no mortgages. Within months, many western banks collapsed, and vast tracts of land, with mortgages foreclosed, became the property of the Bank of the United States. The state banks, more than the Bank of the United States, bore responsibility for this "panic." They were the ones who had charted the course of reckless lending. And overall, the Second Bank had contributed significantly to what stability of currency and regularity of operation there was. Nonetheless, in a rural America where financial woes were blamed on eastern financial interests and where localism and fear of centralized govern-

[10] The First Bank of the United States was established in 1791 and expired in 1811 when Congress refused to renew its charter. Then, in 1816, the Second Bank of the United States was chartered, with powers similar to the First Bank: it was allowed to establish branches in the main towns, was the depository for all National Government funds and could issue notes to be redeemed in specie on demand. The Second Bank had twenty-seven branches and through a system of "branch drafts" assumed the power to extend (or contract) the currency supply far beyond what the charter envisioned. It became the dominant influence in credit manipulations affecting industry, commerce, and agriculture. The Bank handled the government's funds efficiently, and served as a vehicle for indirect national regulation of state bank notes.

mental activity was pervasive, the Bank of the United States became a convenient symbol of the hated "money power." Andrew Jackson's encounter with the "monster bank" is well known. The struggle assumed the intensity which it did as an outburst in agricultural America against the whole array of currency and credit manipulations, and, beyond this, against the development of a money-based economy.

Regional Economic Differences

In the first half of the nineteenth century, the principal geographic regions of the United States developed along different lines economically and came to have conflicting political interests, differences in political style and even in political culture. The Northeast was the center of financial activity, trade, and, as the period progressed, manufacturing. In 1850, this section accounted for three-fourths of the country's manufacturing employment, concentrated in industry in which capital requirements were relatively modest, such as cotton goods, boots and shoes, men's clothing, and leather and woolen goods.[11] With 37 percent of the country's population in 1850, the region had 81 percent of the urban population, 211 of the 236 places with more than 2,500 inhabitants.

The West of this first period was the "Old West," now the North Central states. (As late as 1850 there were fewer than 200,000 people in the territory out of which the Mountain and Pacific Coast states were later carved.) Early in the nineteenth century, a tremendous migration across the Appalachian Mountains began, with Ohio, Indiana, Illinois, and Missouri growing the fastest. These states were the frontier in the Rural Republic. The economy of the Old West was heavily agricultural, and wheat and corn were the most important cash crops. The region needed a large investment in transportation and related overhead facilities to move these staples. Wheat and corn could be most efficiently produced, given the state of agricultural technology, on "family-size" farms, and slavery extended only into the border state of Missouri. The region's limited manufacturing was of the resource-oriented variety, the processing of raw materials, as in lumber, meat packing, and flour milling.

The American South underwent extraordinary economic changes in the first half of the nineteenth century. In 1800, it was a land of small farmers. Jefferson was disliked by many of the old Tidewater families

---

[11] Douglass C. North, *The Economic Growth of the United States, 1790–1860* (Englewood Cliffs, N.J.: Prentice-Hall, 1961; New York, Norton Library, 1966), pp. 115–160.

in Virginia, but he was a great hero during his lifetime throughout most of the South. Apparently the vast majority of Southerners then thought of themselves as good Jeffersonians and accepted his optimism about the future of democracy. Slavery was assumed to be dying, and a buoyant equalitarianism was much more characteristic than the privileged life of the mansions along the Potomac. The South of the small farmer seemed more likely to survive than the South of the planter, for the old families of the Tidewater region were having bad times as their lands lost fertility. But several interrelated developments in the early nineteenth century transformed the cotton culture from a troubled to a highly prosperous enterprise, and slavery from a dying to a vigorous institution. The most important of these were the invention of the cotton gin, a machine for cleaning cotton, by Eli Whitney; the opening up of extremely rich soil perfectly suited for the cotton culture in Georgia, Alabama, and Mississippi; and, with the peace which followed the Napoleonic Wars, an enormous demand for raw cotton in the textile manufacturing centers of the American Northeast and of England. The South produced only 3,000 bales of cotton in 1790, about 73,000 in 1800. But production increased to more than 500,000 bales in 1825, more than 1 million in 1835, 2 million in 1850, and 5 million in 1859.[12]

With the growth and prosperity of the cotton economy after 1815, slavery was transformed from a dying institution into one that was aggressively expansionist, and its supporters came to defend it more passionately. The extension of the plantation system made southern society much more highly stratified and increased inequalities in the distribution of income. Power came to rest with the planter class.

The net effect of these changes was to set the South further and further apart from the rest of the country. The differences in political culture, modest at the turn of the century, had become a chasm by the eve of the Civil War: the culture of the region became much less popular and equalitarian, and began assuming all kinds of anti-liberal, quasi-aristocratic postures. Early in the nineteenth century, politicians in the South and West had actively pursued an alliance against the commercial and financial interests of the Northeast. But this agricultural alliance soon foundered on the growing differences in culture, style, and interests of the family-farm, free-soil West and the slave-owning, plantation South. The planters, as the region's power elite, opposed public investments in human capital—for example, education—and the South began slipping

[12] U.S. Bureau of the Census, *Historical Statistics of the United States, Colonial Times to 1957* (Washington, D.C.: U.S. Government Printing Office, 1960), p. 302.

behind the rest of the country. The ratio of children, in school to
(white) population in 1840 was one-twentieth in the slave-holding
states, one-fifth in the free states.

The first seven decades in American history possess a coherence
partly deriving from the fact that this was then an agricultural society.
Agricultural interests were far from consistently united. Indeed, as we
have seen, slavery and its various accompaniments proved an in-
superable obstacle to effective cooperation between agrarians South and
North. Nor was there some coherent commercial and then industrial
interest which farmers felt compelled to oppose. But there were incessant
pressures to develop business (in contrast to agriculture) and thus to
erode the economic foundation of Jefferson's republic. These sustained
continuing—although uneven and often confused—conflict. Majoritarian
agriculture could at times successfully resist the demands of commercial,
financial, and manufacturing interests, but, perched on the edge of the
industrial revolution and culturally receptive to it, it could not but
ultimately succumb.

The Localized Society and the Claims of Nation

Another distinctive characteristic of the United States in the years
before the Civil War was the localized nature of society. A big geographic area, a predominantly rural population, and the relatively primi-
tive state of communication and transportation technology all contributed
to this localism.

In 1790, 95 percent of the inhabitants of the new nation lived on
farms or in small villages. There were no cities as large as 50,000, and
only twenty-four with as many as 2,500 persons. As Figure 3.2 shows,
urbanism proceeded slowly in the first half of the nineteenth century; in
1850, 85 Americans in 100 were rural dwellers. This rural population
was scattered over a land area which grew through annexations from
just under a million square miles when the Constitution was ratified to
3 million at mid-century. People and goods moved through this vast
expanse (outside of waterways) either by animal or on foot. There were
no railroads until 1830, and in 1850 only a promise of the vast railroad
network to be (166,000 miles of road operated in 1890), with 9,000
miles of track in service. In communications, the same pattern can be
seen. The telegraph, moving messages over hundreds and thousands of
miles instantaneously, was an enormous advance over the previous communications—limited by the speed at which animals could transport
written messages. By 1895, the United States would be crossed with a

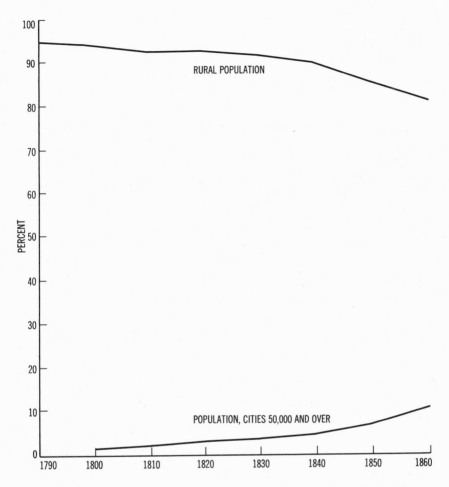

Figure 3.2. Percentage of the Population Rural and in Cities 50,000 or Over, United States 1790–1860*

*Source: *Historical Statistics of the United States,* pp. 7, 14. (The census defined as urban the population of all incorporated places of 2,500 or more. The entire population living outside such incorporated places was classified rural.)

vast grid of telegraph lines, more than 800,000 miles of wire. But the first telegraph service (between Baltimore and Washington, D.C.) did not begin until 1844, and at mid-century, the telegraph, like the railroad, was still only a promise of social transformation.

The Politics of Localism

In this localized society, "states' rights" had a basic legitimacy which most of us cannot now grant such appeals. Today, "states' rights" often serves to mask such objectives as the continuance of racial segregation:

"Let Mississippi handle race relations within its borders" means only "Let white supremacy remain untampered with." But for the followers of Jefferson and Jackson, commitment to state political autonomy involved no such hypocrisies. The position of the states as the principal units of government rested on a very large measure of social and economic independence of the various geographic parts. Later, of course, a mix of technology and economics would impose a massive interdependence on the society. But in pre-Civil War America there was really no integrated national economy, no nationalized cultural product; Maine and South Carolina were separated by weeks of arduous travel.

Americans had another reason to pay much more than lip service to the idea of substantial state autonomy. The centralizers of governmental authority in the seventeenth and eighteenth centuries—the relevant experience for early-nineteenth-century Americans—were the great European monarchs such as Louis XIV of France. States' rights, the relative independence of the constituent governmental units, was seen by many as a democratic principle; it carried the image of independent farmers free to govern themselves without the fetters of an overriding central authority.

The Claims of Nation

Even in this era of maximal localism, the appeal to *nation,* the impulse of nation-building, was felt. Some Americans pursued national integration more arduously than others, and the ensuing conflict figured prominently in the agenda. What were the specific matters at issue?

First, of course, there was the argument over the shape of the national political union. Instead of thirteen independent states loosely aligned under the Articles of Confederation, some wanted an effective national government, and they got it in 1789. The argument over the Constitution was an argument over nation-building. What distinguished the coalition that came together to put the new regime across? In its ranks were nationalists who wanted a strong union to make America respected in the community of nations. Alexander Hamilton was a nationalist in much the same sense—though not the same style—as Charles de Gaulle of France in our own time. They worshiped at the same shrine of national greatness. Another important group of supporters—overlapping with the first—were men of trade and financial affairs, convinced that a national political union was a prerequisite for economic development and prosperity. They insisted upon a government able to provide a congenial setting for economic growth: a big union in which goods could move freely; a strong navy protecting American shipping; support for infant industries; and above all, perhaps, national confidence and sense of purpose. On the other side, cool toward if not opposed to the Constitution, was a large portion of American farmers who had not been especially troubled by the operation of government under the Articles of Confederation.

Conflict over the pursuit of national integration did not stop with the ratification of the Constitution. Two distinct interpretations of the nature of the Union were debated throughout the first half of the nineteenth century, and only on the battlefields of the Civil War was there any resolution. The nationalizers, quite naturally, insisted that the Union had been brought into existence not by independent states but by the people as a whole: "We the people," the Preamble to the Constitution proclaims, formed the Union. The authority of the federal government is derived from this national community. "The Union," said Lincoln, "and not themselves [that is, the states] separately produced their independence and their liberty. . . . The Union gave each of them whatever of independence or liberty it has. The Union is older than any of the states, and, in fact, it created them as states." No state, according to this conception, could nullify an action of the national government with which it disagreed or secede from the Union, because the national Union had not granted the states such authority. The opponents of this "national idea" spoke of state sovereignty; the United States was established through agreement among thirteen independent states, and the Constitution was a kind of treaty among sovereigns. The states agreed to give up some powers to the national government, but they continued to be the fundamental political communities. "From this theory," Beer writes, "it also was plausibly inferred that the states had the right to interrupt the compact and, if necessary, to nullify an unconstitutional act, to interpose their authority to prevent its execution and in the final resort to secede from the Union."[13] Nullification and secession now suggest conflict over race, but before the Civil War states invoked the "right" to nullify legislation—citing the compact theory—in a variety of policy areas. In 1832, for example, the South Carolina legislature passed an "Ordinance of Nullification" declaring that recently enacted tariff legislation was not binding on its citizenry. The legislature further stipulated that if goods were seized for failure to pay tariff duties, the owners of the goods might recover twice their value from the federal

[13] Samuel H. Beer, "Liberalism and the National Idea," *The Public Interest* (Fall, 1966), p. 73.

officials who seized them. This led to Jackson's celebrated comments about hanging John Calhoun—the South Carolina political leader—and his strong defense of the Union: "I consider, then, the power to annul a law of the United States, assumed by one state, incompatible with the existence of the Union. . . . To say that any state may at pleasure secede from the Union is to say that the United States is not a nation. . . . Disunion by armed force is treason."

The argument over the extent to which national integration should be pursued can be seen in the matter of "internal improvements"—such public works as roads and canals. John Quincy Adams and Henry Clay were two political leaders who vigorously supported internal improvements as an instrument for nation-building. In his first message to Congress, Adams asked for a network of roads and canals, which "by multiplying and facilitating the communications and intercourse between distant regions and multitudes of men, are among the most important means of improvement." Through such public works, he felt, government lands would so increase in price as to underwrite an endowment of education and science on a scale never previously conceived. Adams' proposal and others like it were vigorously opposed as calling for actions beyond the scope of the national government. States' rights, limited national activity, substantial independence of the autonomous units were taken seriously indeed in the localized society.

In sum, the agenda of politics in pre–Civil War America bore ample testimony to a tension between national integration and state autonomy. And although major steps in nation-building were taken—especially in creating and securing a national government—the appeal to states' rights had a breadth and legitimacy in this period which it was never again to enjoy.

Before Bigness: The Society of Modest Scale

The period before the Civil War was extraordinary in its equalitarian distribution of resources. The age of bigness had not arrived. The United States, rejecting the patterned inequalities of aristocratic society, had not yet entered into the patterned inequalities bred of resource concentration and bureaucratic development of an industrializing society.

The great concentrations of capital that occurred with industrialization were not to be found in the Rural Republic. The largest manufacturing firms of this period were small indeed compared to those of a half century later. There were prosperous men, but fortunes were modest by the standards of 1900. Louis Hacker has observed that a few hundred thousand dollars was a respectable merchant-capitalist fortune in the 1850s.[14] So modest was the wealth of men of means, and so tenuous its base, that severe reversals often occurred. Thomas Jefferson was reduced to financial ruin and James Madison to near bankruptcy by the excess of entertaining too lavishly at their Virginia estates! Senator Thomas Hart Benton of Missouri, a major political figure between 1820 and 1850, went through recurrent boom and bust, and at one point had his home sold from under him by creditors—an event which caused little surprise and was not seen to reflect badly on Benton. Such turns of fortune were commonplace in an age in which wealth was measured in thousands rather than millions of dollars and rested on such flimsy foundations as land speculation and the whims of the market on cash crops.

The resources required to compete effectively in the communications of ideas were limited. Political communication was accomplished, beyond the reach of the human voice, by local newspapers—typically small, short-lived, and requiring little capital. In New York, the largest city, the *Morning Herald* was started (1835) on $500, and the *Tribune* (1841) on $3,000. Quite literally, any man with a few thousand dollars and the ability to compose a written sentence could set up his own newspaper and compete effectively in the process of idea dissemination.

This society of modest scale didn't require much of government. Government paralleled other social institutions: it was small. All national governmental expenses for all purposes from the formation of the regime to the Civil War totaled about $1.7 billion, and the largest outlay in any single year was $74 million in 1858. Not only was government small, but it didn't get bigger over this period. National expenditures per capita were $2.00 in 1800, $2.00 in 1860! Figure 3.3 shows that per capita expenditures fluctuated between $1.00 and $2.00 over the entire seventy-year span, rising a bit above that level only in war years.

To understand the political agenda of the Rural Republic we must keep very much in mind that it was a society before bigness. Business interests sought governmental support, to be sure, but they were not big business. In general, political competition before 1860 is sharply distinguished from that of the following period by the modest "wallop" of the contending interests. There was no argument about "big government" because no one was advocating big government—unless a tortured

[14] Louis Hacker, *The Triumph of American Capitalism* (New York: Simon and Schuster, 1940), p. 323.

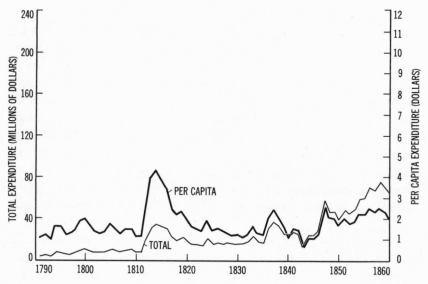

Figure 3.3. Federal Government Expenditure, Per Capita and Total, 1790–
1860*

* Source: *Historical Statistics of the United States,* pp. 7, 711.

construction of *big* is invoked. In 1792, the "big government" of
Alexander Hamilton was expending the grand sum of $5 million! It is a
simple but important fact that political conflict in the years before the
Civil War was not touched by the matter of an expansive role for government in regulating and supervising the economy or in any active sense
assuring the welfare of the citizenry. Andrew Jackson and Franklin
Roosevelt are sometimes lumped together as "strong presidents." Unless
the depiction is intended only to refer to strength of personality and
assertiveness, linking them thus badly confuses matters. Jackson's
presidency operated in the context of a limited, largely negative state;
Roosevelt's in the positive, managerial, and welfare state.

Ethnicity: The Early Rumbles

Conflict among groups defined by ethnocultural identities and attachments is as old as society. Such struggles have loomed especially large
in the United States, a country built on massive waves of immigration
from a variety of religious and ethnic traditions. *E Pluribus Unum,*
imprinted on the banner which waves from the eagle's back in the Great
Seal of the United States, initially suggested the forming of one nation
from thirteen sovereign states, but we see it today a tribute to the
creation of a sense of American national identity from so many national

and ethnic identities. Thus understood, the quite extraordinary movement from *pluribus* to *unum* has been demeaned by syrupy utterances so often heard at holiday observances. It has in fact been a hard journey attended by much of the ugliest in our national existence. The competing claims of ethnocultural groups for economic values, recognition, and influence have generated bitter conflict and, all too often when the contenders were grossly unequal in strength, harsh discrimination. At the same time, a real accomplishment is lost sight of when only the failures in ethnic and religious group relations are remembered. An American can be forgiven for boasting that probably no other country has grappled as successfully with such heterogeneity. The struggles of ethnocultural groups for a place in the sun, then, involves at once some of the worst and best in the American historical experience.

In the pre–Civil War years, the United States had not attained the ethnic diversity which was to follow, and conflict between ethnocultural groups was not as salient. There was a large Negro population, of course—16 percent of the total in 1850—but most were slaves and thus excluded from political life. Race was a continuing issue, and after 1850 one of extraordinary importance, but it was not an issue resulting from demands made by Negroes; instead, groups of whites felt variously threatened by proposals regarding slavery and its extension (see pages 103–108). The white inhabitants of the United States at regime formation were mostly from the British Isles, and the 1790–1860 immigration came mostly from Great Britain, Ireland, Germany, and other countries of Northern Europe. Table 3.1 shows that only a trace of the pre–Civil War immigration came from Eastern, Central, or Southern Europe. The Irish, and to a lesser extent the German, immigrants, accounted for a significant growth in the Catholic population. It was this division between an Anglo-Saxon Protestant majority and an Irish Catholic and German Catholic minority which generated the sharpest ethnocultural conflict up to the Civil War.

Throughout American history, the fears and resentments of established ethnic groups as "newer" Americans have sought recognition and influence have been manifested in nativist movements. Such movements display a lot of commonalities, although their immediate targets have shifted over time. They have not burned steadily, rather have blazed brightly only to largely disappear as if burned out. As Lipset and Raab have noted, "they [have not] become durable political movements, or create[d] viable national political parties. They [have] failed because their single-minded and bigoted emphasis did not equip them for the

TABLE 3.1

Immigration by Country, 1820–1859*

	1820–1859 (IMMIGRATION FROM ALL COUNTRIES: 4,908,774)	1820–1829 (IMMIGRATION FROM ALL COUNTRIES: 128,502)	1830–1839 (IMMIGRATION FROM ALL COUNTRIES: 538,381)	1840–1849 (IMMIGRATION FROM ALL COUNTRIES: 1,427,337)	1850–1859 (IMMIGRATION FROM ALL COUNTRIES: 2,814,554)
Great Britain	15.6	20.5	13.8	15.3	15.8
Ireland	38.9	40.2	31.7	46.0	36.6
Germany	30.4	4.5	23.2	27.0	34.7
Scandinavia	.8	.2	.4	.9	.9
Other Northwestern Europe	5.5	9.3	8.4	6.4	4.4
Central Europe	–	–	.1	–	–
Russia and the Baltic States	–	.1	.2	–	–
Other Eastern Europe	–	–	–	–	–
Italy	.3	.3	.4	.1	.3
Other Southern Europe	.4	3.0	.5	.2	.4
All other	8.1	22.0	21.5	4.1	6.9

*Source: *Historical Statistics of the United States,* pp. 56–59. (All data are expressed as percentages of the total immigration in the specified period.)

kind of coalition politics needed by a national party in America."[14] These nativist movements have been similarly fueled. A new identifiable ethnocultural group (or new groups) arrives in substantial numbers. Since much of the Catholic immigration of the nineteenth and early twentieth centuries and the Negro migration in the contemporary period settled in the cities, the setting for *overt* hostility has been largely urban. The new arrivals bring with them a "strange" or "foreign" culture which many among the established groups resent and cannot understand, and bring "un-Protestant" or "un-American" values and styles. Their growing numbers represent a more tangible threat to the political and economic position of the established groups. They have, or soon gain, the vote, which can be used to sustain new leaders and a hitherto minority party. And they are often seen as competitors for jobs. In addition, the new immigrants typically are low men on the socioeconomic totem pole. They inhabit the worse slums. The stresses and strains of their economic deprivation and exposure to a strange and in many ways hostile culture contribute to a higher incidence of types of behavior which in and of themselves are displeasing to the established population. Billington observes that in the 1830s the "disproportionately large number of foreign born in almshouses [was] repeatedly emphasized by writers who made a conscious effort to depict them as lazy and indolent, content either to accept public charity or beg upon the streets but unwilling to do the necessary hard work which the country required."[15] In 1850, Billington found, more than half of those convicted on criminal charges were foreign-born (though the foreign-born were just 11 percent of the population), and the proportion on public assistance was ten times as high for first-generation immigrants as for the native-born.[16] Looking at such data, Lipset and Raab conclude that part of the nativist resentment of the new immigrants in 1830–1850 (as later) was a reaction to such behavior, wrongly seen as characteristic of the entire group: "The typical characteristics of slum dwellers of the period were stereotyped as Catholic, just as today they are often identified with Negroes, Puerto Ricans, or Mexicans. Much of the negative feeling about Catholics then was the reaction of the clean middle class to the poorest, least educated, dirtiest, most criminal section of the urban population."[17]

[14] Seymour Martin Lipset and Earl Raab, *The Politics of Unreason: Right-Wing Extension in America 1790–1970* (New York: Harper & Row), Chapter 2.
[15] Ray Allen Billington, *The Protestant Crusade 1800–1860* (New York: Holt, Rinehart and Winston, 1952), pp. 194–195.
[16] *Ibid.,* p. 324.
[17] Lipset and Raab, Chapter 2.

Before the Civil War, Catholics were the prime target of nativist bigotry, especially Irish Catholics. It was with the large Irish immigration of the 1830s and 1840s that nativist movements took form. "Native American" associations sprang up, and in 1843 the Native Americans in New York established a third party, taking the name *American Republicans*. The decision to enter the electoral arena directly reflected both the growing strength of the nativist appeal and dissatisfaction with the major parties. The American Republican party quickly spread to other cities along the east coast, and enjoyed impressive successes in the 1844 elections: the nativists elected six congressmen from New York City and Philadelphia and mayors in New York and Boston.

The American Republicans were unable to sustain themselves as an electoral force, disappearing from the ballot in a few years. But in 1854 a much stronger nativist party was organized nationally—the American, or, as it was popularly known, the "Know-Nothing" party. With an anti-Catholic and nativist appeal, the Know-Nothings established themselves as the largest or second-largest party in many states North and South, and helped deliver the coup de grace to the tottering Whigs. While a number of developments, coming together, accounted for the successes of the American party, there is little question that the principal precipitant was the rapid growth of the Catholic immigrant population. Between 1850 and 1855, 2,118,000 immigrants came to the United States, 41 percent from Ireland and 34 percent from Germany. The total immigration in these six years was greater than in the thirty years from 1820 through 1849. A number of studies show that the Know-Nothings received some of their heaviest support among the Protestant working class of the cities. The strongest Know-Nothing ward in Baltimore, for example, was inhabited mostly by Protestant mechanics and workingmen.[18] A large majority of the Boston and Worcester Know-Nothings apparently were Protestant "mechanics."[19]

The struggles between recent Catholic immigrants and older-stock Protestants were carried out around a series of specific issues debated before legislative bodies and in election campaigns. For example, nativist groups repeatedly sought immigration restrictions. In New York state in the early 1840s, there was a lively struggle over proposals to share state

[18] Lawrence F. Schmeckebier, *History of The Know Nothing Party in Maryland* (Baltimore: Johns Hopkins Press, 1899), p. 67.

[19] Gerald P. Daly, "Manifestations of Nativism in Massachusetts with Special Reference to The Know-Nothing Movement" (Honors Thesis, Dept. of History, Harvard University, 1963), pp. 82–83; George H. Haynes, "A Chapter from the Local History of Know Nothingism," *New England Magazine* (September, 1896), pp. 84–96.

support for education, which had gone exclusively to the Protestant-oriented Public School Society, with the parochial schools operated by the Roman Catholic Church.[20] Intermittently, however, the struggle boiled over into acts of extra-legal violence. As early as 1806, there was a bloody riot in New York City involving gangs of nativists and Irish. The Philadelphia riots of 1844 were especially severe: a Catholic Church was burned, thirteen persons were killed, and the militia had to be brought in to re-establish order.

In the mid-1850s, as the deepening crisis over slavery absorbed national attention, the differences among white ethnocultural groups were shoved aside. This was to be only temporary. With the greatly enlarged and diversified immigration of the half-century after the Civil War, conflict involving groups defined by their ethnic and religious identifications was to attain a prominence in the political agenda greater than in the ethnically more homogeneous America of the pre-War period.

The Party System, 1790–1860: A Structural Overview

Americans in 1790 had experience aplenty with *factions*, the assorted cliques which seek to influence governmental activity that were omnipresent in political life before and after egalitarianism, but no experience at all with *party* in the modern sense, an institution for political linkage in a society of mass participation. Alliances began to take shape in Congress in the 1790s, and many—probably most Americans who thought about it at all—viewed this with skepticism if not alarm. After having watched contending groups take ever more definite shape around two of his first Cabinet appointees, Hamilton and Jefferson, Washington issued his famous warning against the dangers of party in his Farewell Address of September, 1796:

It [the spirit of party] serves always to distract the Public Councils and enfeeble the Public administration. It agitates the Community with ill-founded jealousies and false alarms, kindles the animosity of one part against another, foments occasional riot and insurrection. It opens the door to foreign influence and corruption, which find a facilitated access to the government itself through the channels of party passions. . . . A fire not to be quenched; it demands a uniform vigilance to prevent its bursting into a flame, lest instead of warming it should consume.

[20] Lipset and Raab, Chapter 2.

James Madison defined a party or faction (for the two words were used interchangeably) in *The Federalist* as "a number of citizens, whether amounting to a majority or minority of the whole, who are united or actuated by some common impulse of passion, or of interest, *adverse to the rights of other citizens, or to the permanent and aggregate interests of the community.*" And he then referred to methods "of curing the mischiefs of faction." Jefferson, though he was in fact the chief architect of the first political party, seems never to have thought in terms of an institutionalized party system as a regular part of the American political structure. There are many indications of his confusion. Thus in a letter to John Adams in 1813 he remarked that "the same political parties which now agitate the U.S. have existed thro' all time." A curious statement indeed from a political leader who had helped establish the world's first party system! (Some of the points at issue were, of course, not new, but the parties *as institutions* had no precursors.) And while president in 1804, Jefferson had written William Short that "the party division in this country is certainly not among its pleasant features. To a certain degree it will always exist: and chiefly in mercantile places. In the country and those states where the Republicans have a decided superiority, party hostility has ceased to infest society." He went on to lament that he had been quite prepared to offer the Federalist leaders a few minor places in his government if they would cease to be an opposition force, but that they had spurned this! There was, in sum, even among the most prescient of Americans of the day no real picture of party as a regular, necessary instrument through which the views of a citizenry are organized and expressed in an egalitarian polity.

But if Americans were somewhat uncertain as to what they were about, they nonetheless went ahead rapidly with the building of parties. The first stirrings of party were in the conflict between Hamilton and Jefferson in Washington's administration, a division which was part of a much broader argument over public policy in the new regime. As the dispute deepened, Hamilton turned to his friends in Congress, Jefferson to his, and with this factional ties between executive and legislative leaders became much tighter.

The incipient parties arose, then, from divisions in national rather than state politics.[21] Party lines became clear in national politics before they did in state competition. The Republican party of Jefferson made

---

[21] For an excellent description of this, see Noble E. Cunningham, Jr., *The Jeffersonian Republicans* (Chapel Hill: The University of North Carolina Press, 1957).

its first electoral thrusts by endorsing candidates for Congress and for presidential electors in the several states; party tickets for state legislatures and other state offices came later.

By what date had the "factions" become something more than mere cliques, become modern political parties? The question can be better put this way: By what date were the Federalists and Republicans competing in a fairly sustained manner for support among a mass electorate, offering symbol referents (party labels) around which the electorate could rally? Estimates vary. Thus William Nisbet Chambers thinks that "we may speak of a Federalist party proper by the late months of 1793 and the early months of 1794."[22] Certainly the outlines of opposing factions in Congress were clear by then, but the date is a bit early if one holds up seriously the criteria of constituency organization, party tickets, and the regular use of the party symbol. In 1796, for example, candidates for Congress in most of the states ran without any reference to party labels. There is no question, however, but that by the end of Adam's administration, parties in the modern sense were on the scene.

Constituency organization began to appear first in the Middle Atlantic states, especially Pennsylvania and New York. The earliest organization commonly involved some system of "committees of correspondence": a committee of state party notables would contact influential citizens throughout the state, asking them in turn to call meetings of "our friends in your town." Republicans tended to take the initiative in introducing party machinery, but the Federalists usually followed soon after with similar structures. Washington's leaving the presidency in 1797 was an important spur to party organization and activity, because instead of an administration much revered and "above party" there was the Adams presidency as a convenient target for Jeffersonian scorn. The election of 1800 saw dramatic extensions of party organization, and diligent Republican organizational activity in support of Jefferson clearly contributed to his victory.

The Republican Association of Bucks County, Pennsylvania, is an example of an early, highly developed constituency organization. It would elicit admiration from any modern party manager. A February, 1803, communication from the County Republican Committee to the electorate indicates just how quickly party activity matured there. "Time was in this county when a few men met at a court, erected themselves into a committee, and assumed the power of forming a ticket for the

22 William Nisbet Chambers, *Political Parties in a New Nation* (New York: Oxford University Press, 1963), p. 50.

county. A few others constituted in like manner, formed, perhaps, a counter ticket, and left the citizens at large a choice of two evils." But all this, happily, had changed: "Our tickets are formed agreeably to the representative system; by men elected and specially appointed to the service." Still, the communication went on, new procedures were in order. (1) Henceforth each township in the county would have one vote on the county Republican committee. (2) The representatives from each township would be chosen annually in a popular election conducted on the same day and at the same place as the regular township officer elections. (3) Any voter would be able to participate in this election of town committeemen "provided he professes to be a democratic republican," and has supported the party for at least six months. (4) The county committee thus elected would meet at specified and well-publicized times to make nominations for the various county offices—state representatives, sheriff, coroners, county commissioners, etc.[23] Few local parties, however, were this organizationally elaborate. Party organization in the early years of the nineteenth century in most places was rudimentary, and variations in practice from state to state were marked.

One thing which differentiated the first party system from those which followed was that no one active in public life in the early nineteenth century had been born either a Federalist or a Republican. There were no loyalties strong and deep on which to build. We know that one thing which sustains and stabilizes a party system is the identification of large portions of the population with the parties. And in a country with ongoing parties these attachments are formed along with other identifications (ethnic, religious, class, etc.) as individuals grow up and are "socialized," the product of persistent interactions with family and friends. Partisanship thus is "inherited," or passed on from one generation to another.[24] The absence of inherited loyalties in the new party system of the first period, together with the rudimentary character of party organization and the prevailing tendency to see party as, at best, a necessary evil, made the new party growth relatively superficial. The roots of party simply did not run deep.

The two-party system which developed in the 1790s began to de-

[23] "The Republican Committee of Bucks County, To Their Constituents," (February, 1803), in Noble Cunningham, ed., *The Making of the American Party System 1789 to 1809* (Englewood Cliffs, N.J.: Prentice-Hall, 1965), pp. 110–113.

[24] For further discussion of the development of party identification in the United States, see Angus Campbell *et al.*, *The American Voter* (New York: John Wiley, 1960), especially Chapter 7.

teriorate in the early years of the nineteenth century as the Federalists proved unable to compete with the Republicans nationally. Last electing a president in 1796, reduced to a New England base after 1800, the Federalist party disappeared entirely from the national scene after 1816.

In 1816 the Congressional Caucus of the Republican party nominated the last of the Revolutionary notables with a claim to the presidency, James Monroe, by a narrow 65–54 vote over the popular secretary of the treasury, William Crawford of Georgia. The Federalists offered what was to be their last presidential nominee, Rufus King of New York. King managed to collect the electoral votes of only three states, Massachusetts, Connecticut, and Delaware. After 1819, the Federalists competed on a statewide basis only in Massachusetts and Delaware. As a national force the party was dead, the heirs of Jefferson supreme, and the young democracy was without structured party competition. All sorts of politicians scrambled behind the broad Jeffersonian Republican standard. "Party organizations decayed, ideological and programmatic differences were blurred, and many Federalists in search of office joined their erstwhile enemies. With each passing year, Jefferson's vision was increasingly coming to pass—'We are all republicans, we are all federalists'—although the emphasis fell on the former term."[25]

Monroe served two terms as a man without a party; since all claimed to be of one party, obviously party as an instrument for discipline or as a symbol for the faithful to rally about was not operative. He could not exert discipline over Congress, and Congress in turn was too fragmented to act coherently.

When the president bowed to the two-term tradition in 1824, a struggle over who was to be the nominee ensued and the caucus system collapsed. As long as there had been party competition, those in the electorate dissatisfied with the caucus choice could look to the opposition party. But with the disappearance of the Federalist opposition, the Republican caucus choice—if not challenged within the party—was assured of the presidency. At the same time, popular participation was on the rise and the caucus, never a popular instrument, more and more seemed anti-democratic, a small closed group of party leaders selecting the president. Inevitably in this situation, ambitious men would not passively acquiesce to a caucus defeat.

---

[25] Paul Goodman, "The First American Party System," in Chambers and Burnham, eds., *The American Party Systems* (New York: Oxford University Press, 1967), p. 85.

In 1824, William Crawford, despite a serious illness, was the choice of the caucus, but only 20 percent of the senators and representatives voted. Disregarding this action, three other candidates plunged into the contest: John Quincy Adams, who had been Monroe's secretary of state; Henry Clay, the House leader from Kentucky; and Andrew Jackson, the hero of the Battle of New Orleans. In a four-way race, no candidate received a majority of the electoral vote (although Jackson gained a plurality of the popular vote in the first election in which a substantial number of states provided for the popular selection of presidential electors) and the House of Representatives was left to choose among the three leaders—Jackson, Adams, and Crawford. The story is well known that Clay backed Adams who had been second in both the popular and electoral vote, a natural enough decision in view of the strong commitment of both men to internal improvements on behalf of national integration, and Adams became president. In the course of Adams' presidency, the split between the "Adams men" and the "Jackson men" became ever more formally structured, and Adams and Jackson did battle again in 1828, with the latter victorious. The first party system had collapsed and a second was taking shape. Behind the breakup of the Democratic-Republican party and the emergence of a new two-party system was the simple fact that one-partyism was unnatural in a large, diverse, democratic society with a rising level of popular participation. Conflict among men contending for office was inevitable, and so was the structuring of this conflict.

The struggle between the Republicans and the Federalists had at the outset a very clear policy or issue component which was largely absent in the formative years of the second party system: the latter was imposed less by issues than by the demand for a structuring of alternatives in a democratic society. There were real policy differences, but these followed more than precipitated the emergence of the new parties.

After 1828 the new party system was extended and perfected in several stages, as standard party symbols assumed wider frequency, and as party competition was extended into more and more states. In 1832, the new system was well established in New England and the Middle States, but the opposition to the Jackson party lacked a persistent standard and operated variously under the Adams, National Republican, and Antimasonic labels. And the South was politically monolithic, with virtually all politicians claiming at least vague attachment to the Jackson banner; conflict at the state and local levels tended to be unstructured. In 1836, with Martin Van Buren of New York the candidate of what

was widely recognized as the Democratic party, two-party competition
was extended into the South; where Jackson had encountered only
token opposition in the southern states (other than Kentucky) in 1832,
Van Buren polled slightly less than 50 percent of the popular vote. The
anti-Van Buren or Whig parties that emerged in the South and West
between 1834 and 1836—together with those in the Northeast that
had taken shape earlier—lacked in 1836 national cohesion and leadership: in the presidential election that year, the opposition standard was
carried by Hugh Lawson White of Tennessee in the South, by William
Henry Harrison of Indiana in most of the rest of the country except
Massachusetts, where it was native son Daniel Webster. Finally, in
the election of 1840, the new system assumed mature form. Whigs and
Democrats were competing in a national party system which reflected
maturity bred of a half-century of experience and experiment. "In every
region of the country, and indeed in every state, politics was conducted
within the framework of a two-party system, and in all but a handful
of states the parties were so closely balanced as to be competitive."[26]

The second party system, pitting Democrats and Whigs, differed
from the first in a number of structural regards. Competition was vastly
more uniform and consistent at the state level. It was a national system,
with parties organized in all, not just some of, the states. Party machinery
assumed more standard form throughout the country. And the basic
electoral setting in which the second system operated differed vastly
from the first, what McCormick has called a " 'hidden revolution' . . .
in the electoral environment" between 1800 and 1840: presidential
electors came to be chosen by the people on general tickets rather than
by state legislatures; conventions replaced caucuses as the principal
instrument for making nominations, for the presidency and for lesser
offices as well; property qualifications for voting were dropped, universal
white male suffrage was achieved, and the electorate was greatly expanded. By 1840, a party structure had been achieved which has
endured for more than a century, to our own day.

The Parties: Positions in the Agenda

How did the major parties of the Rural Republic—Federalists and
Republicans, then Democrats and Whigs—position themselves in the

[26] Richard McCormick, "Political Development and the Second Party System,"
in Chambers and Burnham, p. 102. See, too, for a careful and detailed description
of the emergence of the second party system, McCormick's *The Second American
Party System* (Chapel Hill: University of North Carolina Press, 1966).

conflict of the period? What was the scope and substance of inter-party policy differences?

Federalists and Republicans

The Federalists in the early years of the new regime were the party of the "national idea"; and in the same tentative sense, the Democratic-Republicans represented the "parochial idea" of state autonomy and a more independent agricultural economy. Those political leaders of the 1790s who held forth a bold and coherent vision of a national union, strong politically and integrated economically, who saw their interests better protected and promoted by national than by state and local authority, were for the most part Federalists. When the Republicans gained power in 1801 they did not, of course, set about systematically dismantling the national union; quite the contrary, they maintained in all essentials the system which the Federalists had bequeathed them. And after 1812, the Federalist remnant, in decline and disarray following repeated defeats, did forsake its old posture as the party of national integration.[27] Still, the Federalists in their short life as a major political party had given the new nation its clearest statement of the national idea.

The United States in the first years after regime formation was an agricultural nation, and no party could have competed without the support of farmers. To describe the Federalists simply as a mercantile party and the Republicans as a party of agricultural interests would be wide of the mark. It was the case, however, that trade and commercial interests, such as they were in the new society, looked to the Federalists to represent their interests. And the Federalists were so closely identified

[27] The Federalist abdication was complete with the Hartford Convention of December 1814. Strong opposition to the 1812–1814 war with England had developed in New England, the Federalist bastion. The American war effort had been badly managed, and one disaster followed another—enough to cause unrest throughout the country—but New England's commercial interests had suffered severely from the British Admiralty's blockade of the Atlantic coast. It was in this setting that Massachusetts invited representatives of the other New England states to a meeting to discuss the war and to plan their future course in the event that the national government was further discredited or, through defeat, unable to protect its members. Every delegate to this Convention, which met in Hartford in late 1814, was a Federalist. The Convention did little, but, unfortunately for the Federalists, only thirty days after it adjourned news was received in Washington of the "great American victory" at New Orleans, and one week later a peace treaty was signed at Ghent. The Federalists were seen as plotting, with the country at war (and, at that, a war of glorious victories!), something smacking of secession or nullification. Ironically, this delivered a final blow to a party which had begun as the custodian of American nationalism.

with the "moneyed" interests that they suffered politically in a society in which most people plowed fields.

The Federalists are sometimes described, quite wrongly, as the party of "big government" in these early years of the new regime. As we have seen, no one at that time was advocating anything approaching "big government." The confusion has arisen from a failure to distinguish between a commitment to nation-building and support of positive government. The Federalist party was the vigorous proponent of the national idea, and thus willing to do what needed to be done to establish an effective national authority. But the claims of national integration in the first period did not in any sense require wide-ranging, positive government.

The Jefferson party was somewhat more popular, less elitist, than its Hamiltonian opponent—although the difference in this regard is easily overstated. The Jeffersonians frequently attacked the Federalists as monarchists, "monocrats," and assorted aristocrats who opposed the new Republican institutions. This was nonsense. And in the relatively deferential politics of the late eighteenth and early nineteenth centuries, the Republican leadership was hardly "just plain folks" doing the people's business. In the Jeffersonian ranks were many well-placed agriculturalists and in some instances, as in Delaware, men of commerce. Still, in 1800 the Federalist party stood in national political life as the home of the American elite. A recent, careful study concludes that "the established elites in most states were Federalist; their challengers were Jeffersonian. . . . Old wealth and respectable callings were but two of many distinguishing characteristics of the American elite, which tended toward Federalism in its politics in 1800. Another was education. The higher the attained level of formal schooling, the more likely was a firm Federalist commitment."[28] The precipitous decline of the Federalists is related to this, for as the party of the American elite they responded more slowly than their opponents to the emergence of a popular and democratic style.

Both Federalists and Republicans had their factions. The Federalists were badly hurt during the administration of John Adams (1797–1801) by the continuing warfare between the so-called "High Federalists" and the party's moderate faction, which Adams represented. The High Federalists were the more elitist, clearly antidemocratic element of the

[28] David Hackett Fischer, *The Revolution of American Conservatism* (New York: Harper & Row, 1965), pp. 203, 208.

party.[29] The Republicans, for their part, had a factional division between pragmatic or moderate leaders such as Jefferson who came to defend the national union they picked up from the Federalists, and to grant the legitimacy of some manufacturing enterprise; and such extreme states' rights proponents as John Taylor of Caroline County, Virginia, who waged a continuing polemical battle against any departure from pure agrarianism.

The Democrats and Whigs

Students of American parties in the first half of the nineteenth century disagree on the extent to which the Whigs can be considered descendants of the Federalists and Democrats the bearers of the old Jeffersonian-Republican standard. Obviously there was no direct lineague in people and organization: that is, the surviving Federalists did not simply re-group in the Whig party, nor the old Jeffersonians in the Jackson party. And most of the men who became the Democratic and Whig leaders in state party systems throughout the country in the 1830s came to public life *after* the time at which the Republican-Federalist division had ceased to exist. There were new men and new organizations. The question of continuity rests, then, on whether the *position* of the Whigs in the political agenda of the 1830s and 1840s *approximated that* of the Federalists at the turn of the century, and the position of the Democrats that of the Republicans. As usual, it seems, with the doctrinally promiscuous and eclectic American parties, the answer to the question of policy continuities is not clear.

In *The Promise of American Life,* written a half-century ago, Herbert Croly located what he considered an important policy continuity from Jeffersonian-Republican to Democratic in the nineteenth century. No "measure of legislation expressive of a progressive national idea," wrote Croly, "can be attributed to the Democratic party [a party which] cannot become the party of national responsibility without being faithless to its own creed."[30] In Jeffersonian and Jacksonian democracy, Croly found accompanying the political doctrine of "trust the people" an economic doctrine of "extreme individualism." The Jeffersonians and Jacksonians concluded that "good government, particularly on the part of Federal officials, consisted, apart from routine business, in letting

[29] For further discussion of Federalist factionalism, see William Nisbet Chambers, *Political Parties in the New Nation* (New York: Oxford University Press, 1963), especially Chapter 6.

[30] Herbert Croly, *The Promise of American Life* (New York: Macmillan, 1914), pp. 163, 171.

things alone."[31] In contrast, the Hamiltonian Federalists, the Whigs (and after the Civil War the Republicans) sought to use the central government "not merely to maintain the Constitution, but to promote the national interest and to consolidate the national organization," a policy which implied "an active interference with the national course of American economic and political business and its regulation and guidance in the national direction."[32] In other words, Croly argues that there is policy continuity linking Federalists and Whigs, and Jeffersonian Republicans and Jacksonian Democrats; the former, albeit imperfectly, were the "nationalizing" parties, and the latter the parties of the provincial idea. But this is a bit too neat. Jefferson, after all, proved an able defender of the national union, and contributed to its territorial expansion with the Louisiana Purchase. And Andrew Jackson resisted Calhoun and the nullifiers, and thus defended the national idea. Recall his famous toast at a Jefferson Day dinner in 1830, in which he proclaimed, "Our federal union, it must be preserved!" Still, central to both Jeffersonian and Jacksonian ideology was a commitment to state autonomy, the belief that the interests of the American people would best be promoted and preserved by the minimal involvement of a national authority. And Whig leaders such as Daniel Webster and Edward Everett, like Hamilton before them, were readier to use the federal government to promote national integration.

We detect a similar policy continuity from Federalists to Whigs and from Jeffersonian Republicans to Democrats in economic policy. In a society so decisively agricultural as the United States before the Civil War, no political party could compete effectively for national power exclusively through appeals to mercantile and industrial interests. But the Whigs like the Federalists before them were the far more consistent proponents of business enterprising nationally. "The Whig Modernists looked toward an increasingly dynamic, complex, and industrialized society. . . . [In contrast] the Democratic traditionalists looked backward to the late 18th century and found inspiration in Jefferson's idyllic vision . . . of the negative state functioning in Arcadia, that is, in a sparsely-settled, simple agrarian country."[33] There is some overstatement in this description of the Whigs as committed to a vision of a complexly industrialized society, but they *were* the party of business, 1840s-style. A recent study shows that in a series of economic policy clashes after 1828,

[31] *Ibid.,* p. 49.
[32] *Ibid.,* pp. 39–40.
[33] Lee Benson, *The Concept of Jacksonian Democracy* (Princeton: Princeton University Press, 1961), pp. 105–106.

more and more New York City businessmen deserted the Democratic party. Some left during the Bank Veto campaign of 1832,[34] others a year later, after Jackson removed federal deposits from the Bank of United States. Still others defected following the Panic of 1837 and the "independent Treasury" or "Subtreasury" proposal.[35] "As important as were the defections, perhaps even more significant was the fact that the Democratic response to the bank war and Panic of 1837 temporarily solidified the New York City business community into an anti-Democratic force. It may be difficult now to comprehend what terrors the Subtreasury scheme would have imposed on the merchants . . . but the businessmen of that day did not have the balm of historical perspective to soothe them."[36] By 1840, nearly 85 percent of the wealthy citizens of New York City were Whigs.

The rapid movement in the first half of the nineteenth century toward a more popular political style did contribute an important difference to Whig-Democratic conflict, compared to that between Republicans and Federalists. Hamilton's party, wedded to a much more deferential style of political life, openly expressed contempt for "the people" and fear of them. The Whig party in 1840 may have resembled the Federalist as a coalition in which voters of high socioeconomic status were concentrated, but the Whigs had successfully abandoned the highly elitist rhetoric of the Federalists and had adopted the equalitarian style with a passion. The Whig presidential campaign of 1840, "Tippecanoe and Tyler too," was an effort to replace discussion of issues with campaign hoopla and emphasis on the standard-bearer (who was a popular war hero). The Whigs showed that they, as much as their Democratic op-

[34] See pages 65–66 for a description of the Second Bank of the United States. Jackson vetoed a bill rechartering the Bank for a second twenty-year term.

[35] After the Panic of 1837 broke, the newly elected president, Martin Van Buren, tried to make the national government independent of all banks by proposing legislation that would place government funds in an "Independent Treasury" in Washington and a series of subtreasuries throughout the country—instead of in state banks or, as was the case under the First and Second Banks of the United States, in a national bank. Van Buren's proposal also contained provision for the government to issue its own currency, in place of banknotes which were serving as currency. (The Independent Treasury bill did not pass until 1840; it was repealed in 1841 and re-enacted in 1846, surviving then until the Civil War.) It was widely believed that separating banks from the government would be bad for business. Editorialized the *National Gazette* of Philadelphia: "It is the incarnation of the Bentonian-Jacksonism—a sophisticated sermon on the favorite text of 'Perish commerce—perish credit,' and an ingenuous appeal to the irrational passions of the worst party in the country" (quoted in Agar, p. 259).

[36] Frank Otto Gatell, "Money and Party in Jacksonian America: A Quantitative Look at New York City's Men of Quality," *Political Science Quarterly* (June, 1967), pp. 244–245.

ponents, understood this remarkably equalitarian society, and were both ready and able to play the game of democratic politics. Beyond this, they had developed the intellectual foundation of what was to serve the Republican party after the Civil War so well as a legitimizing ideology—democratic capitalism.

We think of the Whigs in the age of Harrison as stealing the egalitarian thunder of the Democrats, but actually they did more than that. They transformed it. For if they gave up Hamilton's hatred of the people, they retained his grandiose capitalist dream, and this they combined with the Jeffersonian concept of equal opportunity. The result was to electrify the democratic individual with a passion for great achievement and to produce a personality type that was neither Hamiltonian or Jeffersonian but a strange mixture of them both: the hero of Horatio Alger.[37]

Thus, the more elitist of the two parties had learned to live with democracy.

The scope of government in the years when Whigs and Democrats did battle remained limited, and all contenders looked to a negative state. There is simply no basis for the argument advanced by Benson and others that the Whigs were advocates of the "positive liberal state" and the Democrats of the "negative liberal state."[38] The parties shared the highly individualistic visions and values of liberalism. They agreed upon the desirability of economic arrangements in which acquisitive, capitalist men were able to work their way without governmental interference. No one wanted positive government in the sense of a state supervising, ordering, and directing the flow of life of the society. The Whigs, like the Federalists before them, were somewhat more willing to use governmental power to promote national integration and business enterprise, but the promotion they advocated was modest indeed: setting up a national bank, funding state debts to enhance the financial confidence in the country, building canals and roads to facilitate the flow of goods. This is hardly the positive state!

For well over a century after the beginning of a substantial immigration from Catholic Europe (around 1830), conflict between "old-stock" Protestants and "new-stock" Catholics figured prominently in the American political agenda; and for this entire period the Democrats were distinguished from their major party opponents by a generally greater support of the latter's interests. It would be quite wrong to call the

[37] Hartz, pp. 111–112.
[38] See Benson, pp. 104–109.

Democrats "the Catholic party," for they were a national party appealing to a variety of groups and interests. They were especially strong in the South, an overwhelmingly Protestant and old-stock region. But in national politics the Democracy continued to resist nativism and anti-Catholicism; backed policies which Catholic Americans favored; gave Catholics entree into leadership positions in their organization, especially in the northeastern cities; and were rewarded with the votes of large majorities of Catholics. Nativism and anti-Catholicism often found only tentative or limited support in the national arena from the Whigs and Republicans—engaged as these major parties were in the kind of coalition-building necessary for national power—and boiled over in such third-party challenges as that of the Know-Nothings in the mid-1850s. But what *major party* articulation there was came *consistently* from the Whigs and, subsequently, the Republicans.

In the 1840s, the Whigs flirted with nativist groups, trying to give just enough to win their support without losing the support of others. Sometimes they didn't give enough. In 1843, we have seen, the Native Americans felt that Whig support of their position was insufficient, and organized their own party, the American Republican. But in 1844 the Whigs struck a tacit alliance with the nativists in which they backed the latter's local and congressional candidates and received in turn American Republican support for their presidential ticket. The Whig's vice presidential nominee, Theodore Frelinghuysen, was a prominent nativist. Their New York gubernatorial candidate in 1844 was Millard Fillmore, who went on to become vice president and president (1849–1853), and then in 1856 the presidential nominee of the Know-Nothing party, the larger successor to the American Republicans.

In their 1840 platform, the Democrats put themselves on record as flatly opposed to nativist demands for immigration restriction, insisting that the United States should be a haven for "the oppressed of every nation," and proclaiming further that the open door was a "cardinal principle" of their party's creed: "That the liberal principles embodied by Jefferson in the Declaration of Independence, and sanctioned in the Constitution, which makes ours the land of liberty and the asylum of the oppressed of every nation, have ever been cardinal principles in the democratic faith; *and every attempt to abridge the present privilege of becoming citizens, and the owners of soil among us, ought to be resisted with the same spirit which swept the alien and sedition laws from our statute book*" (emphasis added). In their 1844 platform, before the growth of nativist sympathies indicated by the formation of the American Republican party, the Democrats repeated this plank verbatim. They repeated it again in 1848, in 1852, and 1856, when the Know-Nothings were challenging them on the national scene. Surely the meaning of this was not lost—on either recent immigrants or nativists. Before all this the Whigs were silent; not once in their platforms from 1844 through 1856 (there was no Whig platform in 1840) did they mention immigration. As a major party they would not take over the nativist demands for restriction, but neither would they repudiate such demands.

In the years after 1840, when such movements were attracting substantial support, the Democrats continued to attack nativism and its partisan expressions, the American Republicans and the Know-Nothings. The Whigs, for their part, were engaged in quiet and limited cooperation. Studies of the electoral responses of the various ethnocultural groups to this agree that old-stock Protestants were not polarized but fairly evenly divided between the two big parties, while Catholics of whatever ethnic group were overwhelmingly Democratic.[39] Benson estimates that in 1844 "about 95% of the 'Catholic voters' supported the Democrats in New York State."[40] A large majority in both big parties were Protestants, for the United States before the Civil War was an overwhelmingly Protestant country.

The Parties in Electoral Competition

In American electoral history, we have noted, the contenders in the national two-party system have rarely been evenly matched. Most of the time, one party has been clearly ascendant. The Jeffersonian Republicans and later the Jacksonian Democrats were the "suns" of the Rural Republic, the Federalists and Whigs the orbiting "moons."

Republicans vs. Federalists

The life of the Federalist party as an alliance able to compete effectively for national power was a short one. They elected Adams by the slight electoral vote margin of three in 1797, then lost narrowly in the presidential election of 1801, with Adams and Jefferson again the contestants. Thereafter, only in 1813, with De Witt Clinton of New York as their candidate, aided by disaffection over the war with Eng-

[39] See, for example, Edward Pessen, *Jacksonian America: Society, Personality, and Politics* (Homewood, Ill.: Dorsey, 1969), especially Chapter 10); and Benson, Chapters 8 and 9.
[40] Benson, p. 187.

land, did they challenge effectively. In Congress, the Federalists' strength showed the same precipitous decline. They controlled both houses from the emergence of party blocs in the Second Congress up to the election of 1800, except for the House of Representatives from 1793 to 1795. After that, they were, as Figure 3.4. shows, a weak minority in both houses until their disappearance in the early 1820s.

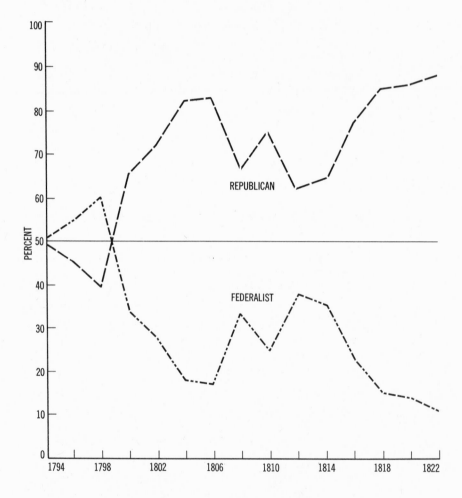

Figure 3.4. Republican Percentage of Seats, U.S. House of Representatives, 1794–1822*

* Source: *Historical Statistics of the United States,* pp. 691–693.

Regional variations in party strength were sharp in the first party system (1796–1820). As the Federalists declined after 1800, they were thrown back upon an almost exclusively New England base. They won

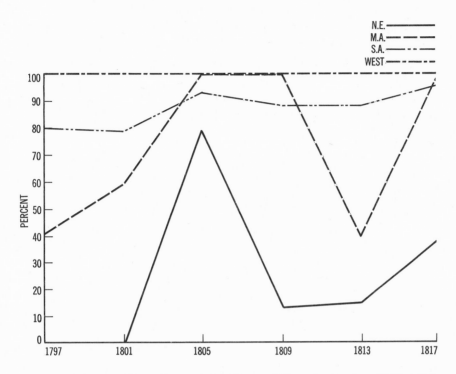

Figure 3.5. Republican Share of the Electoral Vote, by Region, 1797–1817

a majority of the electoral votes in New England in every presidential election from 1797 through 1817, except in 1805. On the other hand, they managed to secure a majority in another of the principal geographic regions on only two occasions—the Middle Atlantic states in 1797 and again in 1813. Outside of Maryland and Delaware, the Federalists never had southern strength, and as Figure 3.5 shows they failed to win a single electoral vote from any of the "Western" (in this period trans-Appalachian) states. Five states gave a majority of their electoral votes to the Federalists in the 1797–1817 presidential elections, Delaware joining four New England states. Twelve states in the union for all or most of the period returned Republican majorities, five never giving the Federalists a vote. (Virginia, not far behind, cast only one Federalist vote.)

Whigs vs. Democrats

We have noted that the second party system was constructed at a time of significant democratization in American political life, including the completion of the movement to popular election of slates of presidential electors, the dropping of property qualifications for voting, and

THE FEDERALIST STATES (*percent of all electoral votes cast*)		THE REPUBLICAN STATES (*percent of all electoral votes cast*)	
Connecticut	100	Georgia	100
Delaware	100	Kentucky	100
Massachusetts	83	South Carolina	100
Rhode Island	67	Tennessee	100
New Hampshire	64	Ohio	100
		Virginia	99
		Pennsylvania	93
		North Carolina	91
		Vermont	78
		Maryland	66
		New York	61
		New Jersey	52
		Louisiana	100 (two elections)
		Indiana	100 (one election)

the development of popular electioneering techniques. Together such
changes produced a dramatic increase in the level of voting. The election

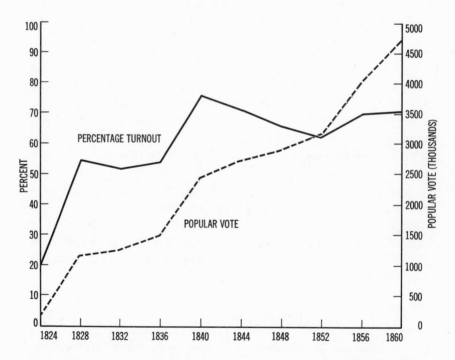

Figure 3.6. Popular Vote and Percentage Turnout, Presidential Elections,
1824–1860

of 1824 was the first in which the popular vote was sufficiently large to permit a description of the outcome in popular vote terms. But it was the election of 1828 that marked the full democratization of the presidency. As Figure 3.6 shows, in this two-way race between the incumbent, Adams, and the challenger, Jackson, the total popular vote was triple that of the preceding presidential election, and the portion of adult white males casting votes increased to the same degree. In 1840, there was another substantial increase in popular turnout, with the introduction of sustained popular electioneering. The percentage of white males of voting age casting ballots was actually slightly greater between 1840 and 1860 than in the 1950s and 1960s.

The two decades after 1832 were a period of exceedingly close national two-party competition. The Whigs, casting aside the old Federalist fear of "the people," engaging in popular electioneering with a passion, and nominating army generals in four of the six presidential contests, gave the majority Democrats stiff competition (Figure 3.7): they won the presidency twice, in 1840 and in 1848. The Democrats' ascendancy in Congress was much clearer. They won a majority of the House seats in all but two of the eleven congressional elections (Figure 3.8) between 1832 and 1852, and controlled Senate majorities in nine of the eleven, in all but the twenty-seventh and the twenty-eighth (1841–1845). There was, then, a long stream of Jeffersonian-Jacksonian con-

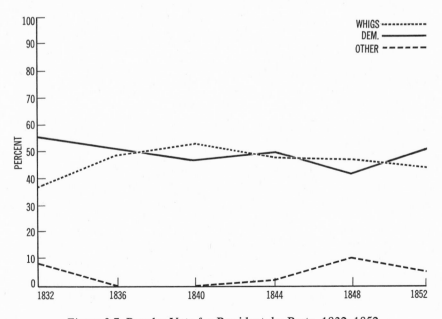

Figure 3.7. Popular Vote for President, by Party, 1832–1852

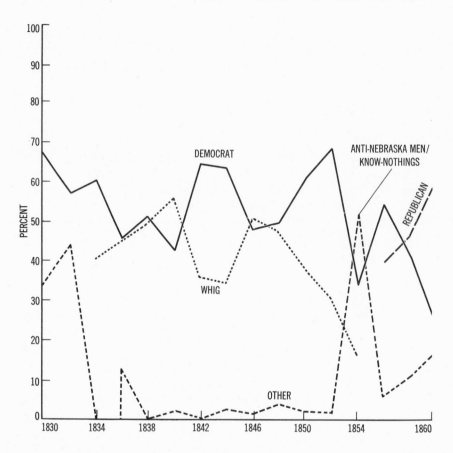

Figure 3.8. U.S. House of Representatives, Membership (Percentage of the Seats), 1830–1860*

* Source: All figures except those for 1854, 1856, and 1858 are from *Historical Statistics of the United States,* pp. 691–692. Figures for 1854 are from Francis Curtis, *The Republican Party* (New York: Putnam, 1964), p. 219. Figures for 1856 and 1858 are from U.S. Congress, *Congressional Globe,* 35th and 36th Cong., 1st Sess., 1857 and 1859, p. 1. (The Whigs are replaced by the Republicans in the 35th Congress.)

trol of the national legislature from 1800 until, in the mid-1850s, anti-Nebraskan and subsequently Republican majorities began to appear.

The United States had not only relatively close two-party competition *nationally* in the second party system, but even competition throughout the states and regions. In the presidential elections of 1828 and 1832 there had been a continuation of the pronounced sectionalism of the previous party system. In 1828, Jackson carried every southern state (including his native Tennessee by a margin of 95 percent to 5 percent),

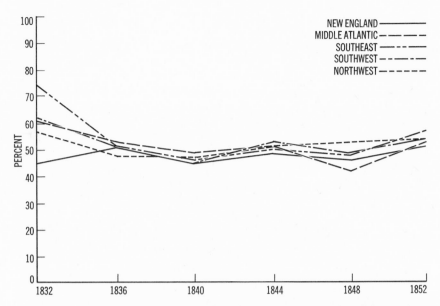

Figure 3.9. Democratic Percentage of the Two-Party, Presidential Popular Vote, by Region, 1832–1852

winning a total of 86 percent of the popular vote in the region. On the other hand, Adams carried every New England state and got less than 75 percent of the vote only in Maine and New Hampshire. In 1832, Jackson repeated his sweep of the South (74 percent of the two-party vote in the Southeast, 63 percent in the Southwest), while the Whig candidate Henry Clay won the three southern New England states (twenty-six of his forty-nine electoral votes) and gathered 54 percent of the two-party vote in New England, the only section he carried. Beginning with the presidential election of 1836, however, and for four elections thereafter, the United States had less regional variation in voting than at any other time in history (Figure 3.9). The two parties were separated by eight percentage points or less in twenty-two of the twenty-five regional contests between 1836 and 1852 (five elections in each of five regions). The Democrats won a plurality of the popular vote in New England in two of the five elections, and in three of five elections in the Middle Atlantic States, the Southeast, the Southwest, and the Northwest.

Source of Evenness of Competition

The close competition did not result from some sudden disappearance of regional social and economic differences. Rather it was that for a

brief period the parties found themselves able to cope with such differences—a commentary both on characteristics of the party system and
on the relatively low intensity of issues related to and invoking competing sectional interests.

The second party system had a maturity the first had lacked. The big
change had occurred in the minority party, of course, as the Whigs
demonstrated a much surer feel than the Federalists had for the role
and responsibilities of the opposition party in a democratic polity. Unquestionably it is good strategy for the minority party to look to presidential nominees with appeals not narrowly partisan or doctrinal; the
regularity with which the Whigs did this for two decades after 1832
had a lot to do with the evenness of competition. Here was a patchwork
party, not without "principles" (understood in terms of prevailing policy
commitments of its national leadership) but strenuously pursuing popular support on something other than doctrinal grounds.

But however ardently the Whigs and Democrats sought backing
throughout the country, they would not have managed to secure it if
the conflict of the day had not cooperated. Simply put, the two decades
after 1832 were a time when the matters being argued did not, for the
most part, involve competing regional interests of high saliency. Above
all, arguments over race and slavery, although they occurred throughout, did not dominate the agenda prior to the 1850s. When race finally
moved center stage, both parties were unable to cope with it—unable,
that is, to find a position which would satisfy North and South—and
they split over it.

State Party Systems

Between 1832 and 1852, a relatively balanced and competitive two-
party system was operating in most states. Still, there was considerable
variation in party strength from one state to another, as Figure 3.10
shows. Each state is located in this figure on the basis of voting in the
six presidential elections, by the percentage of the total two-party popular
vote which it gave to the Democratic candidates, and by the percentage of
elections in which the Democrats carried the state. Those states located
near the center of the figure were the most competitive, with competition
declining with movement to the lower left and upper right quadrants.
States in the former quadrant, of course, gave majority support to the
Whigs, states in the latter to the Democrats.

The Middle Atlantic states, which had been the real battleground

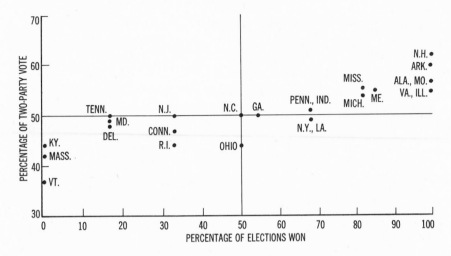

Figure 3.10. The Competitiveness of States, Democratic Performance in Presidential Voting, 1832–1852

in the early Federalist-Republican contests, remained among the most competitive in the second system. New England, the old Federalist stronghold, was the most consistently Whig. Southern states had been the bulwarks of Jeffersonianism, and were among the most strongly Democratic—although Tennessee, North Carolina, Georgia, and Louisiana divided their support evenly between Whig and Democratic candidates.

One curiosity is the polar positions of New Hampshire and Vermont. New Hampshire, a staunch Federalist state, became the most heavily Democratic; and Vermont, loyal to Jeffersonianism produced the largest Whig majorities. Richard McCormick, whose investigations of the state party systems of this period are the most complete, finds the explanation primarily in the quality of party leadership:

Isaac Hill and his associates were unusually gifted politicians, and surely much of the credit for the remarkable strength of the Democracy in New Hampshire must be ascribed to their genius. Ezra Meech in Vermont, on the other hand . . . can be set down as [a] poor political leader. There must obviously be limits to which political leadership can advance a party in a particular state, but those limits are flexible, and, given the loose character of American political parties, they allow considerable scope for the exercise of political talents.[41]

[41] Richard McCormick, *The Second American Party System* (Chapel Hill: University of North Carolina Press, 1966), p. 97.

It is a valuable counterbalance to the easy tendency to deal exclusively
with broad social and economic factors as determinants of party success
and failure to note that the biggest spread in party strength was between the sister states of New Hampshire and Vermont, states similar
in social and economic structure. The New Hampshire–Vermont polarization is also a commentary on the nature of party competition in this
period, eschewing doctrine and emphasizing the personal attributes of
candidates, and on the low saliency of sectional issues; for state party
leadership could not otherwise have been so influential.

The Parties in Subpresidential Elections

Regional differences in party strength are somewhat greater in voting
for subpresidential officers. In six Congresses beginning with the twenty-
seventh (1841–1843), for example, the Democrats won 69 percent of
the seats from the southern states, 67 percent from the Northwest (what
we now call the North Central states), but only 37 percent of the New
England seats. And the percentage variation would have been even
greater were it not for an occasional maverick state in each region.
For example, Ohio accounted for two-thirds of the Whig congressional
victories from the entire block of northwestern states over this twelve-
year span.

Still, if comparison is made to any other time in American history,
1832–1852 is distinguished for relatively balanced party competition
throughout the country. McCormick's summary is instructive:

What was most striking about the parties by the 1840s was that two-party
alignments had been established throughout the nation and that within each
region—and in most states—these parties were balanced and competitive.
They were similarly aligned for contesting both state and national elections.
They tended to adopt similar forms of organization, engage in similar functions, and employ similar campaign techniques. There was, indeed, a nationalization of institutional forms and political styles. There was also a
nationalization of political identities. Voters everywhere thought of themselves as either Whigs or Democrats. Everywhere, too, heightened inter-
party competition stimulated increased voter participation.[42]

It was this party system that the events of the 1850s tore asunder.
Ironically, slavery, a rural and agricultural institution, provided the
issue which split the agricultural majority South and West, bringing
to an end the more than fifty years of agricultural—and thereby

[42] *Ibid.*, p. 342.

Jeffersonian-Jacksonian—ascendancy. As the smoke of battle cleared after 1865, a new, rapidly industrializing society took shape, and with the new society, a new majority party. Before turning to this, however, we must examine the events of the 1850s around race and slavery in some detail, so momentous were they for American public life.

Race, Conflict, and the Party System

The political events of the 1850s surrounding slavery and union require some separate treatment here, because in their magnitude and centrality they constituted an abrupt departure from the agenda of the first period. For more than a decade, American political life was dominated by a single cluster of issues—and a cluster which was not a simple extension or product of the general lines of American sociopolitical development.

Conflict around race did not, of course, appear *de nouveau* in the 1850s. The representation of slave states was argued at the Constitutional Convention in 1787; the result was the well-known compromise wherein three-fifths of the slave population would be added in computing the total state population for apportionment of seats in the House of Representatives. The Missouri Compromise of 1820—providing for the admission of Maine as a free state and Missouri as a slave state—was an important example of the continuing effort of politicians to resolve conflict over the balance of power between North and South. But nothing before 1850 approached the scale and intensity of the ensuing decade. For the country at large, race had been until then "another issue" with which politicians had to deal.

Why did conflict around slavery grow in intensity in the 1850s, bursting the boundaries of the party system and finally of the political system itself? There can be no final agreement on anything so complex. Slavery, we have noted, was flourishing economically at mid-century, and those who considered it a moral wrong and/or a political threat could not comfort themselves that it would "wither away" as they might earlier. In the otherwise equalitarian and democratic life of mid-century, slavery and its attendant social manifestations in the South stood out ever more prominently as an "unnatural" institution. The moral argument, that slavery was an abomination, an institution with no place whatsoever in a free society, was scarcely heard in 1820. But this position gained strength dramatically as the first period drew to a close. The political culture of the South had become increasingly differentiated from that of the North and West. And the population of the free states was expanding faster than that of the slave states. In 1800, exactly half the population of the United States resided in slave states; in 1850, only 40 percent. With this, the careful political balance between slave and free states was being upset.

In Congress at mid-century there was a cadre of southern representatives firmly committed to the maintenance of slavery, and anxious that their political position not be weakened. As the country pushed west, this concern naturally came to focus on whether the newly settled territories would be slave or free. In January, 1854, Stephen A. Douglas, a Democratic senator from Illinois, introduced a bill with the immediate purpose of organizing the Great Plains as the territory of Nebraska to expedite his pet project, a transcontinental railroad. As a sop to the South, Douglas provided for an extension of the principle of states' rights, leaving it to the people of the new territory to determine whether or not to allow slavery. This would repeal the Missouri Compromise of 1820 which prohibited slavery north of 36° 30'. Southern Democrats, ascendant in the congressional party, eagerly took up the measure and succeeded in persuading the Democratic president, Franklin Pierce, to make it a party commitment. The reaction in the North and West was extreme, fed by the now large cultural antagonisms between those regions and the South. The Free Soil movement which had been growing slowly—running on a Free Soil ticket in 1848, former President Martin Van Buren had won 10 percent of the national vote—gained impetus. The Whig party, a national patchwork pieced together by a judicious mixture of popular electioneering and candidates of a nonpartisan flavor, was ill-equipped to withstand the sectional strains. The Democrats, an older and sturdier coalition, were enfeebled by the stranglehold of the southern Democratic congressional bloc and of southerners in national Democratic politics, especially through the two-thirds rule which operated at the party's presidential nominating conventions.[43] The two-thirds rule enabled southern Democrats to exert a veto in the 1850s over the party's nominees, with the result that weak "neutralists"—Pierce and Buchanan—were nominated (and elected) in 1852 and 1856.

In this context of a southern-dominated Congress and a weak presi-

---

[43] The two-thirds rule, which was adopted at the first Democratic presidential nominating convention in 1832 and retained at every subsequent quadrennial convention through 1932, required support from two-thirds of the convention delegates, rather than a simple majority, for the nomination.

dency, crisis after crisis arose in the 1850s: "Bleeding Kansas," the growing outrage and reaction of Northerners over the return of fugitive slaves, the Supreme Court decision in the Dred Scott case, the physical attack in the Senate chamber by Congressman Brooks of South Carolina on Senator Sumner of Massachusetts, the ill-fated raid led by John Brown on Harper's Ferry. With each crisis, emotions North and South rose, and the parties fragmented.

The Whigs collapsed completely. They had been committed, more consistently than to anything else, to national integration, to the Union. True to this, they were the parents of the Compromise of 1850; it was devised by Clay and strongly supported by Webster, the two most prominent Whig leaders. Introduced as a middle ground on which North and South could stand together, it provided for the admission of California as a free state and for an end to the slave trade in the District of Columbia; and to balance these concessions to the North, a stronger fugitive slave law, and the organization of the rest of the land taken from Mexico into territories, with no provision as to whether slavery would be allowed. It was a bold effort at accommodation. In 1852, with yet another general as their standard-bearer—Scott, whose political views, if any, were unknown—the Whigs had run strongly in the popular vote North and West, only 150,000 votes behind the Democrat Pierce. But after the immense popular reaction to the enactment of the Kansas-Nebraska bill in 1854—which had the immediate effect of sweeping a majority of Anti-Nebraskans into the House of Representatives in the elections in the fall of that year—a number of movements formed to demand a party pledged to prevent any extension of slavery.

Some of these Anti-Nebraska state conventions, claiming to be the true descendants of Jefferson, who had backed the Northwest Ordinance of 1787 whereby slavery was banished from the land north of the Ohio River and east of the Mississippi, called themselves *Republicans*.[44] But this Republican movement was only one branch of widespread agitation against the Kansas-Nebraska legislation, and could not in 1854 be identified as the beginning of a major new party. That the Whigs were dying was clear. But it probably seemed likely to most contemporary observers that the Know-Nothings would become the core of the new party. The rallying point for a new party proved to be not

[44] One such meeting, held even before the Kansas-Nebraska bill was passed but after it had been introduced, was in Ripon, Wisconsin, and it is this one which lays claim to being the founding of the Grand Old Party. Surely no one at the time saw it as that. It was but one of a plethora of such conventions.

nativism, however, but opposition to the extension of slavery. The nativist movement itself, meeting in convention in Philadelphia in 1856, split over the question of slavery and the Nebraska act.

Astute Whig politicians such as Thurlow Weed of New York, seeing their old party disintegrating, decided upon the infant Republican movement—for it was then more movement than political party—as the most likely successor. And in 1856, with General John Charles Frémont as their nominee, the Republicans ran a strong second to Buchanan and the Democrats, as a strictly sectional party, with no pretense of support in the South. The remaining Whig politicians, gathering in Baltimore, endorsed former President Millard Fillmore, who had been nominated previously as the candidate of the southern wing of the American (Know-Nothing) party. Fillmore's overwhelming defeat made it clear to remaining Whigs outside the South that if they wanted any part in future public life, they had better cast their lot with either the Democrats or the newly formed Republicans.

As the intensification of the northern reaction around slavery eroded the position the Whigs had occupied as a party of union and accommodation, so at the same time the heightening of sectional feelings in the South weakened them there. The Whigs had won a majority of the electoral votes cast by the southern states in 1840, and carried five of the eleven states which were to form the Confederacy in 1848. But in 1852 they won only Tennessee, and Fillmore failed even there four years later. The Democrats had become the party of regional loyalty, the partisan rallying point of an embattled South.

The Democratic party did not disintegrate, but rather split into two camps. Douglas was finally moved to break with Buchanan and the southern Democrats—after the president had recommended that Congress accept the pro-slavery constitution approved at a convention attended only by the pro-slavery minority of the territory and admit Kansas as a slave state—and in the frenzied atmosphere was quickly declared an enemy by southern Democrats whom he had tried so long to accommodate. Meeting in Charleston in convention in 1860, the Democrats consumated their split. Douglas was the clear choice of the northern Democratic majority, but the southern wing opposed him. When the convention refused to accede to the southern demand for federal protection of slavery in every territory, the southerners walked out. The Convention then adjourned, met again in Baltimore, and nominated Douglas on a platform which still looked to accommodation. But the southern wing rejected compromise, met in Richmond, and nominated John Breckinridge of Kentucky.

The election of 1860 was really two separate elections. Outside the South, it was a contest between Douglas and Abraham Lincoln, the former Whig who carried the Republican banner. Sectional antagonisms were at fever pitch, and the accommodationist northern Democratic appeal was decisively rejected. In the South, the only real competition was between Breckinridge and John Bell, the candidate of the Constitutional Unionists, the descendants of the old southern Whigs. Bell carried two rim-South states—Virginia and Tennessee—and one border state, Kentucky. The parties had split completely on sectional lines. Table 3.2 shows the intense sectionalism of the presidential voting of 1856 and 1860.

TABLE 3.2

The Partisan Division of the Presidential Vote,
by Region, 1856 and 1860 (as Percentages)

| | REGIONS | | |
PARTY/YEAR	North	Border	South
1856			
Democrat	41.8	51.3	58.2
Republican	45.6	00.3	00.0
Whig-American	12.6	48.4	41.8
1860			
Republican	54.0	6.0	00.2*
Northern Democrat	35.7	21.8	9.5
Southern Democrat	8.2	31.9	50.4
Constitutional Unionist	2.2	40.4	39.9

* This percentage represents the 1,929 Republican votes cast in Virginia.

Slavery proved to be the last major issue on the agenda of the Rural Republic. It was in a sense exclusively an issue of an agricultural society, for quite apart from any considerations of morality, slavery is impossible in an industrial system. And it was fought out primarily in rural America. The decisive break was between family-plot, free-soil farmers who came to see the extension of slavery as a threat, and the southern wing of agriculture, the plantation owners who had the slaves and the dirt farmers who threw in their lot with the slave owners out of fear of what an end to slavery, liberating millions of Negroes, would do to them and their place in society.

In the 1850s and through the Civil War, the American political agenda was dominated by the momentous issues of slavery and the Union. Their saliency temporarily masked the magnitude of transformations occurring in American life. In 1850, this was an agricultural nation. After 1870, the commitment to industrialism was decisive, and the balance of power shifted from farm to factory, from farmers to a town and city middle class, from a system of extraordinary independence and localism to one pervasively linked by the bonds of national communications, transportation, and economic integration. The census of 1870 was the first to show a majority of workers in nonagricultural pursuits. The years immediately after 1850, then, are the twilight of the Rural Republic. They would have been that even if the tensions around slavery and union had been peaceably resolved. As it was, the last years of the Rural Republic were a time of unparalleled bitterness and violence, dominated by a war which was—by the measure of American lives—the most costly in our history.

4

The Parties in the Industrializing Nation

When the South capitulated in 1865, the United States was poised at the start of a massive movement toward industrialism. Six decades later, that transformation had been completed. This was a period defined, then, by the dynamic of industrial nation-building—with all the rewards, pain, tensions, and political problems of such an enterprise.

The Society and Its Political Agenda

The Politics of Rapid Industrial Growth

In the years since World War II, the terms "developing nations" and "underdeveloped countries" have come into general use. A big part of the "development" envisioned is economic, and the type of economic development principally industrialization. There has been a major emphasis on transforming agricultural societies—in Latin America, Africa, and Asia—into industrial systems. This enterprise has not been an easy one, and the strains and tensions which have attended it have everywhere been substantial.

The transforming of rural and agricultural societies into urban and industrial began, we know, not in the twentieth century but in the nineteenth in Western Europe and in the United States. Clearly, the requirements and problems of American industrialization then were in many ways very different from those before the "developing nations" today. Still, it is useful to keep in mind that the great transformations America experienced in the half-century or so after the Civil War as it engaged in industrial nation-building are part of a larger process of social change that has subsequently enveloped our planet. The supplanting of rural-agricultural societies by urban-industrial societies is one of the most momentous and far-reaching developments in human history.

The Industrial Order Takes Shape

In the years from the Civil War to the Great Depression, the United States developed as the leading industrial nation, with about one-third of the world's manufacturing capacity. The per capita national product of this country *tripled* in the half century after 1870. In the 1860s, a clear majority of American workers were in agricultural pursuits; but the agricultural labor force began a precipitous relative decline—absolute as well after 1910—leaving at the end of the 1920s fewer than one American family in four employed in any form of agricultural activity. The American population, largely rural in 1865, was massively redistributed as big cities and industrial towns grew up, and sometime between 1910 and 1920 a majority, as the census saw it, became urban dwellers. In place of an economy of small farms and cottage industry there was an economy of scale, dominated by industrial giants. Changes of such magnitude were felt throughout the social system and surely rewrote the American political agenda.

Just why and how rapid industrial growth took place in the United States after 1860 cannot readily be set forth. This is part of the bigger problem of the conditions for economic growth and development, one that contemporary economics has grappled with not altogether successfully.[1] It is clear that the United States owes its rapid industrialization

[1] Walt W. Rostow, for example, has set forth theoretical stages through which economies may move into sustained growth, in *The Stages of Economic Growth: A Non-Communist Manifesto* (Cambridge: Cambridge University Press, 1960). The stage relevant to the discussion here Rostow calls "the take-off," a brief interval of two or three decades during which the economy develops growth in a more or less automatic fashion. Rostow finds three specific conditions essential to "take-off": (a) a rise in the rate of capital formation to 10 percent or more of the national product; (b) the development of manufacturing sectors with high rates of growth; and (c) the rapid emergence of a sociopolitical framework able to exploit the impetus to expansion. The "take-off" stage in the United States he places between 1843 and 1860. Rostow's view, however, is categorically rejected by other economic historians, including Douglass North and Simon Kuznets, in Douglass C. North, *Growth and Welfare in the American Past* (Englewood Cliffs, N.J.: Prentice-Hall, 1966), pp. 85–89; and Simon Kuznets, "Note on the Take-Off," in W. W. Rostow, ed., *The Economics of Take-Off into Sustained Growth,* Proceedings of the International Economic Association Conference, 1960 (New York: St. Martin's Press, 1964). North states flatly that "the case of the United States lends no support to the Rostow hypothesis, nor does that of any other country" (p. 87).

in part to technological innovations which transformed basic production processes; partly to the quality of the labor force—a result both of an extensive investment in human capital and of a wide dissemination of cultural values admirably suited to the task at hand (including orientation to work, savings, and the use of machines, and receptivity to science and technology); and partly to the development of a system of financial intermediaries able to move savings to underwrite the construction of railroads, steel mills, and other forms of industrial capital. If the precise mix of technology, cultural environment, and economic arrangements is somewhat unclear, the end product of the mix in the American situation after 1860 is dramatically evident.

In 1860, 10.5 million Americans comprised the labor force, with more than 6 million in agriculture. Sixty years later, the labor force had quadrupled, non-farm employment had increased by more than 700 percent, while farm employment had less than doubled. Figure 4.1 shows the dramatic change in the relative proportions of the labor force in agricultural and non-agricultural pursuits. Twin developments—the

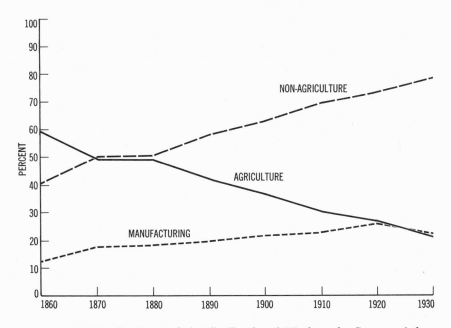

Figure 4.1. Distribution of Gainfully Employed Workers, by Sectors of the Economy, 1860–1930*

* Source: U.S. Bureau of the Census, *Historical Statistics of the United States, Colonial Times to 1957* (Washington, D.C.: U.S. Government Printing Office, 1960), p. 74.

mechanization of agriculture, which enabled an even smaller portion of the labor force to provide enough food, and the growth of industry, with its huge labor demands—required a redistribution of the population from farm and village to town and city. The number of urban places (over 2,500 population) increased from 163 in 1860 to nearly 10,000 sixty years later, as the rural population dropped from over 80 percent of the total to less than half. It was a time for the building of great cities. At the outbreak of the Civil War, no American city had a million people, and only three (New York, Boston, and Philadelphia) were over 250,000. But by the eve of the Depression, the great cities had been built: New York had grown from 800,000 to 7 million; Boston from 175,000 to 800,000; Philadelphia from 550,000 to 2 million; Chicago from 100,000 to more than 3 million; even on the West Coast, the much newer city of Los Angeles was well over a million. If we understand *urbanization* to be a process in which the population density (i.e., persons per square mile) in cities grows progressively greater, the period from the Civil War to the Depression was when most American urbanization occurred. (Since the Depression, the United States has not so much urbanized as *metropolitanized;* the principal component of growth has been a high population flow to what was countryside surrounding the core cities).[2]

The productive capacities of the American economy were extended enormously. If 1899 is taken as the base year, and an index of manufacturing production devised, with 100 representing production in that year, the index figure for 1865 becomes 17. By 1913, it had jumped to 203, and by 1928 to 303.[3] Although the United States had been a relatively wealthy nation in the first half of the nineteenth century, total productivity, figured on a per capita basis, had not grown significantly. The ceiling for an agricultural nation of abundant land and good climate

[2] Leo Schnore, for example, has shown that most core cities have been decentralizing since 1950—the population density of the core declining. The extensive growth has been in suburban and exurban areas. Even in the case of the newer cities of the South and West, only a few have in recent years been centralizing—the density of the center still increasing. The rapid growth of southern and western cities is largely accounted for by their ability to annex surrounding territories; they are, thus, typically far less underbounded than are the older cities of the Northeast. (Leo F. Schnore, "Municipal Annexations and the Growth of Metropolitan Suburbs, 1950–1960," *American Journal of Sociology,* 67 [January, 1962], p. 414.)

[3] This index of manufacturing production was developed by Edwin Frickey, *Production in the United States, 1860–1914* (Cambridge, Mass.: Harvard University Press, 1947), and reprinted in *Historical Statistics of the United States,* p. 409. The 1928 index figure is an approximation based on a projection of the Frickey index, which ends in 1914.

had been reached. But after the Civil War, with industrialization, the total productive capacity increased rapidly. The per capita gross national product in 1865 (in 1929 dollars) was just a little over $200; it grew to more than $400 in 1890, and to more than $800 on the eve of the Depression.[4]

As America industrialized, the size, complexity and resources of economic enterprises expanded enormously. Technological advances required larger units of operation for efficient use. For example, oil refineries in the 1850s were small, and typically cost only $400 or $500 to set up; by 1900, the cost of an efficient refinery had increased to between $1 and $2 million. In steel production, the development of the Bessemer and Open Hearth process had the same effect: it became possible to produce a lot more steel more efficiently, but the technology required much larger capitalization. Advances in transportation, especially the filling out of a railway system, created a national consumer market. To deal with this, business began establishing national marketing networks: Thus the Singer Sewing Machine Company set up its own network of retailing and repair agencies, Swift (meats) a chain of branch offices that sold to and sometimes controlled local retail stores. This process in which manufacturers expanded forward to the consumer market is part of what economists call *vertical integration;* the other part, which occurred at this same time, is expanding backward to the production of raw materials. The fully integrated company, as it appeared in the late nineteenth century, controlled every stage in the life of its product; from the supply of the necessary raw materials to the marketing of the finished goods. To take one prominent example, by the early 1890s Standard Oil was fully integrated from the oil well to the retail pumping station.

In this same period, the corporation replaced the proprietorship and the partnership as the dominant form of business organization. Providing for limited liability and for the raising of capital for expansion through the sale of stocks and bonds, the corporation created a new type of economic actor in the stockholder who shared in earnings but not, typically, in management.

At the beginning of the twentieth century—roughly 1898 to 1906— a great wave of corporate mergers resulted in *big business* in the modern sense of the term. In 1901, the first billion-dollar company—United States Steel—was formed through mergers. Other companies, such as

---

[4] These data are from *Historical Statistics of the United States,* p. 139.

American Tobacco, American Smelting and Refining, and American Can, attained massive size in this manner. As with the earlier move to vertical integration, the basic objective of the mergers was *market control*. In some instances this was realized to the extent of monopoly power, setting the stage for the anti-trust activity of the early twentieth century.

Entrepreneurial Businessmen As the New Political Class

The place held by land-owning farmers as the political class of the Rural Republic was assumed by entrepreneurs large and small in the last half of the nineteenth century. From the displacement of the former and the commitments of the latter came some of the key features of conflict in the second period.

"There is no other period in the nation's history when politics seems so completely dwarfed by economic changes," writes the historian Richard Hofstadter, "none in which the life of the country rests so completely in the hands of the industrial entrepreneur" as the three or four decades after 1865.[5] For what values and objectives was this business power exercised? What visions drove the men of the new business elite? Probably, most sincerely believed they were engaged in an enterprise from which the entire society was profiting. A later generation is more aware of the harshness of the industrial system which the "robber barons" built and directed; still, we should not be surprised that businessmen saw themselves playing a role of enormous social utility. Wasn't evidence of this all about? The productivity of the economy was rapidly expanding. New and cheaper methods of production were being developed; the price of petroleum, to take one example, fell from 36¢ a gallon in 1863 to 8¢ a gallon in 1885. And Horatio Alger stories were common enough, as children of the lower-middle class from small villages and farms became titans of industry, to make plausible the claim that here was a system offering almost limitless opportunity to the industrious, the frugal, the enterprising. Much has been made of John D. Rockefeller's likening himself to an American beauty rose: "The growth of a large business is merely a survival of the fittest. . . . The American beauty rose can be produced in the splendor and fragrance which bring cheer to its beholder only by sacrificing the early buds which grow around it. This is not an evil tendency in business. It is merely

[5] Richard Hofstadter, *The American Political Tradition* (New York: Vintage Books, 1958), p. 164.

the working-out of a law of nature and a law of God."[6] " 'All is well since all grows better,' became my motto," wrote Andrew Carnegie, "my true source of comfort. . . . Nor is there any conceivable end to his march to perfection. His face is turned to the light; he stands in the sun and looks upward."[7] The whole system, through industrialization, was moving ahead; progress was real, despite some harshness; and the business class were the leaders, the movers, and doers of this socially beneficent enterprise. It was a comforting and not altogether implausible view.

The business class wanted an industrial America under its custodianship. It wanted the entire social system bent to the needs of industrialization, wanted governmental power committed to policies and programs on behalf of the ascendant industrial order: the protective tariff, a national banking structure, aid to Pacific railways, a program of sound money, a docile labor force, high profits able to mount at the expense of labor. All these objectives generated opposition, and the opposition at times gained victories, but overall, the business position on the principal agenda items of the period triumphed.

At the national level, Congress and the Supreme Court with great consistency responded in a manner satisfactory to business interests. After 1857, for example, Congress proceeded to enact a series of tariff measures which established increasingly high protective duties. Americans whose political experience is confined to the years after World War II may find it hard to appreciate that, in sheer volume of argument and in persistence, the tariff was the number one domestic political issue between 1870 and 1930. Manufacturing interests defended high tariffs to keep foreign-made competitive products out, justifying their position in terms of the development of the American industrial system. Consumer interests, and especially those in agricultural sections of the country, argued that high tariffs, by increasing the costs of imported goods which consumers had to purchase, were in fact an instrument for taxing consumers to enhance business profits.[8] Not until the Underwood-Simmons Act in Woodrow Wilson's first administration was a broad tariff reduction effected.

[6] Quoted in Richard Hofstadter, *Social Darwinism in American Thought* (Boston: Beacon, 1959), p. 45.

[7] Quoted in Hofstadter, *loc. cit.*

[8] High tariffs were not uniformly supported by industrialists and low tariffs by consumer-agricultural interests. Some agricultural producers wanted, and received, high tariff protection. Some industrial producers didn't face foreign competition.

Some of the important battles over industrialization were fought out in the courts, and after 1890 the Supreme Court proved a generally reliable ally of the business community through its interpretation of such major legislation as the anti-trust laws, and by declaring acts which business found unpalatable to be in violation of the Constitution. Most of the statutes declared unconstitutional were state rather than national; some state legislatures were far readier than Congress to pass minimum-wage and maximum-hour legislation, measures defining employer liability for accidents sustained by workers, laws to improve working conditions in factories. Many businessmen, probably most, in the late nineteenth and early twentieth centuries opposed such regulatory activity as burdensome, unnecessary, and an illegitimate intrusion into their contractual relations with their employees, and the Supreme Court of the United States for the most part agreed. For example, the State of New York passed a labor law with the avowed purpose of protecting the health of workers. It provided that employees in bakeries could not be required to work more than sixty hours in a week or more than ten hours per day. In finding this statute in violation of the Constitution, the Court concluded that there was insufficient justification for the infringement of the freedom of contract of employer and workers. Speaking for the majority of the Court, Justice Peckham argued that

it is unfortunately true that labor, even in any department, may possibly carry with it the seeds of unhealthiness. But are we all, on that account, at the mercy of legislative majorities? A printer, a tinsmith, a locksmith, a carpenter, a cabinetmaker, a drygoods clerk, a bank's, a lawyer's or a physician's clerk, or a clerk in almost any kind of business would come under the power of the Legislature, on this assumption. . . . Scarcely any law but might find shelter under such assumptions, and conduct, properly so-called, as well as contract, would come under the restrictive sway of the Legislature. Not only the hours of employees, but the hours of employers, could be regulated, and doctors, lawyers, scientists, all professional men, as well as athletes and artisans, could be forbidden to fatigue their brains and bodies by prolonged periods of exercise. . . .[9]

What can we say about such a construction? The legislature of the state of New York, after substantial medical testimony, came to the conclusion that there was a serious hazard to the health of employees forced to work excessive hours in extremely hot bakeries. Could the Court's majority really have believed that the next step would be legislation forbidding scientists to use their brains more than so many hours a day? The ques-

[9] *Lochner* v. *New York*, 198 U.S. 45.

tion can be put differently: was Peckham a fool (for the argument sounds foolish) or a knave (raising a false issue in hopes of throwing the slow-witted off the track)? Probably neither. We must understand that a very large majority of the men who thought about such things were convinced that the crash construction of an industrial society was a worthy objective, and were willing to go rather far in giving business-men their head in this enterprise. They did differ, of course, as to precisely how far, as the Lochner case illustrates, but Peckham's ma-jority opinion is intelligible only in a context in which most were committed to the basic beneficence of crash industrialization.

Were businessmen committed to laissez faire? Not in the literal sense of "Government keep completely out of the area of business enter-prise!" There *was* a powerful ideological inheritance from early liberal-ism which held that the good state was the negative state, and that individuals could most fully realize themselves and society's rapid ad-vance if government saw as its job merely to turn men loose; and specifically that economic life should be free of government meddling. In the first period, we have seen, most of the claims for governmental intervention were from the ranks of the nascent business community, and were fairly consistently resisted by men of the Jeffersonian and Jackso-nian persuasions. After the Civil War, however, as the move to indus-trialization became a frantic rush, and as businessmen found themselves ascendant politically and economically, they very often felt that being left alone was quite enough. Then, the old ideological inheritance of laissez faire proved handy: it was a way of legitimizing what was in fact in their interest. Still, the record of the period shows that businessmen were not at all reluctant to seek governmental intervention when they felt they needed it, as in the development of Pacific railways, in pro-tective tariffs, in legislation assuring "sound money." The real importance of laissez faire appears not in its influence on the behavior of business-men, but in the allies which it brought them, in the intellectual justifica-tion it gave to "hands off" in the many areas in which a business class would profit from "hands off."

Businessmen as a political class were not, of course, as united as the above discussion may at times have suggested. They were of many per-suasions and types, frequently differed, often were in the most violent competition with one another, and not infrequently disagreed as to the proper policy objectives and responses. In the Pullman Strike of 1894, to take a prominent episode, George Pullman was not universally defended by his fellow business leaders. Indeed, many saw him as responsible for the strike and its violence through a failure to respond to legitimate worker demands. Mark Hanna was a prominent Cleveland industrialist who made his millions and then went on to become Republican national chairman and a United States senator from Ohio. There was the celebrated episode in the Cleveland Union Club at the time of the strike when Hanna cursed Pullman for refusing to arbitrate, for refusing to "meet his men half way." When someone suggested that Pullman deserved credit for his "model town," Hanna allegedly exploded: "Oh hell! Model———! Go and live in Pullman and find out how much Pullman gets selling city water and gas ten percent higher to those poor fools!" Hanna was a businessman, and certainly a defender of business interests, but he defined business interests differently from George Pullman. Such divisions among the proponents of a business society were not unimportant and not infrequent.

The Supportive Culture

Businessmen were never anything more than a distinct minority of the population of the United States, and their ascendancy has often been explained too simplistically. They did have economic muscle, but their rule was not primarily sustained by an unbroken string of bribes and intimidation. "Rule by the people" was imperfectly attained then as now, but there can be no doubt that "the people" who had some effective say in decision-making far exceeded in numbers the business class, and that "the people" thus construed could have imposed legislation altering the course of American industrial development had they chosen. "Had they chosen" is nebulous, and may imply a condition never present. We are trying to suggest only that however imperfect the machinery of American government from the standpoint of majority rule, businessmen could not have enjoyed the ascendancy which they did if a large number of people who were not businessmen and who did not profit directly from the financial machinations of businessmen had not been willing to acquiesce in business programs and policies. What we must see is that the American cultural setting was broadly supportive of the enterprise which the Carnegies and Rockefellers and Fords directed.

The cultural orientation of a people is a complex matter on which little systematic work has been done. There is no book on the political culture of the United States in 1900, although there are books dealing with components of the political culture of that time. Here, we can only suggest the referents when we speak of a supportive culture. In the preceding chapter, we mentioned the basic receptivity of Americans to entrepreneurial activity and their attitudes toward work and saving and machines and technology. All these things, however we may take them for granted, are not "natural" cultural components shared by all the people by dint of their humanity. They are cultural traditions which Americans brought with them and which were fostered by the prevailing conditions of the new world. When Hartz describes America as "born liberal," he means in part the pervasive sharing of these cultural commitments. And they were shared by men who were farmers as well as by men in cities. There was, then, nothing approaching a "war" between peasantry and bourgeoisie, but rather the more manageable conflict between enterprisers in agriculture and enterprisers in commercial, financial, and industrial activity.

What is sometimes called the "Protestant ethic" can better be seen as a cultural component admirably suited to industrial nation-building, a component which posited the moral necessity of people doing the things which needed to be done for the system to industrialize quickly: for example, working for longer hours and harder than they needed to for food and shelter in the interest of capital accumulation. When the Soviet Union began its rush to industrial development after 1918, it turned to the totalitarian state as an instrument for forcing people to do what had to be done to accumulate capital. It was possible to complete the immense task of industrialization in the United States with a minimum of state direction and intervention in part because the culture was so strongly supportive. The "captains of industry" of the post–Civil War period were not unnatural heroes for Americans. In their commitment to hard work, thrift and industry, and the use of technology in the building of a richer and more prosperous society, they spoke to values broadly disseminated.

There were regional differences in receptivity. In the Northeast where industrialization came earliest, the commitment was stronger than in agricultural areas South and West. This became one of the props of a sectional politics. In the presidential election of 1896, the Democratic candidate, William Jennings Bryan, ran on a program strongly critical of the course of American industrialism and swept the South and West, but he was badly beaten in the industrial Northeast. The thesis sometimes advanced that the urban working class voted for Bryan's Republican opponent, William McKinley, chiefly because they had been told not to report back to work if Bryan were elected appears to lack substantiation. While some employers undoubtedly did try to influence the voting of their employees, the magnitude of Bryan's setback can be understood only as the rejection by men in all sectors of the economy of the style, cultural values, and economic premises of a man from the agricultural heartland.

The Reactions in Rural America

It is not possible to embark upon the transformation of a rural and localized country of farms into an urban and interdependent nation of factories without strains and dislocations, and without the interests of some being neglected or denied. In the last three decades of the nineteenth century in the United States, these strains and this neglect were felt with particular intensity in the hinterland, giving rise to wave upon wave of protest. Many of the grievances of agricultural America were immediate and specific, but behind them was a more diffuse reaction bred of the passing of a familiar and valued world. Is it surprising that a man could compare in his mind's eye the America of Jefferson to that of McKinley and find the former more appealing, more compelling?

One major set of complaints arose as many farmers, needing credit to bring themselves through years when the depressed prices of cash crops was insufficient to sustain their operations and to buy the machinery required to compete in an increasingly mechanized agriculture, found themselves burdened by heavy debts. As debtors, farmers became inflationists, seekers of schemes to get in circulation dollars worth less in actual purchasing power than those with which their debts had been incurred. This brought, of course, them into conflict with the financial community and with business generally, which had an equally direct stake in "hard money," in a stable currency. Like the tariff, the monetary question arose again and again. The words changed but the music was always the same.

The Depression of 1868 elicited the agrarian demand for inflation through monetary policy. The plan then advanced by the inflationists was a simple one. During the Civil War the national government had printed nearly a half-billion dollars in paper money—known as "greenbacks"—and had issued United States Bonds redeemable after periods of five, ten, or twenty years. Since these bonds contained no specific promise of redemption in gold, the inflationists urged that they be redeemed at once with newly printed greenbacks. Like the original greenbacks, the newly printed ones would be legal tender for all debts. This proposal had the double virtue—to its backers—of being both inflationary and a means of retiring a tax-free investment on which "moneyed interests" were receiving a return in gold. This initial commitment to the paper-money standard survived the 1870s and the early 1880s, and was a principal plank of the Independent party, popularly known as the Green-backers. "Corporate control of the volume of money," proclaimed the Greenbackers in their 1880 platform, "has been the means of dividing society into hostile classes, of the unjust distribution of the products of labor, and of building up monopolies of associated capital endowed with the power to confiscate private property. It has kept money scarce, and scarcity of money enforces debt, trade and public and corporate loans. Debt engenders usury, and usury ends in the bankruptcy of the borrower. Other results are deranged markets, uncertainty in manufacturing enterprise and agriculture, precarious and intermittent employment for the laborers, industrial war, increasing pauperism and crime, and the constant intimidation and disenfranchisement of the producer and rapid declension into corporate feudalism. . . ." The Greenbackers broadened their appeal, including other pet agricultural grievances such as the enormous acreage in public lands granted to railroads, the excessive railroad rates, and the importing of "cheap" foreign labor.

Farmers had begun in the late 1860s to organize *granges* to study and discuss their troubles. The study groups rather quickly evolved into political action groups, with such objectives as cooperative buying and selling and combating monopolies. Frequently unable to get satisfaction from the regular political parties, the Granger movement turned to a variety of "independent" and "anti-monopoly" parties, and managed to get "Granger laws" regulating rates for railways and grain warehouses enacted. In the 1880s, two National Farmers Alliances took shape, one in the West, the other in the South, and success spurred these alliances, together with the Grangers and remnants of the Greenbackers, to form the People's or Populist party.

Populism was, then, a joining together of agrarians West and South in an effort to wrest national power from the business class. "The railroad corporations will either own the people or the people must own the railroads," read the People's party platform of 1892. Government-supported industrialization enriches a few while impoverishing many: "From the same prolific womb of governmental injustice we breed the two great classes of tramps and millionaires." The key Populist planks spoke for agrarian-based popular reform. They urged government ownership of railroads, telegraphs, and telephones; called for a graduated income tax; favored the parcel post to break the hold of the express companies; advocated restrictions on immigration, which was providing factory labor and swelling the cities; supported such measures to end the control of public office by the "interests" as popular election of United State senators, the Australian ballot, and the initiative and referendum. There was as well the familiar demand for inflationary currency, but here the hopes of farmers now rested on the free coinage of silver rather than on paper money.

The argument between farmers West and South who advocated the free coinage of silver and Eastern. business, committed to the gold standard, enflamed popular passions as no other issue in the 1890s. Remote as it seems today, the reader should understand why it commanded the intensity of feeling which it did then, and for this some background is needed. From 1792 to 1873 the American money system in theory was bimetallic. Up to 1834, the mint ratio for the two metals had been fixed at one to fifteen (coins of fifteen units of silver equaling in value coins of one unit of gold). In fact, on the market, gold was worth nearly sixteen times as much as silver, so it paid to take silver to the mint to be coined, while gold was of greater value if used as a metal. In 1834, the ratio was changed to sixteen to one; gold became slightly overvalued at the Mint, and silver almost disappeared from circulation. Then, in 1873, the coinage laws were again revised. Since bimetalism had really never worked and was a nuisance, it was abolished. The silver dollar was removed from the list of coins which could be struck freely at the Mint. At that time, few cared, for the emphasis of currency inflationists was on paper money. But in the late 1870s and 1880s, rich new silver mines were discovered, the price of silver dropped dramatically, and westerners came to the conclusion that silver might be a more practical form of inflation than paper. In the 1890s, it in fact took about thirty-two units of silver to equal the value of one unit of gold, and thus the demand for free coinage of silver at the old ratio of sixteen to one was seen by debtors as an inflationary panacea. On the other side, matching this oversimplified faith in free coinage of silver was an equally simplistic attachment of businessmen to gold. In 1896, the business interests of America could genuinely believe that the free silver forces were tampering with "sound money" on which American prosperity depended, and William Jennings Bryan, as the candidate of the Silverites, could lay down the gauntlet to business: "You shall not crucify mankind upon a cross of gold!"

The Populists were too late. By 1896 industrial capitalism was firmly entrenched. The aroused farmers received little support from the growing numbers of foreign-born workers in the factory towns of the East and the Middle West. After 1896 it was clear to all that farmers had become permanently a minority interest, able to bargain with the controllers of American public policy, but never again to command.

This dissent in agricultural America from some features of industrialization had two faces and is not easily understood. There were appeals for reform which later became law in the administrations of the two Roosevelts and Woodrow Wilson. This side has a distinctly modern ring and gives rise to the temptation to establish the Populists as the intellectual precursors of the reformist movements of the twentieth century. To do so would be to overlook the other side. Populism was a movement of "little America," of the small towns and farms against city life. "The great cities," said Bryan in 1896, "rest upon our broad and fertile prairies. Burn down your cities and leave our farms, and your cities will spring up again as if by magic; but destroy our farms and the grass will grow in the streets of every city in the country. . . ." It was a reaction of provincials against cosmopolitans and their worldliness or secularism. "The very words, 'provincial' and 'cosmopolitan,'" writes the historian Herbert Agar, "are a sign that a nation has entered a new stage of history. There were no cosmopolitans in America in 1850, and thus no provincials. The words are meaningless in a land of farmers and country towns." But as the country industrialized and urbanized, the cultural gap between the big city and the farm, "the New Yorker and the hayseed," widened. Populism was also nativistic, bitterly resenting the "importation of foreign pauper labor" that was crowding into the great cities, swelling the ranks of industry, leading the assault on the style and traditions of an older America, the America of the small town and farm and the Protestant church. Bryan the Populist was Bryan the religious fundamentalist, Bryan the prohibitionist, and Bryan the provincial.

Just as it is easy, looking at one side of Populism, to fall into the error of seeing it the forerunner of New Deal liberalism, so looking at the other, a posture of simple derogation comes easily. There was nothing "unnatural" or "shameful" in the Populist resistance to the massive transformations of American life. "In Jefferson's Arcadian plans," Agar writes, "America was given a thousand years to reach the Mississippi. In fact, she had fifty years to reach the Pacific Ocean and another fifty to reach the great stone deserts of mass-industry and finance."[10] Quite understandably, the vision of the Populists was focused on the past, not on the future, on an older, simpler, agricultural society rather than on a more humane industrialism.

[10] Herbert Agar, *The Price of Union* (Boston: Houghton Mifflin, 1950), p. 559.

Were the Populists and those in related movements "progressives"? Only if any opposition to the domination of urban capitalists is called progressive. Farmers in the West and South believed they were being shabbily treated by the Eastern "money power," and they lashed out against it. Bryan was from Nebraska, and his home state consistently sustained this "progressive" position. Today, Nebraska is commonly thought of as a "conservative" state. The people there probably have not undergone some astonishing transformation. The "progressivism" of 1896 was rooted in the profound dissatisfaction of agricultural America with business; once this condition diminished, the other orientations—always present—came to command our attention.

The Reactions of an Urban Working Class

Industrialization produced a decline in the power and influence of agricultural America. It created, too, a large industrial work force. When the Civil War broke out, there were about 1 million production workers in manufacturing enterprises in the United States; the number grew to more than 8 million over the next seventy years. In coal mining, a major extraction industry, there were 30,000 production workers in 1860; in 1920 there were more than 700,000.

Paralleling this growth of the industrial work force was an expansion of the size of the employing companies. Prior to 1860, most manufacturing establishments were small, with fewer than fifty employees. Employer-employee relations were fundamentally altered when, in place of a refinery of $500 capitalization and twenty employees there was Rockefeller's Standard Oil Company with 66,000 workers (1907). The large corporation impersonalized worker-management relations, and removed whatever softening occurred with the personal contact and possible friendship of owner and employee. The individual worker found himself at a decided disadvantage in dealing with the employer. This situation, of course, led to trade union organization. There was little unionization in the United States prior to the Civil War, what there was being limited to such small craft unions as the Stonecutters, Hat Finishers, and Blacksmiths. After the war, there was heightened activity, beginning with the National Labor Union and, in the 1870s and early 1880s, the Knights of Labor. Finally, with the founding of the American Federation of Labor in 1881, unions achieved permanent national organization. Their position still was precarious. They faced strong opposition from most employers; the general use of government power for pro-employer, anti-union objectives; and a public orientation that denied the legitimacy of the unionization enterprise. Membership grew slowly. The Knights of Labor reached their peak membership of 700,000 in 1886, and it was not until 1915 that the AFL had 2 million members. Most industrial workers before the Depression were outside unions. And the suppression of strikes was sometimes bloody. In 1894, in one of the most violent and highly publicized labor episodes, the workers of the Pullman Company struck. That spring, Pullman had imposed wage cuts of 25 percent without any reduction of the rents on housing in the "model town" wholly owned by the company. The wage cut was especially offensive because Pullman had just paid more than 2.5 million dollars in dividends, and held undistributed surplus profits of about $25 million. The men asked for higher wages, were turned down, and their spokesmen were fired. They then went on strike, supported by the American Railway Union, which voted to boycott all Pullman cars. When Pullman was backed by the General Managers Association of Railroads, the strike spread throughout the country. The attorney general of the United States, Richard Olney, intervened to secure a blanket injunction against obstructing the railroads (which, if obeyed, would naturally have broken the strike.) The injunction was ignored, and the Cleveland administration sent in troops to "restore law and order." The troops in fact precipitated violence, and on July 7 seven workers were killed and many were injured.

The rapid industrial growth of this period was financed by what most in a later and more affluent generation would call—and what some contemporaries *did call*—the exploitation of labor. To put it simply, workers put in long hours at low pay to permit a high rate of profit and capital investment by management. In 1900, the average annual earnings of American industrial workers were around $500 a year, and the work week was sixty hours. Not only were wages low, but they did not rise significantly with the substantial increases in productivity between 1870 and 1915. Paul Douglas has concluded that there was no improvement whatever in real wages before the enormous expansion of output in this period.[11] A more recent investigation by Albert Rees found that the average hourly earnings of all workers in manufacturing did increase a bit, from 16¢ in 1890 (in constant 1914 prices) to 22¢ in 1914.[12] In any case, workers did not benefit greatly from increased productivity,

[11] Paul H. Douglas, *Real Wages in the United States, 1890–1926* (Boston: Houghton Mifflin, 1930).
[12] Albert Rees, *Real Wages in Manufacturing, 1890–1914* (Princeton: Princeton University Press, 1961), p. 4.

and crowded tenements, slums, and ghettos were part of the picture of industrial nation-building.

American trade unionism, as represented by the principal labor organization, the American Federation of Labor, was business unionism, committed to accommodation with private capitalism. The AFL worked for better wages, shorter hours, more satisfactory working conditions, and remedial social legislation. It rejected the two chief orientations of European trade union movements of the time—socialist and syndicalist. Significantly, it also rejected the idea of forming its own (labor) party and sought instead to move the two major parties toward positions which it favored. Economic satisfactions and dissatisfactions have an important relational component: American industrial workers were certainly deprived by our standards, clearly had dissatisfactions; but the fact that they could see themselves as better off than their counterparts in other countries apparently checked the most intense dissatisfactions which in Europe sustained strongly anti-system labor movements.

The weakness of American socialism is striking. At no time in the period was the American political agenda influenced significantly by demands for a broad-gauged transformation of the economic order. The small socialist parties which did contest nationally—Socialist Labor, Social Democratic, and Socialist—were forced to curiously adulterate their ideology. Socialism means something quite specific: the *common control of the instruments of production*. Either a party is committed to that or it isn't socialist. It is one thing to find private capitalism in an age of rapid industrial growth excessively harsh—even some industrialists did that—and something else to favor the systematic nationalization of industry. In this regard, the platforms of the American Socialist parties in the 1890s and the early twentieth century make strange reading. They typically begin with obeisance to standard socialist rhetoric. But when they turn to specific proposals, they emphasize such remedial social benefits as a shorter work week, more vacations, a minimum wage, a system of old-age and survivors insurance for workers, and employment and accident insurance. The Socialist party platform of 1912 contains under the heading *political demands:* "The separation of the present Bureau of Labor from the Department of Commerce and Labor and its elevation to the rank of a department." We are not suggesting that American socialists did not understand what they were about, only that the climate in which they operated was so profoundly unsympathetic that they were compelled to shift their public appeal from socialism to social reform. Compared to their counterparts in western Europe, American socialist movements were weaker, less cohesive or class conscious, and never did mount an attack on private capitalism that offered any substantial chance of success.

The Reactions of the Urban Middle Class

In 1900, dissent in agricultural America was waning before increased prosperity and the clear supremacy of the new industrial order; and opposition originating in the industrial work force was proving too weak to alter the direction of American industrialization. In this context, a third reform movement rapidly gained strength. Its social base was urban and middle-class, and its vision of the just society was not of an agricultural past or noncapitalist future, but rather of what William Allen White called "a new highly socialized industrial order." The maturation of a business society, then, built not only business conservatism but also a new kind of reformism in a new social collectivity.

A portion of the urban middle class that grew rapidly after the Civil War had qualms over the direction of industrialism from the outset. But it lacked a public philosophy with which to challenge the emerging order, and it could not offer any politically viable alternative to the world businessmen were building. What public philosophies were available to it? Socialism surely was unpalatable. Since it welcomed an urban and industrial order it could hardly adopt the posture of agrarian reaction. It wound up, then, for a time clinging forlornly to the old liberal doctrine of the negative state, while condemning the excesses of the industrialists. It did not see (at least, it did not see clearly) that by adhering to the liberal principal of negative or limited government *it was in fact rejecting a far more basic liberal commitment to the dispersion of power.* At its best, liberalism had been profoundly suspicious of concentrated power, and its insistence on limited government grew naturally from this. But the concentration of resources and power was imposed by industrialism. The question had become: How could the industrialists be checked?

The extent of the intellectual confusion of the urban middle class in the late nineteenth century is beautifully illustrated by *The Nation,* one of the political journals which spoke to it. *The Nation* championed negative government and extreme industrialism. As the farm protest against the railroads grew louder, the magazine's opposition to state regulation brought it to the side of the railroads.[13] *The Nation* defended the trusts

---

[13] For an excellent general treatment of the policy commitments of *The Nation* from the Civil War to the New Deal, see Alan Pendleton Grimes, *The Political Liberalism of the New York Nation, 1865–1932* (Chapel Hill: University of North Carolina Press, 1953).

on the grounds of reduced costs to consumers and attacked "the whole scheme of criminal legislation against Trusts and monopolies, federal and state, which has all been enacted within a few years at the demands of agitators. . . ."[14] It assimilated large industrial corporations into its individualism, denouncing the modest efforts of organized labor as interference with the natural and proper bargaining between the individual employee and "individual" employer.

It would be easy to dismiss a magazine which defended trusts, attacked labor unions, and denied the legitimacy of governmental intervention in the economy on behalf of the poorer classes as an apologist pure and simple of business interests. But *The Nation* in the late nineteenth century was not that. It strongly opposed slavery, advocated protecting the vote of Negroes; it backed civil service reform to check the spoils system, and the direct primary and proportional representation to curb the power of the bosses. It struggled at the time of the Spanish-American War to resist the imperialistic course on which the United States had embarked with such enthusiasm. In short, "within the framework of the old liberalism *The Nation* fought the good fight for human freedom, honest government and pure society."[15] Here was no business journal. The political thinking of the editors of *The Nation* in the late nineteenth century were typical of an urban middle class which had been reared on the assumption that intervention by the state was generally bad, and which was broadly sympathetic to the process of industrial growth. It was political thinking which tried to preserve a modified version of the "shopkeepers theory" of economics in industrial America. Grimes's summary is instructive: "It failed to see that government, to be effective, must possess a jurisdiction at least as great as the corporations or groups which are subject to its authority. It failed to see that liberty is not necessarily enhanced by the absence of governmental restraint, but by the absence of restraint wherever it may occur. It failed to see that liberty, upon examination, always becomes a question of whose liberty to do what? and that, therefore, in a democracy, determinations of liberties always involve the utilitarian criterion of social consequences."[16]

The development of the Progressive movement in the early twentieth century was a radical departure in the thinking of the reformist middle class, a belated recognition of the "new world" of industrialism. The Progressives were committed to positive government, to the use of gov-

---

[14] "Pools, Trusts and Monopolies," *The Nation*, LXV (1897), p. 44.
[15] Grimes, pp. 116–117.
[16] *Ibid.*, p. 120.

ernmental power to restore the imbalance that had occurred with the growth of private business and to manage a far more complicated and interdependent society. In the language of the time, the Progressives sought to use government "where necessary as an agent of human welfare." "Lord, how we did like that phrase," wrote William Allen White in his *Autobiography,* " 'using government as an agent of human welfare.' " Herbert Croly, through his many writings, especially *The Promise of American Life,* was perhaps the most coherent and insightful Progressive ideologue. And Theodore Roosevelt became the movement's most prominent political spokesman.

Theodore Roosevelt as president, the Progressive party of 1912, Woodrow Wilson in his administration's commitment to the "New Freedom" all received support from a wide assortment of American publics. Many of the Progressives were old-time agrarian radicals, and saw the movement as an extension of their earlier efforts. But the vision of the Progressive movement under Roosevelt and Wilson was new. Richard Hofstadter concludes that "essentially, the New Freedom was an attempt of the middle class, with agrarian and labor support, to arrest the exploitation of the community, the concentration of wealth, and the growing control of politics by insiders, and to restore, as far as possible, competitive opportunities in business."[17] And James McGregor Burns describes the leadership of the Progressive effort as coming "largely out of the nation's waxing, upper middle class in the cities. They were mostly businessmen, editors, lawyers, with the scattering of professional workers, college professors, writers, doctors, and clergymen. Most of them born and bred Republicans, they had kept their distance from other reform movements, from the country populists, the silverites, the trust busters, the city labor groups."[18]

Late in the second sociopolitical period, then, a strong reform movement developed in the urban middle class. It sought to end entrepreneurial government—government conducted along the model of private economic activity; to conserve national resources; to restore economic competition; to distribute income somewhat more equitably; to provide more humane conditions for industrial labor; and generally to supervise and regulate economic activity. The public philosophy of urban

[17] Hofstadter, p. 255.
[18] James MacGregor Burns, *The Deadlock of Democracy* (Englewood Cliffs, N.J.: Prentice-Hall, 1963), p. 114. In this new reformism, rural America received short shift. The Progressive party platform of 1912, for example, devoted fewer than 150 of its 6,500 words to the needs of farmers. The two short paragraphs were quaintly titled "Country Life."

middle-class reform had been clearly formulated by World War I. It was not, however, the ascendant public philosophy of the society. That ascendancy was not to come until a decade of turmoil following the Great Depression.

Industrialization and Sectional Politics

It is quite clear that the net effect of industrial growth and technological development in the twentieth century has been to further nationalize or integrate the various geographic regions of the country. But in the early stages of industrialism the result was the opposite, a heightening of differences between the industrializing and economically ascendant Northeast and a vast rural hinterland.

As early as 1880, more than three-quarters of the labor force in New England and the Middle-Atlantic states was employed in non-agricultural pursuits. This extensive industrialization gave the region some distinctive economic interests: the strong commitment to the protective tariff and to "sound money" are examples. But the impact was much wider. Urbanization necessarily accompanied industrialization. The factories needed labor, more than the mechanization of agriculture could free from American farms; and there was a great importation of labor from agricultural sections of southern, eastern, and central Europe.

The early industrialization of the Northeast sustained a long period of economic ascendancy and greater prosperity for the region. Table 4.1 provides one measure of this economic advantage, comparing personal income per capita, expressed as a percentage of the United States average, for the Northeast, Great Plains and South. In 1900, personal per capita income thus was nearly three times as high in the Northeast as in the South.

The concentration of economic and political power in the Northeast which followed industrialization was resented and at times resisted by the other regions. Herbert Agar is probably not exaggerating when he writes that "the chief domestic issue in America from the Civil War to the time of Franklin Roosevelt . . . [was] the issue of economic colonialism. How can the provinces—especially the South and West—save themselves from what is popularly known as 'Wall Street'?"[19] Economic historians now have considerable doubt about the validity—in a literal sense—of many of the charges the hinterland hurled at the Northeast and the "money power": for instance, that the prices of agricultural

[19] Agar, p. 444.

TABLE 4.1

Personal Income Per Capita:
Northeast, Great Plains, and South, 1860–1930*

	1860	1880	1900	1920	1930
Northeast	139	141	137	132	138
Great Plains					
(West North Central States)	66	90	97	87	82
South	72	51	51	62	55
United States	100	100	100	100	100

* Source: Richard A. Easterlin, "Regional Income Trends, 1840–1950," in Seymour E. Harris, (ed.), *American Economic History* (New York: McGraw-Hill, 1961), p. 528.

commodities fell more sharply than the prices of other goods because the latter were held up by monopolistic practices, and that the interest rates charged by banks and other lenders of money were so high as to be extortionate.[20] In fact, the financial plight of agriculture, and thus of the South and Great Plains states, found its basic cause in an excessive expansion of acreage under cultivation. An oversupply of agricultural commodities led to lengthy periods of depressed prices.

In short, a vast process of world-wide adjustment was taking place in which the demand for agricultural commodities was growing rapidly, but the supply was growing in vast surges. Inevitably, there were times of high prices and above normal profits countered by other times of very low prices and no profits at all. When deficient crops resulted from poor rainfall or other untoward conditions in any area, the outcome was still more catastrophic, coupling a low yield to low prices. Aggravating the difficulties caused by wide fluctuations in the prices of agricultural commodities was the fact that prices in general were falling.[21]

The half-century or so after the Civil War saw a highly sectionalized politics in which a series of political movements based in the South and West challenged the Northeast: the Readjusters, Independents, Greenbackers, Populists, and Bryanites. None of these movements enjoyed any significant successes in the northeastern corner of the country. At times there was talk of an alliance of the disadvantaged of the cities and

[20] For an economic analysis of such arguments, see Douglass C. North, *Growth and Welfare in the American Past* (Englewood Cliffs, N.J.: Prentice-Hall, 1966), pp. 137–144.
[21] *Ibid.*, p. 144.

the country, but this was never put together. The politics of industrialization was a sectional politics, with the several regions perhaps further
separated in basic political concerns than at any other point in American
history.[22]

The Growth of the State with the Building of a Society of Scale

America before the Civil War had been a society of modest scale:
small economic enterprises, small towns and farms, a high degree of
localism and independence—and small government. All this changed
with the coming of industrialism. Between 1870 and 1920, the population of the country tripled, reaching 106 million. The great cities were
built. Huge industrial and financial institutions were established. In
place of small family farms producing foodstuffs of their immediate
areas, there were big corporations drawing resources from throughout
the country (and indeed the world) and servicing national markets.
Developments in one sector increasingly came to have effects throughout
—in contrast to the economy in 1790, with high insulation and autonomy
of the small producing units. The economy came under the domination
of large industrial aggregates engaged in oligopolistic competition. A
new communications technology made activity in one sector the immediate property of the entire nation. This was the half century in which
all the major electronic media except television were developed. There
were 3,000 telephones in the United States in 1876, 340,000 in 1885,
4.1 million in 1905, and 13.3 million in 1920. Radio came later, but by
1929, over 10 million families owned radio sets. A new transportation
network was established, centering on the railroad and the motor car.
The physical mobility of the population was vastly extended. Miles of
railroad track in operation increased from 8,800 in 1850 to 82,000 in
1880 to 406,000 in 1920. Motor vehicle registrations jumped from
8,000 in 1900 to 2.5 million in 1915 to 26.5 million in 1929. In the
latter year, nearly 4.5 million new cars were sold.

With these increases of scale in other parts of the society, there was
a marked expansion of governmental activity. Industrialization produced

[22] The profound "apartness" of the South was the result not only of the extreme rurality of the region in a period of industrialization (in 1880 about 25
percent of the labor force in the South was in non-agricultural pursuits, in contrast to 75 percent in the Northeast), but, of course, of the legacy of race and
the Civil War. In the half-century after the Civil War, most Negroes remained
southern dwellers, and the preoccupation with race and race relations was thus
fundamentally a southern concern. The South, too, was the conquered provinces,
and constructed an elaborate mythology on the North, the War, and Reconstruction. On this mythology the politically "solid South" was built.

massive concentrations of resources, and it became increasingly difficult to act as though this had not occurred, as though there were still the "natural" regulation of competition among many small producers. Maximum hours regulations made little sense—and wasn't suggested— when most Americans were independent farmers; it was quite a different matter when millions entered the ranks of factory labor, working for big corporations. And pure food and drug legislation didn't seem imperative when most people lived on farms and consumed what they produced; but the call for this regulation became increasingly insistent with the growth of big cities and the development of corporations serving national markets.

Paralleling this growth of regulatory activities was a comparable expansion of government services. An industrializing society required far higher investments in education than an agricultural society: total public expenditure for education grew from approximately $90 million in 1875 to $258 million in 1902, $558 million in 1913, and $2,243 million in 1927. New possibilities and requirements in transportation brought a comparable increase in governmental service activity through the construction of highways—from $175 million in 1902 to $1,809 million twenty-five years later.

The expansion of government service activities took place mostly at the state and local level. Federal expenditures were only moderately higher in the 1870–1915 period than they had been before the Civil War, and the increase was largely accounted for by defense, veterans' pensions, and interest on the debt. Figure 4.2 shows the remarkable stability of per capita federal expenditures over a half-century: $6.10 in 1875, $6.80 in 1900 and $7.20 in 1916, the last year before American entry into World War I. Between 1900 and 1916, when state and local spending increased sharply, national government expenditure was static.

After the extraordinary demands of the war, spending did not fall back to the old pre-war level. Expenditures had hovered around $5 to $7 per capita in the half-century after the Civil War, but were between $25 and $30 from 1922 up to the Depression. In 1926, with a conservative Republican president, federal per capita expenditures were nearly *four* times as high as a decade earlier, under a liberal Democrat! Striking as this is, it should not be surprising: *the basic level of government activity in the United States has always been a function of the social setting, not of the particular administration.* The big increase after World War I signaled the entry of the United States into a third great sociopolitical period, with different demands on government than those

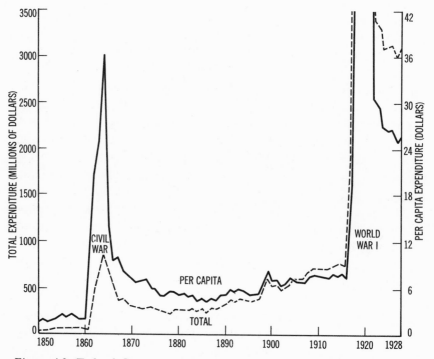

Figure 4.2. Federal Government Expenditure, Per Capita and Total, 1850–1928*

* Source: *Historical Statistics of the United States,* pp. 7, 711. (For the years 1918, 1919, 1920, and 1921, the per capita and total expenditures are, respectively: $123.0, $177.2, $60.1, and $47.1, and $12,696.7, $18,514.9, $6,403.3, and $5,115.9 million.)

of the previous period. In 1902, all units of government in the United States expended slightly more than $1.6 billion; two decades later, the figure had risen to $9.3 billion. This 600-percent expansion, unaffected by war and in a period of relatively stable prices, points to some far-reaching sociopolitical changes which we will explore in the next chapter.

The Politics of Ethnic Heterogeneity

After the Civil War, the American citizenry became far more variegated ethnically, first as Negroes became citizens, and second as the country took in millions of immigrants from eastern, central and southern Europe to meet the labor demands of industrialization. A major change in ethnocultural composition thus occurred just as the population was moving from rural and agricultural to urban and industrial.

The Politics of Race

In 1866 and 1867, the "radicals" in Congress seized power from the politically inept president, Andrew Johnson, and imposed their own plans for reconstruction of the defeated South in place of his. The South was divided into five military districts, each under a major general. A state would be readmitted to the Union only when it had set up a government based on universal male suffrage and had ratified the Fourteenth Amendment. The Bureau of Refugees, Freedmen and Abandoned Lands (commonly called the Freedmen's Bureau) was re-established; it worked largely in the area of relief, but it also set up schools and tried to protect the employment rights of Negroes. The Fifteenth Amendment to the Constitution was ratified, providing that "the right of citizens of the United States shall not be denied or abridged by the United States or by any state on account of race, color or previous condition of servitude." And when Ku Klux Klan terrorism threatened to bring about the collapse of the entire "radical" Reconstruction program, various enforcement acts were passed. It isn't hard to demonstrate inadequacies in this second or "radical" reconstruction, but at least there was a recognition, advanced for the time, that something more than the literal act of emancipation was needed.

In the 1870s, however, northern interest in protecting the rights of Negroes waned, and there were sharp policy reversals. One of these was the Compromise of 1877. The presidential election in 1876 had ended with neither candidate having an unchallenged electoral vote majority. The outcome hinged on twenty disputed votes—nineteen from three southern states—and the Republican candidate, Rutherford Hayes, allowed his friends to promise that the last northern troops would be withdrawn from the South if he were permitted to receive these votes and assume the presidency in peace. Hayes did assume the presidency in peace, northern troops were withdrawn, and Negroes were left to the custody of whites upon their pledge they would protect them in their constitutional rights. After 1877, northern opinion on race moved steadily away from insistence upon the principles of Reconstruction, with point after point being conceded, so that a decade and a half after the war, North and South were not far apart. Race was again a "southern question," to be dealt with in the South.

The southern debate on race between 1877 and 1900—when things were largely settled for a half-century with the erection of the Jim Crow system—was of great moment for American social and political life, and we need to look at it closely. Recent research has made us aware of how vigorous that debate was, undermining a view which long prevailed that once "home rule" was reestablished southern whites immediately and more or less unanimously rose up in righteous indignation at the horrors of Reconstruction, established complete segregation, and excluded Negroes from public life. In fact, before the South gave in to the doctrines of extreme racism, several alternate philosophies of race relations were put forward, the most politically muscular of these being the *conservative* position.[23]

The term *conservative* is used with all sorts of meanings; in this context it refers to a posture assumed by many southerners of the "better sort," men of wealth and high social status. It was paternalistic, reflecting a kind of *noblesse oblige*. In the words of Governor Thomas Jones, an Alabama conservative: "The Negro race is under us. . . . He is in our power. We are his custodians . . . we should extend to him, as far as possible, all the civil rights that will fit him to be a decent and self respecting, law-abiding and intelligent citizen. . . . If we do not lift them up, they will drag us down."[24] As the position of a large segment of the Southern upper class, the conservative philosophy looked to race relations based on civility, moderation, and generosity. It pursued racial accommodation.

For a decade and a half after the end of Reconstruction, men committed to this conservative philosophy were ascendant in state party systems throughout the region. They supported Negro suffrage, appealed to Negroes for their votes, supported the establishment of schools for the newly freed slaves. A good example of the conservative approach is the administration of former Confederate General Wade Hampton in South Carolina. Hampton served as governor from 1876 to 1879, when he was elected to the United States Senate. He clearly went further in his efforts to attract Negro electoral support than any twentieth-century South Carolina governor. The title of a Hampton campaign book is indicative: *Free Men! Free Ballots!! Free Schools!!! The Pledges of General Wade Hampton . . . to the Colored People of South Carolina 1865–1876.* As governor, he appointed more than eighty Negroes to public office.[25]

No thought should be entertained that the conservative alternative

[23] See C. Vann Woodward, *The Strange Career of Jim Crow* (New York: Oxford University Press, 1957).
[24] Quoted by Woodward, pp. 29–30.
[25] *Ibid.*, pp. 36–37.

was some racial paradise. It *was* vastly different from the pattern of race relations which developed in the 1890s. In the decade and a half after the end of Reconstruction, Negroes were participating in public life throughout most of the South much more actively than they would again until the late 1950s, and generally were subjected to much less systematic discrimination. The elaborate biracial (Jim Crow) system was not part of the policy of southern conservatives from 1877 through the early years of the 1890s. What, then, occurred that led to Jim Crow?

The story is a complex one, and much of the answer lies beyond the scope of our analysis. But some basic developments can be sketched. We have referred to the waves of protest which swept across agricultural America in the 1870s, 1880s, and 1890s. The South was overwhelmingly rural, and Populism as a radical agrarian protest representing small and marginal farmers became, around 1890, a potent force. In 1890, the People's party gained control of eight southern state legislatures. At the outset, southern Populism proclaimed itself a movement of the disadvantaged, white and black, and thus was a second alternative to extreme racism. This attempt to build an alliance of poor whites and poor blacks around common economic grievances failed, and even for the brief time it was pursued, Negrophobes in the Populist ranks opposed it. Nonetheless, it was an extraordinary episode in southern politics. C. Vann Woodward is right when he states that the Populists in the early 1890s took steps "sometimes drastic and, for the times, even heroic."[26] For example, the Georgia Populist leader Tom Watson, who was to be the party's national standard-bearer in two extremely unsuccessful presidential races, announced that it was the objective of his party to "make lynch law odious to the people." In 1892, a Negro Populist who had spoken extensively in support of Watson was threatened with lynching; he fled to Watson for protection, and 2,000 armed white farmers responded to the call for aid, remaining on guard for two nights. Watson told whites and blacks: "You are made to hate each other because upon that hatred is rested the keystone of the arch of financial despotism which enslaves you both. You are deceived and blinded that you may not see how this race antagonism perpetuates a monetary system which beggars you both."[27] If you stand up for your rights and work with the People's party, Watson promised, the party will "wipe out the color line and put every man on his citizenship irrespective of color." This was heady stuff, extraordinary since racial

26 *Ibid.,* p. 44.
27 Quoted by Woodward, pp. 44–45.

fears ran strong among the whites to whom the Populist appeal was addressed. The conservative Democrats had, after all, portrayed themselves with at least some plausibility as the defenders of Negroes against the racial fanaticism of the "poor whites."

In view of these impressive early efforts, it is particularly ironic that the Populists were to play an important role in the creation of Jim Crow. The economic upheaval which propelled the Populists ahead around 1890 was extensive, "more profound in its political manifestations than that which shook them [the southern people] in the Great Depression of the 1930s."[28] The Populists, then, were a real threat to the economic and political position of the conservatives. Thoroughly frightened by the prospects of a poor man's coalition, the conservatives resorted to raising the specter of "Negro domination." Having previously resisted Negro disenfranchisement, they now took the lead in supporting it, with the clear intent of depriving the radicals of black support. And, not accidentally, some of the formal mechanisms for Negro disenfranchisement—such as the poll tax and literary tests—succeeded in disenfranchising a goodly number of poor whites as well.

At the very time the conservatives were thus raising racial animosity, they were compounding their offense by taking advantage of their control in the black belt to pile up big majorities of Negro votes *against* Populist candidates and *for white supremacy!* Woodward writes: "Some of these votes were bought and some intimidated, but in the main they were merely counted for the ticket, however they voted or whether they voted or not. Time after time the Populists would discover that after they had carried the white counties, fradulent returns from the black belt counties padded with ballots the Negro did or did not cast were used to overwhelm them."[29]

Not surprisingly, the Populist experiment in interracial collaboration collapsed before this combination of race-baiting and fraudulent use of Negro ballots. Many of the Populist leaders turned on blacks with a vengeance, blaming them for their party's troubles. Others, realizing that the blacks were victims rather than culprits, nonetheless became converts to white supremacy via expediency. Watson, who had taken his lumps while pursuing an alliance of the poor of both races, reversed himself and went on to build a successful political career on virulently anti-Negro appeals.

Both the conservatives and the Populists shifted to the cause of white supremacy, then, but from sharply different assumptions as to the

28 *Ibid.,* p. 60.
29 *Ibid.,* p. 62.

likely effects of the elimination of Negroes from public life. Populists like Watson concluded that only after Negroes were eliminated from politics could Populist principles gain a hearing, that race would have to be eliminated as an issue separating white men before the lower-class white majority could stand united against "the interests." This interpretation was not totally lacking in foundation. Southern progressives after 1900 did have considerable success against corporations and railroads, against insurance companies and trusts. They did democratize politics by introducing the primary system, and through corrupt-practices and anti-lobbying legislation. And they scored some gains in the field of social legislation: the protection of factory workers, the restriction of child labor, consumer protection. But basically, the premise of the conservatives was the one borne out in the decades following the 1890s. By making white supremacy the overriding issue, they shifted the structure of political conflict in a manner salutary to their economic interests: instead of poor whites against more prosperous whites, it became whites against blacks. Attention was directed from the economic disadvantages of lower-class whites to their status superiority over blacks. Lower-class whites were persuaded—and it must be added many were quite ready to be so persuaded—that the fundamental political issue was keeping Negroes in their place; they then had no qualms about supporting conservative political leaders who were effective proponents of white supremacy.

Southern leaders thus came together in the late 1890s and early 1900s behind the systematic exclusion of Negroes from public life and their assignment to segregated and generally inferior public facilities: disenfranchisement; dual school system; separate parks, playgrounds, and swimming pools; exclusion from restaurants and hotels used by whites; and so on. The formal legislative props of this Jim Crow system stood for a half-century and were not massively challenged until the mid-1950s, with the start signaled by *Brown* v. *Board of Education of Topeka* and its companion cases.

Southerners were not alone responsible for the redrawing of the political agenda which culminated in Jim Crow. Northern opinion swung completely away from any insistence that the civil rights of Negro Americans be protected. The northern press showed more sympathy for southern whites and quickly acquiesced to the new "southern solution." Federal courts, through their emasculation of Reconstruction legislation passed to protect Negroes and by their discovery of constitutional sanctions for systematic segregation, aided and abetted the capitulation to Jim Crow. Paralleling the developments in the South, then, was a general weakening of the outside forces which had helped check some of the more overtly racist "solutions."

Jim Crow did not immediately or "naturally" emerge once the force of Yankee arms was removed from Dixie in 1877. It came twenty-five years later, and then the product of national and regional developments some of which were quite distinct from race. Among the many "might-have-beens" in American history is this: that the course of social and political development might have been different if another resolution of the competing and contradictory pressures around race had emerged at the turn of the century.

The Politics of the "Melting Pot"

Outside the South, ethnic group conflict was among whites of different European backgrounds, and was fueled by the largest immigration in history, of about 32.5 million people between 1860 and 1929. The big supply of underemployed labor at this time was not in Britain and northwestern Europe—an area also industrializing—but in the still agricultural countries of central, eastern and southern Europe. Table 4.2 shows that 43 percent of the 1860–1929 immigrants came from these areas, although they accounted for less than 1 percent of the immigration in the four decades before the war. Between 1900 and 1921, the years of peak immigration, more than 10 million people moved to the United States from central, eastern and southern Europe. The immigration from these countries in the first decade of this century alone was greater than from *all countries* between 1820 to 1859. More people emigrated to the U.S. between 1890 and 1914 than in the preceding hundred years stretching back to the ratification of the Constitution.

The ethnic composition of the United States was thus massively changed. In 1820, the country was home to about 9.6 million people who, except for the nearly 2 million Negroes, were mostly of British stock. A century later, when the doors were closed by severely restrictive immigration legislation, Americans of British descent were still the largest ethnic bloc but were far from the overwhelming majority they had been, numbering instead roughly 40 percent of the *white* population.[30]

[30] As difficult as it is to estimate the national origins or "stock" of the American population—because of such things as marriage across "stock" lines—the 40 percent estimate for British stock seems pretty sound. Two separate U.S. Bureau of the Census investigations arrived at it. For the first, see the *Statistical Abstract of the United States 1929*, p. 105; and for a discussion of how these estimates were arrived at, see William S. Bernard, *American Immigration Policy* (New York: Harper & Brothers, 1950), pp. 281–288. For the second and apparently better executed estimate, also by the Census Bureau but unpublished, see the discussion in Theodore White, *The Making of the President 1960* (New York: Atheneum, 1961), pp. 225–227.

TABLE 4.2

Immigration by Country, 1860–1929*

	1860–1929 (IMMIGRATION FROM ALL COUNTRIES: 32,515,120)	1860–1869 (IMMIGRATION FROM ALL COUNTRIES: 2,068,860)	1870–1879 (IMMIGRATION FROM ALL COUNTRIES: 2,751,137)	1880–1889 (IMMIGRATION FROM ALL COUNTRIES: 5,247,568)	1890–1899 (IMMIGRATION FROM ALL COUNTRIES: 3,885,593)	1900–1909 (IMMIGRATION FROM ALL COUNTRIES: 8,202,387)	1910–1919 (IMMIGRATION FROM ALL COUNTRIES: 6,347,380)	1920–1929 (IMMIGRATION FROM ALL COUNTRIES: 4,295,510)
Great Britain	10.6	25.8	21.1	15.5	8.5	5.7	5.9	7.9
Ireland	8.1	20.7	15.4	12.9	10.4	4.2	2.6	4.8
Germany	13.5	35.0	27.3	27.5	14.9	4.0	2.7	9.0
Scandinavia	7.1	4.7	7.6	12.2	10.1	6.0	3.8	4.8
Other northwestern Europe	2.4	3.4	4.3	3.8	2.6	2.2	2.6	3.2
Central Europe	15.3	0.3	2.5	6.8	24.2	24.4	18.2	10.1
Russia and the Baltic states	10.2	0.1	1.3	3.5	10.7	18.3	17.4	2.1
Other eastern Europe	1.1	0.0	0.0	0.1	0.3	1.9	1.8	2.1
Italy	13.8	0.5	1.7	5.1	14.2	23.5	19.4	10.1
Other southern Europe	2.6	0.4	0.7	0.4	1.2	2.9	5.4	3.8
All other	15.3	9.2	17.8	11.6	2.9	6.9	20.3	42.0

* Source: *Historical Statistics of the United States*, pp. 56–59. (All data are expressed as percentages of the total immigration in the specified period.)

The six decades from the Civil War to the Depression, then, were the time of building an ethnically heterogeneous nation, and it was when our ethnic "growing pains" were the sharpest. Certainly it was the time when the conflicting styles and interests of *white* ethnocultural groups were most salient in the political agenda. The contemporary observer is struck by the openness, blatancy, of ethnic hostilities and prejudice. For example, *Harper's Weekly,* an important national magazine, attacked Francis Kernan, who was running for governor of New York State in 1872, on the grounds that "he is a Roman Catholic and will obey the orders of the Church."[31] In 1921, vice-president-elect Calvin Coolidge wrote in a national magazine that "biological laws show us that Nordics deteriorate when mixed with other races."[32] At about the same time, James J. Davis, who served as secretary of labor under Presidents Harding and Coolidge, proclaimed that old-stock Americans were "the beaver type that built up America, whereas the new immigrants were rat-men trying to tear it down; and obviously rat-men could never become beavers."[33] Such statements by "respectable" public men were legion.

Hostility and prejudice were not confined to a single ethnic group. Since old-stock Protestants were the "established" and numerically superior, their prejudices were "controlling" and demand special attention, but this should not imply they were somehow the principal claimants of vice and their ethnic opponents of virtue. The most important ethnic antagonisms tended to be organized around Protestant vs. Catholic, but the overall mix was much more complex. There were, for example, important divisions in American Protestantism, and fundamentalists contributed disproportionately to nativist movements and to anti-Catholicism. After 1890 the United States received a large Jewish immigration from the countries of central and eastern Europe, and anti-Semitism became more prominent. Jews encountered hostility not only from native Protestants, but from Catholic immigrants who were themselves on the receiving end of discrimination. For example, in 1902 the tensions between Jews and Irish in New York City erupted in open violence when a Jewish funeral procession, passing through an Irish

[31] Quoted by Alvin P. Stauffer, *Anti-Catholicism in American Politics, 1865–1900* (Ph.D. dissertation, Department of History, Harvard University, 1933), p. 44.

[32] Calvin Coolidge, "Whose Country Is This?", *Good Housekeeping,* 72 (February, 1921), p. 14; quoted by Seymour Martin Lipset and Earl Raab, *The Politics of Unreason: Right-Wing Extremism in America 1790–1970* (New York: Harper & Row), Chapter 4.

[33] Quoted by Lipset and Raab, Chapter 4.

district, was pelted with iron nuts and bolts. When the police, largely Irish, intervened, it was with abusive language and physical brutality against the Jews.[34] We focus, then, on Protestant antagonism toward Catholics not because it was the sole manifestation of ethnocultural tensions, but because it was the most substantial.

The largest anti-Catholic movement outside the South in the latter part of the nineteenth century was the American Protective Association (APA), organized in 1887. In the mid-1890s, the APA was to claim 4 million supporters. It was a secret organization, with rituals, costumes, and associated paraphernalia similar to those of the Ku Klux Klan. The objectives of the APA were spelled out in an 1894 program: the defense of "true Americanism" against the "subjects of an unAmerican ecclesiastical institution" by the curtailment of immigration, by making it harder for an immigrant to attain citizenship, and by preventing any public assistance to the schools operated by the Catholic church.[35] The APA practiced a virulent anti-Catholicism, requiring every recruit to swear never to vote for a Catholic, employ one (if a Protestant were available), or go out on strike with one. It distributed a series of bogus documents which it claimed to be secret Catholic communications, like one supposedly addressed to American Catholics by Pope Leo XIII, freeing them from any requirement of loyalty to the United States and requiring them "to exterminate all heretics."[36] The APA apparently had its greatest strength among low-status Protestants in urban areas, especially in fast-growing sections of the West.[37]

The APA largely disappeared after 1896, in part because of intense internecine struggles. Nativism, however, showed no sign of abating. It did experience a significant shift in its base of support, from eastern and urban to rural small town and heartland.

This inverted the structure of former anti-Catholic movements and marked an historic transition in the character of Protestant nativism. During the nineteenth century the tradition drew its main strength from the larger towns and cities where Catholics were actually settling. Even in the 1890s, when the excitement invaded the midwestern countryside, in a grotesquely jin-

34 John Higham, "Anti-Semitism in the Gilded Age: A Reinterpretation," *Mississippi Valley Historical Review*, 43 (1957), p. 578.

35 See Lipset and Raab, Chapter 3; John Higham, *Strangers in the Land* (New Brunswick, N.J.: Rutgers University Press, 1955), pp. 83–85; and Humphrey Desmond, *The A.P.A. Movement* (Washington: New Century Press, 1912), *passim*.

36 Lipset and Raab, Chapter 3.

37 *Ibid.*

goistic form, anti-Catholic xenophobia remained primarily an urban movement. But in the twentieth century it re-emerged most actively in rural
America, where adherents of the hated faith were relatively few.[38]

There had been, we have seen, more than a touch of nativism in
such rural movements of the late nineteenth century as Populism, but
this "darker side" had been submerged in an effort to unite the economically disadvantaged against the "interests." "During the nineties,
the Populist party, whose strength lay almost exclusively in the Midwest
and Southern rural Bible Belt areas, while showing nativist and even
anti-Semitic aspects, concentrated on seeking to regain the conditions
which would sustain a stable agrarian society and focused the fire of its
attack on urban controlled banks, railroads, and monopolies."[39] After
1900, however, agriculture-business conflict lost its saliency. First, the
matter of control and direction had really been settled; it was apparent
that "the conditions which would sustain a stable agrarian society" would
not be regained. Second, farmers generally were experiencing relative
economic prosperity, a marked improvement over late-nineteenth-century
conditions, and this took the edge off their antagonism toward "the
interests." At this same time, businessmen, their victory over rural
America complete, found themselves confronting more insistent demands
from the industrial work force they had built—a work force significantly
populated by the newer immigrants. Put differently, conflict shifted from
efforts by agrarians to hold back industrial ascendancy to the matter of
the quality and shape of an industrial society: instead of businessmen
and urban immigrants against farmers, it more and more became
businessmen *vs.* immigrants-as-industrial-workers.

At the time the shape of conflict was thus changing and the agriculture
vs. business dimension losing its intensity, rural concern over cultural
transformation was growing. The immigrants streaming into the cities
brought styles of life and social values which the parochialism of rural
America could not readily accommodate. The earlier nativist movements
had been triggered mostly among *proximate* groups; here, physical
propinquity did not matter. What was perceived as the challenge was a
far-reaching cultural change; the erosion of "traditional" Protestant
styles and values. As immigrants from Catholic Europe consolidated
their positions in the great cities, the nativist protests shifted in scope,
from the immediate and concrete—Protestant urbanites finding their

[38] Higham, *Strangers in the Land,* p. 181.
[39] Lipset and Raab, Chapter 3.

neighborhoods upset and their jobs threatened—to the more abstract and categoric—Protestant parochials seeing the issue as, quite literally, "Whose society is this going to be?" The shift in geographic base, then, merely followed a more fundamental change in the scope of the protests.

The big issues in the conflict of white ethnocultural groups after 1900, such as Prohibition, display this broad cultural dimension. The Prohibition movement became a major political force, its efforts culminating in the ratification of the Eighteenth Amendment in 1919: "After one year from the ratification of this article, the manufacture, sale or transportation of intoxicating liquors within, the importation thereof into, or the exportation thereof from the United States and all territory subject to the jurisdiction thereof for beverage purposes is hereby prohibited." The movement for Prohibition was closely associated with the Protestant fundamentalism of rural sections. While the immediate objective was a ban on the sale of alcoholic beverages, the whole struggle was heavily symbolic: the real enemy was the "different ways" of many of the new Americans.

It was in the 1920s, after the largest immigration in American history (15.8 million people between 1900 and 1921) that the largest nativist movement in American history appeared, the second Ku Klux Klan. The first Klan had been established in 1866 by former Confederate soldiers as a resistance movement, opposed to the freedmen and their Yankee supporters. The second Klan was founded in Atlanta in 1915, but unlike the first, it was not restricted to the South. It was a national movement which reached an extraordinary membership of 3 million, dominating "for a time the seven states of Oregon, Oklahoma, Texas, Arkansas, Indiana, Ohio, and California."[40] And unlike the first Klan, the second was not motivated primarily by a defense of white supremacy, but was an extremist expression of Protestant fundamentalism and moralism. It paraded on the American scene in the 1920s, anti-Catholic, anti-Semitic, anti-immigrant, anti-Negro, against "vice and immorality"; it was anti-Communist as well. "The Klan was to be the last major purely Protestant nativist movement. . . . [It] formed a bridge between the traditional forms of nativist protest and those which were to come on the extreme right. Not only was it anti-immigrant and jingoistic, it also was anti-radical and specifically anti-Communist."[41]

[40] Frederick Lewis Allen, *Only Yesterday* (New York: Harper and Brothers, 1931), p. 66.
[41] Lipset and Raab, Chapter 4.

In the 1920s, after two decades of steadily growing demands, the United States for the first time in its history erected major barriers to immigration. The first restrictions were imposed by the 1921 Immigration Act; immigration from a given country was limited to 3 percent (per year) of the number of *foreign-born* persons of that nationality in the U.S. in 1910, as determined by the census of that year. In 1924, an even more restrictive measure was passed and the basis for computing the country quotas changed not once but twice. Temporarily, the 1924 Act said, the annual quota for any nationality will be *2 percent* of the number of foreign-born persons of that nationality in the U.S. in *1890*. But after 1927, it went on, "the annual quota of any nationality . . . shall be a number which bears the same ratio to 150,000 as the number of inhabitants in continental United States in 1920 having that national origin . . . bears to the number of inhabitants in continental United States in 1920. . . ."[42] In other words, immigration would be limited to 150,000 a year from all quota countries, and the quota of each would be determined by the percentage of the population in 1920 of each national stock or origin. How could it be determined what percentage of the American population in 1920 was of British stock, of German stock, of Irish stock? It really couldn't. Among other things, men and women had married across "stock" lines. "Foreign-born" had at least been a manageable concept. "National origins" was not. But the Act was passed, and a committee composed of the secretaries of state, commerce, and labor, with expert assistance from the Census Bureau, was set up to work out the quotas. The job could not be reasonably performed, and everyone was unhappy. In all, three different and conflicting estimates of national origins and hence quotas were prepared and submitted before one, the fourth and still different, was accepted and put into use in 1929. Behind all the maneuvering as to the base from which the quotas would be computed, of course, was the fact that each change of base gave a larger quota to some countries and a smaller quota to others. The final formula gave the lion's share of the 150,000 immigrants to Britain, with substantial chunks to Ireland and the countries of northern Europe, as the following quotas show:[43]

Great Britain:	65,721
Ireland	17,853
Germany	25,957

[42] 43 *Stat.* 159 (1924).
[43] *Congressional Record,* June 5, 1929, p. 2384.

Scandinavia, Belgium,	
and the Netherlands	11,918
Poland	6,524
Russia	2,784
Italy	5,802
Czechoslovakia	2,874
Hungary	869
Yugoslavia	845

The massive immigration of the sixty years after the Civil War—produced by the labor needs and opportunities of industrialism—left the United States a country of great ethnic heterogeneity. Early American immigration had come predominantly from Britain and western Europe, but the "new" immigration drew heavily from the eastern and southern sections of the Continent. Neither the economic nor the political ascendancy of Americans of the "older" ethnic groups was seriously challenged nationally in this period. For the newcomers, it was a time of settlement and adaptation—in language, culture, economic activity, and political involvement. As the period drew to a close, however, it was clear that Americans of the new immigration were increasingly restive in their subordinate status and increasingly able to challenge the old; that the politics of the next period would reflect the ethnic diversity this period had established.

The Party System, 1865–1925: A Structural Overview

The first fifty years after regime formation was a period of development of democratic electoral institutions; universal white male suffrage was achieved, the presidency transformed into a popular office, and parties organized as vehicles for popular electioneering in the American condition. There has been little basic structural development in the electoral system generally, and specifically in the parties, since 1840. There was, however, one important set of structural changes in and around the party system in the post–Civil War period— that spurred by the Progressive movement between 1900 and 1920. The thrust of these changes was in the direction of further democratizing parties and electoral competition. In most states, direct primaries replaced conventions as the vehicle for conferring party nominations. State constitutional provision was made for the referendum, recall and initiative. And at the national level, the Seventeenth Amendment, ratified in 1913, provided for the direct popular election of senators in place of selection by state legislators.[44] Still other electoral changes, such as the institution of national preference primaries to choose candidates for the presidency in place of the nominating conventions, were backed by the Progressives but were not adopted.

What precipitated this assault on existing party procedures and the accompanying call for more popular involvement in the affairs of state? The United States had moved in the 1890s into a markedly sectional politics: while there was competition between the parties nationally, in most states one party or the other was clearly ascendant. Voters thus found themselves lacking any real opportunity to express their preferences. The party organization controlled the nomination, and in the absence of effective biparty competition in the general election, the majority nominee was usually elected easily. Without inter-party competition, the only meaningful contest became that for the nomination of the majority party, and direct primaries were a way of letting the electorate control the outcome of that contest. In general, in a setting where the party organizations were not made responsive and responsible by vigorous competition, the cry went up to weaken, even dismantle, them.

Since the Progressives wanted policy change and were often thwarted by the regular party leadership, it is not surprising that they looked for ways to go over the heads of the regulars to the people, and thus became the spokesmen for party and electoral reform. Their attack on the regular party leadership was part, too, of a larger struggle of rival social and economic elites.

The attack on the political party came . . . from people involved in institutions at higher, extra-community levels of social organization. Very frequently they were themselves involved in newer forms of decision making. In Pittsburgh, for example, they came from the upper levels of society, from the highest echelons of the corporate world, and from the advanced segments of professional life. In Chicago the Municipal Voters League was composed of men from the city's dominant social and economic groups. In Seattle and Des Moines the drive was spearheaded by the chambers of commerce. The characteristics of the candidates whom these reform groups backed, as contrasted with those whom they opposed, indicated that they

[44] In 1920, the Nineteenth Amendment was ratified, forbidding states to deny women the right to vote. The granting of women's suffrage completed the formal enfranchisement of all major classes of American citizens. Women's suffrage was backed by the Progressives, but its achievement was not directly associated with the Progressive movement as were the other electoral and party changes referred to above.

preferred as decision makers those from their own levels of institutional organization and from occupational groups associated with corporate business and professional life. Those who sought political reform, therefore, were far more involved in a cosmopolitan than a local world, far more receptive to the political processes inherent in the corporate rather than the party system of decision making.[45]

An elite of growing social and economic prominence sought to alter the existing electoral and party arrangements as part of its effort to achieve greater influence over the direction of public policy.

When regular party activity resumed after the Civil War, a national two-party system was quickly reestablished. The Democrats, badly fragmented by the struggle over slavery and union, regrouped with surprising speed and were again one of the contenders for national power. Their opponents were the Republicans, the new party formed in the crisis of the 1850s; born a sectional party, it was not to achieve substantial mass support among southern whites for nearly a century. The old Whig party had vanished utterly. This two-party system was to survive the entire period, and beyond.

A number of "third" or minor parties appeared—most lasting only a short time. Only two became significant contenders for national power, and these only briefly. The People's party, a descendant of earlier agrarian protest movements, was strong in the South and West in the late 1880s and 1890s. And in 1912, the Progressive party had former Republican President Theodore Roosevelt as its nominee and thereby gathered the highest vote percentage ever by an American "third" party— 27 percent, second to the Democrats' 42 percent, 4 percent ahead of the Republican nominee Taft. But Roosevelt should really be seen as the candidate of a wing of the Republican party, rather than of a true third-party movement.

There were other minor party efforts. The Prohibition party entered a nominee for president in every election after 1868. They reached their high mark in popular vote total and percentage in 1892, with 271,000 votes, 2.3 percent of all ballots cast. Socialist parties appeared in the 1880s and contested regularly thereafter. In 1912, Socialists made their best American showing, as Eugene V. Debs received 900,000 votes, 6 percent of the total. In 1924, with the two major parties nominating eastern conservatives, the maverick Republican senator from

45 Samuel P. Hays, "Political Parties and the Community-Society Continuum," in Chambers and Burnham, eds., *The American Party Systems* (New York: Oxford University Press, 1967), p. 177.

Wisconsin Robert LaFollette ran on a Progressive party line and won nearly 5 million votes.

The overwhelming dominance of the Republican and Democratic parties in the six decades after the Civil War is revealed by the fact that over this period third-party candidates managed to win just 123 electoral votes: 22 by Weaver, the Populist nominee, in 1892; 88 by Roosevelt in 1912; and 13 by LaFollette in 1924.

The Parties: Positions in the Agenda

The Parties and Industrial Nation-Building

Within twenty years after the Civil War, the Republican party, which had been born of the tensions surrounding slavery, was firmly established as the party of rapid industrialization, the party of the agenda. More completely and consistently than their Democratic opponents, the Republicans articulated and represented the dominant policy thrusts in the age of industrialization.

Surely the Republican party that took shape in the 1850s was not a business party. The one basic common commitment of that coalition was opposition to the extension of slavery into the territories. In 1861, the Republicans assumed the presidency and the Civil War began, a war hardly popular with American business. "Coming so soon after the Panic of 1857, this forceful severance of relations with the South plunged Northern business into a new decline. Huge debts became uncollectable, ships and factories were made idle by the unavailability of cotton, while war threatened to bring new taxes, new regulation, new government interference with a normal functioning of trade. Northern businessmen made no secret of their opposition to the war with the South."[46] Throughout the industrial North, from a wide range of industries, business spokesmen urged peace. But once started, the war soon proved to be a bonanza for business: "During the War the spoils of that conquest were bestowed lavishly upon many manufacturers in the form of lucrative contracts, cheap labor, high tariffs; railroad men and land speculators got huge grants from the public domain; bankers received war securities to market at handsome premiums; trade was facilitated by nationaliza-

[46] Thomas C. Cochran and William Miller, *The Age of Enterprise: A Social History of Industrial America* (New York: Harper & Row, 1961; first published in 1942), p. 91.

tion of the currency, by the creation through government loans of a great reserve of credit for business purposes."[47]

The status of the Republican party, as the party of business, then, was first promoted by the war-created ties. It was solidified by the party's strategic position as the majority in the North, and by the Democrats' legacy in ideology and geographic base of support. Although the presidential elections from 1868 until 1896 were close, the Republicans lost the presidency only to Grover Cleveland. As the majority, they were the party with which ascendant business interests had to deal, and the relationship proved mutually satisfactory. The GOP had little ideological baggage to get in the way of policies supportive of industrialization. The Democrats were in a quite different position. They were, after all, *the party* of the Rural Republic, the party of Jefferson and Jackson. They had a strong commitment to states' rights. For many leaders of the Democracy, the good society was agricultural. The party retained its old objections to high tariffs and continued to press for reductions: Even Grover Cleveland, a "gold" Democrat strongly sympathetic to business interests, urged tariff reduction when he was president. The Democracy was a less congenial setting for the new political class of entrepreneurial business, too, because of its geographic base of support. It was dominant in the South, the most heavily agricultural region of the country. Thus, while both parties had rural wings, the Democracy's was much larger and stronger. The Republican weakness in the South left its agrarian wing generally subordinate to the business-oriented northern bloc.

The behavior of the Democrats is especially interesting because it displays the intense pressures which have often operated in the minority party, pushing in opposite directions, one set toward "me tooism," the other toward a frontal assault on the ascendant positions. Some interests are persistently dissatisfied with the resolution of "the big issues"; in the late nineteenth and early twentieth centuries, these issues involved the course of American industrialism, and the biggest cluster of dissent was among southern and western farmers. The majority Republicans were firmly committed to support of business custodianship, and this agricultural dissent had its only opportunity for effective national voice through the Democracy. The nomination of William Jennings Bryan in 1896, 1900, and 1908 represented the intraparty triumph of agrarian discontent. The opposing wing of the Democratic party, on the

[47] *Ibid.*

other hand, wanted to minimize differences with the Republicans over industrial nation-building. The three occasions when the party nominated Grover Cleveland (1884, 1888, and 1892) were victories for this "me too" stance.

When the minority party says "me too," those interests strongly opposed to the course the nation is following are left unrepresented by the two-party system. If they are sufficiently numerous, the result commonly is a strong third-party movement. When the Democrats nominated Cleveland and turned their backs on agricultural dissent, the Populists mounted a strong third-party effort. Their 1892 national platform found both of the big parties equally culpable:

We have witnessed for more than a quarter of a century the struggles of the two great political parties for power and plunder, while grievous wrongs have been inflicted upon the suffering people. We charge that the controlling influence dominating both these parties have permitted the existing dreadful conditions to develop without serious effort to prevent or restrain them. Neither do they now promise us any substantial reform. They have agreed together to ignore, in the coming campaign, every issue but one. They propose to drown the outcries of a plundered people with the uproar of a sham battle over the tariff, so that capitalists, corporations, national banks, rings, trusts, watered stock, the demonetization of silver and the oppressions of the usurers may all be lost sight of. They propose to sacrifice our homes, lives, and children on the altar of mammon; to destroy the multitude in order to secure corruption funds from the millionaires. Assembled on the anniversary of the birthday of the Nation, and filled with the spirit of the proud General and Chief who established our independence, we seek to restore the government of the republic to the hands of "the plain people" *with which class it originated.*

The Parties and Urban-Based Reform

After 1900, as it became patently clear that farmers had become a permanent minority interest, there was a shift in the origins of demands for change—from rural to urban. Accompanying this shift in origin, quite naturally, was one in content. The source most muscular politically, we have seen, was a portion of the urban middle class; the substance of the demand was often subsumed under *progressive.* The objective was not basic change: the industrial system under private direction was accepted, even applauded. There was a new readiness to use the state to right a perceived imbalance.

Both political parties felt and expressed these new demands, and each elected a president who represented them: the Republican Theodore Roosevelt and the Democrat Woodrow Wilson. But in the early twentieth century, the Republicans seemed more likely to be the partisan instrument for the extension of these demands and ultimately for their mature statement. Theodore Roosevelt gave the United States its first administration clearly committed to urban middle-class reform. "The great development of industrialism," he said in 1905, "means that there must be an increase in the supervision exercised by the Government over business enterprise." He worked for conservation against resource exploitation; secured passage of stronger interstate commerce legislation, an employers' liability act, a pure food and drug act; and urged, although unsuccessfully, such measures as workman's compensation, an inheritance tax, and the valuation of railroad properties.

Roosevelt's growing commitment to reform sharpened the split in the Republican party between progressives or reformers and the "Old Guard." Although Taft was elected president in 1908 as Roosevelt's handpicked successor, he became dependent as president upon an alliance with the party's conservative wing, ascendant in Congress, and the stage was set for the struggle of 1912. Splitting with the Republicans, who renominated Taft, Roosevelt ran as the Progressive party nominee on a platform which called for the prohibition of child labor, the eight-hour day, effective legislation to prevent industrial accidents and occupational diseases, a comprehensive program of old-age and survivors' and accident insurance, an income tax, a graduated inheritance tax, and a variety of political reforms, including direct primaries, the direct election of United States senators, and the required registration of lobbyists.

In 1909, Herbert Croly published his extremely influential *The Promise of American Life*. It was a strong summons to master the social consequences of industrialization, to "unite the Hamiltonian principle of national political responsibility and efficiency with a frank democratic purpose which will give a new power to the Hamiltonian system of political ideas and a new power to democracy."[48] It would be necessary, Croly argued, to vigorously assert public as opposed to private and special interests, to abandon Jeffersonian individualism and to invoke positive government "for the benefit of a genuinely individual and social consummation."[49] Croly was not overly optimistic about the capacity of either party to combine the "national idea" and the "democratic idea," using government for such high national and democratic purposes as

---

[48] Herbert Croly, *The Promise of American Life* (New York: Macmillan, 1909), p. 154.
[49] *Ibid.*, p. 153.

the harnessing of industrialism on behalf of the people. But from the vantage point of 1909, he placed what hope he had in the Republicans:

The Republican party is still very far from being a wholly sincere agent of the national reform interest. Its official leadership is opposed to reform; and it cannot be made to take a single step in advance except under compulsion. But Mr. Roosevelt probably prevented it from drifting into the position of an anti-reform party—which if it had happened would have meant its ruin, and would have damaged the cause of national reform. *A Republican party which was untrue to the principle of national responsibility would have no reason for existence; and the Democratic party, as we have seen, cannot become the party of national responsibility without being faithless to its own creed.*[50]

Why would Croly look to the Republican party, so much the party of industrialization, as the most likely instrument for national reform? Because the reform he sought would come not from those nostalgic for a rural past but from those who accepted industrialism while seeking to master its social consequences. The Republicans were the party of the urban middle class, and it was to a portion of that class that Croly was looking, from which progressivism sprung. "Those who sought political reform," Samuel Hays writes, "were far more involved in a cosmopolitan than a local world. . . . The reform image of an appropriate decision-making system also arose from the cosmopolitan world. The reformer's model was the business corporation. . . ."[51] Industrialization, in other words, had created a cosmopolitan middle class committed to national action, to efficiency and expertise, to the effective administrative regulation of industrialization for broad national purposes. In 1909, this cosmopolitan middle class was Republican.

For men like Croly, the Democracy was backward looking, its heart in a rural past. As the party of Jefferson and Jackson, it had continued to champion the provincial idea, the concept of states' rights and limited government. Croly's comments on Bryan as a reformer are instructive here. Bryan had been pushed into public prominence by serious economic distress in farm sections of the country in the 1890s, and his sympathies were laudable. But, Croly reasoned, Bryan was a failure as a reformer because he did not understand what was required for reform. At heart, he remained profoundly suspicious of governmental power and was unwilling to use it to achieve coherent national change.

[50] *Ibid.*, p. 171. (Emphasis added.)
[51] Hays, p. 177.

He proposes in one breath enormous increases of federal power and responsibility, and in the next betrays the old Democratic distrust of effective
national organization. He is willing to grant power to the federal authorities,
but he denies them any confidence, because of the Democratic tradition of
an essential conflict between political authority, particularly so far as it is
centralized, and the popular interest. . . . His advocacy of public ownership
[of railroads] was the most courageous act of his political career; but he
soon showed that he was prepared neither to insist upon such a policy or
even to carry it to a logical conclusion. Almost as soon as the words were
out of his mouth, he became horrified at his own audacity and sought to
mitigate its effects. . . . In the one and the same speech, that is, Mr. Bryan
placed himself on record as a radical centralizer of economic and political
power and as a man who is on general principles afraid of centralization
and opposed to it. . . .[52]

The source of Bryan's confusion seemed obvious to Croly. The thinking
of the "Peerless Leader" was perfectly consistent with the traditional
ideas of Jacksonian Democracy. Bryan failed because he was a good
Democrat!

The confusion and inconsistency of Mr. Bryan's own thinking is merely the
reflection of the confusion and inconsistency resident in the creed of his
party. . . . Jeffersonian and Jacksonian Democrats alike have always dis-
trusted and condemned the means whereby alone the underlying purpose
of Democracy can be fulfilled. . . . The remedial policy which he proposes
for the ills of the American political body are meaningless, unless sustained
by faith in the ability of the national political organization to promote the
national welfare. . . . He is possessed by the time-honored Democratic dis-
like of organization and of the faith in expert skill, in specialized training,
and in large personal opportunities and responsibilities which are implied
by a trust in organization.[53]

Bryan was a provincial, his party the provincial party. The struggle for
the effective reform of industrialism, Croly felt, would be fought out
within the Republican party, which, as the party of industrial nation-
building, at least understood and accepted the new society.

In 1909, Croly's interpretation was probably shared by a large majority of the reform-minded urban middle class: the Republicans were
a better bet than the Democrats. Even in the 1920s, after the Democrats
had given the country Wilson and the Republican conservative wing had
turned the party away from what Croly saw its proper role, the GOP was

[52] Croly, pp. 158–159.
[53] *Ibid.*

still more attuned to the industrial order than the Democrats and was in that sense a more likely instrument for the "new" reform. It was a short jump intellectually from the New Nationalism of Theodore Roosevelt to the New Deal of his cousin; it was a much bigger jump from the business Republicanism of the 1920s. But it was perhaps a greater jump still from the Democratic party of the 1920s to the Democratic party of Franklin Roosevelt in the 1930s.

In the campaign of 1928, Herbert Hoover, more than his Democratic opponent Alfred E. Smith, showed recognition of the complex needs of a mature industrial system. Hoover called for a shorter workday, higher wages for labor, collective bargaining, and more stringent controls on the use of labor injunctions. He urged greater expenditures for public education, for public works, and for farm relief. "Far more than Smith," writes David Burner after a careful review of the 1928 contest, "the Republican candidate looked forward to the day when in the words of his acceptance speech, 'poverty will be banished from this nation.' "[54] Smith was a provincial, very much in the old Democratic tradition despite his obvious difference in style from the leaders of the rural wing who opposed him. "While endorsing a limited number of reforms, Smith in his acceptance speech complained of the proliferation of government agencies and their rising costs; insisted that 'Government should interfere as little as possible with business' and at the same time noted that a few corporations were making outrageous profits; advocated putting the tariff on 'a strictly business basis'; and called for 'fearless application of Jeffersonian principles'."[55] Little wonder that Samuel Beer, looking back on the 1928 campaign, is "tempted to speculate what would have happened if Al Smith had won in 1928 and Hoover had taken office in 1932 free of the obligation to defend the policies that had led to the collapse."[56]

The Republican party offered much to the captains of rapid industrialization, relatively little we would say to the foot soldiers, to the growing industrial labor force. But in this period it did not need to offer much, for it was not confronting the Democratic party of Franklin Roosevelt, aggressively courting labor on an expansive program of social amelioration. It faced the Democratic party of Cleveland and Bryan and Smith. When the Democrats picked up major urban working-

[54] David Burner, The Politics of Provincialism: The Democratic Party in Transition, 1918–1932 (New York: Knopf, 1968), pp. 194–195.

[55] Ibid., p. 195.

[56] Samuel Beer, "Liberalism and the National Idea," The Public Interest (Fall, 1966), p. 75.

class support in the 1910s and 1920s, they did so largely on ethnocultural rather than economic appeals.

The Parties and Race

In their early years, the Republicans supported policies relating to Negro Americans which sharply distinguished them from their partisan opponents. Born in the 1850s of the intense northern resistance to the extension of slavery, the party prosecuted, over continuing Democratic opposition, a war which maintained the national political union and ended slavery.[57] In the immediate postwar years, the parties remained far apart on race. However imperfect Reconstruction was, it was some effort, and it was *Republican* policy. The Democratic party opposed Reconstruction, favored an easy return to the Union of the southern states under white control. Thus, its national platform in 1868 urged the "immediate restoration of all the states to their rights in the Union," and "amnesty for all past political offenses, and the regulation of the elective franchise in the states by their citizens." In a revealing letter to Ex-Governor William Bigler of Pennsylvania in 1868, Samuel J. Tilden —who was to become in 1876 the Democratic presidential candidate— maintained that "the restoration of the ten absent states to the Union, with the rights and privileges of the other states, and with their local governments *in the hands of their white population,* must be the absorbing question."[58]

More than abstract, philosophic differences about the proper relationship of whites and Negroes are involved here, of course. The Republicans had little support in the white South, the Democrats a lot. White southerners were a feeble voice in one party, strong in the other. Still, the parties did differ on race in the Civil War and in the immediate post-war years, and their differences had a lasting effect on electoral loyalties. "From Reconstruction until Franklin D. Roosevelt," V. O. Key wrote in his monumental study of southern politics, "most southern Negroes, in so far as they had partisan inclinations, were habitually Republican in the tradition fixed when they had a taste of political power."[59] On the other hand, most southern whites were Democrats.

[57] See Eric L. McKitrick, "Party Politics and the Union and Confederate War Efforts," in Chambers and Burnham, pp. 117–151. McKitrick emphasizes the continuing and coherent nature of Democratic opposition to the Union war effort.

[58] John Bigelow, ed., *Tilden's Letters and Literary Memorials* (New York: Harper and Brothers, 1908), I, 217. (Emphasis added.)

[59] V. O. Key, *Southern Politics in State and Nation* (New York: Knopf, 1949), p. 286.

After the withdrawal of northern troops in 1877, Republican strength in the white South was largely restricted to some 150 counties strung along the Appalachian highlands where cotton was not farmed, slavery had not been a revered institution, and a highland yeomanry had not wanted to fight a rich man's war, and thus where secession had been opposed.

Clear-cut party differences on race were, however, short-lived. The general swing in northern opinion in the 1870s was reflected in Republican policy. The party of industrial nation-building proved no champion of black advancement. Indeed, the national Republican party began after 1877 a long period of ambivalence toward its Negro adherents— torn between encouraging Negro representation in southern Republican organizations and in southern delegations to the party's national conventions as a rather inexpensive symbol of continued fidelity to the cause of the men it had emancipated, and a desire to rid itself of the stigma in the South of a "Negro party" in order to compete more effectively for the support of southern whites.

The Parties and Ethnic Cleavage in White America

The South excepted, a good case can be made for describing the Republicans as the party of American Protestantism. The case rests, however, on the same limited and equivocating association we have come to expect between party and social group or agenda position, in view of the diffuse, undisciplined, nonprogrammatic, "many things to many people" character of the American umbrella parties. The GOP flirted with nativist movements and sentiment, but never forgot that it was a national party and on occasion repudiated nativism—as with the APA in 1896—in pursuit of its coalition interests. The Democrats in national politics were aligned with fair consistency against nativist and anti-Catholic movements. The Democracy was the principal channel through which "newer-stock" Catholics moved into positions of leadership in the American political system, while the leadership of the Republican party was almost exclusively Protestant. From the Civil War to the Great Depression, the Republicans apparently retained the allegiance of a clear majority of non-southern Protestants, while the Democrats were the partisan home of a very large majority of Catholic Americans. The South was, of course, a major exception to this general relationship; the white population of the region was overwhelmingly old-stock Protestant—and overwhelmingly Democratic. The southern wing of the Democracy, in league with rural elements elsewhere, generally controlled party affairs nationally until the 1920s, and the impact of this leadership was to greatly soften the ethnocultural confrontation of the two major parties.

The question of public aid to Catholic schools was an important one in the post–Civil War years, and the parties were sharply divided. In 1876, James G. Blaine of Maine, then Republican leader in the House of Representatives, introduced a Constitutional amendment providing that no governmental aid of any kind could be given to any school or any other institution under the control of a church. Interestingly enough, the proposed amendment specifically allowed the reading of the Bible "in any school or institution," at a time when Catholics opposed Bible reading in the schools because of the general use of the Protestant version. The Blaine amendment failed to get the necessary two-thirds majority in a straight party division, the Republicans voting in favor and the Democrats against. But the GOP did not let matters end here. Their 1880 platform called for passage of the Blaine amendment, noting that while the Constitution "wisely forbids" Congress from enacting legislation aiding any religious body, "it is idle to hope that the Nation can be protected against the influence of *secret sectarianism* while each State is exposed to its domination" (emphasis added). So a Constitutional amendment expressly forbidding state legislatures to appropriate public monies for the support of sectarian schools was called for. Catholics could not be expected to feel especially close to a party which labeled their church "secret sectarianism." "Watch out, America!" the Republicans were saying. "The Catholics are getting strong in certain states, and may succeed in getting the legislatures of those states to provide aid to their schools, unless we stop them." Of course, the Republican position cannot be dismissed simply and solely as "anti-Catholic bigotry." It was quite possible for one to wish Catholics well in every way, and still feel that public money should not go to their church schools. In any case, the Republican party *did* strongly align itself against aid to parochial schools—something which the Catholic hierarchy (and presumably many of their communicants) wanted.

In 1884 the Republicans nominated Blaine for the presidency, and it has sometimes been suggested that his defeat resulted from an anti-Catholic remark by a Protestant minister at a Blaine rally in the last of the campaign. In welcoming the Republican nominee to a meeting of clergymen, the minister described the Democracy as a party "whose antecedents have been Rum, Romanism, and Rebellion." First, this suggestion of a relationship between the remark and the subsequent defeat of Blaine is not substantiated by the election data. The elections of 1876–1892 were extraordinarily close, and in four of the five the Republican nominee trailed slightly in the popular vote.

Republican led (+) or
trailed (−) nationally by:

1876	− 51,746
1880	+ 9,457
1884	− 23,737
1888	− 95,096
1892	−365,516

When elections are this close, there is no way of untangling the factors which shifted the handful of votes who made the difference between victory and defeat. Blaine actually made the second best Republican showing, and did so against a popular Democrat, Grover Cleveland; Cleveland's narrow victory in New York State, which was decisive in the electoral vote count, could easily be explained by his being a New York native. But the larger error in the assertion that "Rum, Romanism and Rebellion" beat Blaine is the implicit suggestion that the minister said something new. In fact, innumerable Protestant clergymen and Republican politicians had been making comparable remarks throughout the party's history.

The APA, we have seen, was the strongest nativist movement of the late nineteenth century, and it operated largely within the Republican party. Democratic leaders were for the most part highly critical of the organization.[60] As with the Whigs and the Native Americans a half-century earlier, Republican politicians entered various informal alliances with the APA. Here again, however, the hetereogeneous character of the major parties and their promiscuous search for allies served to blur the relationship between party and position in the ethnocultural divide. In the election of 1896, the Republican leadership saw an opportunity to win support among the rapidly growing Catholic immigrant population of the cities. This opportunity was presented first by the depression which occurred during the second Cleveland (Democratic) administration, but more clearly by the success in 1896 of the rural wing of the Democratic party in nominating a fundamentalist Protestant, William Jennings Bryan, who then proceeded to run a kind of agrarian crusade.

[60] See Humphrey Desmond, *The A.P.A. Movement* (Washington, D.C.: The New Century Press, 1912), pp. 33–34; and Walter Nugent, *The Tolerant Populists* (Chicago: University of Chicago Press, 1963), pp. 154–155.

As long as it was McKinley vs. Bryan, with McKinley standing for the industrial society against Bryan's agrarianism and fundamentalist Protestant style and concerns, the new immigrants, like other urban dwellers, could be persuaded to give substantial support to the Republicans. In 1896, then, McKinley rejected APA support: "Thus, instead of increased influence with the GOP as a result of what it thought was its major contribution to the 1894 victory, the Order found itself on the outside. Men who had been elected with its suport repudiated it. This political rejection by the party of Protestantism with which it identified seems to have contributed to its rapid decline thereafter."[61]

In the first three decades of the twentieth century, the Democratic party was deeply divided, far more than the Republicans, by the heightening ethnocultural tensions in American society. As Burner observes, "the Democracy had attracted the extremes—the most aggressively Jeffersonian or Populist of the farmers, particularly in the South, and the most powerful of the urban immigrant machines."[62] A party thus bifurcated inevitably became the battleground when such issues as prohibition, immigration, and the Klan assumed high saliency in the national political agenda, because these two wings were diametrically opposed on each. In the course of this struggle the center of power within the Democracy shifted decisively, away from the rural, southern and heartland, Protestant and "dry" wing, toward the faction which can be characterized as urban, eastern, Catholic and "wet." This shift resulted in large measure from the great waves of immigration of the late nineteenth and early twentieth centuries, which swelled the ranks of the latter.

These contending Democratic blocs cannot easily be distinguished in terms of "liberalism vs. conservatism," or by their relative willingness to use governmental power to aid the disadvantaged. Their differences were ethnocultural, of style and status. Their conflict looms large in the career of Alfred E. Smith. Smith was born in New York City, attended Catholic schools there, entered ward politics, and rapidly worked his way up the political ladder until in 1918 he won the New York governorship. He lost in the Republican landslide of 1920, but won again in 1922, 1924, and 1926, altogether serving four terms. In 1924, he sought the Democratic presidential nomination, losing it after a Convention struggle in which he was deadlocked with William Gibbs McAdoo through 100 ballots. When it had been made so painfully obvious that neither Smith

61 Lipset and Raab, Chapter 3.
62 Burner, p. 6.

nor McAdoo could win, the Convention left them and on the 103rd ballot nominated a New York lawyer, John W. Davis, as a compromise candidate. Smith's contest with McAdoo reveals in sharp outline the conflict of the two big Democratic factions.[63] McAdoo was a dry and Smith a wet, McAdoo a Protestant, and Smith a Catholic; McAdoo had strong support from the Klan, which made Catholics a prime target, while Smith had been in open warfare with the hooded knights.[64] Smith was stopped in 1924, but the tide was moving with the forces backing him; four years later he easily won his party's nomination. In the Northeast, the Democrats were the party of the newer ethnocultural groups led by an old ethnocultural minority, Irish Catholics, and this wing had achieved clear ascendancy in the Democratic presidential party.

Despite the deep schism in the Democracy between the rural and Protestant and the urban and Catholic wings, the party was easily distinguished from the Republicans on ethnocultural issues in the 1920s. In the South the Klan worked within the Democratic party, of course—there really wasn't any Republican party—but elsewhere, Burner concludes, "the Klan allied itself primarily with the Republicans and made overtures to the Democracy in most cases only when it desired to widen its already considerable influence. . . . Outside the South the Klan usually assumed a Republican coloration; and at times it encountered organized Democratic opposition."[65] The relatively conservative 1924 Democratic presidential candidate, James W. Davis, denounced the Klan, and Smith, the 1928 nominee, had long been at war with it. There were surely a lot of Democratic prohibitionists, but all three presidential nominees in the 1920s were "wets," and were denounced by the "dry" forces; Smith, of course, was an especially good target.

On immigration restriction, the party differences were somewhat less sharp. In the 1921 and 1924 debates, for example, the Naional Association of Manufacturers—closely aligned with the Republicans—insisted that immigration remain open to all. Industry had long been an advocate of open immigration, because of quite straightforward economic interests: it felt it needed the continued supply of foreign labor. (The American Federation of Labor, on the other hand, urged that immigration be curtailed, again because of straightforward economic interests.) Both parties delivered large majorities of their congressional delegations in

[63] For the best treatment of Democratic factionalism in the 1920s, see Burner, especially Chapters 3, 4, and 7.

[64] As governor of New York, Smith had signed bills practically outlawing the Klan in that state.

[65] Burner, pp. 84–85.

TABLE 4.3

U.S. House of Representatives Roll Call Votes on the 1921 and 1924
Immigration Acts

LEGISLATION		DEMOCRAT		REPUBLICAN	
		Number	*Percent*	*Number*	*Percent*
IMMIGRATION ACT OF 1921 Passed Conference Report (May 13, 1921)	Yea	90	70	186	62
	Nay	14	11	18	6
	Not Voting	25	19	95	32
		129	100	299	100
IMMIGRATION ACT OF 1924 Passed (April 12, 1924)	Yea	157	77	164	73
	Nay	37	18	33	15
	Not Voting	10	5	27	12
		204	100	224	100
Passed Conference Report (May 15, 1924)	Yea	143	70	165	73
	Nay	33	16	27	12
	Not Voting	28	14	34	15
		204	100	226	100

support of the restrictive immigration acts of 1921 and 1924, as Table 4.3 shows. Still, there were clear differences between the parties on this issue. The Republican platforms of 1920, 1924 and 1928 carried strong statements on the need for curtailment of immigration. In 1920, for example, the party declared that "the immigration policy of the U.S. should be such as to insure that the number of foreigners in the country at any one time shall not exceed that which can be assimilated with reasonable rapidity, and to favor immigrants whose standards are similar to ours. . . . No alien should become a citizen until he has become genuinely American." The Democrats, on the other hand, confined themselves in 1920 and 1924 to statements opposing Asian immigration, and in 1928 to a brief and bland endorsement of the existing legislation.

The net result of party differences on the ethnocultural issues we have described was that decisive majorities of Catholic voters continued to back the Democrats. Working with newly discovered interviews which the

parties had conducted systematically with all voters in certain midwestern towns and counties in the 1870s, Richard Jensen has discovered
extraordinarily high Catholic support for the Democracy:

TABLE 4.4

Party Affiliation of Voters in an Illinois Township and an Indiana
County by Ethnic-Religious Identification of the Voters, 1870s*

GENESEO CITY AND TOWNSHIP, ILLINOIS
(1877)

Ethnic Group	Denomination	Percentage Republican	Percentage Democrat	Number
Old Stock	Congregationalist	96.5	3.5	74
	Unitarian	96.0	4.0	25
	Methodist	91.4	8.6	70
	Baptist	90.9	9.1	22
	Presbyterian	72.5	27.5	29
	No denomination	69.0	31.0	400
German	Lutheran	66.7	33.3	60
Swedish	Lutheran, Methodist, other	96.3	3.7	72
German	Catholic	25.0	75.0	16
Irish	Catholic	0.0	100.0	52
Other	Catholic	7.7	92.3	13

HENDRICKS COUNTY, INDIANA
(1874)

Denomination	Percentage Republican	Percentage Democrat	Percentage Other or None	Number
Christian (Disciples)	73.6	23.7	2.7	291
Methodist	72.8	21.9	5.2	232
Presbyterian	64.3	31.4	4.3	70
Missionary Baptist	57.4	38.6	4.0	101
Roman Catholic	4.2	83.3	12.5	24

* Source: Richard Jensen, "The Historical Roots of Party Identification" (paper
presented to the Annual Meeting of the American Political Science Association,
New York, September, 1969), pp. 2, 13.

The data are limited, but other investigations suggest that the picture
they convey is generally valid.

David Burner has brought together data on the voting of ethnic-religious groups between 1916 and 1932 in several large cities. These are not directly comparable to Jensen's, of course, for an individual may vote for a party other than his own in a given election in response to short-term forces. Burner shows, for example, that immigrant groups who resented Wilson's World War I policies deserted the Democrats in

TABLE 4.5

Party Support of Voters in New York, Chicago and Boston by Ethnocultural Identification of the Voters, Presidential Elections, 1916–1932*

	Percentage Democrat	Percentage Pepublican	Other
New York			
Irish			
1916	64	36	–
1920	47	50	3
1924	63	25	12
1928	82	18	–
1932	81	19	–
Italian			
1916	63	37	–
1920	47	50	3
1924	48	44	8
1928	77	23	–
1932	79	21	–
Chicago			
Polish			
1916	73	27	–
1920	55	45	5
1924	51	37	12
1928	83	17	–
1932	85	15	–
Boston			
Italian			
1916	67	33	–
1920	43	50	7
1924	45	35	20
1928	95	5	–
1932	78	22	–

* Source: Burner, pp. 235–236, 241, 243. These are data not on the actual vote of individuals, but on the vote in districts in which the overwhelming majority of the residents were of the specified ethnic group (typically 85 to 90 percent).

large numbers in 1920. Many Irish-Americans did not want to go to war on behalf of England—a hated enemy—and expressed this in the 1920 presidential voting. The Burner investigation nonetheless shows a decided Democratic preference among Catholic Americans.

These data provide some basis for suggesting that in the first twenty-five years of this century the Republicans made gains among Catholic Americans because of their status as the party of industrialism and the strength of the Democrats' rural Protestant wing. The combination of the Depression and the capture of the Democracy by urbanites ended this, however.

The Parties in Electoral Competition

Patterns in Voter Turnout

We have seen that with the culmination of a set of developments, including the democratization of the presidency, the loosening of suffrage requirements, and the introduction of popular electioneering techniques in the 1830s, voting turnout surged enormously. The election of 1840 was the first with a substantially complete mobilization of the eligible electorate; 80 percent of the adult white males cast ballots. For the rest of the nineteenth century, high voter turnout was sustained, far higher than was to be realized at any time in the twentieth century. Between 1840 and 1900, presidential election turnout nationally never dropped below 70 percent, and outside the South it was mostly between 80 and 90 percent. Before 1876, the level of voting in the South was only modestly lower than in the North, but the gap widened significantly in the next two decades and massively after 1896. That the gap got so much larger is all the more extraordinary in view of the substantial drop in voter turnout in the North after 1896, which reached the post-1840 low in the 1920s. The average presidential turnout in the eleven southern states was only slightly more than 25 percent for the elections between 1904 and 1948 (in contrast to about 65 percent between 1868 and 1896), about 68 percent outside the South (or nearly 20 percent lower than the 1868–1896 average).[66]

[66] These data on voter turnout are from the most complete study to date: Walter Dean Burnham, "The Changing Shape of the American Political Universe," American Political Science Review, LIX (March, 1965), pp. 7–28; and Burnham, "Sources of Historical Election Data," mimeographed, Institute for Community Development and Services, Michigan State University, November, 1963. The problems in estimating the size of the eligible electorate are substantial.

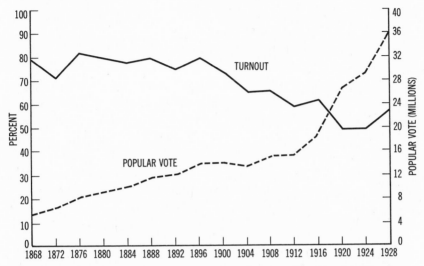

Figure 4.3. Popular Vote and Percentage Turnout, Presidential Elections, 1868–1928*

* Source: Figures on popular vote are from *Historical Statistics of the United States,* pp. 686–688. Figures on percentage turnout are from Walter Dean Burnham, "Sources of Historical Election Data."

The pattern which these data reveal—extremely high voter participation in the nineteenth century followed by a steep decline beginning after 1896 and lasting through the 1920s—appears in voting for lower offices as well. For example, Burnham has calculated that the average turnout in off-year congressional elections was 63 percent from 1876 to 1896 but only 48 percent between 1900 and 1916 and 35 percent from 1922 to 1926.[67]

Another way to describe these changes in voter participation is to ask what proportion of the potential electorate at a given time were "core" or regular voters—voting in virtually all elections; what segment voted occasionally but not regularly and thus were of the peripheral electorate, and what percentage were habitual non-voters. Burnham concludes that in the late nineteenth century, approximately 65 percent of the potential electorate were core, 10 percent peripheral, and about 25 percent nonvoters. In contrast, in the 1920s, little more than one-third of the electorate were core voters, about 16 or 17 percent peri-

One example is the problem imposed by the piecemeal extension of women's suffrage. The general enfranchisement of women was achieved with the ratification of the Nineteenth Amendment in 1920, but various states had granted them the vote prior to that.

[67] Burnham, "The Changing Shape of the American Political Universe," p. 10.

pheral voters, while fully one-half were outside the active voting universe.[68]

What produced this decline in voter participation? A number of factors converged, and while they can be identified, their relative importance is hard to assess. One major factor was the establishment of a heavily sectional party alignment after 1896. This "system of 1896" weakened party competition in wide areas of the country, and appeared as the virtual destruction of inter-party competition in the South. In the absence of effective competition between the parties, the incentive to vote was diminished. If it is certain that the candidate of Party A will win, why expend the effort to vote? High turnout is in part a function of high, sustained partisan competition.

Several other developments contributing to the decline in voter participation involve the adding of new groups to the electorate who were either unable or unwilling to exercise the franchise at the level of the old electorate. Negroes were given the vote and then effectively disenfranchised. The United States took in millions of immigrants after 1880, many with a native language other than English; a period of time was often required to "come of age politically," to become accustomed to the processes of American electioneering, to establish party loyalties, to perceive the desirability of regular participation. The 1910–1930 period was, of course, the time in which the diminishing effects of immigration on voter participation would be greatest: the percentage of foreign-born had reached its high point, and not enough time had passed to permit a full assimiliation into the regular processes of American political life. Also in the early twentieth century, women entered the electorate, and not all were quick to seize their new privilege; initially they voted at a decidedly lower rate than men.

While these variables undoubtedly account for much of the drop in voter participation, the development nonetheless suggests the need for a bit of caution in dealing with the matter of the correlates of voting and nonvoting. Contemporary survey research data show a positive relationship between education and voter turnout: the higher the level of formal education, the higher the rate of voting. But a much higher proportion of Americans voted between 1840 to 1900 than between 1920 and 1960—although the level of formal education was much higher in the latter period. The lower educational level in the United States during the latter half of the nineteenth century did not preclude mass

[68] *Ibid.*, pp. 22–23.

political participation more intense and consistent than that of recent decades. The same discrepancy between what current research would lead us to expect and nineteenth century electoral experience appears in the relationship of rurality to voter participation. Studies in the 1950s and 1960s have shown consistently that turnout is lower for people with rural residence than for urban dwellers, presumably in part because of greater physical difficulties in voting. Nineteenth-century voters, of course, typically confronted even greater physical problems, because transportation was far slower. But the rural America of 1840–1900 produced higher voter participation than the metropolitanized America of the 1960s. As Burnham concludes, American society in the nineteenth century "was quite adequate both in partisan organization and dissemination of political information, to the task of mobilizing voters on a scale which compares favorably with recent European levels of participation," (and, we might emphasize, which exceeds contemporary American levels of participation).[69]

Patterns in Competition

After the fragmentation of party during the 1850s and the Civil War years, the two-party system quickly reformed, with the new Republican coalition the principal competitor to the Democracy. In one tenuous sense the Republicans can be described as the majority party of the entire six decades between the war and the Great Depression. Only two Democrats won the presidency in this period—Grover Cleveland in 1884 and 1892, and Woodrow Wilson in 1912 and 1916. In fact, however, the two-party system that was reestablished after the Civil War was one of extraordinarily even competition. Indeed, the five presidential elections between 1876 and 1892 are unmatched in American history in sustained closeness. The major parties were not separated by more than three percentage points in popular vote in any of these elections, and by less than one point in 1880, 1884, and 1888. Then, with Mc-Kinley's defeat of Bryan in 1896, the Republican national presidential majorities sharply expanded. The party had averaged 47 percent of the national vote in the five elections between 1876 and 1892; it won 54 percent in the next eight elections (excluding 1912 when the party split) against the Democrats' 40 percent. If a presidential "landslide election" is defined as one in which the winning candidate has a margin of 10 percent or more over his principal opponent, there was nothing approaching a landslide after 1872 until 1904. The big pluralities so

[69] *Ibid.,* p. 22.

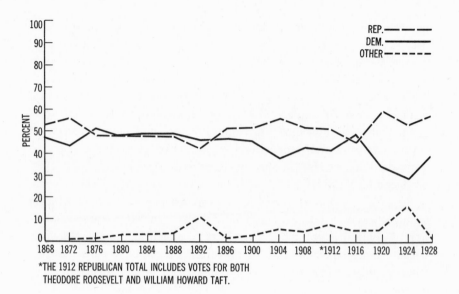

*THE 1912 REPUBLICAN TOTAL INCLUDES VOTES FOR BOTH
THEODORE ROOSEVELT AND WILLIAM HOWARD TAFT.

Figure 4.4. Popular Vote for President, by Party, 1868–1928

common in the presidential elections of the twentieth century were non-existent in the latter half of the nineteenth.

The election of 1896 is often described by social scientists as one of critical importance, a "converting" election in which the majority party

MAJORITY PARTY

		Victory	Defeat
ELECTORAL CLEAVAGE	Continuity	"Maintaining"	"Deviating"
	Change	"Converting"	"Realigning"

Figure 4.5. A Typology of Presidential Elections*

* Source: This typology was suggested by Gerald Pomper, "Classification of Presidential Elections," *Journal of Politics,* Vol. 29 (August, 1967), pp. 535–566. Pomper has modified or refined categories introduced by Angus Campbell and his colleagues in *The American Voter* (New York: John Wiley, 1960), pp. 531–538; and in *Elections and the Political Order* (New York: John Wiley, 1966), pp. 63–77.

(the Republicans) strengthened its position through the conversion of strategic social groupings to its banner. Figure 4.5 shows the classification scheme or typology in which the definition of 1896 as a converting election is located.

Since Republican majorities after 1896 were significantly larger than before, it is hard to argue that this election or more generally this period in some sense involved "conversion." But in what way? Precisely what happened to the lines of partisan competition in the 1890s? Campbell writes that "the Election of 1896 divided the country again as the East and Midwest overcame the Populist challenge of the South and West."[70] V. O. Key concludes that the Democratic defeat in 1896 "was so demoralizing and so thorough that the party made little headway in regrouping its forces until 1916."[71] In his study of the "System of 1896," E. E. Schattschneider argues that a new party cleavage resulted from an extraordinary reaction of people of substance all over the country to the radical agrarianism embodied in the Populist movement: Northern conservatives were so badly frightened by this agrarian challenge represented in the 1896 election by the candidacy of William Jennings Bryan "that they adopted drastic measures to alarm the country . . . [and] as a result the Democratic party in large areas of the Northeast and Middle West was wiped out or decimated, while the Republican party consolidated its supremacy in all of the most populous areas of the country."[72] In the South, the reaction by conservatives resulted in their being "willing to revive the tensions and animosities of the Civil War and the Reconstruction in order to set up a one-party sectional southern political monopoly in which nearly all Negroes and many poor whites were disenfranchised." In effect, then, according to Schattschneider, men of means in the northeastern and north-central states, finding themselves severely threatened by the Bryan Democrats, rallied to the Republican party and succeeded in convincing a majority of their fellow citizens that a Democracy tinged with Bryanism was "dangerous." At the same time, southern conservatives persuaded their fellow citizens of the need to close ranks behind the Democratic party on behalf of white supremacy in the South on an issue which prevented a working alliance of agrarian radicals within the region with those outside.

While part of this commentary on the meaning and results of 1896

[70] Campbell *et al., Elections and the Political Order,* p. 74.

[71] V. O. Key, "A Theory of Critical Elections," *Journal of Politics,* 17 (February, 1955), pp. 3–18.

[72] E. E. Schattschneider, *The Semisovereign People* (New York: Holt, Rinehart and Winston, 1960), p. 79.

can be accepted, some new construction and emphasis is needed. First, Bryan ran a very strong race in 1896, losing to McKinley by only slightly more than 4 percent in the popular vote. Bryan did in fact succeed in putting together a coalition South and West: he won 64 percent of the vote in the South, 65 percent in the West, and slightly over 50 percent in the border states. Only in the Northeast, where he picked up just 36 percent of the vote, was he severely rebuffed. And one need not conjure an image of Bryan severely frightening conservatives to explain this setback. He ran as a sectional candidate, strongly appealing to the popular hinterland distrust of the Northeast, its cities, its "money power." His style of politics could hardly have aroused strong enthusiasm among any major social group in the urban and industrial East.

The key to an explanation of the change in electoral alignments following 1896 seems to lie in the larger matter of society and political agenda. After the Civil War the United States entered a period of great industrial growth, but industrialism did not mature overnight. The Democrats were able to quickly pick up the pieces after Civil War fragmentation and run head to head with the Republicans because American politics and, in turn, American society, were in many important ways similar to before the war. In 1875 the United States was not the rural republic of Jefferson or Jackson, but neither was it the industrial state of 1910 or 1920. The social groups and interests which sustained the Democracy were still strong. What happened in the 1890s was that the transition from rural and agriculture to urban and industrial reached a critical tipping point; after the Election of 1896 there was no question as to the shape of the new America or the groups who would direct it. The growing Republican ascendancy after the 1890s appears to reflect more than any other single fact the emergence of the industrial state and its accompanying agenda. The election of 1896 was important in the same way as the election of 1932 was to be. Since the Democratic party challenged the new agenda just as it was being drawn up, the appeal of the Republicans to those social groups oriented to the new agenda was strengthened. The 1896 presidential election, then, was by itself important, but the fundamental development was the maturation of industrialism and the success of the Republicans in establishing themselves as the party of industrialism. Democratic domination in the South was furthered by the massive rurality of that region in this era of industrial nation building.

The pattern of presidential voting is essentially reproduced in voting

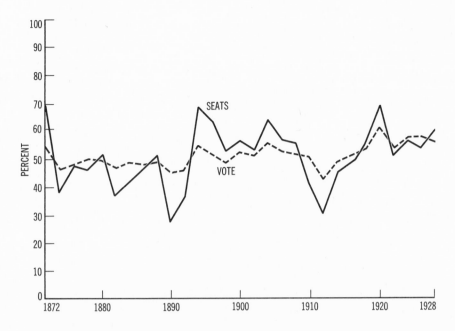

Figure 4.6. Republican Percentage, Two-Party Vote and Seats, U.S. House of Representatives, 1872–1928*

* Source: *Historical Statistics of the United States,* pp. 691–692; Donald E. Stokes and Gudmund R. Iversen, "On the Existence of Forces Restoring Party Competition," in Campbell *et al., Elections and the Political Order,* p. 183.

for other offices. Figure 4.6 shows the same extreme closeness of congressional contests from 1870 through the mid-1890s. The Republican and Democratic shares of the major party vote for candidates for the House of Representatives (the Senate was not selected by popular vote) hugged the 50 percent line, with the Republicans doing slightly less well than in the presidential balloting. The Democrats gained a modest majority of the congressional ballots over these years, and a rather consistent majority in House seats. Then, in the 1894 elections the GOP won a big congressional majority and continued to do so in the elections through the 1920s, dipping to less than 50 percent of the popular vote only three times—in 1898, 1912, and 1914.

Party competition in the various regions of the country declined in the 1890s and thereafter, and regional voting patterns became more sharply differentiated. Figure 4.7 shows a consistent but modest Republican majority in presidential voting in the Northeast from the Civil War through 1892. Then, the margin widened decisively. Presidential elec-

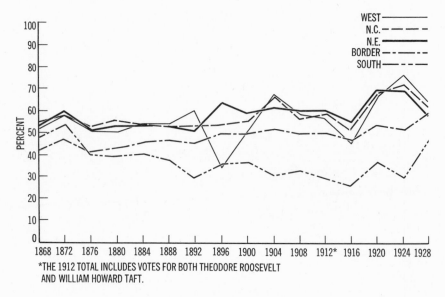

Figure 4.7. Republican Percentage of the Two-Party Presidential Popular Vote, by Region, 1868–1928

tions really were not competitive in this section from 1896 through 1928, except in 1912, when the Republicans split. The GOP was never competitive in the South after Reconstruction. The Democratic margin did increase as the period progressed, but it was already massive in 1876—twenty percentage points. Figure 4.7 shows the extent to which the Northeast and the South moved apart in their electoral performance after 1890: thus, in 1884, the Republican votes in the Northeast and in the South were only twelve percentage points apart; in 1904, the Republicans got 62 percent of the popular vote in the Northeast and just 30 percent in the South, a 32-percent differential. The border states were consistently among the most competitive in presidential voting after 1896.

Figures 4.8 and 4.9 give a more detailed picture of the general decline in party competition in states throughout the country after the mid-1890s, which outside the South was mostly at the expense of the Democrats. Each state has been plotted by two indices of competitiveness, in Figure 4.8 for presidential elections between 1868 and 1892, in Figure 4.9 for those from 1896 to 1928. These indices are the percentage of the presidential elections in the time span in which the Republicans won the state's electoral votes, and the Republican percentage of the

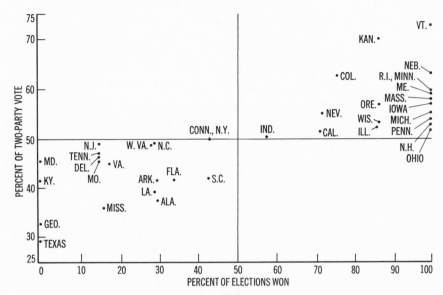

Figure 4.8. The Competitiveness of States, Republican Percentage of the Two-Party Presidential Vote, 1868–1892

popular vote from the state for the cluster of elections. States located near the center in the figures were closely competitive. Those in the upper corner of the top-right cell were Republican-dominated, in the lower corner of the bottom-left cell solidly Democratic. In the first time span, the Democrats held majority status—as defined by these two indices—in about half of the states: eighteen were Democratic-majority states, nineteen Republican-majority, while one—Connecticut—gave the Republicans a slight majority of the total popular vote but went Democratic in a majority of the elections.[73] The Democrats were strong in the South and in the border states, but managed as well to win modest majorities in two important northeastern states, New York and New Jersey. In the second time span, however, the Democracy gained ascendancy only in the eleven states that formed the Confederacy.

The drop in competitiveness is striking. In 1868–1892, twenty-eight of the thirty-eight states fell within the 55-percent lines; that is, the majority party did not average more than 55 percent of the popular vote. But in the second span, only twenty-one of forty-eight states fell within the 55-percent lines. In twenty-two, the majority party averaged

[73] Several states were in the Union for only one of the presidential elections in this time span, and were not included in the graph. They are Idaho, Montana, North Dakota, South Dakota, Washington, and Wyoming.

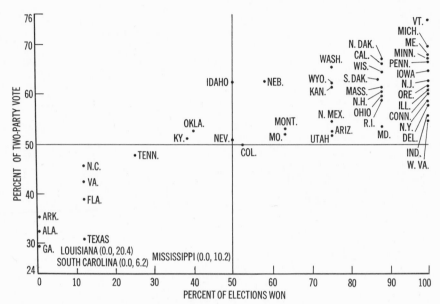

Figure 4.9. The Competitiveness of States, Republican Percentage of the Two-Party Presidential Vote, 1896–1928

better than 60 percent of the presidential ballots cast, a highly noncompetitive status that only ten states occupied for 1868–1892.

We have seen that the 1896–1928 time span was a time of low interparty competition, both nationally and in state party systems. It was also a time when the states were going in opposing electoral directions. Schattschneider refers to the "universality of political trends" as a situation in which a party making a gain nationally would gain more or less uniformly in states around the country. Trends were not universal between 1896 and 1928: the national performance of a party typically was made up of extremely disparate state preformances. To put this more simply, voting was not *nationalized* but highly *sectionalized*. One statistical tool which permits us to describe efficiently the extent of nationalization in voting is the *standard deviation*. This can describe the composite pattern of state deviations from the national performance of a party. If, for example, the Democrats secured 47 percent of the vote nationally and exactly 47 percent in each state, the standard deviation would be zero. The more substantially and frequently the state percentages depart from the party's percentage nationally, the higher the standard deviation.[74] Figure 4.10 shows that the standard deviations

[74] The standard deviation is easily calculated. Where σ is the standard deviation and X the individual deviation from the mean: $\sigma = \sqrt{\dfrac{\Sigma X^2}{N}}$

Figure 4.10. Standard Deviations of Differences of Democratic Vote for President by State, from the Party's National Percentage

for state votes were consistently higher in the four decades after 1890 than in any period in American electoral history.

The election of 1832 was one in which the parties' national totals were achieved through highly disparate state performances. Following this election, sectional differences declined, then rose sharply again in the 1850s. After the Civil War, there was a brief period in which the parties engaged in fairly uniform competition across the country. Then, the deviation of individual state votes from the parties' national totals rose precipitously, reaching successive peaks in 1896, 1904, and in 1924 Figure 4.10 paints a dramatic picture of the high-water marks of sectionalism in American politics. A pronounced nationalization began at the end of this sociopolitical period.

The Parties in the Industrializing Nation

The years from the end of the Civil War to the 1920s could be described as two district periods, with the 1890s a transitional decade.[75]

[75] Looking at electoral behavior, Burnham has demonstrated this convincingly (W. Dean Burnham, *Critical Elections and the Mainsprings of American Politics* [New York: W. W. Norton, 1970]).

We have chosen to refer to them as a single period because they share a preoccupation with industrial nation-building: the transformation of a rural and agricultural society into one that was urban and industrial.

This transformation was extraordinarily rapid by any historical standard but still was accomplished in stages, and these stages are reflected in the pattern of party conflict and competition. The Republicans did not, for example, achieve decisive electoral superiority immediately after the Civil War. That ascendancy came at the turn of the century, after the coalition of interests built up around the emergent industrial order had achieved decisive influence in the society. The Republicans established themselves as the party of business custodianship and industrial nation-building, but this position could not confer clear majority status until the social and economic changes occurring with industrialization had made business custodianship a *fait accompli*.

From 1870 to roughly 1900, the deepest policy conflicts in the United States involved agrarianism vs. industrialism. Whose society was this going to be? It was the Democracy, the only partisan survivor from the Rural Republic, which gave the most consistent major party representation to the claims of agricultural America, to the resentments of the hinterland West and South at the encroachments of eastern "moneyed" interests.

By the turn of the century, however, it was apparent to everyone whose society this was to be. With the decisive triumph of industrialism, the lines of partisan conflict shifted. The urban middle class, a creature of industrial development, came to sustain a critique of industrialism that started from a full acceptance of industrialism. Middle class reformism was felt in both parties, but at least until the administrations of Woodrow Wilson was clearly stronger in the GOP. The urban working class grew rapidly and by the 1920s was heavily Democratic, although for ethnocultural rather than economic reasons. The rural wing of the Democracy was still strong, but now showed more anxiety over the cultural assaults of its urban brethren than with the economic control of its old business foe. The Democratic party became the battleground for these two groups of "outsiders" in an age of business supremacy.

Party conflict and competition thus evolved with the maturation of the enterprise of industrial nation-building. The Republicans were throughout, however, the vehicle through which those interests which directed this enterprise worked; and once established, their majority status was secure so long as the conceptions and commitments which guided the building of an industrial society were widely shared. Only when the agenda was fundamentally changed were the Republicans displaced.

What produced this change? Basically success. The transition from a relatively simple ruralism to a complex industrialism was accomplished. The interests of people and the needs of society in an age of mature industrialism were very different than they had been when the task was industrialization. The Great Depression dramatically announced the arrival of a new sociopolitical period.

5

The Parties in the Industrial State

The Great Depression which began in 1929 did not so much create as abruptly signal the emergence of a new social setting. It shifted national attention from one set of concerns to another with unaccustomed speed. It is often noted that Franklin Roosevelt was re-elected to the presidency in 1936 on programs very different from those on which he ran in 1932, which is true, for the Depression rocked him, his party, and a large portion of the population into new ways of thinking about many relationships in American public life.

The Society and Its Political Agenda

Scale, Interdependence, and the Managerial State

Long before the Depression, there had been some recognition that an emergent society of scale and interdependence would require much more management, regulation, and policing than Americans had been accustomed to. Croly had written eloquently of an expanded managerial role for the state. Theodore Roosevelt and the Progressives in 1912 had articulated an ambitious program of public responsibility. And a number of concrete legislative steps had been taken. For example, the Sherman Antitrust Act was passed in 1890 and the Clayton Antitrust Act in 1914. Various regulatory commissions were established, including the Interstate Commerce Commission (1887), substantially strengthened in the administration of William Howard Taft; the Federal Reserve System in banking (1913); the Federal Trade Commission (1914); and the Federal Power Commission (1920). There had been extensive experimentation by state governments and some by the national government in protective labor legislation: laws regulating hours of labor, methods and time of wage payment, employer liability, and factory conditions.

Still, in 1929 the response in American political ideology and public institutions lagged far behind the realities of the industrial state. It was in this context that the Depression began, an event so massive as to alter significantly American social relations and even more to underline the degree to which these relations had already been changed. The Depression eroded confidence in some of the institutions and procedures and in the ascendant elite of the industrializing society. Its severity and the extraordinary size of the segment of the population which suffered from it overrode powerful inertial tendencies, creating a massive receptivity to political and economic innovation. The Depression demonstrated that a big, complexly integrated economy could not be allowed to operate without central direction, that in place of the "panics" of less integrated economies there was the potential in the industrial state for system-shaking collapses.

It fell to the Roosevelt Administration, then, to begin constructing the managerial state. Not surprisingly, this was not a precisely conceived enterprise. The Administration's deliberations and initiatives in 1933, 1934, and 1935 show contradictory demands, a sense of groping, a large measure of confusion. But out of these efforts the managerial state gradually took form, with several key components:

(1) The "policeman" functions of government were greatly expanded. New regulatory bodies such as the Security and Exchange Commission (SEC) were established to watch over various sectors, in the case of the SEC to protect investors and the overall state of the stock market through orderly procedures in securities exchange.

(2) Government became committed to a systematic intervention on behalf of disadvantaged groups, groups whose resources would not permit them to compete without such intervention. One of the most notable developments here was the passage of the National Labor Relations (Wagner) Act in 1935, making it unlawful for employers to refuse to bargain collectively, to interfere with labor's right to organize, to discriminate against union members, or to control unions.

(3) The managerial state appeared, too, in decisions to give regular governmental direction to activities previously handled informally through private channels. In 1935, the Social Security Act was passed. A year earlier, Roosevelt had told Congress that the American people demanded "some safeguard against misfortunes which cannot be wholly

eliminated in this man-made world of ours." Two of the most important programs included in this omnibus legislation were unemployment compensation and retirement insurance financed by equal contributions by the employer and the employee.

(4) Finally, government assumed the responsibility for smoothing out business cycles, controlling inflation, preventing excessive unemployment, promoting adequate growth—in short, for maintaining and extending prosperity. There were conflicting theories as to how this should be accomplished, but one ultimately was decisive. Its intellectual father was an Englishman who has given his name to the prevailing directions of modern economics, John Maynard Keynes. Keynes capped an extraordinarily varied career, during which he had provoked British opinion with his unorthodox views on economics, with the publication of *The General Theory of Employment, Interest and Money* (1936). Basic to Keynesianism is the rejection of the assumption of classical economics that in bad times government should encourage lower wages and prices, while promoting rigorously balanced budgets; instead, Keynes argued, government should deliberately unbalance the budget by heavy spending and lower taxes. The Keynesian movement swept economics, and American government assumed, imperfectly, the role Keynes prescribed. The real impact of Keynes, as of Marx and Freud, was not in specific analysis or prescription but in basic reconceptualization, a rethinking of the responsibilities of government in economic life.

We get an additional perspective on the expansion of the role of the state from data on public expenditures. In the early years of the country, per capita spending by the national government had averaged between $1 and $2: $2 in 1800, $2 in 1860. While precise state and local data in this period are not available, it seems that in 1860 state and local governments were expending about $5.50 per person, nearly three times the amount flowing from Washington. After the Civil War, spending leveled out modestly higher: between 1866 and 1916 national government expenditures were between $4.50 and $8 per capita—$7.75 in 1870 and actually something less, $7.56, in 1915; and state and local spending increased slowly from about $7 per capita to $25 at the outbreak of World War I. Then, in the 1920s, a pattern of massive and continuing increases in government spending appeared. Federal per capita expenditures in 1925 were nearly 3.5 times that in 1915. They further quadrupled between 1925 and 1941. And after the big World War II jump, they continued to climb sharply: $226 in 1948, $398 in 1956, $660 in 1966, $850 in 1968. Combined state and local spending

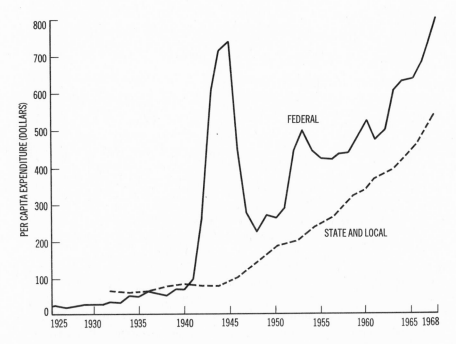

Figure 5.1. Per Capita Federal and State and Local Government Expenditures, 1925–1968*

*Source: U.S. Bureau of the Census, *Historical Statistics of the United States, Colonial Times to 1957* (Washington, D.C.: U.S. Government Printing Office, 1960), pp. 711, 726; U.S. Bureau of the Census, *Historical Statistics of the United States, Colonial Times to 1957; Continuation to 1962 and Revisions* (Washington, D.C.: U.S. Government Printing Office, 1965), pp. 96, 100; U.S. Bureau of the Census, *Statistical Abstract of the United States, 1968* (Washington, D.C.: U.S. Government Printing Office, 1968), pp. 407, 381; and *Statistical Abstract of the United States, 1969,* p. 407.

dropped below the federal level during World War II and stayed below it—for the first time in history—when peace returned.

The Humanization of Industrialism

Countries which have traversed that vast distance from agricultural to industrial have followed different routes: the American course, for example, in which direction was left to the private sector, and the Soviet Union's, where the state guided things. But the enormous demands falling with disproportionate severity on the working class, the foot soldiers of the industrial revolution, stand as a stark and simple constant. In every country that has rapidly industrialized, large numbers of people have been relocated over a generation or two from the conditions of

TABLE 5.1

Distribution of Family Personal Income by Each Fifth and Top
5 Percent of Families, for Selected Years 1929–1947*

	1929	1935–36	1941	1944	1946	1947
Total	100.0	100.0	100.0	100.0	100.0	100.0
Lowest Fifth	12.5	4.1	4.1	4.9	5.0	5.0
Second Fifth		9.2	9.5	10.9	11.1	11.0
Third Fifth	13.8	14.1	15.3	16.2	16.0	16.0
Fourth Fifth	19.3	20.9	22.3	22.2	21.8	22.0
Highest Fifth	54.4	51.7	48.8	45.8	46.8	46.0
Top 5 Percent	30.0	26.5	24.0	20.7	21.3	20.9

* Source: Herman Miller, *Income Distribution in the United States* (Washington, D.C.: U.S. Government Printing Office, 1966), p. 21.

rural and agricultural life to those of the city and factory. Big cities have grown up, and a mixture of inadequate planning and inadequate resources has produced teeming slums. In order for there to be enough "cream"—profits skimmed off for capital plant expansion—the bulk of the working class has been required to work long hours at wages approaching subsistence. Historical data are extremely fragmentary, but it seems clear that in colonial times the small amount that was produced was divided fairly evenly. As the nineteenth and early twentieth centuries progressed, however, income became more unevenly distributed.[1] By 1910 when dependable estimates of income distribution first become available, the 5 percent of the families with the highest income were receiving approximately 30 percent of the total personal family income, the highest fifth of the families in excess of 50 percent, while the 40 percent of the families with the lowest incomes received little more than 10 percent.[2] With the New Deal, this process of growing inequalities was halted, and for a time reversed. Between 1929 and 1947, the share of the lowest two-fifths rose from 12.5 percent to 16 percent, while that of the top 5 percent dropped from 30 percent to 21 percent.[3] While hardly radical, this redistribution was symbolically important. Through the years of industrial nation-building, growing inequities had been countenanced. Now there was greater receptivity to demands for a wide extension of economic values.

[1] See Herman E. Krooss, *American Economic Development: The Progress of a Business Civilization,* (Englewood Cliffs, N.J.: Prentice-Hall, 1966), p. 20.
[2] Krooss, p. 21; and Herman Miller, *Income Distribution in the United States* (Washington, D.C.: U.S. Government Printing Office, 1966), p. 19.
[3] Miller, p. 21.

The big factor in the humanization of industrialism was not formal government action, but the capacity of a mature industrial system—once managed so as to avoid depressions—to produce so much more in goods and services. Thus per capita personal income (expressed in constant 1958 dollars), after a Depression low of $898 in 1932, jumped to $1,423 in 1941, $1,805 in 1950, $2,153 in 1960, and $2,882 in 1968. This capacity to produce a big and ever-enlarging pie "socialized" business, smoothed the rough edges of labor-management relations, and in general permitted a shift in the primary commitment of the system—from building industrialism rapidly with minimal regard for the short-run human costs to using industrialism for some larger measure of popular enrichment.

In the 1930s, we know, poverty was exceedingly widespread. The Depression occurred in a society in which in good times the large majority of the population was living only modestly above subsistence. In 1929, 70 percent of the families earned less than $4,000 (in dollars of 1962 purchasing power, less than $2,250 in 1929 dollars) and nearly a third less than $2,000 (under $1,125 in 1929 dollars). There was little margin, then, and the economic collapse which began in 1929 produced acute distress that was not confined to some small segment of the population, but rather extended to a majority. Per capita personal income dropped 25 percent between 1928 and 1933 (in constant dollars). Such widespread deprivation in a society which had felt the expanding productive capacities of mature industrialism produced a political climate in which economic have-nots were successfully mobilized. It was a time when the economically deprived were organized effectively to use the power of numbers to advance their interests. Thus Harrington writes that "perhaps the most dramatic case of the power of the majority poor took place in the 1930s. The Congress of Industrial Organizations literally organized millions in a matter of years."[4] And the Roosevelt administration spoke to this majoritarian economic deprivation and was handsomely rewarded. There was a majority coalition waiting to be mobilized around a shared economic privation.

The 1930s were the high point in the potency of appeal to economic have-nots, and really the last stand of *majority* deprivation. The great economic gains that began with World War II did not eliminate poverty, but they transformed it from a condition of the many to one of a distinct minority. The social meaning and psychological impact of economic deprivation is very different when it is minoritarian than when it

[4] Michael Harrington, *The Other America* (Baltimore: Penguin, 1963) p. 15.

is majoritarian. Arthur Ross has written of poverty in the 1960s in terms of "the sense of failure and despair eating at a man who cannot make the grade (and who knows that his family knows it)."[5] Poverty in the 1930s *was not* a mark of *personal* failure. And the majority poor of the 1930s contained the necessary core of leadership skills. Harrington was referring to this when he wrote that "the poor were all mixed together. The bright and the dull, those who were going to escape into the Great Society and those who were to stay behind, all of them lived on the same street. When the middle third rose, this community was destroyed. And the entire invisible land of the other Americans became a ghetto, a modern poor farm for the rejects of society and of the economy."[6]

We now have several strands to draw together, all relating to the politics of poverty in the third sociopolitical period. The attack on economic privation had been relatively weak in the years of rapid industrialization although the objective condition was most severe. It was after the process of industrial nation-building was completed, after a major industrial plant was at hand, that the introduction of severe privations through the Depression created a situation deemed intolerable. Put differently, the poverty of the 1930s was not considered "natural," but rather man-made bungling, an aberration which should have been avoided, which by its presence was proof that new approaches in public policy were required. The economic misery of the Depression was more than painful, it was *unnecessary*. Those experiencing economic deprivation were not some modest minority, but a large majority of Americans. The majority poor were rich in political talent, and mounted a political attack which achieved impressive successes.

Thus the third period was defined to an important degree by the high political saliency of majoritarian economic deprivation. When the economy recovered and proceeded along a course of massive growth, the many were transformed from have-nots to haves, and American society and politics very greatly altered. Precisely when the United States entered the "age of affluence"—defined as a condition in which literal economic deprivation is experienced by only a distinct minority—can certainly be debated. But there seems little question that the entry was made by the 1960s, and we argue in the following chapter that this entry delineates the terminal boundary of the third period.

[5] Arthur M. Ross, "The Data Game," *Washington Monthly* (February, 1969) p. 65.
[6] Harrington, pp. 17–18.

Social, Economic, and Political Power:
Ascensions and Displacements

The Twilight of the Entrepreneurs

The transition from one societal setting to another involves the emergence of new social groupings and/or a significant alteration in the power position of existing groups. A class of land-owning agrarians was ascendant in the United States before the Civil War, which is not to say they always got their way, or that they always saw themselves as a coherently defined group doing battle with others; but simply that their views on public policy and expectations as to the general orientations of the society were controlling. Industrialization displaced this old agricultural class and ordained the steady advance of an urban entrepreneurial elite.

The entrepreneurial middle class directed the United States in the years of industrial nation-building, dominating economic life and, to a lesser but still substantial extent, politics from approximately the 1880s through the 1920s. This elite was displaced in the 1930s, and the manner of its displacement left it embittered and for a time at war with the new political coalition which had assumed national power.

Anyone who has examined the reaction of businessmen to Franklin Roosevelt and the New Deal in the years after 1934 must be struck by the disparity between the raw intensity of the business hostility and the objective "damage" done to the position of businessmen by the New Deal. Franklin Roosevelt won the presidency in 1932 with appeals which—for a country beset with economic crisis—were exceedingly temperate, hardly tinged with economic radicalism. Indeed, he at times berated his Republican opponent, the incumbent president Herbert Hoover, for failing to achieve a balanced budget! And there was little in the first two years of Roosevelt's administration to disturb businessmen seriously; Roosevelt in fact was widely praised in business circles. Then, beginning in the latter months of 1934 business opposition rapidly intensified. In 1935, 1936, and 1937, there welled up a vast bitterness against the president from what his secretary of interior, Harold Ickes, later called "the grass roots of every country club in America." Never has any president of the United States been denounced by businessmen with such vehemence as Roosevelt encountered in the latter half of the 1930s.

One possible source of this intense animosity can readily be discounted. Business did not hate Roosevelt because he was an economic radical. He was no ideologue bent upon imposing some socialist program on America, but a pragmatist, picking and choosing among possible economic responses in terms of what was possible on the one hand, and what would seem to bring results on the other. He quite clearly wanted businessmen to behave in a manner more responsive to public interests, but he never entertained any idea of a fundamental alteration of the structure of ownership and control of business enterprises. The Roosevelt administration did take a "turn to the left" in 1935, and pushed through legislation which most businessmen opposed: the Wagner Act, Social Security, an inheritance tax and an estate tax, gift taxes to prevent evasion of the inheritance tax, more steeply graduated taxes on large incomes. But these measures carried no threat to the basic position of business.

The outlines of Roosevelt's response to business are clear and not unfriendly: to put private capitalism back on its feet. Himself a scion of the American upper class, FDR assumed office in the midst of the greatest crises in the history of the American economic system, at a time when the combination of private capitalism and political democracy was under vigorous assault and indeed in retreat throughout most of the Western world, and firmly committed himself to a program designed to maintain both political democracy and private capitalism; and he achieved a large measure of success in restoring public confidence in such a system.

The intensity of the business reaction to Roosevelt becomes quite intelligible, however, if attention is shifted from what the New Deal actually did to the larger transformations in which American business was caught up. First, the idea of the positive state, of government as the permanently established manager in the industrial society of scale and complexity, clashed with the deep commitment in American ideology to the negative state. You get the free society—indeed, more generally, the good society—if government stands back, interferes little, confines itself to insisting that individuals and groups fight it out within the boundaries of a constitutional system. This prescription proved generally valid in the context of the extraordinarily equalitarian distribution of resources of the Rural Republic. It became increasingly less valid as massive resource concentration in the private sector became a fact of life in the industrializing society. But the ideological commitment to the negative state remained strong, and we will not understand the phenomenon if we assume that the commitment of businessmen to it was purely as a prop for their immediate interests. The massive commitment to classical liberalism in the American experience, buttressed by its fine fit to the facts of life for the first seventy or eighty years after regime formation, meant that businessmen (and many other Americans as well) confronted the policy initiatives of the New Deal, edging toward the positive state, with the ideal of the negative state a prominent part of their ideological baggage. As James MacGregor Burns put it, "The business community has become the prisoner of its own idea system."[7]

Secondly, and this appears to be far more fundamental, business experienced with the Depression a profound change in status, position, and role. Businessmen had done something more than rule during the period of industrial nation-building; they had *reigned*. The country was engaged in a great enterprise, and they were its guides. They occupied center stage and received the applause. Society was indeed getting better, and they were the chosen instruments for this betterment. Then, almost overnight, with the Depression, instead of cheers there were boos and catcalls. Instead of being the custodians of American prosperity, the builders of the American dream, they were presiding over an economic system in unparalleled collapse and appeared powerless to effect a remedy. In this situation, along came Roosevelt and the New Deal, and things—haltingly and imperfectly, to be sure—began to improve. "Roosevelt had robbed them [businessmen] of something far more important than their clichés and their money," Burns has written; "he had sapped their self-esteem." "The men who had been the economic lords of creation found themselves in a world where political leaders were masters of headline, of applause, and of deference. Men who felt that they had shouldered the great tasks of building the economy of the whole nation found themselves saddled with the responsibility for the Depression. Men who had stood for Righteousness and Civic Virtues found themselves whipping boys for vote-cadging politicians."[8]

American businessmen in the last half of the nineteenth century and the early years of the twentieth, more than any other group, were the spokesmen for what Croly called "the principle of nationality." They played a powerful nationalizing role, tearing asunder the localized society of Jefferson and Jackson. But in the 1930s, this older business nationalism found itself confronting a "new nationalism" not so very different from the one Theodore Roosevelt had earlier proposed but

[7] James MacGregor Burns, *Roosevelt: The Lion and the Fox* (New York: Harcourt, Brace & World, 1956), p. 239.
[8] *Ibid.*, p. 240.

much stronger. In the new nationalism, *government* was the instrument for bringing in left-out groups, for supervising, policing, and managing the complex system which had been developed. Businessmen lost their position as custodians of the national idea.

The intense hostility of a large segment of American business to the Roosevelt administration can only in small part be accounted for by the objective threat to business interests which Roosevelt's policies posed. The New Deal was simply the convenient target for a series of frustrations and resentments experienced by many businessmen as they saw themselves charged with the responsibility for economic collapse instead of applauded for growing prosperity, and as their long domination of the country's nationalizing impulses was challenged. The New Deal had not brought about these displacements and transformations, but it came to symbolize them, and this led businessmen to launch an assault of unprecedented ferocity.

New Claimants

Labor. One of the principal new claimants for power and recognition was organized labor. Industrialization had created a large urban working class; what remained in 1929 for it to assume real political power was effective organization. This organization was achieved in the decade after 1935. Figure 5.2 shows the total trade union membership, 1900 through 1968, and the percentage of the non-agricultural labor force in unions. At the turn of the century, American labor unions had fewer than 1 million members, and only 4 percent of the workers outside agriculture were organized. After a brief spurt around the end of World War I, membership leveled out in the 3 millions in the 1920s and early 1930s, just slightly more than 10 percent of the non-agricultural workers. Then, a combination of the new political climate which followed the Depression, the general encouragement of the Roosevelt administration, the formal legislative support provided by the Wagner Act, and the vigorous initiatives of a new generation of labor leaders produced a surge in membership, to 10 million on the eve of World War II and more than 14 million when the war ended.

This was the "heroic age" of American labor. Between 1936 and 1938 alone, over 4 million new union members were added. It was the period when labor won its great victories: in 1937, for example, General Motors was compelled to recognize the United Auto Workers, CIO, after a bitter strike; and United States Steel, which had beaten back organizing strikes on three occasions in 1901, 1910, and 1919, con-

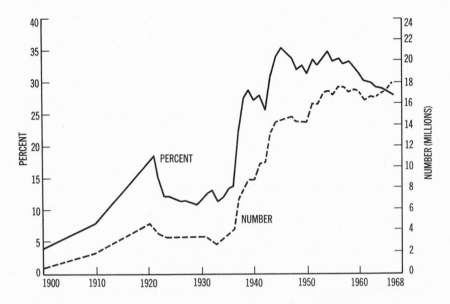

Figure 5.2. Labor Union Membership, Excluding Canadians, Number, and as a Percentage of the Non-Agricultural Labor Force, 1900–1968*

*Source: For 1930–1968, U.S. Department of Labor, *Handbook of Labor Statistics, 1968* (Washington, D.C.: U.S. Government Printing Office, 1968), p. 300; for 1900–1930, *Historical Statistics of the United States,* pp. 73, 97.

sented to negotiate with the Steelworkers Organizing Committee without a strike. It was in this period that labor launched a big new effort aimed at the unskilled and semiskilled workers of the mass production industries. The American Federation of Labor had been built on a craft union basis: that is, workers were organized by their skill or craft—like carpenters, bricklayers, meat cutters, and railway carmen. The extraordinary growth of such mass production industries as automobile manufacturing had created a situation which these craft unions were not equipped to handle, in which a major industry employed tens of thousands of workers, many of them unskilled or semiskilled, in a wide variety of functions not neatly encompassed by the old skill or craft lines. In 1935, a minority in the AFL, including John L. Lewis of the United Mine Workers and David Dubinsky of the Ladies' Garment Workers, formed a Committee for Industrial Organization, with the purpose of encouraging industrial unions in mass production industries. The ensuing struggle between two approaches to unionization rapidly escalated; in 1938 the Executive Council of the AFL formally revoked the charters of the rebel industrial unions, and the Committee for Industrial Organization transformed itself into a permanent Congress of Industrial Organizations.[9]

In certain areas, organized labor achieved more impressive advances than the data on the entire labor force presented in Figure 5.2 would suggest. More than 80 percent of the wage earners in a score of the country's most important industries, including construction, automobiles, steel, and clothing, were unionized in the ten years after the passage of the Wagner Act.

The economic power of this immensely invigorated American unionism was quickly felt. Important, too, was a new political role, as unions provided friendly candidates with funds and with a powerful source of electoral support. Indeed, so rapid was the increase in the power of organized labor that in 1947 a congressional majority was persuaded that unions had become too strong. This conclusion was expressed legislatively in the Labor-Management Relations (Taft-Hartley) Act. Taft-Hartley forbade coercing employees to join unions and prohibited unions from engaging in secondary boycotts. It outlawed the closed shop (by which all workers in a unionized industry could be compelled to join the union as a condition of employment). And it restored the use of injunctions in labor disputes, giving the attorney general the power to issue an injunction postponing a strike for eighty days if the president certified the labor dispute as a threat to national health or safety.

Union membership in 1968 would be only 3 million higher than in 1945, and a substantially smaller percentage of the work force. The conditions which have produced this relative decline are discussed in the next chapter. Here we need only note that the building of trade unions as a major economic and political force was accomplished in the ten years after passage of the Wagner Act, that the proportion of non-agricultural workers in unions in 1945 was the highest it was ever to be, and generally that 1935–1950 was the high point in the impact of unions in American society.

The advances made by labor in the third sociopolitical period were shared by other social groups—their membership overlapping substantially—who had been excluded or placed in a subordinate position in the years of industrial nation-building. In Chapter 4 the big post–Civil War immigration was described. While these new Americans came from a wide variety of national origins and fared very differently in terms of

---

[9] The AFL and the CIO merged in 1955, forming a single labor federation, the AFL-CIO.

acceptance or integration, up to the 1920s many remained on the periphery of American social, economic, and political life.

Then came their movement into the much-maligned American mainstream. It had taken time to master the language, time for children and grandchildren to reach adulthood with a sure feel for the demands and styles of life in the broader society. Another major factor in the enhancement of the power position of the newer immigrants involved a general improvement of the economic position of the working class, in which they were heavily concentrated. Having "come of age politically" in the United States, their economic position strengthened, the 1880–1920 immigrants and their children became a major component in a newly ascendant political coalition.

Negroes. The "Jim Crow" system erected in the South at the end of the nineteenth century had not only survived but was scarcely challenged in the 1930s. It was a pervasive pattern of discrimination, rooted in law and custom, and enforced by legal and extralegal violence. Negroes had no voice in the social, economic, and political decisions which affected them. Their disenfranchisement was virtually complete. All public facilities in the region, including playgrounds and parks, theaters, restaurants, and hotels were rigidly segregated—as was, of course, the entire school system. And, perhaps worst of all, Negroes could not expect white law enforcement officials to protect them, and confronted courts of law which were in fact instruments for maintaining white supremacy. This meant, of course, that they frequently had to endure whatever harassments and brutalities whites chose to mete out. Between 1882 and 1936, at least 3,275 Negroes were lynched in the American South.

It was in the third period that the assault on Jim Crow finally began, very slowly at first but with a rush by the end of the period that importantly affected the course of American political life. In the New Deal, there was little along the lines of a formal legislative or judicial attack on white supremacy. The advances in the position of Negroes which were achieved were largely spin-offs from legislation designed to benefit the lower-income strata generally. Race advancement organizations such as the NAACP were still forced to operate with a highly circumscribed program: it could not yet be, "End Jim Crow," but was instead, "End the worst abuses under Jim Crow," such as lynching.

In the 1940s and early 1950s, the pace of civil rights activity quickened appreciably. Perhaps most influential was the intervention of the federal courts against the institutions of white supremacy in the South.

A great variety of cases are involved, but two are especially notable. The landmark *Smith* v. *Allwright* (1944) decision of the Supreme Court ended the white primary, the most important "legal" device excluding Negroes from electoral participation. The South was a one-party region, so general elections were mostly uncontested and the only meaningful contests were in the primaries of the Democratic party. The Fifteenth Amendment to the U.S. Constitution clearly guaranteed Negroes the right to vote, but did its guarantee apply to primary elections? The white South said no, that the Democratic party was a private organization which could exclude Negroes if it so chose. It did so choose, and Negroes were cut off from the only elections that mattered. The immediate impact of *Smith* v. *Allwright* and related decisions was to expand dramatically Negro electoral activity, especially in the cities of the outer South: while fewer than 250,000 Negroes were registered in all of Dixie when World War II broke out, 1 million were registered a decade later.

The best known of all the civil rights cases, of course, is *Brown* v. *Board of Education of Topeka* (1954). The immediate finding of the Court in this and its companion cases was the unconstitutionality of the South's Jim Crow school system. But the real power of *Brown* was in the crystal clarity of its signal that the highest court in the United States would declare the entire Jim Crow system to be in violation of the spirit of the American constitutional order.

Up to the mid-1950s, the civil rights movement mostly pursued juridical solutions, and civil rights questions had high public visibility only in the South. Then, on a chilly December 5 in 1955, Mrs. Rosa Parks refused to give up her seat on a bus to a white man, and in so doing precipitated the Montgomery (Alabama) Movement. Direct-action demonstrations and civil disobedience quickly became the distinctive modes of operation of the civil rights movement. In the North, for the first time since the immediate Civil War period, *mass* public attention and condemnation was fixed on southern race relations. It seems clear that a majority of northerners, and an overwhelming majority of northerners in positions of influence, had concluded that "Jim Crow must go." The steady increase of federal government intervention against the institutions of white supremacy in Dixie followed naturally from this consensus.

The great civil rights battles of the decade after *Brown* and Montgomery were battles against Jim Crow: Little Rock; the sit-ins which began January 31, 1960, at a Woolworth's in Greensboro, North Carolina; Oxford, Mississippi; Birmingham, Alabama. The final battle took place in Washington in 1964 and 1965, and culminated in the passage of major civil rights legislation directed specifically at Jim Crow. Full equality had not been achieved, but Jim Crow was dead.

Throughout this period, we have seen, the civil rights movement pursued a *southern strategy*. This is hardly surprising. The problems confronting Negro Americans in the South were of a radically different dimension than in the North. It was not wrong to see the North as a purgatory to which Negroes could flee from a southern hell. As long as Jim Crow stood, North and South were far apart. It was in this period that *northern opinion* was effectively mobilized against *southern race relations*. Once Jim Crow was eradicated, however, the differences separating North and South in racial matters were greatly reduced, and a pronounced nationalizing of the politics of race ensued.

Why was it that Negro Americans, so long excluded from effective participation in their country's social, economic, and political life, emerged in the period we are discussing into a far higher—if still imperfect—level of citizenship? Complex social change does not tolerate simple explanations, and we will attempt here only to suggest the direction in which explanation lies.[10] On the one hand, the political position of Negroes was strengthened. Their mass movement to the urban North after 1920 helped persuade increasing numbers of northern politicians to be more solicitous of their interests.[11] By the time of the presidential election of 1964, more than 3.5 million Negroes were registered to vote outside the South, and these voters were strategically concentrated in the major cities of the big industrial states. Urbanization within the South brought more and more Negroes into population centers where collective political action was far more easily accomplished.

At a very different level, the Jim Crow system came to be seen by increasing numbers of Americans as totally without intellectual or moral justification. White supremacy was an idea whose time had passed. The United States was at birth an egalitarian nation, but egalitarianism has never been a complete or a static phenomenon. Throughout American history, there have been successful attempts to include within the "men"

[10] I have discussed these matters at much greater length elsewhere. See my *Negro Political Leadership in the South* (Ithaca, N.Y.: Cornell University Press, 1966).

[11] The following data on the percentage of the total Negro population of the United States living in the eleven states of the old Confederacy in selected years indicate the scope and timing of the Negro migration:

1830	92.8%	1930	78.7%
1870	90.6%	1960	52.3%
1920	85.2%	1964 (estimated)	49.0%

whom Thomas Jefferson said are "all created equal" new social collectivities previously excluded. American social structure and ideology have made it impossible to reject permanently the demands of such groups.

Negroes started out exceptionally disadvantaged, and for a long time their demands for inclusion in the mainstream of American life were faint. In the third sociopolitical period, however, the denial of the American commitment to egalitarianism always contained in the condition of Negroes was impressed on national consciousness. The cumulative impact of social science research came to be the preclusion of any intellectually respectable defense of white supremacy. The war-hastened collapse of colonialism permitted peoples of color to walk on the world stage as masters of their nations. The ever more impressive and better publicized achievements of Negro Americans made the falsity of the charge of biological inferiority ever more palpable. The answer to why the ideological case against white supremacy became so much more persuasive is broader than any of these, however. It is, basically, that the ideas of liberalism had at last come to be applied to the relations of white and black. Developments in American race relations were a logical and necessary working out of egalitarianism.

Power and Technology: America and the World Outside

The relationship of the United States to the world outside from the War of 1812 to World War I cannot precisely be described as *isolation,* for this country was continually involved with other nations through trade, for example, and through occasional acts of unilateral military intervention. On the other hand, if *isolation* is construed somewhat more casually or loosely, it becomes not at all an inappropriate characterization of some of the principal features of American foreign relations.

(1) It was a period in which the United States looked inward. For about four decades after 1776, looking inward had not been possible: there was the war with Britain, continued threats to American integrity imposed by the struggle between France and Britain in the Napoleonic wars, then the second war with England between 1812 and 1814. The outside world was too immediately threatening to be ignored. But in the century after the 1812–1814 conflict, it became possible to turn inward. National independence had been clearly established, Europe was in a period of relative peace, and the technology of the day made the oceans separating America from the great centers of world population very formidable barriers. What was possible coincided with what was desirable: this was the century of continental development, first the push-

ing out to the Pacific, then the massive enterprise of industrial nation-building.

(2) As a corollary of number 1, the United States was not involved in any formal and demanding alliance system. It had not taken responsibility for the maintenance of peace or the balance of power in the principal arena of world power, Europe.

(3) The United States did not develop the instruments needed for a major assertion of leadership in international affairs. Throughout the nineteenth century and up to 1898, the American armed forces never had as many as 50,000 men, except during an internal struggle, the Civil War. Total military expenditures for all purposes reached a pre–Civil War high of $46 million in 1847 during the war with Mexico, and between the Civil War and 1898 a high of $86 million in 1894.

This isolation was ended by developments in the twentieth century associated with the processes of industrialization. Military power became a function of technology and industrial capacity, and the U.S. became the leading industrial nation. The major technological changes which in so many ways had "shrunk" the planet, linking nations more closely together, could not help but impinge on international affairs generally, on warfare in particular. The airplane greatly lessened America's splendid insulation, and the missile was later to end it utterly. Precisely when, indeed because, the United States emerged as a mature industrial state, it ended its insulation-isolation and stood as a world power.

Americans had in the sociopolitical period we describe here to get accustomed to the end of their isolation and insulation in the community of nations, and this at times proved painful. This adjustment calls to mind Ralph Waldo Emerson's image of society as a wave, suggesting that advance and retreat, gain and loss are part of one process. Technological and industrial development provided extraordinary instruments for solving old problems but at once generated new ones, including some relating to the country's emergence as a big power in a shrinking world. The period in which Americans had to adjust to the changing requirements of mature industrialism in domestic public policy was also one in which they grappled with the implications of their nation's position as a world power.

"Until 1914," the historian Selig Adler writes, "the tradition [isolationism] had not withstood a real test. There are few, indeed, who grasped the implications of an American abstention from a balance of power. Arguments about isolation were mild and restrained for it seemed that only an abstraction was at stake. . . . Kaleidoscopic events beyond the sea, however, revealed the unity of a closely knit industrialized world. . . . When war came in 1914, the Great American Debate on foreign policy began in earnest.[12] Foreign policy questions appeared prominently in the political agenda. The first big argument was over what the American response should be to the European war which broke out in the summer of 1914. Then, after the United States entered the war in 1917, raising the strength of its armed forces from less than 180,000 to nearly 3 million men, and shared in the victory, there was the massive struggle over future obligations, centering on the question of participation in the League of Nations. Following a short respite in the 1920s, the events of the 1930s again thrust international affairs into domestic politics with particular intensity.

The initial American reaction to the renewal of hostilities in Europe in the mid-1930s was overwhelmingly on the side of noninvolvement. Three neutrality acts were passed, requiring the president, in event of a foreign war, to proclaim its existence, to withhold the shipment of arms to or for *all* belligerents, and to prohibit loans by American citizens to all governments involved in the war. This legislation reveals the depth of the fear of involvement, the freneticness of the search for a way to stay out, for it committed America to a policy that would embarrass collective security efforts: the legislation failed to distinguish between the parties guilty of aggression and those who were its innocent victims and required that an arms embargo be extended to countries engaging in efforts to punish aggressors!

Roosevelt quite clearly was unhappy with the neutrality acts but felt unable to directly challenge their backers, such was their strength. The Neutrality Act of 1937, for example, passed the House 376 to 16 and the Senate 63 to 6. So he dealt with the opponents of involvement in the most circumspect manner, nibbling on the peripheries, slowly extending commitments while strongly proclaiming his intention to keep American troops out of the struggle. Indeed, so circumspect was the president's handling of the isolationists that the basis was laid for the most venomous of the anti-Roosevelt literature—portraying him as the complete Machiavellian, promising that "your boys are not going to be sent into any foreign wars" while conspiring to send them into war, ultimately inviting the Pearl Harbor disaster to shock American public opinion into support of his objectives. A kinder and more accurate picture reveals a master politician confronting extremely strong opposition to American involvement, believing that the country had no course other

[12] Selig Adler, *The Isolationist Impulse* (New York: Collier, 1961), p. 34.

than stopping Hitler, engaging in an elaborate process of manipulation in which he did not always say what he believed.

After 1937, American opinion, both elite and mass, gradually swung away from intransigent opposition to any involvement in the unfolding European struggle. The most influential precipitants of this shift were the extreme German ruthlessness, and the severity of the threat posed by expansionist Germany to American economic interests, national security, and hopes for something other than a totalitarian world. Step by step, the United States moved closer to war. In 1937 Roosevelt delivered his "quarantine the aggressor" speech: "When an epidemic of physical disease starts to spread, the community approves and joins in a quarantine of the patients in order to protect the health of the community against the spread of the disease." In 1938 the Vinson Naval Expansion Act was passed, and provision was made for the accumulation of strategic materials. In 1939 the arms embargo was repealed. Finally came lend-lease legislation and the destroyer deal with Britain. Under the former, the president was authorized to lend, lease, sell, or barter arms, ammunition, food, or any defense article or any defense information to "the government of any country whose defense the president deems vital to the defense of the United States." Here the break with conventional neutrality was complete.

The several strands of domestic opposition in the 1930s to an assumption of enlarged international responsibilities can be more specifically described. First, there was a widespread desire to avoid the sacrifices of war and to continue what was seen as a long and admirable policy of noninvolvement in the blundering of European nations. The United States had been blessed by insulation; it was hard for a mass public to come to realize that insulation and the isolation it permitted was at an end. The time when the new involvement was thrust upon the country— the Depression years—added to the intensity of popular opposition: there were far too many domestic problems commanding attention and resources to think of involvement in a foreign war. The American people, Elihu Root had written, in 1922 were "only at the beginning of the task" of learning about international relations. The 1930s, ridden with domestic anxieties, were a difficult time for that lesson to be learned.

The extraordinary ethnic diversity of the United States provided a peculiar source of opposition to intervention. There were millions of Americans linked by ancestry if not by birth to countries on both sides of the European struggle; for many, unavoidably then, intervention meant intervention *against* the country in which they or their parents or grandparents had been born. World War I had provided a taste of this "hyphenate isolationism" in the opposition of German-Americans and Austrian-Americans to a U.S. alliance with France and England. On the other side, of course, was the strong pro-British sentiment of east-coast Americans of Anglo-Saxon ancestry. In the 1930s, the ethnic loyalties of German- and Italian-Americans understandably contributed to support for nonintervention. Still another twist was the reluctance of many Irish-Americans to back national sacrifices on behalf of England, an old enemy.

The geographic size and diversity of the United States had often in the past contributed a sectional axis to political conflict, and it did in the 1930s to the foreign policy argument. A sense of remoteness and isolation from European affairs was somewhat stronger in the Midwest than on the eastern seaboard. A *Fortune* poll released in July, 1940, showed about 42 percent of the sample from the Midwest opposed not only to involvement in the war but to coming to the aid of England in any way. In contrast, only 15 percent of the respondents in the Northeast backed this complete neutrality.

The old tradition of agrarian radicalism provided yet another source of opposition to intervention. It was not hard for men reared with fears and suspicions of eastern business to come to see efforts to involve America in a second European war as motivated by the bankers and the munition makers, men bent, as they always had been, on profits and prepared to spill American blood for them. How curious it is that this long-time agrarian distrust of bankers and financial manipulations and the money market and the machinations of men of industry could seem so bold and popular at one point, and so narrow and parochial at another.

An important forum for the contention that the money changers were the real villains in the effort to push America into war was the committee chaired, beginning in the fall of 1934, by the old-time North Dakota Progressive senator Gerald P. Nye. At this time, when business stood indicted at the bar of public opinion for "that most heinous of American crimes—the ruin of prosperity," the "merchants of death" argument, on the role of the munitions industry in World War I, gained considerable popular frequency, and Nye was appointed chairman of a Senate committee to investigate. It appears that he came to the investigation with his mind made up. In any case, the Nye Committee report made public in 1935 concluded that the munitions people and the Wall Street bankers, who had made it possible for the allies to buy the materials of war, had inveigled the United States into intervening on behalf of the side so heavily in their debt. The report had, of course, the purpose not only of passing out guilt for the past, but of sounding an alarm for the future: the munitions makers and the money changers must not again be allowed to dupe us into war.

There are other facets of this Populist-Progressive opposition to American involvement on which contemporary readers can look more sympathetically. Many from this tradition looked with a genuine horror on war, on the suffering that U.S. intervention would surely entail, were genuinely committed to domestic reforms and measures to restore prosperity at home and believed that the nation's energies and resources must be committed to these goals. There should be thoroughgoing reform to make the American masses prosperous, and, this done, we could "till our own garden" regardless of what happened abroad.

The mixture of liberalism in domestic politics and isolationism in foreign affairs found in old Progressives like Borah of Idaho, Johnson of California, Wheeler of Montana, Nye of North Dakota, and the La Follettes of Wisconsin was not to survive in anything approaching its historic form or strength the cataclysmic events which drew the U.S. into World War II. As Roosevelt and his New Deal supporters led the United States to increasingly overt opposition to Germany, the leadership of the opposition to these foreign policy commitments came to rest with domestic conservatives opposed to the New Deal. By the summer of 1940, conservatives controlled the isolationist coalition. In this situation, the liberal isolationists were pulled in two directions, and the position effectively disappeared:

Old-time progressives, like Senators Gerald P. Nye and Burton K. Wheeler, who remained intransigent isolationists, became more conservative in domestic policy, while the liberal Senator George W. Norris overcame the prejudices of a lifetime and veered to support the President. Henceforth isolationism was to become the seminal power of the reaction against 20th-century changes in American life. Resistant forces were to blame intervention in foreign war for changes in the social and economic pattern. The conservative isolationists would remember and utilize the isolationist conclusions of Charles A. Beard, while they would jettison his plans for making isolationism work by expanding the New Deal at home.[13]

The shock of Pearl Harbor effectively ended domestic opposition, making American involvement in the war a *fait accompli*. From Decem-

[13] Adler, pp. 271–272.

ber 7, 1941, until the end of World War II in the late summer of 1945, foreign policy arguments were shoved off the political agenda by the commitment to winning the war. But they quickly reappeared after 1945, as the United States emerged as the most powerful nation, its immense industrial plant intact while Europe was in ruins, in a world which the onrush of technology had made ever smaller. For Americans wishing some respite from the incessant demands of the war years there was little comfort. At once the country was involved in the establishment of a great new international venture, the United Nations, based on American soil. Wartime amity between the United States and the Soviet Union proved short-lived, and Americans saw their country confronting a powerful opponent consolidating its hegemony over central and eastern Europe, a regime whose ideology had long appeared especially threatening. The United States was called upon to play a large role in the economic rebuilding of Europe through the European Recovery Program (Marshall Plan), and to assume leadership in defending Europe through a permanent military alliance, the North Atlantic Treaty Organization (NATO). Crises in Asia rivaled those in Europe, as the government of Chiang Kai-shek was completely routed by domestic Communist forces and fled to Formosa (December, 1949), and then, in the summer of 1950, the Korean War broke out.

The United States, then, found itself in a world in which its security was diminished by the new technology of war, with obligations to the maintenance of peace showing no sign of ever diminishing, leading an elaborate alliance system, with a large defense establishment an apparently permanent burden. The strains and tensions surrounding this vastly altered role dominated domestic political argument in the decade after the war, and were an important source of the reaction to which a junior senator from Wisconsin gave his name—McCarthyism. The sheer magnitude of the international problems before the United States would have generated serious debate; the fact that the country was moving without blueprint, departing massively from past experience, assuming obligations imperfectly conceived, transformed debate into near hysteria.

Since the mid-1950s foreign policy controversies have lost none of their saliency in domestic political debate; indeed with Vietnam and the debate over defense spending they have, if anything, increased. But it does seem clear that the general outlines of the role thrust on the United States as the major industrial state in a nuclear age have achieved much wider recognition and acceptance.

Politics in the Industrial State

No polarity has been invoked as frequently to explain American political conflict in the year since Franklin Roosevelt won the presidency as *liberal vs. conservative*. Yet it rarely intruded in discussions of conflict before the 1930s. Reflecting on this, Samuel Beer has observed that "in politics words are cheap and this striking innovation in political terminology could have been merely verbal. In fact, the New Deal brought into existence not only a new alignment of social forces and a new balance between the parties, but also a new outlook on public policy."[14] We would put it only slightly differently and suggest that *liberal vs. conservative* came into frequency in American political parlance for the first time in the 1930s as a way of describing a type of conflict that gained centrality only when the United States emerged from the enterprise of industrial nation-building into mature industrialism.

Before pursuing this further, we should specify what *liberal* and *conservative* mean. The terms have been used in a variety of ways, but common threads run through many of the constructions. In a wide literature, liberals are described as in some sense proponents and conservatives as opponents of change.[15] There is somewhat less agreement about what kind of change conservatives align themselves against and what kind liberals seek, but by far the most common construction is that the liberal supports change to achieve a more popular or equal distribution of some important social value: a higher standard of living, more and better public education, assurance of adequate health care, etc. Liberals, who themselves may or may not be "little guys," concern themselves with the needs of "little guys" over the "big guys" of the society.

A second component of the polarity is defined by answers to the question, "Who should lead?" Conservatives are inclined to the rule of an elite, typically one whose fitness has been demonstrated by its economic success. Liberals look to rule "by the people" or more precisely to the leadership of spokesmen for the people. If the good society requires a proper balance of competing demands, liberals see this balance as threatened by the acquisition of power and privilege by some elite,

[14] Samuel Beer, "Liberalism and the National Idea," *The Public Interest* (Fall, 1966), p. 71.

[15] See, for example, Wilmoore Kendall and George Carey, "Toward a Definition of Conservatism," *Journal of Politics* (May, 1964), pp. 406–422; Samuel Huntington, "Conservatism as an Ideology," *American Political Science Review*, 51 (June, 1957), pp. 454–473; Clinton Rossiter, *Conservatism in America* (New York: Knopf, 1962).

and conservatives by popular infringements on the elite. These components of the liberal vs. conservative polarity—orientation to change involving claims for a more equitable distribution of dollars and status, and preference for elite or mass rule—can be summarized thus:[16]

WHO SHALL LEAD?

	MINORITY OF WEALTH	"THE PEOPLE" OR THEIR SPOKESMEN
Supports change toward a more popular extension of values	A	B Liberals
Change for what?		
Opposes change toward a more popular extension of values	C Conservatives	D

While the United States has always had some conflict of the liberal-conservative variety, such conflict quite clearly has not always been central. In the years of industrial nation-building, the primary component of change involved the agricultural-to-industrial transformations. Only when the point of transition from *industrializing* to *industrialized* was reached, when the enterprise of basic capital accumulation had been substantially completed, did the *primary demands for change* in the public sector look to more equalitarian extensions of values. And at this point, the old political class of entrepreneurial businessmen aligned itself squarely against change. The business elite further insisted on the continuance of the sociopolitical ascendancy it had enjoyed in the years of industrialization, while "newer" social groups—many the children of industrialism—rejected the legitimacy of this claim and sought a larger voice in governance and full entry into the American mainstream.

To sum up, the liberal-conservative polarity came to have real explanative power—in the sense of conveying a lot of information about the primary characteristics of political conflict—in the United States of the third sociopolitical period, as a business class, its ascendancy challenged, stoutly resisted the efforts of groups of lower socioeconomic status to achieve a more equitable distribution of the fruits of industrialism and to assume a larger role in American social, economic, and political life. We will suggest in the concluding chapter that just as the

[16] For a more detailed discussion of this, see Everett Carll Ladd, Jr., *Ideology in America: Change and Response in a City, a Suburb, and a Small Town* (Ithaca, N.Y.: Cornell University Press, 1969), especially Chapter V.

type of conflict to which liberal and conservative speaks was not central before the third period, so it lost centrality as that period drew to a close. Each sociopolitical period has its distinctive configurations of conflict; liberal vs. conservative captured the essential characteristics of political argument in the New Deal and immediate post–New Deal years.

The Party System, 1926–1970: A Structural Overview

The ground rules governing American party activity and electioneering have not been altered in any basic fashion since 1926, but two sets of changes of considerable significance have been achieved near the end of this contemporary period. One of these is the extension of the vote to Negroes in the South, where formal mechanisms and informal sanctions had long kept the large majority effectively disenfranchised. Beginning in the 1940s, a combination of Supreme Court decisions (especially *Smith* v. *Allwright,* 1944, which ended the white primary), new national legislation (the voting rights laws of 1957, 1960, and, by far the most influential, of 1965), initiatives by the federal executive branch, together with vigorous local campaigns by southern Negroes, brought a majority of the adult black population of Dixie into the electorate.

The second influential change is reapportionment. A series of sweeping Supreme Court decisions beginning with *Baker* v. *Carr* (1962) have required (a) that the several congressional districts in a state be of equal population size; (b) that both houses of the state legislatures be apportioned on a strict population basis; (c) that all these legislative districts also meet rigorous standards of compactness and contiguity (for districts might be equal in population but drawn in such a way as to disadvantage a party or certain social groups, the old technique of gerrymandering); (d) in short, that the letter and spirit of "one man, one vote" be scrupulously observed. Since American state parties had often perpetrated extraordinary malapportionments, these decisions had an immense immediate impact: extensive redistricting and sharp gains and losses in party strength in the state legislatures. While it now seems likely that many early estimates of the policy significance of reapportionment were exaggerated, the context for state party competition was significantly altered.

Still other important structural changes have been advanced though not achieved. In the 1960s, efforts to lower the voting age gained momentum. So, too, did the longstanding proposal to replace the

Electoral College mechanism for choosing presidents by direct popular election. And the presidential nominating convention came under re-newed challenge, especially as to the matter of delegate selection. While the specific incentives for these proposed and achieved changes are varied, the changes all appear to involve some further extension of participation/democratization of parties and elections. This has been, of course, the principal thrust of most of the significant alterations of the electoral ground rules in earlier periods.

The Republican and Democratic parties—both well into their second century by the end of this period—continued along a familiar pattern; organizationally diffuse, internally divided, but unchallenged as rallying symbols for electoral allegiance. This type of two-party system remained intact.

A great variety of "third" parties appeared on the electoral scene. Only five of these, however, managed to get as much as 1 percent of the popular vote in contests for the presidency. In 1932, Norman Thomas was the Socialist party candidate for president and won a little over 2 percent of the vote; this was his electoral high-water mark in six tries (1928, 1932, 1936, 1940, 1944, and 1948), but far below the best Socialist performance in an American national election, the 6 percent of Eugene Debs in 1912. William Lemke, a little-known North Dakota congressman, was the 1936 nominee of a strange one-shot alliance which took the name Union party, and he managed to poll just under 2 percent of the vote. The Union party turned out a pale version of what many in 1935 had expected to be a strong third-party challenge mounted by a collection of Depression radicals and led by Huey Long of Louisiana. But Long was assassinated in September, 1935, and the other radical leaders—Dr. Francis E. Townsend, Father Charles Coughlin, and Gerald L. K. Smith—settled on Lemke.

In 1948 there were two vigorous minor party efforts on opposite sides of the political spectrum: a left-wing challenger, the Progressive party, was headed by Henry A. Wallace, former secretary of agriculture and then vice president (1941–45); the party on the right, the States' Rights party, stood for southern racial protest, and had South Carolina Governor J. Strom Thurmond as its standard bearer. The strength of the Progressives was scattered around the country, their high 8 percent in New York. With just under 2.4 percent of the national popular vote, the Progressives won no electoral votes. On the other hand, with an almost identical popular vote concentrated in the South, the States' Rights party picked up thirty-nine electoral votes, carrying four states.

The strongest third-party movement of the period was the American Independent party of George Wallace in 1968. Founded on white racial protest, it spoke in neopopulist terms to a broad range of grievances of working-class and lower-middle-class whites, won 13.5 percent of the national vote, and seriously threatened to throw the election into the U.S. House of Representatives for decision.

Overall, the ascendancy of the two major parties in national politics remained impressive. Their candidates for president won all but 101 of the electoral votes cast in the 11 elections of this span, or more than 98 percent of the total.

The Parties: Positions in the Agenda

The Republicans and Democrats on the Eve of the Depression

When, in the 1920s, the United States stood at the end of more than a half-century of industrial nation-building as a mature and complexly integrated industrial state, what were the major parties fighting about? What distinguished them? Party platforms give some indication. In their 1928 platform, the Democrats had reiterated many of their historic commitments: to states' rights as "a bulwark against centralization and the destructive tendencies of the Republican party"; to a "reduction of those monopolistic and extortionate tariff rates bestowed in payment of political debts," and to "safeguarding the public against monopoly created by special tariff favors." The shift in the center of power in the presidential Democratic party—not in the congressional Democratic party—from rural to urban had resulted in greater sensitivity to the styles and status needs of the millions of recent immigrants who had settled in the great cities. The nomination of Alfred E. Smith was an important symbolic act, as was Smith's running as a "wet." (In deference to the rural wing of the party, the 1928 platform did not advocate repeal of prohibition; but the 1932 platform did.) The Democrats claimed as much fidelity as the Republicans to business values in an age of business ascendancy, calling in their 1928 platform for the "businesslike reorganization of all departments of government," and a sinking fund adequate "to extinguish the nation's indebtedness within a reasonable period of time." But they showed their old hostility to the unrestricted ascendancy of business, criticizing "the proverbial desire of the Republican party always to discriminate against the masses in favor of the privileged classes," berating the GOP for not enforcing antitrust laws "so that the country is rapidly becoming controlled by trusts and sinister monopolies formed for the purpose of wringing from the necessaries of life an un-righteous profit." There were a few measures in which the Democratic party anticipated what was to be its strong commitment to the humaniza-tion of industrialism. The 1928 platform cited the problem of unem-ployment and urged adoption of "a scientific plan whereby during periods of unemployment appropriations shall be made available for the construction of necessary public works." But there were few such anticipations.

The Republicans, residents in the White House for fifty-two of the previous sixty-eight years, offered themselves unabashedly as the party of business and national prosperity. They had been the party of industrial nation-building, of national economic integration, of the national idea thus expressed. They asserted confidently that their programs and policies had contributed and would continue to contribute to the material ful-fillment of American life, the widest extension of increased prosperity.

Under this Administration a high level of wages and living has been estab-lished and maintained. The door of opportunity has been opened wide to all. It has given to our people greater comfort and leisure, and the mutual profit has been evident in the increasingly harmonious relations between employers and employees, and the steady rise by promotion of the men in the shops to places at the council tables of the industries. It has been made evident by the increasing enrollments of our youth in the technical schools and col-leges, the increase in savings and life insurance accounts, and by our ability, as a people, to lend a hand of succor not only to those overcome by disasters in our own country but in foreign lands. . . . For the Republican party we are justified in claiming a major share of the credit for the position which the United States occupies today as the most favored nation on the globe.

The 1928 Republican platform did not, however, contain more than a trace of the commitment to middle-class reform which Theodore Roose-vent had so persuasively articulated.

On the eve of the Depression, then, party conflict assumed a pattern made familiar by the preceding half-century. There was little to suggest the lines of cleavage which were to become central in the next decade.

Partisan Conflict in the 1930s

Even after the Depression had struck, change was slow in coming. In 1932, the Democrats castigated the incumbent Republicans for the economic crisis which had beset the nation, yet looked back rather than ahead in policy response. Thus, their 1932 platform urged "an immediate and drastic reduction of governmental expenditures . . . to accomplish a saving of not less than twenty-five per cent in the cost of the federal government," and recommended a balanced budget. Victorious in November, 1932, the Democrats under Franklin Roosevelt still moved cautiously. But with the emergence of the "second New Deal" in 1935, the fabric of party conflict was drastically altered. The Democracy nationally became a liberal party in coherent programmatic opposition to a conservative Republican party. The Democrats strongly attacked the business elite, structured their appeals in class terms, and unquestionably heightened the economic and class distinction between themselves and the Republicans. Long the parochials, the Democrats became the proponents of a new nationalism. These differences cast in the Depression years persisted, and party conflict in the third period bore little resemblance to that of the second.

The 1935–1940 span was unusual for the *intensity* and *coherence* of party policy conflict. The Social Security Act, for example, passed not with the support of a two-party coalition, but as a Democratic measure, with Republicans in ineffective but resolute opposition. The key Social Security vote in the House was on a motion to recommit (April 19, 1935):

	DEMOCRATIC		REPUBLICAN	
	Number	*Percent*	*Number*	*Percent*
Yea (to recommit and thus kill the measure)	45	15	95	99
Nay	252	85	1	1

The Democratic party had gained huge majorities under Roosevelt, and for a time remained cohesively behind the program of his administration. The intensity of Republican opposition was produced not only by the genuinely innovative character of the new Democratic policies, but also by a reaction to the bitterness of defeat and the stigma of failure. The Republicans had been "the party of prosperity," but they presided over a great depression. Now the Democrats were riding high, branding them the party of economic collapse, calling for dramatically different policy initiatives. The Republicans felt compelled to defend their stewardship and reject responsibility for the great collapse.

Party Conflict in the Post–New Deal Years

Republicans and Democrats remained divided over domestic economic, regulatory, and welfare policy matters after the policy innovations of the 1930s. The Democrats continued to be more receptive to the interests of organized labor, more willing to spend public moneys for public welfare, more willing to invoke governmental power in new ways in the management and regulation of economic life. But the structure of partisan conflict underwent significant changes, changes involving a greater prominence of *intra-party* vis-à-vis *inter-party* conflict, and thus a lessening of partisan distinctiveness, a blurring of party position, a return, in short, to the historic pattern. Several distinct developments account for this.

Republican Acceptance of the New Agenda.   After a period of all-out war with the new Democratic programs, the Republicans came to accept many of them, at least grudgingly. In 1936, for example, they criticized in their platform the unemployment and old age annuity sections of the Social Security Act as "unworkable." But by 1939, Republicans in the House of Representatives were supporting amendments to the Social Security Act extending benefits to dependents and survivors of insured workers. The party specifically endorsed old-age and survivors' insurance for the first time in its 1944 platform when it advocated "extension of the existing old-age insurance and unemployment insurance systems to all employees not already covered." Partisan differences over Social Security matters did not end; they were apparent in debates on major new programs such as disability insurance and Medicare. But conflict over the *content* of a program is different than over whether or not there should be a program. After 1940, the Republican party was no longer at war with the principle of Social Security, and often joined with the Democrats in supporting increased payments and increased coverage.[17]

Intra-Party Divisions: The Democrats.   Partisan conflict over domestic economic, regulatory, and welfare legislation lost some of its 1930s clarity, too, because of divisions which quickly appeared in both political parties on such measures. In the Democracy a northern-southern split began taking shape in the late 1930s.

[17] For a comprehensive survey of the parties' positions on Social Security, see John P. Bradley, "Party Platforms and Party Performance Concerning Social Security," *Polity,* (Spring, 1969), pp. 337–358.

For those with political memories limited to the events since World War II, the northern-southern Democrat division appears part of the natural order of things. In presidential politics since the war, southern Democrats have shown considerable disenchantment with their party's presidential nominees and national policies, and have sustained two important third-party movements, in support of J. Strom Thurmond in the 1948 presidential election and George Wallace in 1968. In Congress, southern Democrats have often worked in tandem with a majority in the Republican party in opposition to northern Democrats, this so-called "conservative coalition" playing a major and at times controlling role in the flow of legislation. So important did this southern Democratic–Republican alliance against the northern wing of the Democracy become that the principal reporting service on Congress, *Congressional Quarterly,* began treating the conservative coalition as a formal and enduring legislative bloc, and now systematically reports the percentage of all roll calls in which the coalition appears and the regularity with which each member of Congress supports and opposes it. A student of Congress observes that

in a very real sense voting lines in the House during this period [1959–1962, but the same thing could be said for any of the post-war years] were most commonly of a coalitional rather than a party nature on many of the most important matters in three policy areas—domestic issues, foreign policy, and civil liberties. On these issues it was a common matter for the great majority of Northern Democrats and a handful of Liberal Republicans to find themselves opposed by a coalition of Conservative Republicans and Southern Democrats. Such coalition voting muddied the waters of Congressional party politics considerably during this period.[18]

It was not always so. In the early 1930s, for example, southerners were the most loyal of congressional Democrats. They voted against their party majority less frequently than northern Democrats, and rarely worked in tandem with Republicans. Julius Turner tabulated an "Index of Loyalty" for northern and southern Democrats in the House of Representatives in the 1930–1931 session.[19] As Table 5.2 shows, only 10 percent of the southern Democrats had Index of Loyalty scores of less than eighty-five, while 52 percent of the northern Democrats were

18 W. Wayne Shannon, *Party, Constituency, and Congressional Voting* (Baton Rouge: Louisiana State University Press, 1968), p. 95–96.

19 His Index of Loyalty is the same measure which the *Congressional Quarterly* now calls a "Party Unity Score." The Index of Loyalty or Party Unity Score for a congressman measures the percentage of times he votes with the majority of his party when majorities of the two parties are opposed.

TABLE 5.2

Frequency Distribution of Northern and Southern Democrats,
Index of Loyalty; House of Representatives, 1930–1931*

RANGE OF INDEX OF LOYALTY	NORTHERN DEMOCRATS		SOUTHERN DEMOCRATS	
	Number	Percent	Number	Percent
Below 75.1	11	18.0	2	2.0
75.1 to 80	13	21.3	4	4.0
80.1 to 85	8	13.1	4	4.0
85.1 to 90	6	9.8	24	24.2
90.1 to 95	13	21.3	36	36.4
95.1 to 100	10	16.4	29	29.3
Totals	61	100.0	99	100.0

* Source: Julius Turner, *Party and Constituency: Pressures on Congress* (Baltimore: Johns Hopkins Press, 1951), p. 136.

under eighty-five. In the first session of the seventy-second Congress (1933), there were fifty-six roll call votes in which congressmen did not vote unanimously or nearly unanimously for or against a measure, and in none of these contested votes did a majority of southern Democrats and a majority of Republicans oppose a majority of northern Democrats. In other words, if a conservative coalition roll call is defined as one in which a majority of southern Democrats vote with a majority of the Republicans against a majority of northern Democrats, there were no conservative coalition roll calls in 1933 in the House of Representatives.[20] Southern Democrats consistently supported the major legislative proposals of Roosevelt's first administration. They were not "at war" with northern Democrats; they were not voting together with Republicans; they were not part of a conservative coalition blocking legislation desired by a Democratic president.

But in Roosevelt's second term, the conservative coalition began to make its influence felt, appearing in votes on crucial pieces of legislation. By the early 1940s, southern Democrats were departing from their party's majority far more regularly than northern Democrats. While only 10 percent of the southern Democrats had an Index of Loyalty score of less than eighty-five in 1930–1931, 74 percent were under eighty-five in 1944.

[20] These data are from V. O. Key, Jr., *Southern Politics* (New York: Knopf, 1949), p. 375.

TABLE 5.3

Frequency Distribution of Northern and Southern Democrats,
Index of Loyalty; House of Representatives, 1944*

RANGE OF INDEX OF LOYALTY	NORTHERN DEMOCRATS		SOUTHERN DEMOCRATS	
	Number	Percent	Number	Percent
Below 75.1	12	11.3	66	61.1
75.1 to 80	7	6.6	14	10.0
80.1 to 85	7	6.6	10	9.3
85.1 to 90	16	15.1	9	8.3
90.1 to 95	26	24.5	5	4.6
95.1 to 100	38	35.8	4	3.7
Totals	106	100.0	108	100.0

* Source: Julius Turner, *Party and Constituency: Pressures on Congress* (Baltimore: Johns Hopkins Press, 1951), p. 137.

This general picture, of southerners defecting from the majority position much more than northerners in the congressional Domestic party, has continued to be valid in subsequent Congresses. Compare, for example, the distribution of Index of Loyalty scores for the House in 1959:

TABLE 5.4

Frequency Distribution of Northern and Southern Democrats,
Index of Loyalty; House of Representatives, 1959*

RANGE OF INDEX OF LOYALTY	NORTHERN DEMOCRATS		SOUTHERN DEMOCRATS	
	Number	Percent	Number	Percent
Below 75.1	27	18.8	57	58.8
75.1 to 80	17	11.8	12	12.4
80.1 to 85	22	15.3	7	7.2
85.1 to 90	21	14.6	11	11.3
90.1 to 95	38	26.4	10	10.3
95.1 to 100	19	13.2	0	0.0
Totals	144	100.0	97	100.0

* Source: Data compiled from *Congressional Quarterly Almanac*, 1959.

The Conservative coalition, which did not appear on any of the roll calls in 1933, was put together on 9 percent of the contested votes in the House in 1937, 13 percent in 1941, 16 percent in 1945; by the 1960s it had become a prominent force, appearing, for example, on 28 percent of the contested votes in 1960, 21 percent in 1962, and 24 percent in 1968.[21] And these data do not fully state the influence of the conservative coalition, because they do not discriminate as to the importance of legislative measures, and do not record coalition victories. Northern and southern Democrats have been divided, the latter voting with the Republican majority, on many of the most significant pieces of legislation. Thompson has noted that in the Eightieth Congress (1946) the southern Democrat–Republican alliance "succeeded in passing the Taft-Hartley Act and in overriding President Truman's veto of the measure. It reduced coverage under the Social Security Act, overrode Truman's veto of the "rich man's" tax reduction bill and further weakened price and rent controls. The hand of the coalition was also seen in blocking such measures as an effective public housing program, federal aid to education, Civil Rights, an increase in the minimum wage, an adequate farm program and other legislation which President Truman proposed to the 80th Congress."[22]

Finally, it is clear that this southern Democrat–Republican alliance really operated as a *conservative* coalition. Shannon constructed liberalism scales for the voting of northern Democrats, southern Democrats, and Republicans on legislation in key policy areas for the Eighty-sixth Congress (1959–1960). He found that in most areas southern Democrats were clustered on the "least liberal" end of the scale, northern Democrats on the "most liberal," and that southern Democrats resembled Republicans much more than they did northern Democrats. Table 5.5 presents data from three policy areas.

A sharp and influential split appeared in the congressional Democratic party, then, after Roosevelt's first term, with northern and southern Democrats frequently at odds. Why did this division appear when it did, and with such prominence? Race figures in the answer, as indeed it does in most matters involving southern political life. Up until the late 1930s, northern Democrats were not pushing programs bringing them into conflict with their southern brethren in the area of race relations.

[21] These data are from Key, p. 375; Shannon, p. 104; and *Congressional Quarterly Almanacs,* 1960, 1962, and 1968.

[22] Rep. Frank Thompson, in a speech delivered on the floor of the House of Representatives; U.S., Congress, *Congressional Record,* 86th Cong., 2nd sess., 1960, 106, pp. 1441–1442.

TABLE 5.5

Frequency Distribution of House Party Groups on
Selected Policy Scales, Eighty-sixth Congress*

SCALE SCORE	NORTHERN DEMOCRATS		SOUTHERN DEMOCRATS		REPUBLICANS	
	Number	Percent	Number	Percent	Number	Percent
Labor Scale						
1	50	28.1	0	0.0	1	0.7
2	66	37.1	1	1.0	4	2.7
3	15	8.4	1	1.0	4	2.7
4	35	19.7	11	11.3	9	6.1
5 (Least liberal)	10	5.6	82	84.5	128	87.1
Aid to Education						
1	161	90.4	0	0.0	26	17.7
2	7	3.9	8	8.2	3	2.0
3	7	3.9	72	74.2	50	34.0
4	1	0.6	10	10.3	58	39.5
Minimum Wage						
1	161	90.4	13	13.4	27	18.4
2	7	3.9	47	48.5	86	58.5
3	6	3.4	35	36.1	33	22.4

* Source: Shannon, pp. 81–94. The scale which Shannon uses is similar to that suggested by Charles D. Farris, "A Scale Analysis of Ideological Factors in Congressional Voting," *Journal of Politics,* 20 (May, 1958), pp. 308–338. The scales were constructed to provide an ordinal ranking for members of the three party groups analyzed.

Shannon writes that "the South's attachment to the Democratic party since the Civil War, after all, had been largely a matter of two things—the weight of tradition and a convenient means to preserve a racial caste system."[23] As northern Democrats (and the presidential Democratic party) moved to support policies designed to advance the position of Negro Americans, the ground was laid for intra-party conflict.

The new Democratic commitment on race began taking form in the post-war administration of Harry Truman. At the party's 1948 convention, there was a bitter floor battle over an amendment from the

[23] Shannon, p. 112.

floor to substitute a strong civil rights plank for the weaker one which the platform committee had recommended. The strong plank, which carried by a vote of 651½ to 582½, stipulated that

the Democratic party commits itself to continuing its efforts to eradicate all racial, religious and economic discrimination. We again state our belief that racial and religious minorities must have the right to live, the right to work, the right to vote, the full and equal protection of the laws, on a basis of equality with all citizens as guaranteed by the Constitution. We highly commend President Harry S. Truman for his courageous stand on the issue of Civil Rights. We call upon the Congress to support our President in guaranteeing these basic and fundamental American Principles: (1) the right of full and equal political participation; (2) the right to equal opportunity of employment; (3) the right of security of person; (4) and the right of equal treatment in the service and defense of our nation.

Hubert H. Humphrey, then a young Minneapolis mayor, led this successful floor fight for the stronger plank. After it passed, the Mississippi delegates and half the Alabama delegates walked out of the convention. Anti-Truman southerners met in Birmingham and nominated South Carolina Governor J. Strom Thurmond for president on a states' rights and white supremacy platform.

When the national government began to intervene actively in southern race relations after the *Brown* v. *Board of Education* decision (1954), race-related controversy was extended to legislative matters previously fought out without reference to race, and the northern Democrat–southern Democrat split was thereby extended. For example, when big federal aid to education programs were introduced in Congress in the 1960s, southerners saw them against the backdrop of a decade in which agencies of the national government had moved to bring to an end the South's "separate but equal" system of school segregation. Thus, federal aid to education was opposed by some southerners on the grounds that it would enhance federal leverage over southern school districts in pupil assignment policy.

Besides this general suffusion of racial concerns through a wide array of legislation, the resentment felt by many southerners over the commitment of the three post-war Democratic presidents to civil rights made the southern Democratic legislator inclined to support his party's position—even in areas having nothing at all to do with race—vulnerable to attack as simply too friendly to the national administration. Such attacks were unthinkable, of course, until national Democratic administrations began intervening against "the southern way of life." An example of this vulnerability of pro-administration southerners in a period of massive southern alienation from the national government is the defeat of Mississippi Congressman Frank E. Smith. Smith, a strong backer of the Kennedy administration, was beaten in a Democratic primary by Jamie Whitten in 1962, in a campaign in which Whitten made much of Smith's warm support of Kennedy. Whitten could not claim that Smith backed civil rights legislation offensive to the South, but did find him tainted by a general inclination to back the Democratic president. For example, Whitten charged Smith with being "the only Mississippi congressman to vote for such Kennedy administration measures as: foreign aid [and the] special UN appropriations [Congo operation]."[24] A Democratic congressman was defeated, in other words, for the crime of having supported rather consistently a president who was a member of his own party! Southern Democrats, and not just those in the deep South, found it in their interest to show a healthy degree of opposition to their northern colleagues.

The North-South division in the Democracy after 1937 appears to have another important component quite distinct from race. In the period of industrial nation-building and into the 1930s, the South was largely agricultural. From the standpoint of both interests and style, many southerners had reason to dissent from the national political and economic ascendancy of big business. Here was the "traditional" agrarian antagonism to the industrial society. The Republicans were the party of industrialism, and the Democrats were aligned against them; thus loyalty to the Democracy came easily for southerners. But developments beginning in the 1930s and much extended since then have eroded this "natural" Democratic allegiance. First, parts of the South have industrialized, and their spokesmen have found a kinship with the GOP. More importantly, party conflict was massively restructured with the New Deal. Instead of agriculture vs. industry, the principal division became that separating two visions of the urban and industrial nation. This reshaping of conflict made the position of northern business and the Republicans far less unpalatable than it had appeared in the earlier agenda, especially when northern Democrats took on as well the taint of opposition to the South's racial policies. Shannon was approaching this in another way when he observed that "when it is understood that the rural South has felt largely by-passed by the urban revolution and that the Northern Democrats have moved closer to the interests and concerns

---

[24] See Frank E. Smith, *Congressman from Mississippi* (New York: Pantheon Books, 1964), pp. 288–289.

of the Northern metropolis, the dissidence of Southern Congressmen on New Deal–Fair Deal–New Frontier economic issues becomes more easily understood."[25]

A new urban and industrial South, under vigorous attack from northern Democrats, found its historic party loyalty increasingly trying and established in Congress an effective working alliance with conservative Republicans. Democratic-Republican conflict beginning in the late 1930s, then, has been blurred by this massive and relatively stable division within the Democracy.

Intra-Party Divisions: The Republicans. At the same time, the Republicans were developing a new fissure in which a northeastern and industrial wing ascendant in the presidential party did battle with a midwestern and small-town faction dominant in the congressional party. These two loose blocs have been divided in a rather persistent fashion since the late 1930s, and the liberal-conservative polarity generally locates their differences. The "moderate" Republicans assumed a posture vis-à-vis the majority party comparable to that of the Cleveland wing of the Democracy a half-century earlier: they said "us too," accepted the new agenda, and claimed only that they could do things a little better. Conservative Republicans, on the other hand, opposed many of the new functions and responsibilities which the national government assumed with the New Deal and resisted their extension or enlargement. Like the Bryan Democrats of the 1890s, they fought a rearguard action, losing the war but winning impressive short-term victories, especially through their congressional alliance with southern Democrats.

During the years of rapid industrialization, the Republicans had a split with roughly the same territorial boundaries but with very different policy dimensions. The rural wing then was in no sense spokesman for economic conservatism. Quite the contrary. Republicans from agricultural states were tinged with economic radicalism and regularly dissented from business dominance. The list of leading agrarian dissenters in the GOP in the 1920s, for example, included Norris and Howell of Nebraska, Norbeck of South Dakota, Bristow and Capper of Kansas, Brookhardt and Dolliver of Iowa, La Follette and Blaine of Wisconsin, Ladd and Frazier of North Dakota, and Couzens of Michigan. This progressive band, Moos observes, "had been roving the land pouring out ideas and programs unacceptable to conservative Republican leadership."[26] The

[25] Shannon, p. 113.
[26] Malcolm Moos, *The Republicans* (New York: Random House, 1956), p. 362.

latter was concentrated in the Northeast: "If we look at New England in the middle 1920s, the type of Republican in the Senatorial contingent stands out in marked contrast to what we find in the Middle West. From Connecticut we have Bingham and Brandegee; from New Hampshire Moses and Keyes; from Rhode Island LeBaron Colt and Metcalf; and in Maine Frederick Hale. . . . That the foregoing represented the hard-shell conservative wing of the Republican party hardly requires explaining."[27]

We can accept most of Moos's analysis but must take issue with his insistence on placing the agrarian-industrial division in the Republican ranks in a liberal-conservative context. The eastern wing of the Republican party did contain a disproportionate number of leaders committed to industrial nation-building. The policy center of gravity in midwestern and western Republicanism was different, and reflected the prevailing dissatisfaction with business dominance and certain features of a business society. But business in this period was hardly conservative; it was change-oriented, building a new and very different society than that of the agrarian past. The farm Republicans were in one basic sense the conservatives or preservatists: They were trying to hold onto a social order that was slipping away.

After the 1930s, the internal politics of both the Northeast and Midwest changed. In the latter, general prosperity muffled the old economic discontents. Non-agricultural business had expanded enormously, and the small-town businessman became as representative a political figure as the embattled farmer had once been. On the other hand, just as the Northeast had been most strongly supportive of industrial development and was the section in which that progressed furthest and fastest, so in the late 1930s and subsequently the political agenda of the region shifted most completely, reflecting a commitment *to changes to cope with mature industrialism*. To survive politically, northeastern Republicans had to respond to these new demands, and came to provide the strongest support of any in their party for the types of reform which the New Deal initiated. The tension between Northeast and hinterland continued, but around vastly altered policy commitments.

Another contributing factor in the striking changes in intra-party divisions was a shift in position by Republicans in the conflict situation *within* many midwestern states. Prior to the 1930s, the Republican party in the Midwest contained strong representation of extremely disgruntled farmers. In some instances, the principal opposition to the Republicans came not from the Democratic party but from third-party

[27] *Ibid.*

movements such as the Nonpartisan League in the Dakotas, the Farmer-Labor party in Minnesota, and the Progressive party in Wisconsin. Many agrarian progressives were either Republicans, in a third-party movement, or torn between these two alternatives. But in the 1930s and 1940s, they went over in large numbers to the Democrats.

Wisconsin is a case in point. For forty-six years, the La Follettes—father Robert, Sr., and sons Robert, Jr., and Philip—dominated Wisconsin politics, holding continuously either the governorship or a seat in the United States Senate. The La Follettes were Republicans but progressive Republicans often at war with the party's national leadership. In 1924, Robert, Sr. ran for president as a Progressive and won 16.6 percent of the popular vote, a third-party total surpassed only by Roosevelt in 1912. And in 1934, again disgusted with Republican leadership, Philip and Robert, Jr., organized the Progressive party of Wisconsin; under its banner, Robert was elected to the United States Senate and Philip to the governorship.

For all their dissatisfactions, the La Follettes kept coming back to the Republican party. In 1946, speaking to the Progressives at a party conference, Robert, Jr., urged a return to the GOP. He opposed alignment with the Democrats, a party which "is now stalled on dead center. Although it is the party in power with a clear majority, it has been unable to act with sufficient unity of purpose to meet the urgent problems of today." La Follette concluded with this hopeful endorsement of Republicanism: "I am convinced that the Republican party of Wisconsin offers us the best opportunity for the advancement of progressive principles. Wisconsin has always been a Republican State—and by this I don't mean a reactionary state. Some of the most far-reaching legislation ever enacted anywhere in America was enacted in our State when Progressives were in the Republican party. . . ."[28] But in the 1946 Republican primary, La Follette was nosed out for his party's nomination by a relative unknown, Joseph R. McCarthy. Crushed by this defeat, the Progressive party in tatters, many of the La Follette Republicans at last went over to the Democracy.

In Minnesota, the Republicans were dominant for three-quarters of a century after 1857. Until 1918, despite the outpourings of discontent which produced the Grangers in the 1870s, the Farmers' Alliance in the 1880s and 1890s, and the Progressives early in the twentieth century, they had managed to retain the loyalties of the more radical farmers. But in 1918, Republican Governor J. A. A. Burnquist and his "regular

[28] Quoted in Moos, p. 451.

Republican" organization responded violently to the challenge of the latest agrarian protest movement, the Non-Partisan League, and drove the radicals to a formal third-party challenge.[29] Burnquist established a "Minnesota Commission of Public Safety," ostensibly to promote patriotic behavior; in fact, its main function was the harassment of Non-Partisan League candidates. The Commission's chairman charged that "a Non-Partisan League lecturer is a traitor every time. In other words, no matter what he says or does, a League worker is a traitor."[30] The "traitor" charge was directed at the lack of support for the American war effort among some League leaders. Infuriated League supporters responded by leaving the Republicans and organizing the Farmer-Labor party. The Farmer-Laborites proceeded to win the Minnesota governorship in four successive elections, 1930 through 1936.

While the actions of the Burnquist faction had shorn the Republicans of their radical supporters, the Democrats were not yet the beneficiary and functioned as a relatively conservative also-ran restricted to an ethnocultural base of German-, Irish-, and Polish-Catholics. It wasn't until 1944 that Hubert Humphrey and other young Democratic leaders, aided by the appeal of the national party under Roosevelt, were able to bring about a Democratic–Farmer-Labor alliance and thereby turn the Democrats into a broad-based liberal party. Minnesota Republicans were not left a reactionary party—for the political culture of Minnesota has sustained a more progressive politics than that of many states —but they did become the *more* conservative party.

A shift within midwestern Republicanism from agrarian progressivism toward conservatism occurred, then, not only as a result of economic developments that eroded the former position, but through a change in Republican-Democratic competition: transformed state Democratic parties came to appeal more effectively to voters with intellectual roots in the old progressive tradition and to their New Deal heirs.

The new sectional division in which the northeastern component had become the more liberal is nicely revealed by the voting of delegates to Republican presidential nominating conventions. In the conventions of 1940, 1948, 1952, and 1964, a candidate clearly identified as conservative sought his party's nomination against more liberal opposition: Robert A. Taft of Ohio in the first three, and Barry M. Goldwater of

[29] See John Fenton, *Midwest Politics* (New York: Holt, Rinehart and Winston, 1966), pp. 77–81. The Non-Partisan League had supported in the 1918 Republican primaries in Minnesota a full slate of candidates in opposition to the more conservative wing represented by Governor Burnquist.

[30] Quoted by Fenton, p. 80.

TABLE 5.6

Republican Factions: Scale of Consistency in
Four Presidential Nominating Convention Roll Calls, 1940–1964*

	STATES VOTING FOR:				STATES VOTING AGAINST:			
	Taft 1948	*Taft* 1940	*Taft* 1952	*Gold-water* 1964	*Taft* 1948	*Taft* 1940	*Taft* 1952	*Gold-water* 1964
GROUP 1								
Illinois	X	X	X	X				
Louisiana	X	X		X			X	
Mississippi	X	X	X	X				
Ohio	X	X	X	X				
South Carolina	X		X	X		X		
Tennessee	X		X	X		X		
Texas	X	X		X			X	
GROUP 2								
Alabama		X	X	X	X			
Arkansas		X	X	X	X			
Idaho		X	X	X	X			
Kentucky		X	X	X	X			
Nebraska		X	X	X	X			
Oklahoma		X		X	X		X	
South Dakota		X	X	X	X			
Washington		X		X	X		X	
West Virginia		X	X	X	X			
GROUP 3								
Arizona			X	X	X	X		
Florida			X	X	X	X		
Indiana			X	X	X	X		
Montana			X	X	X	X		
Nevada			X	X	X	X		
New Mexico			X	X	X	X		
North Carolina			X	X	X	X		
North Dakota			X		X	X		X
Utah			X	X	X	X		
Virginia			X	X	X	X		
Wisconsin			X	X	X	X		
GROUP 4								
California				X	X	X	X	
Colorado				X	X	X	X	

	STATES VOTING FOR:				STATES VOTING AGAINST:			
	Taft 1948	Taft 1940	Taft 1952	Gold-water 1964	Taft 1948	Taft 1940	Taft 1952	Gold-water 1964
Delaware				X	X	X	X	
Georgia				X	X	X	X	
Iowa		X		X	X		X	
Kansas				X	X	X	X	
Missouri				X	X	X	X	
Wyoming				X	X	X	X	
GROUP 5								
Connecticut					X	X	X	X
Maine					X	X	X	X
Maryland					X	X	X	X
Massachusetts					X	X	X	X
Michigan					X	X	X	X
Minnesota		X			X		X	X
New Hampshire					X	X	X	X
New Jersey					X	X	X	X
New York					X	X	X	X
Oregon					X	X	X	X
Pennsylvania					X	X	X	X
Rhode Island					X	X	X	X
Vermont					X	X	X	X

*Source: Table from Frank Munger and James Blackhurst, "Factionalism in the National Conventions, 1940–1960: An Analysis of Ideological Consistency in State Delegation Voting," *Journal of Politics*, 27 (1965), pp. 375–394.

Arizona in 1964. Frank Munger has recorded the conservative support or opposition of each state delegation at these conventions.[31] States are distributed among five categories ranging with a relatively small

[31] Munger defined a state delegation as supporting the conservative candidate if it gave more than half of its votes to that candidate on the ballot where his strength was most realistically presented: for Senator Taft at the point of his maximum strength on the fifth ballot in 1940; for Taft on the second ballot in 1948; for Taft on the first ballot in 1952, before it became clear that Eisenhower had secured a majority and the switching began; and for Senator Goldwater on his victorious first ballot at the 1964 convention. In table 5.6, the roll calls are arranged in order of increasing conservative support: that is, Taft received the majority support of only seven state delegations in 1948, of sixteen in 1940, of twenty-three in 1952, and Goldwater of thirty-four in 1964. Munger found a high degree of consistency in the sense that states which supported the conservative candidate at one level of conservative strength with only 9 exceptions out of 192 roll call responses supported all conservative candidates of greater overall strength.

distortion from the most conservative to the least conservative. Table 5.6 shows the distinctive regional characteristics of each bloc of states. The last group, those voting against the conservative contender at all four conventions, is largely northeastern, containing all of the New England states, the four Mid-Atlantic states, and only three outside the region—Michigan, Minnesota, and Oregon.

The new divisions which appeared in both the Republican and Democratic parties in the late 1930s were ideological-geographic-institutional. The Republicans' more conservative interior wing was dominant in the congressional party. The eastern industrial state faction, centered in the liberal-conservative polarity further toward the liberal pole, enjoyed a string of successes in the party's presidential nominating politics, with the nomination of Willkie in 1940, Dewey in 1944 and 1948, and Eisenhower in the 1950s. Dissenting southern Democrats had little success in the presidential party but through seniority and other rules of operation of the Congress exercised great power in the legislative process, working in alliance with congressional Republicans in a conservative coalition in many of the most important legislative struggles. These *intra-party* divisions served to blur *inter-party* policy struggles. The Democrats were the liberal party with a powerful conservative wing in Congress. The Republicans were the more conservative party, with a moderate wing ascendant in presidential politics. The policy differences separating congressional Republicans and presidential Democrats throughout the third sociopolitical period were sharp, and easily accounted for by the liberal-conservative polarity. On the other hand, presidential Republicans and congressional Democrats were not polarized ideologically, as indicated by the easy cooperation between the Eisenhower administration and the Democratic leadership in Congress in the 1950s. The presidential Democrats provided the initiative in extending governmental activity in those areas where the New Deal innovated, but the presidential Republicans served as a good "me too" party, accommodating themselves with relatively little difficulty to the Democratic innovations.

Party Conflict: A Note on Foreign Affairs

The suggestion that "politics stops at the water's edge" is one of those massive cliches which contains one grain of validity. While the whole matter of the appropriate foreign policy initiatives and responses has been subject to the most intense political argument, and while disagreement and dissent rooted in foreign policy questions have intruded continuously through domestic political argument since 1930, intra-party splits have been more prominent and inter-party divisions less prominent than in the principal areas of domestic policy. And bipartisanship—the effort to secure the endorsement of policies by both Republican and Democratic leaders—has been more successfully utilized in foreign affairs than in the equally momentous and contentious areas of domestic policy.

We know from studies such as Dahl's[32] that partisan conflict over foreign affairs was much sharper in the 1933–1941 period than after World War II. Between 1933 and 1941, for example, only 40 percent of the votes cast by Democrats in the House of Representatives were in support of neutrality and isolation, in contrast to 87 percent of the votes of House Republicans. Most of the major foreign policy innovations after World War II, however, such as ratification of the Charter of the United Nations, the Greek-Turkish loan, and the European Recovery Program (Marshall Plan), found influential Republican leaders actively involved and working with the Democratic president, and majorities of both parties in favor of the measures.

A variety of factors account for the higher partisanship in the prewar years than after the war. The break with neutrality in the 1930s was made by a Democratic president. The natural thrust of Republican partisanship, then—and these were times of high partisan feelings—brought them to a defense of isolationism. The big difference in the regional bases of Republican and Democratic congressional representation also served in the context of foreign policy argument in the decade before World War II to heighten inter-party splits. Senators and representatives from the South—almost all of whom were Democrats—were more opposed to neutrality and isolation legislation than were either Republican or Democratic delegations from any other geographic region. Dahl suggests that this was due not so much to the demands of public opinion in the South, although opinion there was probably somewhat less isolationist, as to the fact that southern internationalists were overrepresented in Congress "because of the peculiar class character of the southern Democratic party."[33] His argument is that the big differences in public opinion on questions of neutrality and isolation were not geographically defined, but rather between educational and income

[32] Robert Dahl, *Congress and Foreign Policy* (New York: Norton Library, 1964; first published 1950).
[33] *Ibid.*, p. 191.

TABLE 5.7

House of Representative Voting, by Region;
Neutrality and Isolation Legislation, 1933–1941*

	PERCENTAGE FOR			PERCENTAGE AGAINST		
	Total	Democratic	Republican	Total	Democratic	Republican
North Central	79	56	91	16	36	5
West Central	81	60	88	17	40	10
South	32	32	–	59	59	–

* Source: Data are from Dahl, p. 192. The composite percentages were derived from seventeen votes on nine issues in 1933, 1937, 1939, and 1941. Totals do not equal 100 percent because percentages were computed from the base of total membership, and some did not vote.

groups; voters of high income and college education were substantially more "internationalist" than low SES voters.

This difference . . . was characteristic not merely of the South, but every region in the nation. But what makes this significant in the South is the tendency in that region for the high-income and college educated groups to be represented at the expense of the low-income, grade school educated. Had an active two-party system been competing for votes in all strata of the population in the South, there is every reason to suppose that the Congressional delegation would have provided more support than it did for the neutrality-isolationist position. In other words, preferences reflected in the "internationalist" position of the Southern delegation were not entirely those of region but also of class and status groups.[34]

On the other hand, the Republicans drew a much higher proportion of their congressional strength from the interior states of the North where the commitment to isolation *in both parties* was highest. In 1939, 45 percent of the congressional Republicans were from the North-Central states, only 16 percent of the Democrats; 37 percent of the Democratic congressional delegation was southern, while only two Republicans were elected from the eleven states of the old Confederacy. Comparing the voting of congressional delegations from these regions on neutrality and isolation legislation between 1933 and 1941, we see the importance of the marked difference in geographic base for party position.

After the war partisan conflict over foreign policy declined, partly

[34] *Ibid.*, p. 193.

because the lessons of the previous three decades had been well learned; that is, that the consequences could be disastrous if maximum efforts were not made to involve the leadership of both parties behind foreign policy innovations. Wilson's League of Nations mistake would not be repeated. The Truman Administration after World War II was especially careful to take Republican leaders into its counsel at all stages leading to foreign policy departures, and this decision produced handsome dividends. As it was successful, and produced formal Republican as well as Democratic leadership sponsorship, it naturally served to reduce, though not entirely remove, inter-party differences.

After World War II, moreover, the substance of foreign policy controversy was very different than it had been earlier. In the 1933–1941 period, we have seen, southerners were more "internationally minded" than their colleagues from other sections, which is to say they were less wedded to the old tradition of isolation. After the war, being "internationalist" came to mean something quite different, and southerners decidedly were not the most internationalist. Looking at the voting distribution of southern Democrats, northern Democrats, and Republicans on foreign aid measures in the First Session of the Eighty-sixth Congress (1959), Shannon found the southerners the least supportive. Their greater opposition seems to have two principal causes: economic conservatism which included a reluctance to spend money on foreign aid, and the suffusion of racial considerations through foreign policy matters along with others in a wide range of issues. Former Congressman Frank E. Smith of Mississippi has argued that many white southerners came to see the world situation against the backdrop

TABLE 5.8

Frequency Distribution of House Party Groups on the Foreign
Aid Scale, Eighty-sixth Congress, First Session, 1959*

SCALE SCORE	NORTHERN DEMOCRATS		SOUTHERN DEMOCRATS		REPUBLICANS	
	Number	Percent	Number	Percent	Number	Percent
1 (Most liberal)	151	84.8	25	25.8	76	51.7
2	2	1.1	5	5.2	5	3.4
3	3	1.7	2	2.1	3	2.0
4	20	11.2	64	66.0	58	39.5

* Source: Table from Shannon, p. 90.

of American race relations, with foreign aid, the United Nations, and internationalism generally objects of suspicion because southerners found opposition to their racial policies in a world populated by more independent, nonwhite nations.[35] Conservative Republican and conservative Democratic cooperation thus developed in the foreign policy sector.

Party differences over foreign policy have been less intense, too, because the *parties* appear to lack philosophies on such matters comparable in coherence to those they have on domestic welfare and regulatory and economic issues. Party positions in Congress have varied greatly depending on who controlled the presidency and was initiating policy. A study of Republican and Democratic voting in the House and Senate on foreign aid measures in three sessions, 1957 through 1959, found a higher proportion of Republicans than Democrats supporting foreign aid. A Republican president, of course, was calling for large appropriations. This was a reversal from the late 1940s and early 1950s, when, with Truman president, Democrats backed foreign aid more strongly.[36] The situation was again reversed in the 1960s as the Democrats, back in the White House, once more became the more consistent supporters of foreign aid measures. Many in both parties were consistently committed to foreign aid, others were consistently opposed, while a third group appeared to swing with the pulls of party loyalty.

The Parties in Electoral Competition

The presidential election of 1928 was a landslide (if such is thought of as an election in which the winner has at least a ten-percentage-point margin over the runner-up) won by the Republicans; the 1932 presidential election was also a landslide, but with the Democrats victorious. The six presidential elections from 1920 through 1940 are striking both because they encompass a massive reversal of party fortunes, and because of the size of the winner's victory in each: the Republicans won the first three, the Democrats the latter three, and in all six the winner's popular vote margin exceeded 10 percent. In only twelve of the thirty-five presidential elections from 1832 through 1968 did the winning candidate gather over 50 percent of the vote and enjoy a margin of at

[35] Frank E. Smith, *Look Away From Dixie* (Baton Rouge: Louisiana State University Press, 1965), pp. 17–30.

[36] Everett Carll Ladd, Jr. "The Congressional Parties: Cohesion and Conflict," mimeographed. Cornell University, 1960.

least 10 percent over the runner-up. Half of these were consecutive elections beginning with 1920, and all but two were in the twentieth century.[37] Presidential contests were substantially closer in the last century than they have been in our own.

The Electoral Strength of the Party Coalitions

In the 1930s, a new majority party coalition, the Democratic, took shape, ending seventy years of Republican ascendancy. From the beginning of the Depression in 1929 through the 1960s, the Democrats lost only three presidential elections; and only in 1952 and 1956, when their candidate was General Dwight D. Eisenhower, a national hero with strong personal appeal and weak partisan identification, did the Republicans win decisively. Eisenhower's victories were clearly not party victories. Indeed, in 1956, when he beat Stevenson by fifteen percentage points, the Democrats actually increased their share of seats in the House of Representatives.[38]

In two of the ten post-Depression presidential elections, the Republicans benefited from the preponderance of short-term factors but lacked a national hero as their standard-bearer: in 1948, when the Democrats had been in power for sixteen years and had a relatively

[37] These twelve landslides, with the winner's margin over the runner-up in parentheses, are: 1832 (17 percent); 1872 (12 percent); 1904 (19 percent); 1920 (16 percent); 1924 (25 percent); 1928 (17 percent); 1932 (18 percent); 1936 (24 percent); 1940 (10 percent); 1952 (11 percent); 1956 (15 percent); 1964 (22 percent).

[38] There is extensive survey data showing the strength of Eisenhower's personal appeal. The Survey Research Center of the University of Michigan found favorable references to Eisenhower's personal attributes exceeding favorable references to Stevenson's by more than 60 percent in 1952. The 1956 Michigan survey reported a marked decline in Stevenson's personal popularity, unfavorable references to him actually exceeding favorable references, while the electorate's assessment of Eisenhower remained warmly favorable (Angus Campbell et al., The American Voter [New York: John Wiley, 1960], pp. 54–55). In addition, in 1952 the Republicans enjoyed an enormous advantage in short-term issues. The Korean War was still going on. The electorate wanted it ended, and in the normal course of democratic politics looked to the party out of power. The Michigan study found that references to war and peace in 1952 were pro-Republican or anti-Democratic by a ratio of better than seven to one. Two other short-term issues working in the Republicans' favor were "corruption" and "time for a change." The Michigan investigation found frequent pro-Republican references to both.

Pro-Republican references to corruption	546
Pro-Republican references to need for a change	490
Pro-Democratic references to corruption	–
Pro-Democratic references to need for a change	–

See Campbell, p. 50.

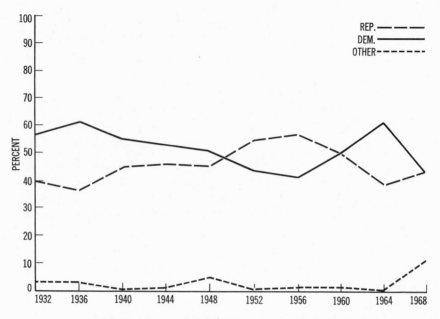

Figure 5.3. Popular Vote for President by Party, 1932–1968

unpopular nominee, and in 1968, when the incumbent Democrats were suffering from their stewardship of an extremely unpopular war, from bitter intra-party feuding, and from a number of war-related ills including inflation and widespread public disruptions. The weakness of the Republican coalition is underscored by the party's inability to convert these short-term advantages into solid victories. In 1948 they lost, and in 1968 they won the narrowest of victories—with Nixon's popular vote margin over Democrat Hubert Humphrey less than one-half of one percentage point.

The Democrats had a majority in the national House of Representatives in all but two of the twenty Congresses from 1930 through 1968, and a majority in the Senate all but three times. Figure 5.4 shows that the Republicans did fare somewhat better in popular voting for the House—single-member district, simple majority systems generally produce this distortion, giving the winning party a higher percentage of seats than of the popular vote—but the Democrats won popular majorities in 70 percent of the Congressional elections in this thirty-year span.

The status of the Democrats as the majority coalition of the third sociopolitical period is evident, then, in their disproportionate share of victories in national voting. It is revealed, too, by data on the partisan identifications of the electorate, for which there are survey data going

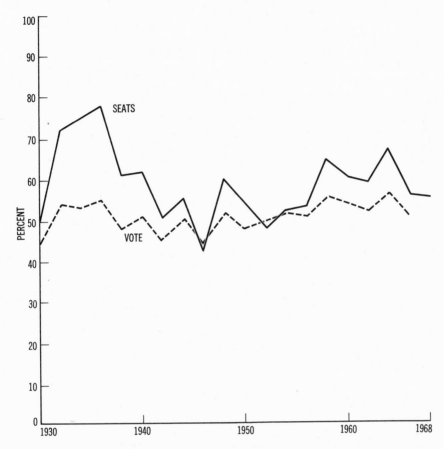

Figure 5.4. Democratic Percentage, Two-Party Vote and Seats, U.S. House of Representatives, 1930–1968*

* Source: U.S. Bureau of the Census, *Statistical Abstract of the United States, 1968* (Washington, D.C.: U.S. Government Printing Office. 1968), pp. 357, 368.

back to the mid-1930s.[39] The Gallup organization has been asking respondents in its national surveys the question, "In politics, as of today, do you consider yourself a Republican, Democrat, or Independent?" Figure 5.5 shows that in the 1940s the Democrats held a lead over the Republicans, but it was slim. Then the Democratic margin gradually widened until, in the mid-1960s, about half the electorate described

[39] Registration is an unreliable index of party strength. There are two chief reasons for this. Many voters, once having registered with a party, leave their registration unchanged even though their identification changes. And since registering with a party is a public declaration, voters may choose to record an "acceptable" affiliation, even though their private commitment is different.

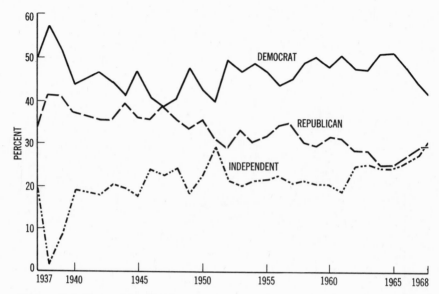

Figure 5.5. Party Identification of the American Electorate, 1937–1968*

Question: In politics, as of today, do you consider yourself a Republican, Democrat, or Independent?

* Source: American Institute of Public Opinion (Gallup), national surveys 1937–1968, made available through the Roper Center for Public Opinion Research (Williamstown, Mass.).

itself as Democratic, only one-quarter as Republican, and one-quarter as independent.

Another survey organization, the Survey Research Center of the University of Michigan (SRC), has been conducting systematic investigations of American voting behavior since 1952, and this gives us some parallel data for comparison. The SRC portrait, presented in Figure 5.6, confirms Gallup's in one basic regard: it shows the Democrats with a large lead over the Republicans in electorate allegiance. And Gallup and SRC frequently agree closely on the size of the three major groupings—Democrat, Republican, and Independent. In 1960, for example, Gallup found that 30 percent of the voting-age population were Republican identifiers, SRC 27 percent; 47 percent (Gallup) and 46 percent (SRC) were Democrats; each survey recorded 23 percent Independents.[40] But one important difference in the SRC and Gallup

[40] SRC breaks down the partisan affiliation of respondents more precisely than does Gallup, as *Strong Democrat, Weak Democrat, Independent Democrat, Independent, Independent Republican, Weak Republican,* and *Strong Republican.* In Figure 5.6, *Strong* and *Weak Democrat* have been combined to yield Democratic identifiers, as have *Strong* and *Weak Republican* to yield Republican identifiers. Independents leaning toward the Democrats and Independents leaning

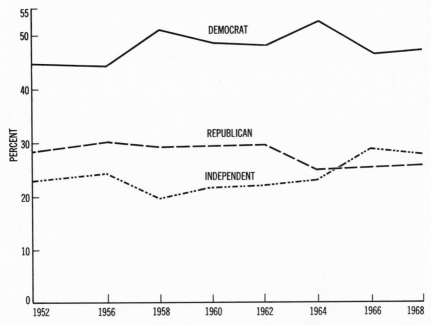

Figure 5.6. Party Identification of the American Electorate, 1952–1968*

Question: Generally speaking, do you usually think of yourself as a Republican, a Democrat, an Independent, or what?
* Source: The Survey Research Center of the University of Michigan; made available through the Inter-University Consortium for Political Research.

portraits of party ties should be noted. The SRC studies show a great constancy in party identification. Apparently, the parties' shares of the underlying allegiance of the electorate have not been affected by short-term considerations such as candidate attractiveness and the issues of the day. Gallup, however, reports substantial fluctuations in voter identification from year to year, suggesting that the identification of some—presumably the less intensely committed—is affected by short-term factors. This discrepancy remains unexplained. On the clear majority status of the Democrats in voter identification, however, there can be no doubt.

The Nationalization of Politics

In the 1840s, we have seen, the two major political parties competed on even terms in all the geographic sections of the country. The Demo-

---

toward the Republicans have been placed in the *Independent* category, together with those who claimed not even the slightest preference for one party or the other.

cratic share of the popular vote in one was not more than a few percentage points above or below that in the other sections, and all were clustered around the 50-percent line. In the two decades after the Civil War, sectional differences in party strength were greater than they had been between 1836 and 1852, but still were relatively modest. In 1884, for example, the Republican percentage of the presidential vote in the party's strongest section—the West—was only 13 percent above that in the region where it ran most poorly—the South. Then in the 1890s, a four-decade period of profoundly sectional alignment began in which (a) the differences in Republican and Democratic strength from section to section were extreme and (b) the increase or decrease in a party's strength from one election to the next did not follow a uniform trend nationally. The Republican percentage of the popular vote in the Western states in 1896, for example, was 24 percent lower than it had been in the previous presidential election, while the party did 12 percent better in the Northeast in 1896 than in 1892. In wide areas of the country there was little real party competition. The sectional differences in party strength after 1896 tended to widen rather than lessen, reaching their apogee in 1924, when the Republican presidential candidate won 77 percent of the votes in the West, but only 29 percent in the eleven states of the Old Confederacy. A full forty-eight percentage points, then, separated the Republican share of the vote in the regions of high and low performance.

In contrast to the extreme sectionalism of the four decades after 1890, the four since 1930 have seen a nationalization of politics, or, as E. E. Schattschneider puts it, the substitution of "a national political alignment for an extreme sectional alignment everywhere. . . ."[41] Schattschneider added a qualification to *everywhere:* "except the South." We can now drop this qualification, for while the South remains a deviating region in which the dimensions of partisan competition depart significantly from other regions, it has felt a powerful current sweeping away from one-party dominance. There has been, too, some diminution of the difference in relative party strengths within the region and outside. Figure 5.7 demonstrates the general decline in sectional differences in presidential voting. In 1904, when the Republican party won a massive victory, it gained over its 1900 performance in only twenty-six states, actually losing ground in nineteen states; in contrast, in 1952, the Republicans improved on their 1948 performance in every state,

---

[41] E. E. Schattschneider, *The Semi-Sovereign People* (New York: Holt, Rinehart and Winston, 1960), p. 89.

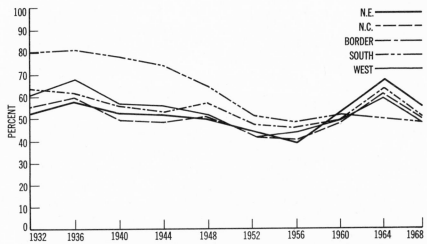

Figure 5.7. Democratic Percentage of the Two-Party Presidential Vote, by Region 1932–1968

did less well in forty-five states in 1954, improved their position in all states in 1956, and did less well in virtually all states in 1958.

Figures 4.8 and 4.9 in Chapter 4 show a growing Republican ascendency everywhere outside the South after the Civil War, and the movement of large numbers of states—North and South—toward one-party domination. After 1932, as the distribution of states in Figure 5.8 clearly points out, this situation was reversed. The Democrats made dramatic gains outside the South. In presidential voting between 1932 and 1968, the Republicans held claim to majority status in only ten states, all in either the Midwest or northern New England. And states throughout the country moved toward more even competition. We can describe a state as highly competitive in the presidential balloting of this period if the minority party won at least 45 percent of the popular vote in the ten elections and carried the state in at least 30 percent of the elections. Thirty-two of the fifty states meet this standard of competitiveness for 1932–1968, only six of forty-eight between 1896 and 1928. Other indicators, for example, data on gubernatorial and congressional voting, reveal the same thing: movement toward a more competitive two-party system throughout the country after 1932.

Social Group Composition of the Party Coalitions

In the 1930s, a major alteration of the American political agenda occurred, and the Democrats succeeded in transforming themselves into the party of the new agenda, thereby laying the foundation for their

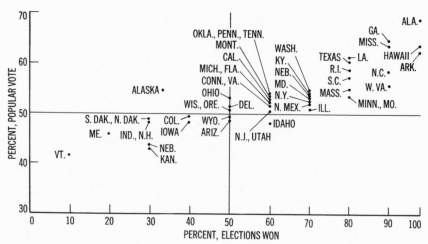

Figure 5.8. The Competitiveness of States, Democratic Percentage of the Two-Party Presidential Vote, 1932–1968

supremacy. We would expect, with the emergence of a new agenda and a new majority party speaking to it, that voters entering the electorate for the first time would show greater long-range allegiance to the new majority than those who were part of the electorate when the old agenda was still largely intact. Party identification, once fixed, is not readily eroded, and new voters, not having developed stable party attachments, should thereby be drawn in greater numbers to the new majority than those anchored by partisan attachments and related political perceptions formed under the old. Data collected by the Survey Research Center in the 1950s strongly indicates that this indeed was the case: "There is reason to believe, however, that a good many of these Republicans who defected into the Democratic ranks during the early years of the Roosevelt period were soon disenchanted. Some erstwhile Republicans never returned to their party, but these party-changers do not appear to have made up a very large part of the long-term Democratic increase. Our inquiries into the political histories of our respondents lead us to believe that a larger component of the gain came from young voters entering the electorate. . . ."[42]

The new majority, in other words, was built less on *conversion* than on success in attracting a disproportionate share of the emerging electorate. We can see from Figure 5.9 that those in the electorate of the 1950s who had begun voting in the 1920s were much less Democratic

[42] Angus Campbell *et al., The American Voter* (New York: John Wiley, 1960), p. 153.

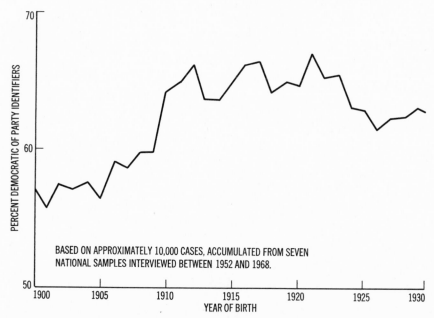

Figure 5.9. Party Identification of Party Identifiers Born between 1900 and 1930*

* Source: Figure from Campbell, *et al., The American Voter,* p. 154.

than those who had first entered the electorate in the 1930s and 1940s. What this means, of course, is that one of the key social group components of the new Democratic majority is defined by age. This is especially important to keep in mind because it is often suggested that the composition of party coalitions should be understood almost exclusively in economic and ethnocultural group terms. The *entire political generation that came of age politically after 1930 was more Democratic than the previous generations.*

This is not to suggest that the parties drew equally on the various economic and ethnocultural groups after 1930. The Democrats backed programs designed to help those in the lower socioeconomic strata, and they drew a far larger share of the allegiance of people in the lower strata, as shown by the representative data in Table 5.9, drawn from the SRC 1952 election study.

The Democrats' greater strength among voters of lower socioeconomic status (SES), variously defined, and, conversely, the greater Republican strength among high SES voters held for all sections of the United States except the South, where Democratic allegiance for a long period was an essential act of regional loyalty and commitment to white supremacy

TABLE 5.9

Party Identification of the American Electorate, 1952,
by Income and Education Groups*

INCOME	DEMOCRATIC	REPUBLICAN	INDEPENDENT
Less than $3,000 (n = 618)	54.2	26.5	19.3
$3,000–$5,000 (n = 653)	51.0	25.4	23.7
$5,000–$7,500 (n = 306)	48.0	32.0	19.9
$7,500–$10,000 (n = 87)	29.9	34.5	35.6
Over $10,000 (n = 64)	15.6	48.4	35.9
EDUCATION			
0–7 years (n = 355)	61.7	20.0	18.3
8–11 years (n = 679)	50.5	26.7	22.8
High school graduate (n = 419)	44.9	32.0	23.1
Some college (n = 147)	41.5	36.0	22.5
College graduate (n = 260)	23.9	39.8	36.3

* Source: The Survey Research Center of the University of Michigan. (All data are expressed as percentages of *n*.)

and higher SES groups were about as heavily Democratic as lower SES groups. Table 5.10 compares the party identification of working-class and middle-class voters for the four principal geographic regions, and points out the striking southern deviation.

The Democrats in the 1930s, 1940s, and 1950s claimed by decisive margins over the Republicans the support of voters in most ethnocultural minority groups, including Catholics and Jews, blacks, and whites tracing their ethnic ancestry to eastern, central and southern Europe. Some of these ethnocultural minorities were longstanding members of the Democratic coalition; for example, Catholics were heavily Democratic in the nineteenth century. But others were brought into the party in the 1930s. Jewish-Americans, now overwhelmingly Democratic, gave substantial support to the Republicans in the 1920s. Fuchs found that the vote in heavily Jewish districts in the big cities of the Northeast ran as high as 80-percent Republican during that decade.[43] Before the 1930s Negroes were predominantly Republican, the result of an historic attachment to the party of Lincoln. But a steady shift to the Democracy began in the 1930s and continued through the 1940s and 1950s. In 1952, SRC found two out of three Negro Americans identifying with the Democratic party, fewer than one in six with the Republicans.

[43] Lawrence Fuchs, *The Political Behavior of American Jews* (Glencoe, Ill., The Free Press, 1956), p. 56.

TABLE 5.10

Class Differences in Party Identification, by Region, 1952*

	WORKING CLASS	MIDDLE CLASS
	Percent	*Percent*
NORTHEAST		
Democrat	42	24
Republican	31	46
Independent	27	30
MIDWEST		
Democrat	47	30
Republican	26	45
Independent	27	25
WEST		
Democrat	57	30
Republican	17	45
Independent	26	25
SOUTH		
Democrat	70	63
Republican	17	17
Independent	13	20

* Source: Data adapted from Campbell, p. 158.

TABLE 5.11

Party Identification of Some Principal Ethnocultural
Minority Groups, 1952*

	DEMOCRAT	REPUBLICAN	INDEPENDENT
	Percent	*Percent*	*Percent*
Catholic (n = 385)	56.1	17.9	26.0
Jew (n = 57)	68.4	0.0	31.6
Negro (n = 135)	66.9	15.3	17.8
Irish** (n = 96)	49.0	21.9	29.1
Polish** (n = 50)	54.0	12.0	34.0
Other Eastern Europe** (n = 99)	56.6	11.1	32.3
Italian** (n = 74)	59.5	16.2	24.3

* Source: The Survey Research Center of the University of Michigan.
** A respondent is thus classified if he, his father, or one of his father's parents
was born in the country referred to.

TABLE 5.12

Republican and Democratic Identifiers, by Family Income, 1952*

	DEMOCRAT $(n = 842)$	REPUBLICAN $(n = 475)$
Less than $3,000	37.7	32.0
$3,000–$5,000	40.1	34.5
$5,000–$7,500	17.8	20.6
$7,500–$10,000	3.2	6.3
Over $10,000	1.2	6.5

* Source: The Survey Research Center of the University of Michigan. (All data expressed as percentages of *n*.)

A large measure of caution is in order in dealing with data like the above. As an example, we noted that voters with high incomes in 1952 were significantly more Republican than Democrat in party identification, with the converse true for low-income voters. A somewhat different picture appears if we ask instead what portion of the electorate which identifies itself as Democratic falls within each income stratum, what portion of the Republican identifiers are drawn from each. While the Republicans drew about 13 percent of their identifiers from families with incomes of $7,500 and above (in 1952) and the Democrats only 4 percent of their supporters from these strata, a very large majority of both Republicans and Democratic identifiers were from families earning less than $5,000. And the lowest stratum furnished roughly equivalent portions of the total support of each party: about a third of the Republicans and just over a third of the Democrats had family incomes of less than $3,000. These data do not refute the argument that the Democrats in this period were a working-class party in competition with a middle-class Republican aggregation, but they do suggest the qualifications which must be understood before the argument can be accepted.

The Parties in the Industrial State

The three decades or so from the Depression era into the 1950s assume coherence as a societal setting around a basic adjustment to the social, economic and political consequences of the American venture in industrial nation-building. Industrialization built a massive urban working class which had to be accommodated within the structure of industrial decision-making and within national political life. It is hardly accidental that labor unions became especially prominent institutions in this period, reaching their greatest influence. The economy of mature industrialism—distinguished by the size and resources of the major producers and by the complex interdependence of the constituent parts —dictated a greatly expanded level of public supervision and management, and the fleshing out of the managerial state was a primary occupation of the period. Industrialization had added enormously to overall productive capacities, and in the industrial state the pressures to use these for a much larger measure of popular enrichment and economic security were strong and persistent.

The Great Depression did not create the conditions calling for these adjustments, but instead dramatized their appearance, strengthened enormously the political hand of those interests inclined toward political change, and telescoped the period in which this change occurred. The social collectivities, such as urban workers, so greatly enlarged by industrialization could not have permanently acquiesced to the supremacy of the entrepreneurs, but the Depression hastened the latter's displacement by de-authorizing them: it made them appear the architects of collapse rather than of prosperity. The United States would certainly have come to the managerial state in any event, but the crisis of the 1930s forced public men to erect it much more rapidly. The foot soldiers of industrialism would have demanded that the new economic capacities be used much more for their benefit even if there had never been a depression, but the drastic increase of privation gave a special saliency to class antagonisms.

These characteristics of the social setting resulted in important changes in the party system, the most obvious of which was the emergence of a new majority party. It was not so much the close Republican association with the majority coalition and the political agenda of the previous period as the unparalleled abruptness of the transition, together with the Republicans' misfortune in holding power when the Depression began, which provided the minority Democrats with their extraordinary opportunity to establish themselves as the party of the new agenda. Never before (or since) was there a reversal of party fortunes so massive or rapid as this one, because at no other time in American history has there been so telescoped a transition from one political agenda to another.

The American parties through most of their history have not been *class* parties: they have not been very sharply differentiated, in either constituency or appeals, by social class. Party conflict in the third sociopolitical period is therefore distinguished by the fact that class was salient. Especially in the 1930s, the Democrats functioned as a working-class party, the Republicans as a middle-class party; both the substance and style of their differences clearly reflected this class line. Even in the 1930s, of course, class "warfare" in the U.S. was muted by European standards of the time, and so then was the class differentiation of the parties. The class divide nonetheless was the deepest it has ever been in the American experience. Furthermore, while declining after the Depression decade, it remained relatively high throughout the period.

The class orientation of the parties was a reflection of the saliency of class in the society. The displacement of the entrepreneurial middle class, the pronounced strengthening of trade unions, the introduction of much more systematic governmental regulation of business enterprise and of some features of the welfare state—both limited but still an abrupt departure from the American past—were all part of a political agenda which emphasized the competing interests of *economically defined* groups.

The class appeals of the parties in the industrial state contributed to a marked nationalization of American politics. Each championed a version of the "national idea" which it took to the entire country: the older business nationalism of the Republicans and the "new nationalism" of the New Deal and the Fair Deal.

In the 1930s, the Democracy was established as the majority party, and it still held this position at the start of the 1970s. This is not to say, however, that the party system has remained largely unchanged. In the concluding chapter, we argue that massive and continuing social transformations since World War II have ushered in a new sociopolitical period, the fourth such fundamental setting in American history, and that this in turn has entailed profound modifications in the structure of party conflict and competition.

6

On the Future of American Politics: The Emergent Society and the Party System

American society and its political agenda in 1970 appear to us sufficiently different from what emerged fully in the 1930s to require consideration analytically as the fourth fundamental sociopolitical setting in the country's history. The effective environment in which political institutions such as parties move and have their being has changed decisively.

Commentary on this is made difficult by the fact that the changes we refer to are so immediately proximate. The 1960s seem to have been, quintessentially, a transitional decade in which more and more components of the new setting took form. We must try to describe the new, then, just as the pieces are being put together. The sociopolitical setting now emergent will be far easier to evaluate in 1980 than in 1970, a threshold year.

The Condition and Meaning of Mass Affluence

In 1958, John Kenneth Galbraith more or less officially labeled American society as "affluent."[1] No one has much questioned the validity of this description. But what precisely does it mean to set American society of the 1950s, the 1960s, and beyond apart from the

---

[1] John Kenneth Galbraith, *The Affluent Society* (Boston: Houghton Mifflin, 1958).

America of earlier times by its possession of the characteristic *affluence?* From its beginning, the United States has been a wealthy country, compared to the others. Most Americans were better off in 1960 than their counterparts in any other country, and dramatically better off than the citizenry of most other countries. But this was true in the 1920s, in the 1880s, in the 1840s. What is understood by the condition of societal affluence, prompting social scientists with rare unanimity to perceive America's entry into it in the 1950s and 1960s?

The Condition of Societal Affluence

We should first state what the usual conception of the affluent society does not mean or require. It does not require economic nirvana, in which everyone finds all or most of his economic desires satiated. Quite clearly, if that were required the United States could not be considered affluent, nor would this or any society ever attain affluence. We know that expectations can rise at least as fast as the gross national product. The affluent society is not one where everyone is "wealthy," where poverty is abolished. In the United States in the 1960s, millions of people—just how many is hard indeed to estimate—experienced literal economic deprivation—inadequate diet, housing not meeting basic standards for health, etc. U.S. government statistical data for 1967 showed about 28 million Americans living in literal poverty.[2] While classification efforts of this kind are bound to leave much to be desired, there can be no doubt that millions of people have gross economic needs that are being met.[3] Poverty, moreover, is almost certainly more extensive than data assessing it as a more or less literal and absolute condition would indicate, because of the relational component. People think of themselves as poor or deprived when their standard of living is below the level which the society in which they live considers "acceptable," even if they have quite enough for food and shelter.

Affluence as a description of the condition of a society means something quite precise and limited: it is a situation in which a "critical mass" of the population of a country does not face problems related to subsistence. Galbraith has observed that the affluent society is one in which

---

[2] See U.S. Bureau of the Census, *Current Population Reports: Special Studies*, series P-23, No. 28, August 12, 1969. A fairly elaborate mechanism of classification is used, including the consideration of family size and farm or non-farm residence. A non-farm family of four with an annual income of $3,388 or less (1967 dollars) was classified as within the poverty level.

[3] For a thoughtful warning on the dangers in such gross statistical estimates of so complex a matter as the amount of poverty, see Arthur Ross, "The Data Game," *Washington Monthly,* 1 (Feb., 1969) pp. 62–71.

literal economic privation is a concern of the *few* rather than of the *many,* is minoritarian instead of majoritarian.

In the 1960s, a large majority of Americans clearly did not need to concern themselves with problems related to economic scarcity, to subsistence—adequate shelter, enough food, sufficient clothing, the necessities of life. "Is the clothing of the desired style?" and "Does the clothing suffice to protect the body from the environment?" are very different sorts of questions. "Mr. Average" in the United States of the 1960s could dwell on questions of the former sort and ignore those like the latter. While many in this majority were not wealthy, they were above subsistence, operating in a setting with very different sorts of economic concerns.

We know that Americans did not wake up one morning to discover that their society was affluent. The productive capacities of the United States have been increasing steadily if not evenly for 130 years. Still, this country's entry into societal affluence is very recent, having occurred in the last two decades. A majority of Americans in 1947, while not in a condition one would want to describe as poverty, had incomes in which the margin over basic subsistence was small. The median family income that year was $3,000, and 81 percent of all families earned less than $5,000. These Americans certainly had little left over when food, clothing and shelter were taken care of. Their economic world revolved around subsistence-type concerns.

Figure 6.1 records the extraordinary advances which occurred in the 1950s and 1960s as the society was propelled into a affluence. The median family income, expressed in dollars of constant purchasing power, jumped nearly $4,000 between 1947 and 1968, an increase of 83 percent. The percentage of families earning $10,000 and over, again in constant dollars, quadrupled—from 10 percent to 40 percent—over this period.

With these massive increases in wealth, an entire range of consumption values previously limited to a tiny elite came within the grasp of a large segment of the population. Cereals no longer sufficed by being nourishing; they had to excite the imagination with delightful shapes and colors. Soaps had to do more than clean; they had to become imaginative toys, or clean without scrubbing. Dog foods came to compete with extravagant claims as to which best titillated the palates of discerning dogs. And leisure, long a "problem" only in its absence, became a problem in its use.

Analysis thus far has emphasized the raw income component of

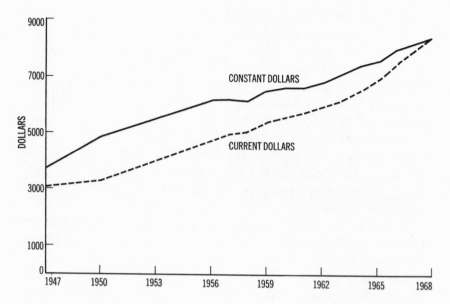

Figure 6.1. Median Family Income in Current and Constant (1968) Dollars, 1947–1968*

* Source: U.S. Bureau of the Census, *Current Population Reports—Consumer Income,* Series P-60, No. 66, December 23, 1969.

affluence. But there is another facet which deserves some attention. Robert Lane, in describing the main characteristics of the *age of affluence,* emphasizes the following:

Provisions against the hazards of life—that is against sickness, penury, unemployment, dependence in old age, squalor—the features now associated with the term "welfare state"; and

A "managed economy" in the sense of conscious and more or less successful governmental use of fiscal and monetary powers to smooth out the business cycle and avoid depressions, as well as to provide for . . . economic growth. . . .[4]

These point to the matter of economic security. To describe a society as affluent, it is not merely enough that a majority of the population have a substantial margin over subsistence; there must also be reasonable assurance that this prosperity will continue. Lane deals with two different dimensions of its continuance. First, individuals are underwritten against such personal catastrophes as serious illness; the "welfare state"

[4] Robert Lane, "The Politics of Consensus in an Age of Affluence," *The American Political Science Review,* 59 (December, 1965), pp. 874.

provisions of government are matched, in many cases surpassed, by the "welfare society" guarantees of private employers—including life insurance benefits, medical care policies, and retirement provisions. Related to this, as one of the things an affluent society does to assure its inhabitants that it is unlikely they will be thrust up against subsistence concerns at some point in the future, are the various provisions for job security pursued and achieved by large blocs of white-collar and blue-collar workers alike. Not only are the many above subsistence, but there are rather substantial guarantees against some personal misfortune changing this. Lane's second observation is that security is provided not only against personal misfortunes but also against *system failure*. The "managed economy" commitment postulates both that it is *desirable* for government to supervise and regulate the economy to assure prosperity, and as well that it is *possible* for government to do this successfully.

In sum, in the United States of the 1960s a large majority of the citizenry have incomes with a substantial margin over subsistence, a considerable guarantee that they are protected from personal misfortune, and apparently substantial confidence that the economy is sufficiently well understood and the machinery adequate to prevent some future collapse.

Political implications

The poor as minority. In his influential *The Other America,* Michael Harrington observes that "unlike the poor today, the majority poor of a generation ago were an immediate (if cynical) concern of political leaders. The old slums of the immigrants had the votes; they provided the basis for labor organizations; their very numbers could be a powerful force in political conflict."[5] The intensity of the Great Depression, the number of people who suffered from it—in 1933, for example, nearly 13 million, or 25 percent of the total population—contributed mightily to the political popularity of appeals to end economic deprivation. And the Depression occurred in a society in which a large portion of the population was under any circumstances directly occupied with scarcity. There was a majority coalition waiting to be mobilized around its economic needs. The Roosevelt administration increasingly directed its rhetoric after 1934 to majority deprivation, and it was rewarded handsomely. Since the 1950s, however, no such majority has been available. "Now any politician who speaks for the very poor is speaking for a

[5] Michael Harrington, *The Other America* (Baltimore: Penguin, 1963), p. 15.

small and also inarticulate minority. As a result the modern liberal politician aligns himself not with the poverty-ridden members of the community but with the far more numerous people who enjoy the far more affluent income of (say) the modern trade union member. . . . Reform now concerns itself with people who are relatively well-to-do— whether the comparison be with their own past or with those who are really at the bottom of the income ladder."[6]

The transformation of interests. There is a profound alteration in the shape of operative political interests in the affluent society and, directly related to this, in the political relations and roles of the various economically defined interest groups. Individuals and groups can be expected to pursue their interests. But what do they deem these interests to be? With affluence, the "luxuries" of times past become "necessities," and large numbers of people come to pursue values which earlier were the concern of a tiny elite or at most a narrow slice of the population. While the American "Mr. Average" of the 1930s was often preoccupied with such basic needs as food and housing, his counterpart in the 1970s worries about getting his son or daughter into college. College and professional school enrollment, just 52,000 in 1870, less than 500,000 when World War I ended, less than 1.5 million before the outbreak of World War II, climbed to over 2.5 million in 1956, 3.5 million in 1960, and 7,250,000 in the fall of 1969. This increase between 1960 and 1969—3,750,000 or more than 100 percent—was about 2.5 times more than the total enrollment in 1940. Some projections show nearly 12 million enrolled in 1985. Assuring his children college educations became an important political interest for "Mr. Average," as the burgeoning legislative appropriations for higher education so amply show.

The growth in college enrollment testifies not only to the possibilities of affluence, of course, but also to the drastic change in job and skill needs in the technological society. The components of social change we have described enjoy only analytic distinctness. Still, only a society of mass-extended affluence can afford to support seven million people of peak physical capacities in college. Higher education, in the past an interest of only the few, has become a pursuit of a very large portion of the American population.

The affluent society expends sums the magnitude of which are totally without historical precedent on education and on research, and the groups organized around this sector have become major interest groups in the total society. In the 1930s, studies of interest groups, justifiably,

[6] Galbraith, *The Affluent Society,* p. 328.

focused on business, labor, and agriculture. In the 1970s, such studies cannot ignore the education and scientific "establishment." Total expenditures by all levels of government for education in 1936 were $2.365 billion. In 1950, they had risen to $15.098 billion. In 1965, the national, state, and local governments were spending approximately $35 billion on education. Expenditures for scientific research and development show this same massive growth. In 1940, all branches of the national government spent $74 million for "R and D." Two decades later, federal R and D expenditures had climbed to $7.277 billion, and in 1967 they exceeded $15 billion.[7]

The centrality of the position of the federal government in this R and D effort is revealed in its share of the funds expended. In 1965, of the $20.470 billion from all sources, $13.790 billion—67 percent—were federal monies.[8] As Galbraith points out, the costs of technological development have become high for even large corporations to assume, and have fallen to government: "the underwriting of sophisticated technology by the state has become an approved social function."[9] Education, research and development, sophisticated technology: in a society which is affluent and at a stage of advanced industrialism (and the two are but different sides of one coin), massive resources are here allocated, the state is the principal supplier of funds, and those interest collectivities organized around them are as representative of the interests and the interest group struggle as entrepreneurial business and trade unions were of an earlier time.

In an age of affluence, organized interests and various collections of individuals do not behave as past experience would lead us to expect them to behave; more to the point, they do not behave as their past position would have required. Organized labor, business, and the relationship between business and labor is a good case in point. Many observers have commented on the transformation of the American labor movement since World War II. Unions are weaker. In the decade after 1956, when the total non-agricultural employment in the United States increased by 12 million, trade union membership declined from 17.5 to 16.9 million. Thirty-five percent of the non-agricultural work force was

---

[7] These data are from U.S. Bureau of the Census, *Historical Statistics of the United States, Colonial Times to 1957* (Washington, D.C.: U.S. Government Printing Office, 1960, p. 613; and *Statistical Abstract of the United States, 1967* (Washington, D.C.: U.S. Government Printing Office, 1967), p. 538. The data exclude expenditures for research and development plant.

[8] *Statistical Abstract of the United States, 1967*, p. 537.

[9] John Kenneth Galbraith, *The New Industrial State,* (New York: New American Library, 1968), p. 174.

unionized in 1954, only 26.3% in 1968. But the weakening of unions involves more than numbers (which to a significant extent is accounted for by the growth in white-collar employment, since white-collar workers have remained generally resistant to the union appeals). Ultimately, the decline of American trade unions is rooted in the reduction of the dependency of workers upon them, and that in turn in affluence and in what affluence does to the primary institution with which unions deal, the business corporation.

In contrast to the situation in previous periods, a broad segment of business leadership is no longer antagonistic to the desires of workers to share—not to the same extent as business leaders, of course, but still to share—in national abundance. There are a number of reasons for this change, but the most basic is a new perception of economic reality which follows from experience with a society of affluence. The assumption that for workers to move to a position of relative economic well-being, business interests—specifically profits—must suffer can no longer be sustained. Indeed, the economy of an affluent society is such that the many must be relatively well off for business to prosper, since the enterprise is geared to the mass production of luxury goods. The highly paid manager of a well-established and secure corporation operating in the comfortable climate of an extremely wealthy society is far less hostile to the desire of workers to share in the good life than was the entrepreneur, operating in an economics of scarcity and, perhaps as important, from a mentality of scarcity. Thus, to a substantial degree the heat has gone out of labor-management relations. Businessmen have not become more saintly, more disinterested; rather, the shape of controlling interests has changed. Well-to-do workers confronting businessmen who are far from hostile are simply not as dependent upon unions, and the unions are denied an heroic role: "A fighting lawyer is a figure of great majesty before a hanging judge. His stature is less before one who places everyone on probation."[10]

The political position of unions changes in yet another way. In the 1930s, when they spoke for "have-nots," they were a force for change in American life. A couple of generations of American liberals grew up with a picture of labor unions as "liberal," "progressive," "change-oriented." And so they were. What we must see, however, is that a picture of "conservative" business resisting change to advance the welfare of "the people," and "progressive" labor backing such change has for the 1970s only the most limited validity. While there are still many

[10] Galbraith, *The New Industrial State*, p. 263.

poor people in the United States, they are not, for the most part, trade union members. A very large portion of the unionized labor force has changed status from "have-not" to at least marginal "have"; for this group, the victory over economic privation has been won. The price of the victory, if one chooses to call it a price, is that they are no longer in any regular or consistent way a force for change. The constituents of the American trade unions, in fact, are often prime opponents of equalitarian change, because demands for such change frequently seek to extend benefits to blacks. The frontier of popular change, then, no longer pits a white working class against a white middle class, but, typically, white lower and lower-middle strata against the black under-class. The new marginal haves find threats to their property and status in the demands of a great mass of urban, black have-nots. Their resistance ranges from passivity (refusal to strike alliances with Negro Americans) to a kind of popular reactionism. If, as Lipset and Raab argue, we see "rightist movements as those which have risen primarily in reaction against the displacement of power and status accompanying change; while left-wing [movements are] seen as impelling social change," then the white working class generally and the rank and file of trade unionists as a relatively privileged segment of the working class in the 1970s will commonly be on the right rather than the left.[11]

The picture must not be overdrawn, and it so easily can be. Trade unions and unionists have not suddenly been transformed into a massive and sustained movement for political reaction. A large majority supported the liberal Democratic nominee for president in 1968, for example, and can be expected to give such candidates important support in future elections. Trade union leaders, moreover, are often more receptive to demands for change than their membership, presumably because they have interests and perspectives closer to other high-status managers than to the rank-and-file worker. Still, there is ample evidence that trade unionists have in this age of affluence been transformed from change-oriented have-nots to change-resistant marginal haves, and as such provide substantive support for rightist candidates and movements. In 1968, George Wallace's reactionary right candidacy received strong support among union members, although the top union leadership were solidly against him and had some success in persuading their membership to return to their normal Democratic home. Table 6.1 shows the levels

[11] Seymour Martin Lipset and Earl Raab, *The Politics of Unreason: Right-Wing Extremism in America 1790–1970* (New York: Harper & Row, 1970), Chapter 1.

TABLE 6.1

Support for Presidential Candidates, 1968,
Among Occupational Groups and by Union/Non-union Membership;
Southerners and Nonwhites Excluded

OCCUPATION	CANDIDATE FAVORED*			UN-DECIDED/ OTHER/ NONE
	Humphrey	Nixon	Wallace	
NON-MANUAL (n = 431)	27	51	13	9
Professional (n = 152)	27	52	9	13
Business (n = 149)	26	51	16	7
Lower white collar (n = 130)	29	51	13	7
MANUAL (n = 456)	26	44	22	8
Skilled labor (n = 169)	28	45	20	7
Unskilled labor (n = 162)	26	39	25	10
Service workers (n = 52)	33	37	25	6
Farm (n = 73)	18	58	21	4
Union family (n = 212)	28	38	26	8
Non-union family (n = 244)	25	48	19	8
ALL RESPONDENTS (n = 1059)	48	28	15	8

	VOTED FOR**			Considered Wallace	TOTAL WALLACE SYMPA-THIZERS
	Humphrey	Nixon	Wallace		
NON-MANUAL					
(n = 350; 406)	42	53	5	5	10
Professional					
(n = 117; 133)	42	55	3	4	6
Business					
(n = 121; 144)	39	55	6	4	10
Lower white collar					
(n = 112; 129)	44	50	7	8	14
MANUAL					
(n = 327; 426)	49	42	9	13	22
Skilled labor					
(n = 171; 212)	47	46	7	13	21

Unskilled labor (n = 119; 162)	55	33	13	14	26
Service workers (n = 37; 52)	41	54	5	5	11
Farm (n = 57; 70)	21	77	2	16	18
Union family (n = 189; 234)	57	34	9	16	25
Non-union family (n = 138; 192)	39	52	9	8	17
ALL RESPONDENTS (n = 894; 1106)	44	49	7	8	15

* Source: Data from Gallup survey (AIPO) 768, September 17, 1968; made available by The Roper Center for Public Research, Williamstown, Mass.
** Data are from Gallup survey (AIPO) 771-k, November 7, 1968, as compiled by Lipset and Raab, Chapter X. (The *considered Wallace* category includes those who thought about voting for him earlier in the campaign but switched to another candidate. *Total Wallace Sympathizers* includes both those who voted for Wallace and those who considered voting for him. There are two *n*'s for each category: the first is of the number who voted, the latter of the total in the sample, upon which the *Sympathizer* percentage was compiled.)

of support for Wallace in the various categories of the labor force in 1968. The data are drawn from two Gallup surveys, one in September, the other following the election in November. Southerners have been excluded because Wallace had a far more substantial appeal in that region as a "local" candidate, and nonwhites for the obvious reason that since his candidacy was uniformly opposed by nonwhites, their inclusion could mask the factor being analyzed—his relative strength among whites in the various occupational groups.

Table 6.1 shows that about one-quarter of the respondents from union families favored Wallace in the pre-election survey, and about the same proportion in the post-election survey acknowledged either voting for him or having thought seriously of it. Wallace's support was markedly lower among white-collar workers, especially among those holding professional positions. While the vigorous activity of union leaders and the late surge by Humphrey joined with traditional Democratic loyalties to send many of the unionists back to the Democratic ranks, it is clear that Wallace—an Alabamian running on a third-party ticket with a reactionary right appeal—enjoyed strong support among working-class whites, especially those in trade unions, outside the South.

The position of labor is part of a broader pattern: popular forces are increasingly change-resisting rather than change-demanding. Mass-extended affluence has made the many positional conservatives. By bringing large numbers of people across the divide between have-not and have, it has muffled many of the tensions and conflicts of earlier industrialism.

New patterns in conflict. Affluence transforms patterns in societal conflict, but does not produce an end of conflict, or even necessarily a reduction in its intensity. For a long time it has been a polite cliche that "money doesn't buy happiness." In the late 1960s Americans began to discover that this polite cliche was actually true. An age of affluence generates new and historically unprecedented types of conflict and dissent.

For one thing, it presents a situation in which collections of very prosperous people play the role of dissidents, a role which in earlier periods of industrialism belonged mostly to the economically deprived and their spokesmen. At one large student demonstration on the campus of a major American university, an elderly matron was heard to exclaim with a mixture of surprise and dismay, referring to a leader of the Students for a Democratic Society (SDS) group which was spearheading the protest, "But he drives a Mercedes!" The incident is small, yet illustrative of something which will loom rather large. The shadow of Marx is a long one, and we find it hard to get from beneath it. "Real conflict is economic, between the rich and the poor, with the rich generally satisfied and the poor at least intermittently dissatisfied and producing the dissidence. Prosperous people are not supposed to protest." But in an age of affluence, when a large majority of the population are by any legitimate historical standard well off, and when conflict between the rich and the poor loses centrality, it is not at all surprising that groups of prosperous people, indeed very prosperous people, act as dissidents. There is nothing at all anomalous about drivers-of-Mercedes-qua-dissidents unless one assumes that the only "real" dissent is economic.

The reduction of classical economic tensions, for a large majority of the population, has had the result of opening the door to new tensions and concerns. One of these involves the problem of distinction. In scarcity-bound societies, the possession of wealth was (is) an important badge of distinction. If you have wealth, you know you are an important person and will continue to be such as long as you retain your wealth. If you are poor, but see a chance to become something other than poor, the accumulation of wealth is an avenue to prestige. But in a society of mass-extended affluence, wealth, unless extraordinary, is not a guarantor of distinction. The power of wealth today is circumscribed by the fact that obeisance cannot be commanded so readily when the many are relatively well off as when they are poor. The wealthy can indeed buy luxury goods, but the meaning of the possession of these is very different when they or comparable artifacts are broadly distributed through the society: the quip, "Why buy a Cadillac when you can get a Chevrolet for the same price?" conveys this precisely.

People get rewards, both psychic and material, from the possession of wealth. The point is only that when many are prosperous, being prosperous does not set you apart, and does not afford that sense of distinction and satisfaction which it did at earlier points in history. The reason that the affluent of scarcity-bound societies were not dissidents is that wealth conferred distinction. It set the possessor apart from the many, stamped him a person of privilege. Society at large knew it. He knew it. The affluent of an affluent society who act as dissidents do not, of course, do so because they are well off; their discontents are often quite outside the realm of economics. Rather, it is that their affluence *neither confers the satisfaction which would submerge other dissatisfactions nor creates the mentality of a privileged class ready to defend its position against all challengers.*

Affluence in one way increases dissatisfactions, and thus conflict, by contributing to a mentality of demand, an inordinately expanded set of expectations concerning what is one's due, a diminished tolerance of conditions less than ideal. Precisely because an affluent society can deliver so much, because its expanding resources create the impression that all good things are possible if only men honestly pursue them, because so many of the things which have vexed man historically and made his life "solitary, poor, nasty, brutish, and short" have been removed, the standards by which acts, conditions, and problems are judged to be "intolerable" have been dramatically enlarged or softened.

The intense unrest in American college campuses in the late 1960s is a complex phenomenon with many causes, but most observers conclude that it is intimately linked to affluence and the problem of distinction. Most investigations have found that the white dissidents (things are obviously very different for blacks) in the campus protests come not from the working class or the lower reaches of the middle class, from groups for whom the attainment of a college degree would be an important step up the social ladder, but rather from the more prosperous business and professional strata, from the upper reaches of the middle class.[12] Most of these "young radicals" have lived all their lives bathed in affluence, and have no experience in anything other than an affluent society (as do their parents). Since in the prosperous suburbs in which many were reared it was quite literally true that "everyone was well off," the condition of affluence was in no sense distinctive or distinguishing. The campus dissidents of the late 1960s are members of the first generation in history for whom both *affluent* and *mass* apply to the entirety of their social experience.

Not all the members of this group, of course, will play the role of dissidents; but neither is it likely that the challenges they have initiated will prove a "passing fancy." The challenges must be seen as part of the changing face of conflict in an affluent society, and specifically that part which occurs when individual affluence ceases to be a badge of distinction. It is sometimes said of young men and women today that "never in history has a generation been so much aware of such a wide array of problems, so sensitive to the gap between 'the calling and the coming' in American life." Without any thought of disparagement, it must be added that never in history has a generation had the luxury of being this sensitive. The sensitivity is real, probably will be heightened rather than diminished, and points to the way the affluent society, having resolved so many of the problems of earlier industrialism, becomes occupied with new ones.

The Technological Society

The notion of American society being transformed by entry into an advanced state of technological development is now commonly encountered; a whole spate of books attests to its wide frequency.[13] What is meant by a "technological society"? The common definition of technology, "the systematic knowledge of the industrial arts," doesn't help us very much. In that sense, it has been appropriate to speak of technology at least since the eighteenth century. What the concept suggests is the reaching of a point in the development of technology—both in its

[12] See, for example, Richard Flacks, "The Liberated Generation: An Exploration of the Roots of Student Protest," *Journal of Social Issues*, 23 (1967), pp. 52–75; and Richard Peterson, "The Student Left in American Higher Education," *Daedalus*, 97 (Winter, 1968), pp. 293–317.

[13] See, as two of the better recent expositions, Galbraith, *The New Industrial State;* and Peter F. Drucker, *The Age of Discontinuity* (New York: Harper & Row, 1969).

extent and in its sophistication—at which the difference from earlier periods cannot properly be described simply as "more." The quantitative progression produces qualitative change. The analogy of a small snowball at the top of an inclination gradual at the start and becoming ever steeper is not inappropriate. The ball of snow begins to roll, slowly at first, and with its small mass it grows but slowly; but as the mass enlarges and the inclination becomes steeper, its growth in size becomes extremely rapid. As it approaches the base of the hill, the innocent little snowball has become a fast-moving boulder of snow. In one sense, both the little ball and the boulder could be called snowballs, but a person in their respective paths could not fail to detect an immense difference. At what point did the little snowball become a boulder? At what point in the development of its technology did the United States become a technological society? The technological society is the payoff period for a century and a half of industrial growth and scientific development. The tools and know-how were accumulated through a process that was painfully slow at the outset. Both became increasingly extensive and elaborate, with a point being reached—in the United States apparently during and just after World War II—at which the "snowball" of technology became a boulder. Its mass had assumed dominating proportions, and its capacity for further growth and development far outstripped any prior capacity.

Stories are often told to illustrate this difference between snowball and boulder. James Conant relates that during World War I, as president of the American Chemical Society, he offered the services of the Society to Newton D. Baker, then secretary of war. He was told that these services would not be necessary since the War Department already had a chemist! And Conant also describes a board headed by Thomas Alva Edison, created to help the Navy, on which Edison placed one physicist because, as he told President Wilson, "We ought to have one mathematician fellow in case we have to calculate something out." Compare this to the reservoir of scientific and technical expertise committed to the weapons and defense efforts in the 1960s. A series of developments merge in the technological society: The manufacturing of new information reaches enormous proportions, as one reads of 50,000 technical journals publishing 1.2 million articles a year; the knowledge requirements of the society become such that extensive resources are committed to education, and what Daniel Bell calls a "vast new array of conglomerations of universities, research institutes, research corporations" become distinctive, even dominate social institutions.[14] The processes of continued technological development become enormously complex and expensive. Galbraith cites the $28,500 which it took to produce the first Ford in 1903 and compares that to the $60,000,000 which it took to engineer and tool up for the production of the first Mustang in 1964. The capacity to control the physical environment, when there is a will to do so and the consequent commitment of resources, appears almost without limit. "Things are in the saddle," Emerson wrote referring to a general materialism, "and they ride mankind." How much contemporary technology is in the saddle "riding mankind" through its sheer scale and complexity.

The technological society and the affluent society are, of course, inseparably linked; the distinction is analytic only. Affluence as defined in the preceding section is a function of a high stage of technological development. There are components of social change, however, which relate more directly to the extent and sophistication of technology than to the wealth which that technology produces, and it is these, and their impact on the political agenda, which we will be discussing in this section.

The Technological Society and Social Problems—the Old and the New

The technological society has the productive capacity, for the first time in history, to end mass economic privation. In it, most men no longer live lives dominated by hard physical labor. Leisure becomes available in abundance and the question is how to use it. The technological society has an unprecedented capacity for environment manipulation. Heat and cold, distance, disease—all, to a degree without historical parallel, succumb to its powers. It dangles before the population the bright baubles of its accomplishments. A complex national communications network, with television the most prominent component, brings *Petticoat Junction* into homes from Biloxi to Butte with (in 1966) more than 71 million television sets in 94 percent of the homes in the country each tuned in to a nationalized cultural package of an average of five hours and thirty-two minutes per day.[15] Electronic computers store and retrieve staggering quantities of information, and guide rockets with pinpoint accuracy. Space travel puts human beings on the surface of the moon. Biological manipulations are performed through which, to

[14] Daniel Bell, "The Post-Industrial Society," in Eli Ginsberg, ed., *Technology and Social Change* (New York: Columbia University Press, 1964), p. 44.
[15] The data are from *Television Fact Book* (Washington, D.C.: Radio News Bureau, 1967).

cite one example, embryos from the wombs of prize ewes are implanted in the womb of a rabbit, the rabbit flown across the Atlantic, and each embryo placed in the wombs of "host" ewes, who deliver in due time, literally, a herd of prize lambs.[16]

The technology is dazzling. Its extension and use have come to be of primary importance to the society. And both are extremely expensive. Thus government has come to be centrally involved in both the extension and use of technology: it underwrites, we have seen, much of the cost; it is intimately involved in its use, from weapons systems to efforts to resolve pressing domestic social problems. All this is new. Prior to World War II, developments in technology occurred "out there" in the private sector, with government only peripherally involved. "Big government" becomes the necessary adjunct of the technological society, for the state is the custodian of the advanced technology.

It is apparently a source of more than a little frustration and concern —sometimes precisely articulated, more often expressed in vague grumblings—that technology is not exclusively beneficent. It has, in fact, thrust upon the public sector in contemporary America new problems. While the scope of this subject goes far beyond our present concerns, it does seem important to suggest a few of these "new" problems since they figure prominently in the emergent political agenda.

The technological society is a society of massive scale: big bureaucratic structures, whether in business, education, or government; big metropolitan complexes as the distinctive residential setting; a massive national communications system; a definition of public problems and their resolution which requires large commitments of resources and puts them quite beyond the reach of individual action. In this technological society of scale and complexity, there appear frustrations involving the loss of a sense of individual control. Consider the middle-level executive who works for International Business Machines and lives in the greater New York City area. It is very, very hard for him to have the feeling that he controls in any way the major social institutions which affect his life. Contrast his situation to that of an equally representative denizen of an earlier America, a clerk in a general store in Skowhegan, Maine, in 1900, or a farmer near Oneonta, New York, in 1845. Certainly the latter didn't have greater control over matters national and global, but he did have greater control over the institutions and processes which directly and immediately affected him. Not only are the institutions with

[16] David M. Rorvik, "Making Men and Women Without Men and Women," *Esquire* (April, 1969), pp. 108–115.

which one deals typically much larger in the technological society than in earlier periods, but the environment with which one has to deal, which affects one's life, becomes vastly extended; this is in part what we mean when we speak of technology "shrinking the globe," or contributing to a powerful nationalization of life. It is technically possible, whether it ever occurs, for a decision made in Moscow to result, in a matter of minutes, in the destruction of Bismarck, North Dakota. Environmental pollution of remote origins can and does detract from the enjoyment of millions. In a small town an individual could see a fairly direct connection between his voice and vote on the one hand and governmental response on the other; he still has his voice and vote in the metropolitan region today, but the connection between these and any kind of governmental response has been stretched almost beyond recognition.

The problem of scale and individual control has important implications for the contemporary status of freedom of expression. In the West in the eighteenth century, the notion of freedom of expression received much more recognition than it had ever been given before. A picture of the necessary conditions for freedom of expression and the threats to it was clearly laid out. An individual was thus free when he was able to say or write what he wanted, and no governmental body would punish him or allow extralegal vigilantes to do so. What, in the eighteenth and nineteenth centuries, were the resources relevant to verbal communication? Since the electronic media had not been developed, a man could reach an audience limited by the distance which an unamplified human voice could carry. The resources of all men were roughly the same. The high and lowly, the rich and poor alike operated in essentially the same situation: the audience for a speech were the people—at the very most a few thousand—who could be collected in a hall, a square, or a field. The written word could carry further, but in eighteenth- and nineteenth-century America magazines and newspapers typically were small enterprises, requiring very modest capital and reaching audiences numbering at most in the several thousands. Things are very much changed now, with a communications technology that makes possible audience of millions. But this new technology requires vast resources, and is not accessible to most in the population. The Nielsen ratings for January-March, 1969, indicated that Walter Cronkite spoke nightly to over 15 million people, and David Brinkley and Chet Huntley to an audience nearly as large. How many Americans, equally aware politically and equally able to articulate their ideas, were denied access to the electronic media and thus able to communicate only to audiences numbering in the hundreds rather than the millions? The concern does not require that the television networks abuse the privilege granted them. Nor is it removed by the assertion that those with access to the media are a microcosm representing the views of the larger society. The point is simply that the resources required to compete effectively in the great democratic enterprise of political persuasion have been enormously extended in the technological society.[17]

There are indications that the political dimensions of reactions to scale, complexity, and the loss of a sense of individual control are becoming more prominent. College student radicalism is a case in point. The big, impersonal, bureaucratized, and change-resistant features of the society have been emphasized in the demands and rhetoric of the campus radicals. The student protests of the late 1960s were in part a reaction to the scale of the technological society, to the bureaucratized university, to the seeming impersonalization of life in the larger society, to the loss of personal control and the threat to personal identity that portends.

The problems which we have described can be thought of as unintended increments of technology. In promoting certain values as intended, there have been payoffs which were both unforeseen and unwanted. These unintended increments of technology are proving to be surprisingly numerous, and are occupying a prominent part of the emergent political agenda. Let us examine a few additional examples briefly.

The effluent society. One of the great triumphs of American technology is the mass production of motor cars; but these motor cars, by their very numbers, are polluting the atmosphere. Environmental pollution has become a major public problem.

Boredom. Throughout history leisure has been a value reserved to the very few. But technology extends it to many. While the precise social costs are hard indeed to estimate, there is little doubt that finding a rewarding use for leisure time is a problem for many, and that the search for an escape from boredom has become frenetic for more than a few.

Old age. The new technology has dramatically lengthened the life span of the average American by freeing him from harsh, unremitting toil, and through medical advances. But never in American history has the position of the elderly been so disturbing. For the old are func-

[17] The matter of the power and representativeness of the media became a major political flap in the fall of 1969 following speeches by Vice President Spiro Agnew. The basic problem outlined here, however, received relatively little consideration in that controversy.

tionally superfluous in the technological society. It doesn't need their labor. Their experience is often invalidated by the rapidity of change; where a half-century ago a grandmother still acted as a repository of folk wisdom, passing on sewing and cooking skills to her grandchildren, there is little of direct functional relevance that a grandmother in the 1960s can bestow. The rapidity of technical change means, typically, that the skills which the elderly of the contemporary period so carefully accumulated are of little relevance to the career lines and life styles of the young. It has not been uncommon in other societies for the relatively few who attained old age to be revered persons, revered because their experiential knowledge was a valued commodity. The technological society extends long life to many, but it consigns them to a life that is often wanting because of the knowledge that their labor is not needed and their technical skills are outdated.

The pangs of interdependence. The technological society is unique in the extent to which its many parts are complexly interrelated. This produces some unwanted byproducts. A relatively modest failure in electrical power equipment in Niagara Falls, New York, can plunge the entire Northeast into darkness. If a small group of fuel oil delivery men decide to strike in New York City, hundreds of thousands of persons may suffer very immediately and directly. How very different from a rural society, where if more fuel is needed one simply swings the axe a few more times. The strike by fuel oil delivery men is not, in itself, a very momentous event; but the society is so extensively integrated that it becomes magnified to serious proportions. These unintended increments of technology collectively loom large.

Science as an Ideology in a Civilisation Technecienne

In the technological society, the exponential growth of bodies of expert information, the increased complexity of public problems as they are defined before the society, and the emergence of a large class of high-status "brain workers" committed to the styles and orthodoxies of rationality and expertise elevate science to the status of a principal ideology offering systematic analysis and prescription as to the issues of public life. The division between the orthodoxies of science and the many varieties of earlier orthodoxies, which we can call "pre-science," becomes increasingly deep and fundamental to the conflict of the fourth agenda.

The political significance of this divide is beginning to be recognized. A conference is held to discuss problems of the central city and the need for metropolitan cooperation, and business executives, city managers, federal government officials, and college professors find they can readily accept a "scientific" statement of both the nature of the problems and how they should be met. They find, too, that differences among them as liberals and conservatives appear much less imposing than differences between them and those not sharing in this scientific view of urban problems. A conference is held to discuss the employment problems of Negro Americans, and again social scientists, bankers, antipoverty officials, and members of a state civil rights commission conceptualize the problem before them in the same way. They accept a "scientific" analysis of the causes of poverty in nonwhite America, and the "scientifically" valid solutions to it. What are the sources of poverty? The scientific orthodoxy speaks of the cycle of poverty; of a socialization of the children of the poor that stifles expectations, which is to say, crushes motivation; of cultural deprivation which is not met by welfare checks. It speaks of the difficulty in ending the cycle, and of the poor as victims not of the machinations of the rich but of the cycle itself. This analysis of cause commits to specific categories of social response. The older orthodoxies, on the other hand, hold up quite different pictures of the causes of poverty, portraying it largely in terms of redistribution. Such descriptions typically cut two ways: either poverty is seen as resulting from the hoarding of the rich, and hence as resolvable through redistribution, or the poor are depicted as victims of their own sloth and lack of talent, and their continuing efforts to take from the industrious the fruits of honest toil and thereby to destroy incentive are to be stoutly resisted. These older orthodoxies are not mere straw men. They are accepted by a large portion of the population.

The new scientific statement, like its earlier rivals, is essentially ideological: specifying responses to a wide range of major political problems that collectively define the "good society." It is shared by people from whom we have been taught to expect—and who until fairly recently did in fact reflect—sharply divergent ideological positions: for example, "conservative" corporation officials and "liberal" college professors. The scientific community is separated from those who do not comprehend the new orthodoxy by a very wide chasm, and this division intrudes with increasing frequency into major national problems.

The Collapse of the Public vs. Private Distinction

Liberal societies like the United States were built on a sharp differentiation between the public and the private sectors, with the former deliberately circumscribed or limited. The immediate experience of eighteenth-century liberals with the use of government power was the great centralizing monarchies of Europe. "Big government" at that time, then, evoked the image of powerful kings trampling the "traditional" rights of various constituent groups in the society. The answer of liberalism to the problem of power was to distribute it broadly, or *pluralize* it, and to restrict government to the essentially *negative* function of policing the society, seeing to it that no one of the various private groups got too strong and abridged the rights of others. There was to be a clear adversary relationship between government and the private sector; it was believed that the assumption of a function by government was on the face of it undesirable and required careful justification before it could be permitted.

As earlier chapters in this book have shown, a rigid circumscription of the public sector proved generally satisfactory in the early years of the United States, but became increasingly unsatisfactory with the immense concentrations of social and economic power in private hands following the advent of industrialization. The 1930s saw a concerted effort to redress the imbalance by expanding governmental activities as a "countervailing" force (and also by building up certain groups in the private sector, such as labor). Since "big business" was a fact of life in the industrial society, and since the pluralism of the society of limited scale was no longer possible, there would have to be a new pluralism operating at a far more rarified level of power, with "big government" and "big labor" keeping business in check.

Business and other groups which had come to profit from the earlier circumscription of the public sector not surprisingly resisted the expansion, and the question, "Should there be more or less governmental intervention?" became a primary source of argument in the agenda. But this argument between *public* and *private* is no longer primary, and the shape of political argument has been dramatically changed by this fact. "Statesmen simply no longer disagree about whether government should be involved; therefore they neither seek out the old criteria for guidance through their disagreements, nor do they really have need of the criteria to justify the mere governmental character of policies. . . . Obviously, the liberal-conservative dialogue made no sense after the establishment of the principle of positive government."[18]

Why is it that in the contemporary period "statesmen simply no

[18] Theodore J. Lowi, *The End of Liberalism* (New York: Norton, 1969), pp. 67ff.

longer disagree about whether government should be involved"? First, because it is apparent that the technological society, by the intricacy of its mechanisms, requires continuing supervision and regulation. Professors of economics, executives of the major American corporations, and trade union leaders are not in any basic disagreement over the primary importance of a large and continually expanding governmental responsibility for the maintenance of prosperity. Galbraith has described precisely the dependence of the present-day corporations on the state, contrasting this to the earlier entrepreneurial enterprise.

The entrepreneurial corporation, from public resources to favorable tariffs to tax concessions, had much to get from the state. And from adverse regulation and higher taxation it had considerable to lose. But apart from the provision of law and order which on occasion it supplied to itself, it was not deeply dependent on the government. The mature corporation by contrast depends on the state for trained manpower, the regulation of aggregate demand, for stability in wages and prices. All are essential to the planning with which it replaces the market. The state, through military and technical procurement, underwrites the corporation's largest capital commitments in the area of most advanced technology.[19]

There is no longer any pretense, among those close to the matter, that "private enterprise" should go its own way, with only a minimal "negative" involvement by the state. When Boeing Aircraft sells 65 percent of its output to the government, Raytheon 70 percent, Republic Aviation 100 percent; (or, to move from the business to the educational sector, when MIT, a "private" university, receives about 85 percent of its operating budget from the federal government), the distinction between *public* and *private* has indeed been violated.

There is yet another way in which the distinction has been blurred. Differences in the styles and procedures of big bureaucratic enterprises —whether government, a business, a university, or a foundation—are few. A large portion of that growing body of "brain workers" in the technological society spend their work lives in the generally comfortable interstices of large bureaucratic structures, and *public vs. private* does not appear especially useful in distinguishing their experiences. They come from similar backgrounds, pursue comparable training (in colleges and universities), and enter work relationships fundamentally the same. The late sociologist C. Wright Mills, in his argumentative but incisive *The Power Elite,* dealt extensively with this subject, although

[19] Galbraith, *The New Industrial State,* p. 308.

from a very different perspective from our own. Mills found in the United States an elite which "now make such key decisions as are made."[20] Those who command three principal institutional hierarchies —the military, the national government, and big business corporations— are not simply a collection of powerful men, but a cohesive and interacting elite; the cohesiveness and interaction, he saw based on "three major keys": (1) Similarities in social background and career lines; (2) Continuous social interaction or intermingling; and (3) Commonality of interests.[21] Without concerning ourselves with where Mills moves from them, we can accept his observations that the historic distinctions separating the military, private business, and government have been eroded by the similarities in the backgrounds, career lines, interests, and life styles of those who occupy these hierarchies. And what Mills describes for those at the top—the elite—appears to hold for a broad assortment of the professionals who man the middle levels as well.

Galbraith took this argument one step further when he observed that government officials, corporation executives, and university professors increasingly work for the same things, that is, share a common motivation. The question of what motivates people to work as they do is an exceedingly complicated one, but the basic point in Galbraith's argument can be handled here. He sees four principal inducements by which individuals can be brought to pursue the objectives of an organization, whatever it happens to be: (1) compulsion; (2) pecuniary motivation; (3) identification, whereby the individual comes to accept or identify with the goals of a group, considering them superior to his own; (4) adaptation, through which an individual commits himself to the work of an organization with the hope and expectation of bringing its goals more closely into accord with his own. In essence, Galbraith's conclusion is that the corporation president, the university professor and the high government official are all motivated by a mixture of identification and adaptation, and that neither compulsion nor pecuniary motivation are *central* for any of them.[22]

We can now come back and try to draw a number of strands together. The public vs. private distinction has collapsed, and there are a number of reasons for this. In the economy of the technological society, there is an extensive interpenetration of the public and private; specifically, business (private) is dependent upon the intervention of government (pub-

[20] C. Wright Mills, *The Power Elite* (New York: Oxford University Press, 1956; Galaxy Books, 1959), p. 28.
[21] *Ibid.*, pp. 19–20, 282–283.
[22] Galbraith, *The New Industrial State*, pp. 128–139.

lic) for a number of the key requisites of its operation. Men on both sides of the old distinction have so much in common: they work for similar kinds of organizations, follow similar career lines, are similarly motivated in their work lives. The massive bureaucratic similarities of the technological society do not deal kindly with the old polarity. The result is the emergence of a kind of corporate state, the end of the old adversary relationship between government and various institutions—principally business—of the private sector. Some of the old rhetoric survives—"the danger of big government," "creeping socialism," "the importance of private enterprise"—but the heat is gone. The question is, "Will the action help the interests I represent?" not, "Should it be conducted by the public or by the private sector?"

Class and Status: Changes in the Cutting Edge of Conflict

Social class has been used in a number of ways in different types of analyses. In one construction, *class* refers quite narrowly to economic position, to groups of people similarly situated in the gradations and sources of their incomes—how much they earn and where they earn it.[23] This is what we understand by the term here. *Class politics,* then, suggests a situation in which the struggle among various economic groupings defined in terms of amounts and sources of income occupies the primary or central place in the political agenda. *Social status,* like *class,* is not without ambiguities, but here it is understood to contain what Weber referred to as "a quality of social honor or a lack of it," in other words, social prestige or esteem.[24] Status and class, thus understood, are certainly not unrelated; as Weber observed, "social honor can stick directly to a class-situation. . . ."[25] The economic position which an individual occupies has a good deal to do with his standing or prestige in the society. But it is clear that a person's social status has many bases

[23] See C. Wright Mills, "The Social Life of a Modern Community," in Irving Louis Horowitz, ed., *Power, Politics, and People: The Collected Essays of C. Wright Mills* (New York: Ballantine Books, 1963), p. 41. Mills takes the sociologist W. Lloyd Warner to task for failing to distinguish between class and status. According to Mills, *class* (properly construed) "swallows up the sheerly economic in all of its *gradations* (amounts) and in all its *sources* (rentier, salaried, wage earner, *et al.*)," while status "points at the distribution of 'prestige,' 'deference,' 'esteem,' 'honor.' "

[24] Hans Gerth and C. Wright Mills, eds., *From Max Weber: Essays in Sociology* (New York: Oxford University Press, 1958), p. 405.

[25] *Ibid.*

other than his income, and satisfactions or dissatisfactions involving some component of status may have little if anything to do with economic position. *Status politics* calls attention to a situation in which people project anxieties about their social status onto political objects. Presumably there never has been a point in American history in which there were not individuals and groups to some extent in competition over status values, in which dissatisfaction with assigned status and demands to alter it did not account for some important part of the political conflict of the society. But the relative saliency of the class and status dimensions of conflict has varied.

In nineteenth-century America, class conflict, strictly defined, was muted. But status conflict was sharp and continuing. This isn't surprising when one notes the big waves of immigration which brought people of different cultural traditions to our shores. Protestants and Catholic, Irish and Yankee, "old" immigrant and "new," "wet" and "dry"—all point in a social and political sense to status groups frequently in conflict. Their struggles often had immediate economic components, but above all their differences were rooted in contrasting life styles, values, cultural attachments, associations—as these were promoted and threatened by developments in American life. Thus, as we have seen, nativist movements arose one after the other to resist "encroachments" by newcomers on the "American way of life." And new immigrants sought greater recognition.

The Depression inaugurated a period in which class politics became relatively more salient, through the combination of severe economic hardship existing in the midst of a major industrial system. The thirties did not produce "class warfare" in the United States, but the conflict between economically defined groups did come to dominate the political agenda, and business and labor were at opposite poles. *Liberal vs. conservative,* the conventional dichotomy, was the ideological statement of this form of class conflict.

Status Conflict

Increasing Saliency. In the affluent society, class tensions have declined markedly, and status-group conflict again occupies center stage. But the dimensions of status politics in the 1970s are very different from those in earlier periods. We can review the reasons for the extremely high saliency of status concerns in the contemporary society and the type of conflict they have generated.

American technology has made possible the reduction of the deepest economic tensions, giving more to many without taking from any through an unparalleled increase of productivity. But status remains in seriously short supply. We became aware that status values are relatively inelastic: to give greater recognition or prestige to one group is, to a significant degree, to take from another, since social status is a relational expression. This is not altogether the case, of course. The proliferation of titles and other such distinctions in bureaucratic organizations is an effort, and in part a successful one, to increase the supply of status values for distribution. But in general the point stands: economic values have proved in an age of advance technology to be far more elastic than status values, and it is easier to meet economic demands than to meet status demands.

Still other developments have combined to make social status and status concerns ever more consuming. (1) There is increased physical mobility, putting many Americans in a situation where they must convince those who have not known them over time of their worth. (2) Bureaucratization has made new occupational demands emphasizing the manipulation of people rather than the manipulation of things; and the new middle-class worker typically lacks the tangible testimony to his worth that the skilled artisan had. The measure of his success is the judgment of others that he is doing well. (3) There is a decline in the value of *experience,* as technology and life styles unfold so rapidly that the experience of two decades past frequently is an accumulation to be unlearned. Few can be certain that by assiduously building up a store of certain forms of experiential knowledge they will be assured of social recognition. (4) The new affluence has freed an increasing portion of the population from a preoccupation with economics, permitting them a preoccupation with status. In a scarcity-bound society, the vast majority were engaged in an endless struggle for food, clothing and shelter. But in the United States of the 1960s and 1970s, the majority are beyond subsistence concerns, and thus can "afford" to devote attention to matters of prestige or standing in the society.

Status Conflict

Blacks vs. Whites. Not all status concerns, of course, are politicized. But many are, and many of the really vexing political conflicts in the United States pivot on status anxieties. Those involving race are primary examples. The most persistent pressures for popular change in America come from blacks, and the weight of these—in housing and schools, for example—falls largely on the *common man* of the metropolitan region, the white person of marginal socioeconomic status. Who has something to lose from efforts to integrate a city school system by busing blacks into white areas? Not Chamber of Commerce executives, ensconced in $75,000 houses in two-acre zones in the suburbs, their children attending elite private schools. While this is putting it too crudely, it is clear that demands for change in the metropolitan region thrusts status concerns to the fore, and thereby bifurcate metropolitan political elites. In a study conducted in Hartford, Connecticut, in the 1960s, we found the Chamber of Commerce urging such programs and projects as low-rent, integrated housing, setting up a corporation to promote it; the busing of black children from declining neighborhoods in the city to schools outside, including suburban schools; greater employment opportunities for blacks; and much greater expenditures for public schools in the city. The columnist Stewart Alsop visited Hartford and wrote a piece for the *Saturday Evening Post* in which he warmly praised the Hartford Chamber. They "have begun to talk like a bunch of damn New Deal spenders," and in this there is great hope for urban America. If cities are to be saved, Alsop concluded, it will be only with the help of enlightened business communities like Hartford's. Businessmen had not suddenly lost sight of their economic interests. Rather it is that in an age of affluence status remains in seriously short supply, and many perplexing domestic problems come to hinge around status concerns; in this situation, those of secure status—and corporation officials are but one group —can afford to be and so become the "progressives," while those of marginal status must resist this "progress." Spokesmen for the white lower and lower-middle classes insist that Negroes should "stay where they belong." And corporation officials find themselves cast in what is for business historically an anomalous role; they become, perhaps in spite of themselves, a socially progressive force.

Conflict between blacks and whites cannot be described solely in terms of social status: there is a quite specific economic dimension, and many in both groups fear that members of the other will inflict physical harm upon them. But the intensity of the division between blacks and whites cannot be understood unless reference is made to their conflicting status claims. Black Americans, as the low group on the American status ladder want to move up, want greater recognition and acceptance.[26] Many whites, in turn, resent and resist the demands by blacks for freer

[26] As demands for integration into the larger society have been stymied, and as advances have increased group confidence and security, there has come to be a greater pride in their cultural distinctiveness among blacks, but this in no way contradicts the argument that enhanced social status is the objective.

entry. A black skin has been made the principal badge of low social status in the United States. In view of this and the extreme sensitivity of the population to status concerns, it is little wonder that integration, whether of schools or neighborhoods, is often so fiercely resisted. The entry of blacks into a neighborhood is a threat to the status of those residing there.

In their valuable little study, Harry and David Rosen describe an attempt to build an integrated housing subdivision in a prosperous Chicago suburb, Deerfield.[27] An organization committed to integrated housing planned to build in Deerfield a fifty-one-house subdivision, with about one-fourth of the houses to be sold to blacks. The houses were to be expensive, and their purchasers would, regardless of color, be of the professional and business classes. The authors describe the intense reaction of this prosperous northern suburb to so limited an attempt at residential integration. Mass protest meetings were held, pamphlets charging a Communist conspiracy circulated, supporters of the subdivision hounded, scurrilously racist documents brought out; and in the end the town of Deerfield decided, by a vote of 2,635 to 1,207, that it needed a park where the subdivision was to be built, and the land was taken for that purpose. How does one explain this reaction? The residents of Deerfield were generally well educated. They were successful people economically, in no sense threatened by the blacks who would move in. There was no substantive basis for fear of a change in the class composition of the community, since the proposed subdivision was to contain expensive homes. The residents of Deerfield were a cross-section of young corporation executives, drawn from all over the United States. It seems impossible to account for the reaction without noting that in the type of society we occupy, people are especially sensitized to status concerns, and blacks are the outstanding symbol of low social status.

Status Conflict

Students. The conflict between blacks and whites is highly salient, but it is not the only instance of conflict between groups defined essentially in status terms. In the late 1960s, protests on college campuses became common occurrences; and as complicated as the matter of their sources is, we get some insights if we view students as a status group.

Higher education has been, for the most part, an elite affair. Even in

[27] *But Not Next Door* (New York: Avon Books, 1962).

the United States, where colleges and universities were established in the nineteenth century as part of the working out of egalitarian and democratic notions,[28] only a very small portion of the college-age population were enrolled before World War II: less than 2 percent in 1870, about 5 percent in 1910, and 16 percent of those aged 18–21 in 1940.[29] The 1.5 million college students in 1940 were still a relatively distinctive or privileged group.

All this was changed by the end of the 1960s, when more than 7 million were in college. There had been a steady growth of enrollment in the first decade after World War II; by 1956, the proportion of those aged 18–21 who were in college was 30 percent, twice what it had been in 1940. Since 1956, the proportion has continued to rise, although more slowly, reaching 34 percent in 1968. But the base of college-age Americans increased so extensively (as the bumper post-war baby crop grew up) that the number enrolled jumped phenomenally: from 2.6 million in 1956 to 3.6 million in 1960, 5.5 million in 1965, and 7.1 million in the fall of 1969. Here, in little more than a decade, was the massification of American higher education.

The student graduating from a college in 1970 could not be assured, as his counterpart in 1910 could, that some position of *relative* economic privilege was awaiting him. The problem of "What will I do now that I am a college graduate?" is especially acute for the large number of liberal arts graduates who lack specific technical skills. They may know that there are positions for them in the burgeoning ranks of white-collar employees, but most of these positions are in no sense special either in salary or prerogatives, and they possess no skills better equipping them for these than millions of their fellow graduates. They are a mass without special skills, looking to very ordinary positions in large bureaucratic institutions.

Just as the outside world which awaits college graduates in the 1970s

[28] Jencks and Riesman observe that "nineteenth-century Americans grouped themselves by occupation, social class, religion, sex, locality, and ethnic background, among other things. As the century wore on almost all these groups felt impelled to set up their own colleges, both to perpetuate their distinctive subculture and to give it legitimacy in the larger society. By 1900 there were special colleges for Baptists and Catholics, for men and women, for whites and blacks, for rich and not-so-rich, for North and South, for small town and big city, for adolescents and adults, for engineers and teachers" (Christopher Jencks and David Riesman, *The Academic Revolution* [Garden City, N.Y.: Doubleday, 1969], pp. 2–3).

[29] These data are from U.S. Bureau of the Census, *Historical Statistics of the United States,* pp. 210–211; and *Current Population Reports,* Series P-20, No. 190.

receives them as mass rather than as elite, so the institutions which they attend, typically, treat them as mass. The enormous increase in the number of people attending colleges and universities has meant a growth in the size of individual institutions of higher education. Where the typical college of a half-century ago was small, permitting extensive face-to-face contact of faculty and students, the representative university of the 1970s has an enrollment of between 10,000 and 35,000 students, with a faculty numbering in the many hundreds to several thousands. The atmosphere, because of this element of scale, is highly impersonal, and it is little wonder that many college students complain that they are simply numbers on IBM cards, small cogs in a large bureaucratic enterprise. The faculty members with whom they deal are more and more caught up in research and administrative responsibilities, and give relatively little personal attention to them. "There can be little doubt," Lipset writes, "that undergraduate students, as such, are of much less concern to the faculty and administration than in earlier periods of American education."[30] There is indication this treatment clashes sharply with expectations, especially of that segment of the student body who come from families of upper SES position.[31] Affluent, having been treated with indulgence, their importance repeatedly affirmed by the rhetoric of the society, they find themselves in institutions where they are part of a great mass, to a significant degree ignored or dealt with impersonally by the faculty, and looking forward to careers for which they can claim no special skill, without any assurance that they will be set apart as people of some importance or distinction.

Along with the massification of what was historically an elite enterprise, and in a direct sense because of it, the university has become more competitive and meritocratic.

. . . it is how well you do, rather than who you are that counts. Hence, young people in a society in which education increasingly determines how well they start in a struggle for place, find themselves facing a highly competitive situation. The pressures to conform to the requirements of the education establishment begin for many middle-class and aspiring working-class youth in elementary school and intensify in high school. Hard work

[30] Seymour Martin Lipset, "American Student Activism," in Philip G. Altbach, ed., *Student Politics and Higher Education in the United States: A Selected Bibliography* (Cambridge, Mass.: Harvard Center for International Affairs, 1968), p. 7.

[31] See, for example, Richard Flacks, "The Liberated Generation: An Exploration of the Roots of Student Protest," *Journal of Social Issues,* 23 (1967), pp. 52–75.

and ability at each level only serve to qualify the individual to enter an even more difficult competition at the next rung in the educational ladder. While some succeed, many must show up as mediocre or must rank low.[32]

The student admitted to a good college in 1928 or even 1950 had made it. Today, his counterpart faces prolonged indeterminancy with regard to his standing in the larger society.

In addition to the problems described above, which seem quite new, there is an old ambiguity in college students' status. There are in any instance, Lipset notes, "marginal men . . . in transition between having been dependent on their families for income, status and various forms of security and protection, and taking up their own roles in jobs and families."[33]

The resultant tensions and dissatisfactions relating to status do not in themselves *produce* student radicalism, but they do contribute importantly to the setting in which so many economically well-off students are psychologically prepared for the role of dissident.

The Established, the Disestablished, and the Nonestablished

We find a disparate collection of Americans with status grievances or dissatisfactions in this age of status politics. They can be thought of as the "disestablished" and the "nonestablished." The "disestablished" include those of the old middle class who have been displaced by some of the primary thrusts of contemporary change, who find so many of the styles and values to which they are attached severely challenged; while the "nonestablished" are those, like blacks, who have never enjoyed high standing in American society. In this construction, the "establishment" becomes those whose technical competence and/or positions in well-established enterprises assure them high social prestige and position.

Conflict typically does not pit the established against the disestablished and the nonestablished, but instead various groups within the disestablishment and nonestablishment against one another, with the establishment looking on, protecting its own interests, occasionally siding with one or another of the contending groups. The various movements of the disestablished and the nonestablished fail partly because they confront at some point the opposition of the establishment and its extensive resources—its command of the major institutions, including the media of communications, business corporations, the executive branch of the national government, the education enterprises—but also because they

[32] Lipset, "American Student Activism," p. 4.
[33] *Ibid.*

cannot work together. What holds one segment together assures that the rest cannot enter a coalition with it. To those seeking revolution in America this proposition can be put: Find some way of making the disparate assortment of the status dissatisfied—including radical students, blacks, and Wallacites—a *coalition,* and success may be yours. But such a coalition does not now appear in order.

Groups within the nonestablished and the disestablished are engaged in bitter and continuing conflict. In these struggles, the established sometimes find threats to their own position: how many leaders of the major business corporations or professors at prestigeous universities would welcome the election of George Wallace to the presidency? At other times, they side with one segment of the disestablished and non-established against another. An example is the uneasy alliance of the leadership of big business and of the black poor on behalf of urban programs opposed by the white lower-middle and working classes. Conflict is sharply altered and political alliances transformed in an age of status politics, as those of secure status intervene selectively in the internecine struggles of the disestablished and the nonestablished.

The New "Political Class": Style, Power, and Public Philosophy

Our notion of "political class" as discussed in the earlier chapters originates in the fact that through long periods of American history certain loose socioeconomic groupings can be identified whose political styles, interests, values, and expectations were controlling for the society.

Interestingly enough, the socioeconomic group which has emerged as the political class of the contemporary period was not seen as one of the principal contenders for influence in the 1930s, and that fact is testimony to the extent of social change. The new class has been described in a number of ways. James Burnham was one of the first to note its ascendancy in his book *The Managerial Revolution.* "Professionals and managers," "new middle class," or the several nouns which John Kenneth Galbraith has attached to its components including "technostructure" and "educational and scientific estate" all refer, if imprecisely, to the same general phenomenon. "Brain workers" occupying professional and managerial positions in the major bureaucratic structures of contemporary American society are as clearly the political class of the new society as farmers were in the America of the first agenda or entrepreneurial businessmen in the second.

Having said this we must acknowledge that the boundaries of this new class are hard to locate precisely. Two decades ago, C. Wright Mills noted that one of the reasons why it was so difficult to come to grips with the question of the behavior of the "new middle class" was the vague nature of its boundary lines: "We can easily understand why such an occupational salad invites so many conflicting theories and why general images of it are likely to differ. There is no one accepted word for them; white collar, salaried employee, new middle class are used interchangeably."[34] Certainly this is the case; in a society like our own, "white-collar workers" is as vaguely inclusive as "manual workers" was in 1875.

We can be somewhat more precise in referring to the boundaries of the socioeconomic group whose political interests and styles, and expectations about and general orientations to public policy, appear to be generally ascendant in contemporary America. Galbraith is helpful when he describes the composition of the "technostructure":

This latter group is very large; it extends from the most senior officials of the corporation to where it meets, at the outer perimeter, the white and blue collar workers whose function is to conform more or less mechanically to instruction or routine. It embraces all who bring specialized knowledge, talent or experience to group decision-making. This, not the management, is the guiding intelligence—the brain—of the enterprise. There is no name for all who participate in group decision-making or the organization which they form. I propose to call this organization the Technostructure.[35]

Closely associated with the technostructure is a large and growing body of educators and research scientists, "the educational and scientific estate." For Galbraith, the "technostructure" and "the educational and scientific estate" collectively comprise the principal components of the new political class.

There still can be no exact set of boundaries for this class; there is not, in some mysterious way, a line which runs between those who are in and those who are out. It cannot be said that the ascendancy of this group is so clear that its interests and orientations are always controlling, or that it is sufficiently cohesive so its interests and orientations can always be located. But our argument does not require these. The United States has become what Giovanni Sartori called a *civilisation tech-*

---

[34] C. Wright Mills, *White Collar* (New York: Oxford University Press, 1951), p. 291.
[35] Galbraith, *The New Industrial State*, p. 71.

necienne, a technological civilization. In this kind of society there is an enormous expansion of certain types of work activity which involve, principally, management and the production and distribution of knowledge; this activity goes on disproportionately in large bureaucratic structures, including those of government, education, and business. Illustrative occupations include corporation, university, foundation, and government managers; scientists and related technicians; engineers; professors—a broad professional and managerial stratum. Since we find Galbraith's *technostructure* somewhat pretentious and imprecise, it seems more to the point to describe it as we have, as a professional and managerial stratum in the technological society. Broad and disparate as this collectivity is, its members seem to have enough in common to permit it to be considered a class; and in numbers, strategic location, and expertise it has sufficient influence to make its political styles, interests, and orientations controlling. It is the *political class* of contemporary America.

Commonalities

What is the basis for suggesting that members of the professional and managerial stratum have enough in common to give them a reasonably coherent social and political role? First, there is the matter of motivation. Galbraith notes that one of the principal characteristics of contemporary economic life is the similarity in the motivations or reasons for work performance of men of ideas and men of business. The sources of their work commitments are now to be found—and this could not have been said for their counterparts a half-century ago—in "identifications" and "adaptations."

With the rise of the technostructure, relations between those associated with economic enterprise and the educational and scientific estate undergo a radical transformation. There is no longer an abrupt conflict in motivation. Like the educational and scientific estate, the technostructure is no longer exclusively or perhaps even primarily, responsive to pecuniary motivation. Both see themselves as identified with social goals, or with organizations serving social purposes. And both, it may be assumed, seek to adapt social goals to their own.[36]

Those of the professional and managerial stratum are, typically, employees rather than owners or persons self-employed; their careers are spent in the fairly comfortable interstices of big bureaucracies. Their jobs involve the manipulation of people and ideas, not the manipulation

[36] *Ibid.,* p. 288.

of things. They are, then, brain workers. They share long, formal exposure to higher education, which means not simply having attended college, but more importantly training and experience in the handling of abstract ideas. The college professor and the corporation vice president, upon meeting, find, often to their mutual surprise, that they "talk the same language," in large measure because both have been trained in and accept the legitimacy of discourse involving abstract ideas. Their educational backgrounds incline them to a similar "scientific" analysis of most of the major public problems. They are among the relatively affluent (although there are very substantial gradations in income within this stratum), and more importantly, perhaps, share in a "mentality of affluence" rather than a "mentality of scarcity." The Carnegie Foundation; the University of Pennsylvania; the Department of Health, Education, and Welfare; and General Electric are all well-established corporate entities, and the managers and professionals attached to them have no reason to doubt their continued prosperity.

As persons whose careers are rooted in big bureaucratic enterprises, they do not fear bigness in the society or specifically in government. "Big government" is not a bugaboo of the professional and managerial stratum. The research scientist, the academician, and the corporate official alike look to government as a supplier of resources and as a guarantor of continued prosperity. Unlike entrepreneurial business in the past, the managerial and professional stratum does not see the good society as produced by atomistic competition, but rather by careful planning and regulation among large-scale enterprises whose existence cannot be put in jeopardy by traditional competition.

Again, there is no suggestion that the members of this professional and managerial stratum always are in agreement, only that there are impressive commonalities. These arise from similarities in training, patterns of motivation, occupational demands and styles, information and conceptualizations with regard to public life and its problems, positions which guarantee both continued affluence and high social status. Whether one is inclined to view this with alarm or with satisfaction, there should be a continuation, indeed an accentuation, of the similarities in political style, interests, and orientation of those in the professional and managerial stratum.

Influence

The position of the professional and managerial stratum as the ascendant political class results from its size, its strategic location and the expertise it commands. This stratum has grown tremendously since World War II. Table 6.2 shows the changes in size of the entire labor force over the seven decades of the present century, and the growth and decline of various of its components both in absolute numbers and as a percentage of all those employed. Between 1900 and 1969 the labor force increased by about 250 percent. But various subgroups had very different experiences as the fabric of the American economy changed.

The number of blue-collar workers increased at about the same rate as the whole labor force, and their proportion was roughly constant. The number of farm workers, which as a proportion of the total labor force had been declining since 1800, began an absolute decline after 1910, relatively slow at first but precipitous after World War II. About 11.5 million people were employed in agriculture in 1910, 7 million in 1950, and only 3.5 million in 1968.

As the number of blue-collar workers held to a steady proportion and that of farmers declined sharply, the big gains were in white-collar employment, which increased by 700 percent. Wearing a white collar is too vaguely inclusive, however; the boundaries of the professional and managerial stratum and its extraordinary growth are revealed by the four remaining categories in Table 6.2. The census headings "professional and technical" and "managers, officials (salaried)" give us aggregate data with the closest fit to the stratum as we envision it. In 1968, more than 16 million persons—better than one-fifth of the labor force—were in such occupations. In 1900, only 6 percent were thus employed, and in 1940 just 10.5 percent, so the expansion has been largely a post–World War II phenomenon. By the end of the 1960s, the professional and managerial stratum had by sheer weight of numbers become a major force. College and university professors and engineers are included in Table 6.2 to illustrate the extraordinary post-1945 growth of specific scientific and technical occupations. There were only 38,000 engineers of all sorts in the United States in 1900, 297,000 in 1940; but at the end of the 1960s, there were 1.2 million professional engineers. College and university professors have had a similar growth curve: 24,000 in 1900, 147,000 in 1940, and more than 600,000 in 1968.

But numbers are not the only or even the primary source of influence. More important is the command of the principal institutional hierarchies of the technological society. This control is not an abstraction; it manifests itself in resources which are brought into play in struggles with other groups. Economic power, of course, is one of these resources, but there are others, such as control of the communications media. Those

TABLE 6.2

Selected Occupational Groups in the United States,
Number in Thousands and Percentage of the Labor Force,
1900–1968*

YEAR	TOTAL EMPLOYED	BLUE-COLLAR	AGRICULTURE	WHITE-COLLAR	PROFESSIONAL AND TECHNICAL	MANAGERS, OFFICIALS, (SALARIED)	FACULTY IN HIGHER EDUCATION	ENGINEERS
1900	(29,030)	35.8 (10,401)	37.5 (10,888)	17.6 (5,115)	4.3 (1,234)	2.0 (1,569)**	0.1 (24)	0.1 (38)
1910	(37,291)	38.2 (14,234)	30.9 (11,533)	21.4 (7,962)	4.7 (1,758)	2.9 (1,065)**	0.1 (36)	0.2 (77)
1920	(42,206)	40.2 (16,974)	27.0 (11,390)	25.0 (10,529)	5.4 (2,283)	2.8 (1,176)**	0.1 (49)	0.3 (134)
1930	(48,686)	39.6 (19,272)	21.2 (10,322)	29.4 (14,320)	6.8 (3,311)	2.9 (1,495)**	0.2 (82)	0.5 (217)
1940	(51,742)	39.8 (20,597)	17.4 (8,994)	31.1 (16,082)	7.5 (3,879)	3.0 (1,548)**	0.3 (147)	0.6 (297)
1950	(59,999)	40.4 (24,266)	11.6 (6,953)	36.0 (21,601)	8.5 (5,081)	4.2 (2,499)	0.4 (247)	0.9 (543)
1960	(66,681)	36.3 (24,211)	8.1 (5,395)	43.1 (28,726)	11.2 (7,475)	5.3 (3,514)	0.6 (381)	1.3 (864)
1968	(75,920)	36.3 (27,524)	4.6 (3,464)	46.8 (35,551)	13.6 (10,325)	7.2 (5,466)	0.8 (615)†	1.6 (1192)

* Source: U.S. Bureau of the Census, *Historical Statistics of the United States*, pp. 74–75; U.S. Bureau of the Census, *Statistical Abstract: 1969* (Washington, D.C.: U.S. Government Printing Office, 1969), p. 223; U.S. Office of Education, *Digest of Educational Statistics, 1968* (Washington, D.C.: U.S. Government Printing Office, 1968), p. 69.

** These figures are estimates derived from Table Series D 72–122, *Historical Statistics*.

† U.S. Office of Education, *Projections of Educational Statistics to 1976–77* (Washington, D.C.: U.S. Government Printing Office, 1968), Table 30, p. 57.

who do not command the electronic media of communications or the mass circulation newspapers and magazines are severely disadvantaged in struggles over public policy. What would have been the fate of the candidacy of George Wallace if the major national media had not been overwhelmingly hostile? What would have happened if they had supported him as strongly as in fact they opposed him? And it must be seen that the opposition of those who command the media to Wallace's candidacy was generic, not personal: they can be counted upon to oppose any such candidacy in any election in the foreseeable future. In 1964, Barry Goldwater was badly defeated as the Republican nominee for the presidency, and surely the widespread hostility of the national communications elite was an important factor. In a case study of public policy formation in one American city, Hartford, Connecticut, we found that those who control the principal media of communication—the mass circulation newspapers and radio and television—regularly sided with other segments of the professional and managerial stratum in the big public policy struggle.[37] That is, *the communications elite tends to reflect the policy judgments of the larger professional and managerial stratum of which it is a part, and functions as a key resource of that stratum.*

The Parties and the Emergent Society

The party system erected in the 1930s has not emerged unscathed from such massive transformations of American society. Here, we take a look at one important set of changes—in the social group composition of the party coalitions. Who are the Democrats and the Republicans in mass constituency terms? How do the parties' respective constituencies differ today from what they were in the 1930s, 1940s, and 1950s? What strains and tensions have resulted from the continued presence in the party coalitions of groups which now stand in a very different relationship than when their *de facto* alliance was first consummated?

The Parties and the Middle Class, Old and New

In the 1930s and 1940s, and into the 1950s, lower-class Americans were Democratic by decisive margins, while those in the middle and

[37] Everett Carll Ladd, Jr., *Ideology in America: Change and Response in a City, a Suburb, and a Small Town* (Ithaca, N.Y.: Cornell University Press, 1969), especially Chapters V and VIII.

upper reaches of the middle class were as decisively Republican. The polarization of these income and occupation groups never was complete —that is, it never approached 100–0—but within the American context of big umbrella parties drawing support from all ranks of the population, it was notable. In fact, recognition that there was a connection between class (or, more generally, SES) and party loyalty became so firmly implanted that many came to think of the relationship as "natural" or likely to persist substantially unchanged. One result was the interpretation commonly encountered in the late 1940s and the 1950s that the growing affluence of the United States, permitting more and more people to move up into the middle class, was inexorably advancing the cause of Republicanism.

This often surfaced in discussions of suburbanization and Republicanism. The suburbs are after all, quintessentially, the home of the new middle class, and their tremendous growth since World War II is testimony to the prodigious expansion of the new middle class. So the argument circulated that the Republican party would ride a suburban wave to victory. In one ecstatic moment in 1952, Republican Senator Robert A. Taft decreed that "the Democratic party will never win another national election until it solves the problem of the suburbs." And it was not only Republican politicians who succumbed to this rosy view. In April, 1957, *Newsweek* declared that "when a city dweller packs up and moves his family to the suburbs, he usually acquires a mortgage, a power lawnmower, and backyard grill. *Often, though a lifelong Democrat, he starts voting Republican.*"[38] And William Whyte observed a bit mystically: "Whatever the cause, it is true that something does seem to happen to Democrats when they get to Suburbia. Despite the constant influx of Democrats the size of the Republican vote remains fairly constant from suburb to suburb."[39]

That "something" which allegedly happened to Democrats in suburbia was in fact, of course, the converting power of high SES. If being a Democrat and having high SES are in some way contradictory, then the move to suburbia which symbolizes a rise in socioeconomic status should precipitate a conversion to Republicanism. Various arguments were made explaining this alleged conversion of Democrats. The one most commonly encountered focused on social status. Children of the "tenement trail," upwardly mobile, arrive in suburbia. Having achieved

---

[38] *Newsweek*, April 1, 1957, p. 42. (Emphasis added.)

[39] William Whyte, *The Organization Man* (New York: Simon and Shuster, 1959), p. 300.

a new and augmented social status, they seek the various symbols and attachments appropriate to it. The older ethnic identifications and big-city associations are sloughed off, and the suburbanite becomes more receptive to the appeals of that respectable upper-status party, the Republicans. Another explanation of conversion depicted suburbs as breeders of conservatives. By moving to the suburb, becoming home-owners and sharing in property tax worries, many Americans were thought to develop an attachment to "financial responsibility" and thereby to the more "responsible" of the two parties. Suburbanites as people of high SES were naturally more conservative, and the GOP was the more conservative party.[40]

Conversion thus postulated was not implausible. As careful an observer as Edward Banfield assumed a 60 percent Republican suburban plurality; he hence predicted that the Democrats' electoral advantage in metropolitan areas would disappear shortly after 1956, and, further, that by 1975 the imbalance between city and suburban populations would be so great that the Republican metropolitan plurality would exceed 2 million.[41] But we now know that the conversion statement, so plausible in many regards, was wrong. The source of the error was in assuming that the relationship between socioeconomic status and party identification would persist: specifically, that the marked preference of the middle class in the 1930s for the Republican party would be duplicated in the vastly larger middle class which developed after 1950.

Perhaps the most obvious indication that it didn't persist is the fact that with the great advances of the American population in income and related aspects of social position since World War II, the Democrats' margin over the Republicans in voter loyalty did not narrow; in fact, it became somewhat greater. Figure 6.2 shows the distribution of the electorate in party identification, and two social indicators which point to the growth of the middle class since 1940.[42]

40 Louis Harris, *Is There a Republican Majority?* (New York: Harper & Brothers, 1954) presents one of the more complete statements of conversion. See also Harry Gersh, "The New Suburbanites of The Fifties," *Commentary,* 17 (March, 1954), p. 217; and Frederick Lewis Allen, "The Big Change in Suburbia," Part II, *Harper's,* July, 1954, p. 50.

41 Edward Banfield, "The Changing Political Environment of City Planning" (paper delivered at the American Political Science Association Meeting, 1956).

42 The basic data on party identification are from the Gallup and SRC surveys as reported in Figures 5.5 and 5.6 in Chapter 5. For 1940–1950, the data are Gallup; for 1952–68, SRC. SRC data are not available for the former period. Our extremely high regard for the SRC investigations leads us to utilize their findings when available. The only other change has resulted from a recomputing of percentages, excluding independents; that is, the Democratic and Republican percentages in Figure 6.2 of this chapter are based on an N of major party identifiers

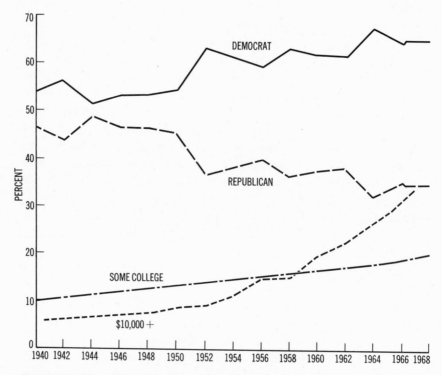

Figure 6.2. Party Identification and the Growth of the Middle Class, 1940–1968

Clearly these data allow us to draw just one limited observation, but it is an important one: that from 1940 through the end of the 1960s, a burgeoning affluence drew a growing proportion of the population into a socioeconomic position commonly referred to as middle-class, with the percentage of families earning over $10,000 and the portion of the population over twenty-five having attended college fairly representative indicators; and as the middle class thus expanded, the Democrats' margin over the Republicans in voter loyalty *not only did not shrink but actually increased.*

A closer look at the partisan identifications of the various socioeconomic groups confirms what Figure 6.3 suggests, that the Democrats in

---

only. This seemed useful since we are now interested strictly in the relative Republican and Democratic strength in the electorate. The percentage of families with annual incomes of $10,000 and higher (in 1962 dollars) is from the U.S. Bureau of the Census, unpublished data. Data on the proportion of the adult population having attended college have been computed from *Statistical Abstract of the United States 1966* and from *Current Population Reports,* Series P-20, No. 182, April 28, 1969. The data are for 1940, 1950, 1960, 1965, and 1968 only.

TABLE 6.3

Party Identification of Income Strata, 1952 and 1968*

1952	OVER $7,500 (1952)	$4,000–7,500 (1952)	UNDER $4,000 (1952)
	(Percent)	(Percent)	(Percent)
Republican	40	29	26
Democrat	24	48	54
Independent	36	23	20

1968	OVER $10,000 (1968)	$,5000–10,000 (1968)	UNDER $5,000 (1968)
	(Percent)	(Percent)	(Percent)
Republican	27 (−13)	26 (−3)	22 (−4)
Democrat	39 (+15)	46 (−2)	56 (+2)
Independent	34	28	22

* These data are from the SRC 1968 Election Study, made available through the Inter-University Consortium for Political Research.

the 1960s were much stronger among the middle class than they had been two decades earlier, that as the middle class grew so did the Democratic strength in the middle class. Table 6.3 shows the party identification of voters in the several income strata in 1952 and in 1968. The strengthening of the Democratic position among those with incomes of the middle and higher range is pronounced. In 1952, Table 6.3 shows, a substantially greater proportion of those with family incomes over $7,500 a year described themselves as Republicans than as Democrats. By 1968, this had dramatically changed. The Democrats were stronger in each stratum, but their greatest gains had come in the highest. In 1968 as in 1952, the percentage identifying with the Democratic party went down with movement from the lowest to the highest income stratum, while the Republican share went up. That had not changed. But in 1968, the Democrats enjoyed a large plurality over the Republicans even in the over-$10,000 stratum. The Republicans received the allegiance of fewer than three voters in ten from families with incomes over $10,000 (the rough equivalent in purchasing power to $7,500 and more in 1952). Only when family income reached $15,000 a year did Republicans begin to receive more support that the Democrats, and even here the margin was modest.

In 1968, the Democrats had a decisive lead among those who describe themselves as "middle-class" or "upper-class." And while nearly half of today's college students are independents, those claiming a party attachment are Democrats by a margin approaching two to one.[43]

	DEMOCRAT	REPUBLICAN
	(Percent)	(Percent)
Middle-class and upper-class (in self-attribution of class position) (n = 448)	56	44
College Students (n = 578)	65	35

There can be little doubt that a majority of the American middle class—imprecise as that category is—at the end of the 1960s were Democrats.

Furthermore, the advantage which the Republicans still hold among those in the *upper reaches* of the middle class disappears among the young. A majority of those over forty with family incomes of $15,000 and higher are Republicans; but a majority of college students from families with such incomes are Democrats:[44]

	DEMOCRAT	REPUBLICAN
	(Percent)	(Percent)
Respondents 40 years and older	39	61
College students	59	41

The Democrats are the majority party in large measure because they have successfully transformed themselves from a party of "have-nots" to a party of "haves." They compete effectively with the Republicans within the massive middle class of this age of affluence. Some important qualifications must be kept in mind. The Democratic party at the end of the 1960s is still substantially weaker among the middle class than among the working class. The upper reaches of the middle class give a clear, although not overwhelming, margin to the Republicans. We have

[43] The data on class are from the SRC 1968 Election Study, those on college students from the *Gallup Opinion Index,* 37 (July, 1968).

[44] These data are for 1968: for the college students, from the *Gallup Opinion Index,* 37 (July, 1968); for respondents forty and older from AIPO surveys 768 (September 17, 1968), 769 (September 24, 1968), and 770 (October 15, 1968).

been describing *party identification,* not actual voting. A number of short-term factors, including specific issues and candidate attractiveness, intrude to affect voting. The 1968 Republican presidential nominee, Richard Nixon, received the support of a majority of middle-class voters, while in 1964 Democrat Lyndon Johnson was the majority choice. It is nonetheless clear—and this is of the utmost importance to an understanding of contemporary partisan conflict—that at the end of the 1960s there were no tensions in the relationship of middle-class standing and Democratic allegiance. For the first time in the twentieth century, the Democrats were the choice of a majority of middle-class voters claiming attachment to one of the principal parties.

How did the Democracy come by this enhanced standing within the middle class? There are three primary precipitating factors. One was identified by Lubell in *The Future of American Politics,* when he wrote of "transplantation" occurring instead of conversion. That is, as large numbers of Americans moved up the socioeconomic ladder, they carried their Democratic identification with them. This is entirely consistent with what we know about party identification: that once formed it tends to persist. Many of those who entered the Democratic party as economic "have-nots" in the 1930s—and their children—retained Democratic loyalties as their social and economic position rose.

The Democrats generally have been thought of as the "poor man's party" and at the outset of the New Deal, they certainly were mainly an aggregation of economic "have nots." The rising prosperity of the last twenty years, however, has suddenly transformed the internal makeup of the Democratic coalition, lifting many of its members to a "have" status. . . . In view of the usual sharp division in voting along economic lines, one might expect people to turn Republican as they mount to better income heights. There has indeed been much of that, particularly in the last few and inflation-haunted years. But in large part, as the poor and underprivileged prospered and climbed they remained loyal to the Democratic party. The new middle class, which has developed over the last two decades, seems as Democratic by custom as the older middle-class elements are instinctively Republican.[45]

A second and related factor involves the *transformation* of the Democracy in tone and style into a party that is inviting to the now affluent. As many of the Democrats of the 1930s shared in a growing national prosperity, the character of their party changed. The rank-and-file began

[45] Samuel Lubell, *The Future of American Politics,* 2nd ed., revised (Garden City, N.Y.: Doubleday, 1956), pp. 61–62.

sending up different messages, and these were received. The Democracy abandoned much of the rhetoric of class struggle on which it had capitalized so well in the 1930s. And the *new middle class qua Democratic identifiers,* finding many like themselves in the party, saw nothing contradictory in being a person of rising socioeconomic status and being a Democrat. They would have perceived a conflict in the 1930s, but not in the 1950s and 1960s when such a large segment of the population was at the same time making the same journey.

Finally, a large segment of the middle class at the end of the 1960s is *new* middle class, that is, it occupies positions created by the economy of advanced industrialism, and thus is not unreceptive to the governmental programs and policies introduced as public responses to advance industrialism. The Democrats are, of course, the principal architects of these policies. The Republican party was the party of industrial nation-building, and was supported by an apparently large majority of the middle class associated with this enterprise. In the 1920s and 1930s (as earlier) the middle class was largely the *old* or *entrepreneurial* middle class. Since it had generally sought and benefited from Republican policies, its opposition to the departures of the New Deal is not surprising. Further, this old middle class was disproportionately Anglo-Saxon Protestant, and the attachments of WASPs in all class positions outside the South to the Republicans has been well established. As the middle class expanded after World War II, its composition was drastically altered. Many of the children and grandchildren of the 1885–1920 immigrants made the socioeconomic jump to the middle class, and their ethnic group attachments inclined them, for the most part, to the Democrats. The new middle class, moreover, had none of the stakes of the old in the earlier Republican programs. For example, it had no experience and no interest leading it into opposition to a substantial governmental role in regulating and managing the economy. The new middle class appears to give general support to the broad outlines of public policy which the Democrats have taken the initiative in defining.

In the 1930s, the Democracy was in a very real way the party of the "little guy," of the "have-not"; and the Republicans of the more secure and prosperous. In 1970, things had not moved full circle, but they had changed substantially, so much as to prompt a young Republican strategist who had worked for Richard Nixon's election in 1968 as special assistant to national campaign manager John Mitchell to proclaim ecstatically that his party was riding a wave to national majority status as the party of 'the people'—the white working-class and middle-class majority—over a Democracy which was the party of the American establishment:

Until the Nineteen-Sixties, the Establishment *was* basically conservative—the perpetuation of exhausted Coolidge-Mellon-Hoover politics—but in recent years, a new, *liberal* Establishment has replaced it. . . . A new Establishment—the media, universities, conglomerate corporations, research and development corporations—has achieved much of the power of the industrial and financial establishment dethroned politically by the New Deal. This new Establishment thrives on a government vastly more powerful than that deplored by the business titans of the Nineteen-Thirties. . . . Liberalism became the creature of Georgetown, Hyannisport and Brattle Street—a long way from Muscle Shoals on anybody's map; its captains were McNamara, Rusk, Dillon and Bundy of Ford Motor Company, the Carnegie Foundation, Dillon, Read and Company, and Harvard. There was no WPA culture or hot dogs for visiting royalty on the New Frontier: the Harvard Chief Executive and his Vassar First Lady brought Casals and *haute cuisine* to the White House.[46]

The Establishment is liberal, and it is solidly Democratic. The Democratic strongholds have come to be "the most expensive suburbs" and the watering places of "silk-stocking Megapolitans" (along with, of course, the Negro ghetto). There are some things right and many wrong in Phillips' book. It *is* a revealing commentary on the extent of change in the social composition of the party coalitions from the 1930s to the 1960s that a Republican strategist would belabor the Democratic party as being the home of the American establishment and thus unmindful of the needs of "the people."

The Parties and the New Ethnic Frontier

All this seems to suggest a rosy future for the Democracy. It has thus far maintained an ascendancy among Americans of low SES, while establishing itself as a major competitor for the support of the vastly expanded middle strata of the affluent society. In fact, its future as the majority coalition is not untroubled. One obvious "trouble spot" is not at all where most observers a decade-and-a-half ago expected, in the expanding circles of affluence, but in an old stronghold of the party.

The Democratic party outside the South came in the 1940s and 1950s to include large numbers of Negroes. For a time, it was able to incorporate them into the old New Deal coalition with little difficulty. But the

---

[46] Kevin Phillips, *The Emerging Republican Majority* (New Rochelle, N.Y.: Arlington House, 1969), pp. 83–88 *passim*.

conflict patterns which appeared fully after 1965 have made it impossible for white and black to rest easily together in one party in urban America. It had been relatively easy to unite blacks and whites in the cities behind a single party standard as long as many in both racial groups had as their most salient political concern an improvement of the standard of living. It is quite another when some of the bitterest conflict revolves around the demands, fears and resentments of blacks and whites as competing status groups.

At the end of the 1960s, both whites and Negroes in the big cities still favored the Democrats, as Table 6.4 shows. But the cracks in the coalition were everywhere.

TABLE 6.4

Party Identification of Whites and Negroes in Cities of
50,000 and More, 1968*

	DEMOCRAT	REPUBLICAN	INDEPENDENT
	(Percent)	(Percent)	(Percent)
Whites (n = 345)	39.4	22.0	38.6
Negroes (n = 149)	86.6	4.0	9.4

* Data from the SRC 1968 Election Study.

Negro Democrats, increasingly confident and politically assertive, with more political muscle provided by the growth of the urban black population, began running candidates from their own ethnic group, or insisting upon racially responsive whites such as John V. Lindsay in New York City. White Democrats, on the other hand, responded to the racial tension by rewarding racially conservative (many of whom were in no sense economically conservative) whites—for example, Louise Day Hicks in Boston, Mario Procaccino in New York, and Samuel Yorty in Los Angeles. In 1968 these racial differences carried over strikingly into presidential voting: Richard Nixon received virtually no support from Negroes, but won 53 percent of the white two-party vote in cities of 50,000 and more.

There is little likelihood that urban Democratic parties will find some easy escape from the dilemma imposed by the racial bifurcation. As long as whites and blacks are at each other's throats, it will be hard for the Democrats to keep both within the fold. The Republicans will benefit— how much cannot be determined.

The Parties and the Protestant-Catholic Divide

The U.S. was built on the immigration of peoples from varied linguistic and cultural traditions, and clashes involving the competing claims of the many immigrant groups for recognition, social standing, power, and influence have dotted the American political landscape throughout our history. As variegated as the ethnic struggles have been, the Protestant-Catholic division has been a great organizer. And the Democracy, we have seen, has been the partisan home of large majorities of Catholic Americans as it has done battle with a series of largely Protestant, and at times anti-Catholic, opponents—the Federalists, Whigs, and Republicans.

The Democrats gave something very concrete to the ethnocultural groups we describe by one of their characteristics, Catholic. For example, when they made Alfred E. Smith, an Irish Catholic, their presidential nominee in 1928, they were extending recognition, acceptance, legitimacy. And in return, they received regular electoral support. With the coming of the New Deal, Catholic status-group attachments to the Democracy were reinforced by economic attachments, since the preponderance of Catholics were in the groups which benefited most from the new social policies. Catholic Americans were an important part of the Rooseveltian coalition.

By the 1960s, however, the position of Catholics in American life had changed in a number of important ways. Many had moved up the socioeconomic ladder and were "haves" rather than "have-nots." They were less and less a beneficiary group, more a contributing group in Democratic welfare policies. Perhaps even more important, most Catholics were no longer "have-nots" in status terms, having gained a large measure of acceptance into national life. The Democratic party can no longer count upon status services as a cement to secure Catholics to its coalition.

The various ethnic-religious groups in white America are no longer status collectivities in serious competition. Religion has lost its saliency as a source of conflict; the greater tolerance of Protestants and Catholics for one another is the result, more than anything else, of the fact there are no longer meaningful status tensions between them. The only politically muscular ethnic chasm separates whites from blacks.

There are plenty of indications that the Democrats cannot now "count on" the "Catholic vote" as they once could. The state of Rhode Island has a largely Catholic population, the heaviest of any state in the

country. Its gubernatorial elections of 1962, 1964, and 1968 are therefore especially interesting. In all three, the minority Republican party
had as its candidate an Anglo-Saxon Protestant, John Chafee. Chafee's
religious-ethnic background was widely known and subject to no confusion. Yet in 1962 he defeated the incumbent Democratic governor,
an Italian Catholic. In 1964 he increased his margin of victory to a
resounding 61 percent to 39 percent, even though his Democratic opponent was Catholic and was running on the same ticket as Lyndon
Johnson, who carried Rhode Island with 81 percent to the 19 percent
for Republican Barry Goldwater. The Democratic nominee in 1964 was
young and personable, and his record bore not the slightest taint of
scandal, which is to say that the outcome cannot be accounted for by
Chafee's overwhelming superiority in intelligence or character. Chafee
again won easy election in 1966 before succumbing in 1968 to a Democrat whose ethnic-religious affiliation was Jewish, a group which is an
exceedingly small minority in Rhode Island. There are reasons, of
course, why Chafee won in 1964 and lost in 1968. The point is only
that the results are incompatible with any picture of white ethnocultural
identifications having much pulling power in electoral behavior.

Another case, not involving Republican-Democratic competition but
providing a striking commentary on the weakening of ethnic-religious
ties in voting, is provided by Gallup survey data from March, 1968,
when Robert Kennedy and Eugene McCarthy were challenging Lyndon
Johnson for the Democratic presidential nomination, just prior to Johnson's announcement of withdrawal. Gallup asked the question: "Suppose
the choice for president in the Democratic convention narrows down to
Senator Eugene McCarthy of Minnesota [with the same question asked,
substituting "Senator Robert Kennedy of New York" for McCarthy]
and President Lyndon Johnson. Which one would you prefer to have
the Democratic convention select?"

| | | | NO | | | NO |
	MCCARTHY	JOHNSON	OPINION	KENNEDY	JOHNSON	OPINION
Protestants	40	42	18	37	41	22
Catholics	37	47	16	33	47	20

In short, Kennedy and McCarthy—both Roman Catholics—were found
by this Gallup survey to be running better among Protestants than
among Roman Catholics; while Lyndon Johnson, a southern Protestant,

was doing significantly better among Roman Catholics than among Protestants.

Looking at the developments we have been describing, a number of Republican observers have voiced satisfaction and have begun to talk optimistically about their party's chances among ethnic-religious groups where historically it has been weak. Phillips, indeed, makes Catholic Americans an important part of "the emerging Republican majority."[47] However, it is far from certain that that optimism is called for. Two important qualifications must be placed upon the interpretation developed thus far.

First, while it seems clear that the ethnocultural groups identified loosely here as Catholic are no longer bound to the Democracy by strong interests as they were in the past, they are still Democratic allegiants. Identifications, once established, persist; the Democratic identifications of Catholics are persisting, although their initial precipitants have quite vanished. Catholics are substantially more Democratic, measured by either party identification or Presidential voting, and there is no indication yet of any significant diminution of the Democratic advantage (see Table 6.5). The "staying power" of party identification is impressive. Presumably there will be an erosion, but it will be slow.

The other qualification is of a quite different nature but is as important. The same developments that appear to be cutting into the Democratic claim on the Catholic vote are cutting into the historic Republican claim on the anti-Catholic or Protestant vote. The Democrats surely gained many votes as the "Catholic party," but they thereby lost many Protestant votes. What has now happened is that Protestant and Catholic no longer identify politically important socioeconomic and status collectivities. No longer will the Democratic or the Republican coalition be held together by ethnoculturally related divisions within white America.

The Parties and the South

No section of the United States has ever committed itself so completely to one political party as the South did to the Democracy for nearly a century after the Civil War. From the 1890s through the 1920s, the Northeast was firmly Republican, but that commitment is tepid by comparison. The South was literally a one-party region; competition was almost exclusively *intra*-party, not *inter*-party. Negroes

[47] Phillips, pp. 175, 186.

TABLE 6.5

Party Identification and Presidential Vote of Protestants and Catholics, 1952–1968*

	PROTESTANT						CATHOLIC					
	DEMOCRAT		REPUBLICAN		INDEPENDENT		DEMOCRAT		REPUBLICAN		INDEPENDENT	
	Number	Percent	Number	Percent	Number	Percent	Number	Percent	Number	Percent	Number	Percent
1952												
Party identification	561	(46)	404	(33)	249	(21)	216	(56)	69	(18)	100	(26)
Presidential vote	296	(36)	521	(64)			148	(52)	139	(48)		
1956												
Party identification	528	(43)	419	(34)	284	(23)	188	(52)	77	(21)	97	(27)
Presidential vote	317	(36)	567	(64)			136	(46)	161	(54)		
1960												
Party identification	337	(43)	273	(35)	167	(22)	142	(64)	34	(15)	46	(21)
Presidential vote	207	(34)	397	(66)			166	(82)	36	(18)		
1964												
Party identification	553	(51)	308	(29)	218	(20)	201	(58)	58	(17)	85	(25)
Presidential vote	496	(63)	296	(37)			214	(79)	58	(21)		
1968												
Party identification	470	(45)	314	(30)	271	(26)	177	(54)	51	(16)	98	(30)
Presidential vote	259	(39)	397	(61)			131	(60)	88	(40)		

* In 1968, 13 percent of the Protestant and 7 percent of the Catholic respondents voted for George Wallace.
Source: Data from the SRC election studies; made available through the Inter-University Consortium for Political Research.

were the only large social group with Republican inclinations, and they were effectively disenfranchised after the mid-1890s.

The South's fidelity to the Democratic party had three great supports. The one best understood is the mixture of experiences surrounding race and the Civil War. The Democracy came to function as the expression of white supremacy and regional loyalty. But important as this prop was, it could not have held up one-partyism for so prolonged a period by itself. Parallel support was provided by the region's status as a predominantly rural and farming area in those years when the dominant national thrusts centered around industrial nation-building: since the Republicans were quickly established after the Civil War as the principal partisan instrument of the interests surrounding industrialization, the Democratic party was the obvious vehicle for the dissenting and minoritarian interests of the agriculture South. The old Confederacy was the last major section to industrialize. The strength of these two supports naturally permitted construction of a third—tradition. Quite tangible interests underlay the South's commitment to the Democracy, but once established, that commitment had a life of its own. For a southerner growing up in, say, 1920, Democratic allegiance was "natural." Wasn't everyone around Democratic? We have repeatedly called attention to the persistence of party identifications; in the South that meant the persistence of massive Democratic loyalties.

By the end of the 1960s, the first two props had been kicked out; the third was still there, but the strains on it were immense and were warping it in strange ways. The Democratic party nationally, since the 1940s, and especially since 1961, had been giving much stronger expression than the Republicans to the attack on white supremacy. Thus race—which had led the region to the Democracy—was now leading it away. The South was the last region to industrialize, but after 1950 it was industrializing with a passion. Much of this new industrialism of the South behaved like industrialism three or four decades earlier in the Northeast: it was, for example, militantly anti–trade union, opposed to large-scale governmental intervention in social and economic life, and generally conservative. As the more mature business interests of the North were swinging significantly toward the Democrats, southern business was finding the Republicans much more acceptable. The region had acquired powerful interest collectivities around industrialization that considered the Republicans a natural home. That left tradition, bent but not completely bowed, as the only one of the three major supports remaining.

A new but relatively weak support of the Democratic party was provided by Negroes. In a final ironic twist, the ethnic group that had
long been Republican and a cause of white southern loyalty to the
Democratic party, had become overwhelmingly Democratic, and, at last
substantially freed from disenfranchisement and now a participant in
political life, was helping to keep up some tottering regional support
for the national Democratic party. But Negroes were leaving the South
in large numbers, and their impact was thus much less than it would
have been had they become voters three or four decades earlier. In
the mid-1960s, only 20 percent of the population of the eleven states
of the old Confederacy was Negro; in 1920 it had been 32 percent. And
the exodus of Negroes, brought on by the almost total collapse of the
relatively unproductive agriculture in which most were traditionally
engaged, still has not ended. Further, even if all of the restrictions and
restraints, both formal and informal, which have kept Negroes out of
southern politics so long are completely removed, Negroes will remain
a deprived group socially and economically, and this deprivation is in
itself a barrier to effective participation. In 1980, Negroes will be less
than 15 percent of the *actual electorate* in the South.

The net result of the developments sketched above has been a drastic
erosion of southern support for the national Democratic party, expressed
first and foremost in presidential voting. What had been consistently
the most Democratic section of the country became in the 1960s the
least Democratic! With only two exceptions in the presidential elections
from 1876 to 1956, the Democratic percentage of the presidential vote
in the South exceeded that in any other section.[48] And for twenty
consecutive elections (until 1956, when Dwight Eisenhower gained a
narrow mojority), the Democrats outpolled the Republicans in the
South, usually by overwhelming margins. Over the course of these
twenty-one elections, the Democratic candidates took 64.2 percent of
the major party vote in Dixie. From this lofty record, Democratic
fortunes declined so precipitously that in 1964 and 1968 the South
was the party's worst region. The Democrats' southern performance in
1964 was 11 percent less than their national share, and in 1968 12
percent less. In 1964, the Republicans did markedly better in the South

---

[48] In 1896, the South was solidly for Bryan, but the western states gave the
"Peerless Leader" a slightly bigger margin; in 1948, the third-party candidacy of
South Carolina Democratic Governor J. Strom Thurmond reduced Truman's
southern percentage to slightly under what he received in the border states.

than in the rest of the country. Hubert Humphrey won only 31 percent of the popular vote in the South in 1968, *nearly 20 percent less than any previous performance* by a national Democratic candidate, and finished last in a three-way race.

TABLE 6.6

Presidential Voting in the South, 1960–1968

	MAJOR PARTY VOTE PERCENT	PARTY PERCENTAGE IN THE SOUTH COMPARED TO PERCENTAGE NATIONALLY
1960		
Democrat	52.3	+ 2.2
Republican	47.7	− 2.2
1964		
Democrat	50.3	−11.0
Republican	49.7	+11.0
1968		
Democrat	30.9	−11.8
Republican	34.6	− 8.8
American Independent	34.3	+20.8

This Democratic decline in Dixie has occurred through a pattern of Republican gains and third-party protests that have not been uniform throughout the South. At its low ebb in the early years of this century, the Republican party was a feeble collection of Negroes (the relatively few not disenfranchised), patronage hangers-on, and "mountain Republicans."[49] It showed its first signs of reviving in the presidential election of 1928, when the Democrats nominated a Roman Catholic, Alfred Smith of New York. The revival began, then, when the national Democratic party came into the hands of a Northern and urban wing. In 1928, the Republicans managed to get 48 percent of the region's

[49] The principal concentrations of mountain Republicans were in southwestern Virginia, western North Carolina, and eastern Tennessee. Slavery was never extensive in these upland areas, and in 1860–1861 their inhabitants showed little enthusiasm for secession and for the planters' war. Key has summarized it nicely: "The upland yeomanry did not want to fight a rich man's war; the Democratic party was or at least became the planters' party and the war party. The Democratic party forced the hills into the War, and for this it has never been forgiven" (V. O. Key. *Southern Politics* [New York: Knopf, 1950], p. 283).

vote, but their fortunes were markedly different in the states of the outer South than in the deep south."[50] Hoover won five southern states with sixty-two electoral votes, and all were in the rim land. His share of the popular vote was 20 percent lower in the deep South.

	OUTER SOUTH		DEEP SOUTH	
	Number	(Percent)	Number	(Percent)
Hoover (R)	1,304,888	53.0	306,573	33.4
Smith (D)	1,149,018	47.0	609,293	66.4

Why would the Bible-belt, solidly Protestant heartland of Dixie stick with a Catholic Democratic nominee while the rim South was defecting? First, because its Democratic attachments were stronger. Less pluralistic, overwhelmingly rural, with a much larger Negro population historically and thus more obsessed with race, the deep South's commitment to the Democracy as the party of white supremacy and regional loyalty was far more complete. The one thing it would not tolerate from the national party was any "deviation" on race, and in 1928 there wasn't any. Unhappy about Smith, it nonetheless voted for him.

The states of the rim South were more diverse socially and economically. Their Negro populations had never been nearly as large proportionally, and their politics never so dominated by racial concerns. They began industrializing sooner, received a greater population movement from other sections of the country, and were less estranged from national life. The Civil War–racial support of Democratic allegiance was weaker, then, and there was more of a socioeconomic base on which to build an opposition party. "Presidential Republicanism," which refers to voting for Republican national nominees even though state and local politics are still one-party Democratic, began in the rim South, and Smith's Catholicism simply gave it a big short-term shove.

The Depression and FDR put a temporary damper on presidential Republicanism, but the further diversification of the region in the World War II and postwar years—especially in the rim South—assured its revival. In 1948, however, the principal electoral inroads into national Democratic allegiance did not result from the gradual construction of a Republican party on the same general policy and constituency base as

[50] The deep South states are South Carolina, Georgia, Alabama, Mississippi, and Louisiana; Virginia, North Carolina, Tennessee, Florida, Arkansas, and Texas comprise the outer or rim South.

elsewhere in the country, but rather from a regional third-party protest. Angered by the civil rights commitments of the national party, the States' Rights Democratic party was launched. The Republicans failed to carry a single southern state, but the States' Rights party took four. And where in 1928 the defections from the national ticket occurred in the rim states, in 1948 they were deep South.

	OUTER SOUTH		DEEP SOUTH	
	Number	*(Percent)*	*Number*	*(Percent)*
Truman (D)	2,186,140	57.1	444,747	32.1
Dewey (R)	1,182,262	31.0	200,707	15.0
Thurmond (States' Rights)	430,603	11.2	731,003	53.0
Other	24,115	.6	6,572	.5

The one thing the deep South would not tolerate in the national party was a racial "betrayal."

In the 1950s, Eisenhower did well in the South, aided by his immense personal popularity and the gradual development of his party's regional base. Following the longstanding pattern, he ran better in the outer South, winning Florida, Tennessee, Texas, and Virginia in 1952 and the same states plus Louisiana four years later.

In the 1960s, the two currents working against the national Democrats in Dixie came together. On the one hand, there was a firm sociopolitical base for the Republicans as the more conservative party, and large numbers of southerners were quite accustomed to voting Republican in presidential elections. On the other, civil rights matters reached high saliency, the national Democrats were clearly committed to advancing the position of Negro Americans, and racial protests by angry whites against the national party became intense. In 1960, Kennedy—burdened, too, by his Catholicism—lost the rim South to Nixon in the popular vote; each won the electoral vote of three states. In the deep South, the Democratic nominee ran well ahead of his Republican opponent but lost the electoral vote of two states—Alabama and Mississippi—to slates of unpledged electors entered as a protest. Then in 1964, historic voting patterns were completely scrambled as the Republican nominee became the expression of the southern racial protest. For the first time, the GOP did better in the deep South than in the rim states, sweeping all five states of the former. For the first time, too, the Democratic southern vote was less than the party's share in the country as a whole, and the Republicans did better in the South than anywhere else.

	OUTER SOUTH		DEEP SOUTH	
	Number	*(Percent)*	*Number*	*(Percent)*
Johnson (D)	4,919,146	56.9	1,177,965	34.1
Goldwater (R)	3,722,914	43.1	2,270,470	65.9

The 1964 election appears to have had a long-term importance—which, of course, the election statistics by themselves do not reveal—in a legitimizing of the GOP. For the first time a white southerner could acknowledge his Republicanism without feeling the slightest tinge of regional disloyalty. The old Civil War repute of the Republicanism as something unbecoming a southerner was pretty much erased.

In 1968, the Republicans again contested strongly for southern support, but as a moderately conservative center party between Wallace on the right and the national Democrats on the left. We can expect that the general demands of national electioneering and memories of the 1964 disaster, when they allowed their party to be closely associated with southern protest, will make this 1968 posture the norm in the future. In the deep South, the party of racial protest won decisively, and the national Democrats were reduced to one-quarter of the vote, their lowest in history. In the rim states it was a close three-way race, with the Republicans ending up on top.

	OUTER SOUTH		DEEP SOUTH	
	Number	*(Percent)*	*Number*	*(Percent)*
Humphrey (D)	3,389,559	33.6	1,188,763	25.2
Nixon (R)	3,995,510	39.6	1,127,147	23.9
Wallace (AI)	2,692,271	26.7	2,388,054	50.7

It seems apparent that the rim and heartland are still on very different courses politically, and that the latter will continue for some time to offer fertile soil for racial protests. There, the national Democrats appear to have been reduced to a political base in the Negro population. The rim states can be expected to sustain a Republican-Democratic competition resembling the national, with both parties generally competitive. Overall, the national Democratic party is now a minority in the South, the region which for so long massively sustained it.

We have referred to the weakness of the *national Democratic party* in Dixie. This is not at all the same as the weakness of the *Democratic party*. State Democratic organizations show no sign of collapsing. The Republicans have made impressive gains in state and local races in the rim states, but they remain generally weaker in much of the deep South. The continued strength of Democratic loyalties focusing on the state parties, as well as the rejection of the national party, are evident in these Gallup data:[51]

"IN POLITICS, AS OF TODAY, DO YOU CONSIDER YOURSELF
A REPUBLICAN, DEMOCRAT, OR INDEPENDENT?"

	REPUBLICAN	DEMOCRAT	INDEPENDENT
	(*Percent*)	(*Percent*)	(*Percent*)
Outer South			
1956 (n = 760)	26	57	17
1968 (n = 1,061)	21	49	30
Deep South			
1956 (n = 398)	13	72	15
1968 (n = 610)	13	41	46

The proportion describing themselves as Democrats has declined, and markedly in the deep South. Here is the protest. But there has been no increase in Republican identifiers. Even in 1968 only one deep South resident in eight took the Republican label, only one in five in the rim states. Here, clearly, is testimony to the pull of tradition, and to the continued success of the *state* Democratic parties in satisfying their constituents. It seems fairly certain that the label *independent* is for many a halfway house in a complete conversion to Republicanism.

The Parties and the Matter of Generations

From the 1930s up to the 1960s, older voters were found consistently to be more Republican than young voters. By the mid-1960s, however, this age-associated difference had completely disappeared, and voters over fifty were giving the Democrats as big a margin of support as twenty-one-to-twenty-nine-year-olds. Table 6.7 shows this striking shift.

[51] These data are from AIPO surveys 571, 572, and 573 (1956); and 765, 768, 769, 770, and 771 (1968).

TABLE 6.7

Party Identification by Age Groups, 1940–1968*

	September 1940 Percent	September 1944 Percent	October 1948 Percent	November 1951 Percent	December 1955 Percent	February 1960 Percent	September 1967 Percent	March 1968 Percent
21-TO-29-YEAR-OLDS								
Republican	31	31	29	24	29	23	22	22
	+15**	+14	+14	+17	+16	+22	+16	+16
Democrat	46	45	43	41	45	45	38	38
Independent	23	24	27	35	26	32	40	40
30-TO-49-YEAR-OLDS								
Republican	37	35	33	30	30	27	27	25
	+ 6	+ 9	+14	+11	+15	+21	+14	+19
Democrat	43	44	47	41	45	48	41	44
Independent	20	21	20	29	25	25	32	31
50 AND OVER								
Republican	41	40	40	39	43	35	30	30
	+ 1	+ 3	+ 2	– 1	– 4	+12	+16	+16
Democrat	42	43	42	38	39	47	46	46
Independent	17	17	19	23	18	18	24	24

* Source: AIPO Surveys 208 (1940), 328 (1944), 430 (1948); and *Gallup Opinion* Index 36 (June, 1968).
** Percentage more (+) or less (−) Democratic.

It seems evident that these changes in the partisan distribution of age groups are accounted for in large measure by the phenomenon of political generations, discussed briefly in the previous chapter (pp. 236–237). We noted there that Survey Research Center investigations indicated that the Democrats became the majority party not so much by converting Republicans from the old electorate as by attracting a decisive majority of the emerging electorate. Table 6.7 provides further confirmation of this interpretation. In 1951, any voter over fifty had come of political age prior to the Depression, in an era of Republican ascendancy, and the Republicans retained a slight lead over the Democrats among this pre-New Deal generation, while twenty-one-to-twenty-nine-year-olds, an entirely post–New Deal generation, gave the Democrats a seventeen-percentage-point margin. By 1968, however, a decisive majority in the past-fifty bracket had their formative partisan experiences in the years of Democratic ascendancy, and were as heavily Democratic as the young.

The Emerging? Majority

In the 1930s the Democratic coalition drew its prime support from economic have-nots, from white ethnocultural groups long on the outside in an Anglo-Saxon culture, and, geographically, from southerners. In 1970, affluence is continuing to thin out the ranks of the former; Catholic Americans are no longer on the outside but on the inside, where they appear as concerned as old-stock Protestants about the way the principal ethnic have-nots—Negroes—are attempting to get inside, and are doing more than a little flirting with the Republicans; and the South is the weakest section of the country for the national Democratic party, while that historic bastion of Republicanism, the Northeast, is the most Democratic. The middle class of the 1930s (as earlier) was solidly Republican, but the much larger middle class in 1970 is Democratic. Republican strategists talk confidently about their emerging majority in which southerners and Catholics are important components, wage a presidential campaign (1968) on behalf of the "forgotten American," and berate the Democracy—long the home of the "little guy"—as the "establishment party." Surely American politics changed mightily between 1935 and 1970!

What does the future hold? First, we can expect the professional and managerial stratum to solidify its position as the new political class. Affluent, cosmopolitan, of high and secure status; in control of the major bureaucratic hierarchies, including universities, big business corporations, foundations, the national news media, and the executive departments of government; expert in the new orthodoxies of science; this stratum will call the tune to which America marches—as much and as imperfectly as entrepreneurial business did in 1900. A significant portion of this stratum is Republican in its loyalties, but like the larger new middle class it became increasingly Democratic during the 1960s. As Phillips and others have noted, this growth of Democratic support has resulted not so much from the conversion of old-line business executives as from the vast multiplication of newer professional and managerial positions in the technological society.[52] There is no indication of a reversal of this Democratic trend, and here is the gloomiest indicator from the Republican perspective. It is not the number of votes of members of the professional and managerial stratum, but their opinion-influencing capabilities, and the fact that as long as this stratum is Democratic, the GOP will be cast in the role of resisting and reacting against the prevailing movement of the society rather than leading it. Here is the strategic role of the political class: it is tone-setting; the party it adheres to disproportionately is thus tone-setting; the other big party thereby becomes the principal home for elites who oppose these tones and directions.

The new political class and the Democrats as its partisan instrument should encounter challenges, often populistic in style, just as previous ruling classes continually met such challenges. It is hardly accidental that in the 1960s with Goldwater and Nixon the Republicans adopted a neopopulistic rhetoric. Wasn't the political class, the "establishment," Democratic? George Wallace left no doubt that, along with blacks, the new political class was a prime target. The American political landscape historically has been littered with assaults in the name of the aggrieved "common man" on national leadership insensitive to his needs. At times these challenges have been strong indeed, but over the long haul of American history they have lacked the resources to succeed.

The most salient development bearing on the party coalitions in the emergent society appears to us to be successful transformation of the Democracy from a low SES aggregation to the perfectly respectable home for the new middle class generally, and specifically for the professional and managerial stratum. From this base, with the often reluctant backing of the black underclass it imperfectly champions, with some "unthinking" support based on the persistence of Democratic

[52] See Phillips, p. 88.

loyalties, with impressive media support for its programs, with judicious manipulations of public policy to meet various constituency needs, the Democratic party should continue as the "sun," although it is not the "sun" that rose with Roosevelt.

Looking beyond specific elections with their peculiar blend of proximate issues and personalities, it is hard to find evidence of a general realignment likely to culminate in Republican ascendancy. If there is an emerging Republican majority, it will have to show up in party identification; there will have to be an increase in the proportion of the electorate which thinks of itself as generally Republican. There is not, thus far, any clear sign of this occurring. Compare, for example, party identification by region in 1956 and 1968.

In the Northeast and the Great Lakes area, the Republicans lost substantial ground over this twelve-year period. Elsewhere, they only maintained the share of the electorate allegiant to them in 1956. Only in the South did the Democracy lose support. Only in the farm belt states, with but fifty-one electoral votes, did Republican allegiants outnumber Democrats in 1968 (according to one of the survey organizations), and then by a statistically insignificant amount. Neither Gallup nor Survey Research investigations have uncovered evidence of the type of swing in party identification on which the case for a new Republican majority could legitimately be constructed.

Social Change and Party Response in the Contemporary Period

One is struck by the fact that contemporary change in political conflict in the United States is greater than what it would appear to be if observations were narrowly limited to party behavior. What are the causes of this lag, and what does it mean for the political system?

One important cause stems from the type of party America has, in the role which the parties now play and indeed have always played. Observers have approached this from a variety of angles, using different vocabularies, but have emerged with roughly the same conclusion. Lowi describes American parties as "constituent" rather than "responsible."[53] The responsible party is the policy-making or programmatic party; it stakes out coherent positions on issues, takes these to the electorate, and, if rewarded with a legislative majority, carries its program into law. By constituent Lowi means "that which constitutes . . . [having] some-

[53] Theodore I. Lowi, "Party, Policy and Constitution in America," in Chambers and Burnham, *The American Party Systems* (New York: Oxford University Press, 1967), pp. 239–241.

TABLE 6.8

Party Identification by Region, 1956 and 1968*

	REPUBLICAN		DEMOCRAT		INDEPENDENT	
	GALLUP	SRC	GALLUP	SRC	GALLUP	SRC
	Percent	*Percent*	*Percent*	*Percent*	*Percent*	*Percent*
NORTHEASTERN STATES						
(139 ELECTORAL VOTES)						
1956 (n = 1,909; 456)	43	42	37	31	20	27
1968 (n = 2,041; 385)	33	30	41	41	26	29
OUTER SOUTH STATES						
(81 ELECTORAL VOTES)						
1956 (n = 1,007; 295)	29	20	56	63	15	17
1968 (n = 1,324; 284)	22	13	46	60	32	27
DEEP SOUTH STATES						
(47 ELECTORAL VOTES)						
1956 (n = 419; 101)	12	10	71	82	17	34
1968 (n = 610; 80)	13	9	41	57	46	34
BORDER STATES						
(36 ELECTORAL VOTES)						
1956 (n = 515; 101)	39	27	49	55	13	18
1968 (n = 301; 140)	22	25	51	45	27	30
GREAT LAKES STATES						
(86 ELECTORAL VOTES)						
1956 (n = 1,108; 303)	40	32	36	35	24	33
1968 (n = 1,278; 252)	31	31	35	41	34	28
FARM BELT STATES						
(51 ELECTORAL VOTES)						
1956 (n = 582; 204)	38	37	40	39	22	24
1968 (n = 788; 117)	39	27	36	41	25	32
ROCKY MOUNTAIN STATES						
(33 ELECTORAL VOTES)						
1956 (n = 194; 65)	34	18	43	48	23	34
1968 (n = 274; 41)	34	29	43	49	23	22
PACIFIC STATES						
(62 ELECTORAL VOTES)						
1956 (n = 765; 165)	36	26	46	50	18	24
1968 (n = 912; 193	37	33	42	48	21	19

* Source: Gallup data from AIPO surveys 571, 572, and 573 (1956), and 765, 768, 769, 770, and 771 (1968). SRC data from the 1956 and 1968 Election Studies. (The state "assignments" to each region follow Phillips, with two exceptions. Northeast: New England and New York, New Jersey, Pennsylvania,

thing regular and essential to do—whether intended or not—with the structure, the composition, and the operation of the regime or system." The American parties, he argues, have not, through the long sweep of American political history, been program innovators, but have tended to deal exclusively with the constituent function. They have been instruments for organizing the government, for recruiting leaders, for bringing out the vote, for patching together a disparate array of interests to secure control of the machinery of government. "It is in this sense that party can be termed basically a container, composer, and cumulator, a statistical rather than a rational or conscious order. As such it may be a more or less passive channel for regular expression without influencing or being influenced much along the route. In this it is as much a part of the constitutional process as any institution could be. In other words, party in America continues to make possible a popularly based policy-making process without very much directing the policy outcomes themselves."[54] In Chapter 2, we made essentially the same point in a different context in observing that the American parties have never been instruments for effecting social change. Social change the United States has had aplenty, but the parties have been neither the initiators nor the custodians of it. Instead, they have been receptacles into which the various demands resulting from social change have been poured, and party leaders have, typically, tried to mediate among these demands on behalf of regime stability and system maintenance.

What these descriptions point to, of course, is a type of party which is inherently slow in reflecting and responding to social change. In terms of the larger political system, the parties are conservative. They are not "the first by whom the new is tried."

Over the course of American history, this party passiveness before social change has probably had a salutary effect, contributing to the capacity of the parties to perform a "peacemaking" or "reconciling" function. But in a period of exceptionally rapid and extensive change— and none has been more pronounced in this regard than our own—it

---

Delaware, and Maryland. Great Lakes: Michigan, Illinois, Indiana, and Ohio. Outer South: Virginia, North Carolina, Tennessee, Florida, Texas, and Arkansas. Deep South: South Carolina, Georgia, Louisiana, Alabama, and Mississippi. Border: West Virginia, Kentucky, Missouri, and Oklahoma. Farm Belt: Wisconsin, Minnesota, North Dakota, South Dakota, Iowa, Nebraska, and Kansas. Rocky Mountain: Montana, Wyoming, Idaho, Colorado, Nevada, Utah, Arizona, and New Mexico. Pacific: Washington, Oregon, California, Alaska, and Hawaii. The exceptions are Tennessee and Arkansas; Phillips assigned them to the Border State category.)

[54] *Ibid.*, p. 264.

also has the adverse effect of heightening the sense of unresponsiveness in the political system.

The lag has occurred, too, because of the nature of partisan identification. Party identification is an anchor holding a substantial portion of the electorate in place through all of the vagaries of American electioneering.[55] It is not hard to see why this is so. People develop affective orientations to important group-objects in their environment as part of the basic process of defining self. Whom am I? The question is answered: "A member of this family, but not of those; of this ethnic group but not that one; of this country but not those; of the Republican but not the Democratic party," and so on. Identification begins in childhood with the primary family group, and as the environment in which one moves enlarges a variety of secondary groups become foci for these positive and negative affective orientations. Positive identifications with important group-objects persist because the self is defined in terms of them. It is not an abstract attachment to something "out there," but rather a part of "who I am." People do indeed change their party identifications—Michigan's Survey Research Center has found that about 20 percent of the electorate have changed from one party to another—but since identification to party is one of those group identifications which give individuals a hold on their own identity, we can see why it is not casually tossed aside. This persistence of party identification means that the coalitions at any given moment *will reflect the social divisions of an earlier point in time.* The Republican and Democratic coalitions in 1970, while different in social group composition from the party coalitions of the 1930s, appear to be less different than the gap between American society of the 1930s and 1970s would suggest.

One example might clarify this. The Democratic party of the 1930s gave something quite tangible to white ethnocultural minorities. It offered a level of recognition which was denied them in the Anglo-Saxon-dominated Republican party. It is hard in 1970 to see the Democrats offering these same groups anything so valuable, but voting surveys

[55] For the best general description of the formation of party identification and its persistence for a large portion of the American electorate, see Angus Campbell, *et al., The American Voter* (New York: John Wiley, 1960), especially Chapters VI and VII. They write: "In a survey interview most of our citizens freely classify themselves as Republicans or Democrats and indicate that these loyalties have persisted through a number of elections. Few factors are of greater importance for our national elections than the lasting attachment of tens of millions of Americans to one of the parties. These loyalties establish a basic division of electoral strength within which the competition of particular campaigns takes place. And they are an important factor in assuring the stability of the party system itself" (p. 121).

show large majorities identified with the Democracy: for example, a large majority of Roman Catholics, in 1970 as three or four decades earlier, are Democrats. It is clear that the contemporary distribution is largely a statistical fact bred of the persistence of identifications, while in the 1930s the preference of Catholics for the Democratic party was the result of a conscious pursuit of concrete interests. When a social group attachment to a party coalition is exclusively residual, lacking an interest base, that social group is "ripe" for picking from the coalition as other differentations arise in the population which really matter to people, which really "hit them where they live." But the "picking" process may be slow, given the persistence of identifications based on differentations which once possessed vitality.

There is yet another reason why the American parties are slow in reflecting the politics of the emergent period. As ongoing organizations, they are dominated by men who came of age politically in an earlier period, whose political perceptions and allegiances predate many of the dramatic societal changes which this chapter has chronicled. Such a leadership is not totally bereft of a capacity to adapt; quite the contrary, its continuance demands adaptation. But it seems unavoidable in a period of rapid change that two established, middle-class parties whose elites are heavy with men who began their active political careers in the 1930s and 1940s would be somewhat slow in departing from the style and substance of the earlier agenda. This is especially true of congressional leadership, where power is vested in seniority, where the path to leadership winds through both age and districts which tend to be relatively insensitive to change.

A final principal source of the apparent slowness of the parties' response is even more directly linked to the amount and speed of change in this transition period. Americans in the 1970s find themselves facing a variety of problems growing out of affluence and technology—which were expected to resolve rather than cause problems. It seems clear that a substantial portion of the citizenry has been abruptly disabused of the notion that economic and technological development would certainly produce a happier nation, has been made far more keenly aware of the inordinate complexity of the good society. The perceptible public pessimism seems in large measure the result of the fact that many of our glossier successes have produced a cumulative reality which was unintended, a world nobody envisioned, and that large numbers of "successful people" find themselves dissatisfied before that new society yet lack any coherent "language" for charting a course from their dissatisfactions to public solutions. Indeed, it is often hard to acknowledge the legitimacy of these dissatisfactions since they are not those which the historic critical languages specified; they do not result, that is, primarily from scarcity. Americans in the 1920s know "that something is wrong," but the new "problems of success" are exceptionally misunderstood and a new critical language suited to their resolution is not yet in hand.

Party leaders are, then, groping. They face a troubled society but the sources of the trouble are so recent and unprecedented that they cannot effectively articulate the causes of dissatisfaction or delineate realistic solutions. The U.S. in the early 1970s stands at one of those rare points of massive transformation from one political agenda to another, perhaps more bereft than at the previous junctures of an appropriate critical language. So while contemporary problems may not in any sense be "greater" than in earlier periods, our party leaders seem ill-equipped to respond to them.

What effects has the lag in party response had thus far? For one thing, it appears to have contributed to a decline in the interest and confidence of many, especially younger, Americans in the parties as instruments to work with in resolving social problems. In the late 1960s, the percentage calling themselves *Independents* among twenty-one-to-twenty-nine-year-olds increased sharply, and all major surveys for the first time reported independents outnumbering both Democrats and Republicans. A 1968 Gallup survey of college students found 43 percent describing themselves as independents; in a similar 1969 survey independents were 44 percent.[56] Michigan's Survey Research Center reported that nearly 50 percent of their respondents aged twenty-one to twenty-nine disavowed any attachment to either of the major parties:[57]

	DEMOCRATIC (*Percent*)	REPUBLICAN (*Percent*)	INDEPENDENT (*Percent*)
21–29 (n = 270)	32.7	19.4	47.9
30–39 (n = 284)	52.8	21.1	26.1
40–49 (n = 322)	46.6	25.8	27.6
50 and over (n = 616)	50.5	30.2	19.3

For as long as we have survey data, of course, the proportion of young voters *Independent* has been substantially higher than of the

[56] *Gallup Opinion Index,* 37 (July, 1968), and 38 (June, 1969).

[57] These data are from the SRC 1968 Election Study, made available through the Inter-University Consortium for Political Research.

electorate as a whole, reflecting a lack of time in which to form strong party loyalties and a generally lower level of political involvement. And some of the big increase in the late 1960s undoubtedly had sources outside party response lag. The intense dissatisfaction of many young Americans with the positions on the Vietnam war of leaders in both major parties probably contributed significantly to a short-term deauthorization of party leadership. The assassination of two major political leaders who had exceptional strength among younger voters—John F. Kennedy and Robert F. Kennedy—temporarily detracted from the capacity of party to inspire. Still, there is reason to expect that the failure of both parties to win the measure of allegiance among the young which they did in the past has resulted in part from their inability to respond adequately to the demands of a new agenda to which the young—less attached to the concerns of the previous agenda—are especially sensitive.

Some significant measure of response can, nonetheless, already be seen. The environment has emerged as a major political issue in the 1970s. Awareness that many unintended increments of technology wreak havoc upon our air, water, and landscape surely is not new, but the high political saliency of appeals to "save the environment" is peculiar to the postindustrial state. This is so partly because the steady march of technology makes the problem objectively worse, but also because environmental squalor is made to appear far more unacceptable by the overall affluence of the society. Both Democrats and Republicans are showing that they appreciate the new political muscle of this issue. As it has become clearer that victories in the century-old American quest to produce more and more goods and services do not necessarily contribute to "the quality of life," party leaders have begun to give more public recognition to how complex the mix producing a good society is.

The question, then, is not whether the parties will respond, but whether they will respond fast enough. Parties in America have never been called upon to act as initiators of change, in the manner of the Communist party of the Soviet Union in the first three decades after it seized power, but the American system does require them to be responsive to change. The responsiveness of party leadership in the 1970s in style, rhetoric, and policy commitments appropriate to the new agenda will in significant measure determine how easy or how painful the transition to the new society will be.

Bibliographical Commentary

The literature and sources of data which bear on the subject matter of this book are exceptionally broad and diverse. The following is but a small selection of those which seem to be the most pertinent and useful, and which are therefore commended to the reader who desires to pursue further the themes and concerns of the present study.

A number of writers have tried to come to grips with fundamental dimensions of the American social and political experience. Alexis de Tocqueville's *Democracy in America,* although nearly a century-and-a-half old, remains a monument, an example of the best in big-minded social inquiry. It is available in a good abridged edition (New York: New American Library, 1956) and unabridged in a fine new translation (Garden City, N.Y.: Doubleday Anchor, 1969). Herbert Croly, *The Promise of American Life* (New York: Macmillan, 1909) is another work whose value has not been diminished by the passage of time. Louis Hartz in *The Liberal Tradition in America* (New York: Harcourt, Brace & World, 1955) emphasizes the importance of the absence of an aristocratic tradition. Seymour Martin Lipset, *The First New Nation* (Garden City, N.Y.: Doubleday Anchor, 1967) is a most valuable inquiry in historical sociology. On the contemporary United States, John Kenneth Galbraith, *The New Industrial State* (Boston: Houghton, Mifflin, 1967); and Theodore J. Lowi, *The End of Liberalism* (New York: Norton, 1969) are imaginative and penetrating, although written from very different perspectives.

Maurice Duverger, *Political Parties* (New York: John Wiley, 1959) remains a useful effort at cross-national comparison of party systems. Joseph LaPalombara and Myron Weiner, eds., *Political Parties and Political Development* (Princeton, N.J.: Princeton University Press, 1966) also provides interesting cross-national comparative perspectives. William Nisbet Chambers and Walter Dean Burnham, eds., *The American Party Systems: Stages of Development* (New York: Oxford University Press, 1967) is an excellent beginning in comparative analysis along the temporal dimension. Among the general histories of political parties in the United States written from a more traditional perspective, Herbert Agar, *The Price of Union* (Boston: Houghton Mifflin, 1950); Wilfred Binkley, *American Political Parties: Their Natural History*, 4th ed. (New York: Knopf, 1962); and Malcolm Moos, *The Republicans* (New York: Random House, 1956) are good sources of "names and events" information.

Some very good work has been done on the parties in more limited historical periods, especially for the pre-Civil War years. William Nisbet Chambers, *Political Parties in a New Nation* (New York: Oxford University Press, 1963); Richard Hofstadter, *The Idea of a Party System* (Berkeley and Los Angeles: University of California Press, 1969); Noble Cunningham, *The Jeffersonian Republicans* (Chapel Hill: The University of North Carolina Press, 1957); David Hackett Fisher, *The Revolution of American Conservatism* (New York: Harper & Row, 1965) on the Federalist party; Richard McCormick, *The Second American Party System* (Chapel Hill: University of North Carolina Press, 1966); and Lee Benson, *The Concept of Jacksonian Democracy* (Princeton, N.J.: Princeton University Press, 1961) provide a carefully reasoned and reasonably complete introduction to the early parties. No other period up to our own has been so closely studied, but there are still a number of valuable works. E. E. Schattschneider, *The Semisovereign People* (New York: Holt, Rinehart and Winston, 1960) on the 1890s; Richard Hofstadter, *The Age of Reform* (New York: Knopf, 1955) on the first two decades in the twentieth century; and David Burner, *The Politics of Provincialism: The Democratic Party in Transition, 1918–1932* (New York: Knopf, 1968), for the years specified in the title, are most useful. Samuel Lubell, *The Future of American Politics*, 2nd ed., revised (Garden City, N.Y.: Doubleday, 1956), especially the introduction and Chapter 6, is a penetrating analysis of the changes in partisan competition which occurred in the New Deal and Fair Deal years.

Elections and voting behavior have received extensive study, and an impressive body of literature is available. The especially notable work of the Survey Research Center of the University of Michigan is reported in three important publications: Angus Campbell, *et al., The Voter Decides* (Evanston, Ill.: Row, Peterson, 1954): Campbell, *et al., The American Voter* (New York: John Wiley, 1960); and Campbell, *et al., Elections and the Political Order* (New York: John Wiley, 1966). V. O. Key, Jr., *The Responsible Electorate* (Cambridge, Mass.: Harvard University Press, 1966) argues that this literature has given inadequate recognition to the rationality in voter choice. Gerald Pomper, *Elections in America* (New York: Dodd, Mead, 1968) is an excellent survey of elections and the electoral process. Walter Dean Burnham, *Critical Elections and the Mainsprings of American Politics* (New York: Norton, 1970) is a pioneering effort in the analysis of aggregate voting data.

Publications of the United States Bureau of the Census contain a broad array of economic and demographic data. Especially useful for the amount of material collected in a single source is the Bureau's *Historical Statistics of the United States, Colonial Times to 1957* (Washington, D.C.: U.S. Government Printing Office, 1960). The *Statistical Abstract of the United States* (Washington, D.C.: U.S. Government Printing Office, published annually) is, of course, a basic source. Kirk H. Porter and Donald Bruce Johnson, eds., *National Party Platforms, 1840–1964* (Urbana, Ill.: University of Illinois Press, 1966) is a complete compilation of the texts of major and minor party platforms. Svend Petersen, *A Statistical History of the American Presidential Elections* (New York: Frederick Ungar, 1963) brings together election returns by state for every presidential election up to 1960. Now, more detailed or extensive analysis has been provided for by the work of the Inter-University Consortium for Political Research (Ann Arbor, Mich.) The ICPR has collected and put in machine-readable form election returns by county for president, governors, and members of Congress for every election in American history. This immense collection of material is available on magnetic tape through member universities of the ICPR. Extensive survey data on voting behavior can be obtained through member schools of the ICPR and the Roper Center for Public Opinion Research (Williamstown, Mass.). The former's holdings include the biennial national surveys of the Survey Research Center of the University of Michigan. The Roper Center is a depository for the studies of such survey research organizations as the American Institute of Public Opinion (Gallup) and Roper Research Associates.

Index

Accommodation, politics of, 33, 34, 39, 43
Adams, John Quincy, 72, 80, 81, 84, 87, 93, 97, 99
Affluence, 243–256
  condition of, 244–247
  patterns in conflict, 254–256
  political implications of, 247–248
  technology and, 256–267
Agnew, Spiro, 261
Agriculture
  employment, 279, 281
    decline in, 110
    1800–1860, 62
    1860, 111
  mechanization of, 112
  paper money controversy, 120–121, 122
  populism, 120–124
  price declines, 131
  reaction to Industrializing Nation, 120–124
  in Rural Republic, 60–62
  and tariffs, 115
Alabama
  civil rights movement, 194
  cotton culture, 67
Alaska, open primary, 29
Alsop, Stewart, 270
American Can Company, 114
American Chemical Society, 257
American colonies, aristocracy and, 35
American Federation of Labor (AFL), 126, 191
  founding of, 124
  goals of, 126
  membership of, 125
  merger with CIO, 192
American Independent party, 207
American Institute of Public Opinion, 232
American party system
  advent of, 15–27
    aristocracy and, 16–20
    egalitarianism and, 20–27
  as body of notables, 8
  conflict situations, 34–45
    cultural discontinuity, 37–39
    geographic variations, 45
    social change, 44–45
    system confidence, 39–44
  constitutional setting, 45–53
    electoral system, 46–49
    federalism, 49
    one-man executive, 46
    response to change, 53
    separation of president and congress, 49–53
  electoral competition (1790–1860), 93–103
    race, conflict and, 103–108
    Republicans *vs.* Federalists, 93–95
    source of evenness, 99–100
    state-party systems, 100–102
    in subpresidential elections, 102–103

  Whigs *vs.* Democrats, 95–99
  electoral competition (1865–1928), 166–177
    patterns in competition, 169–177
    patterns in voter turnout, 166–169
  electoral competition (1926–1970), 228–240
    nationalization of politics, 233–235
    party coalition strength, 229–233
    social group composition of coalitions, 235–240
  Emergent Society, 281–311
    the majority, 303–305
    matter of generations, 301–303
    middle class, 281–289
    new ethnic frontier, 289–290
    Protestant-Catholic divide, 291–293
    social change and response, 305–311
    and the South, 293–301
  majority as "sun," 3–6
  majority-minority relationship, 3–7
  meaning of, 7–10
  minority as "moon," 6–7
  as organization, 8
  party identification, 232–233
  as party of mass supporters, 8
  1790–1860 (Rural Republic), 79–108
    Democrats and Whigs, 88–93
    electoral competition, 93–103
    Federalists and Republicans, 86–88
    positions in the agenda, 85–93
    race, conflict and, 103–108
    society and political agenda, 57–79
    structural overview, 79–85
  1865–1925 (Industrializing Nation), 147–179
    electoral competition, 166–177
    nation-building and, 150–152
    the parties in, 177–179
    positions in the agenda, 150–166
    race relations, 157–166
    society and political agenda, 109–147
    structural overview, 147–150
    urban based reform, 152–157
  1926–1970s (Industrial State), 205–242
    electoral competition, 228–240
    foreign affairs, 224–228
    the parties in, 240–242
    positions in the agenda, 207–228
    society and the political agenda, 180–186
    structural overview, 205–207
  spectrum of ideological argument, 31–32
  structure and style, 33–34
American Protective Association (APA), 143, 160, 161
American Railway Union, 125
American Republican party, 78, 160
  formation of, 92–93
  See also Nativism
American Smelting and Refining Company, 114

315

American Tobacco Company, 114
Anti-Catholicism, 92, 143–145, 159
Antimasonic party, 84
Anti-Semitism, 142, 145
Aristocracy, 16–20, 57
    American colonies and, 35
    collapse of, 18–20
    deferential style and, 58
    defined, 17
    nature of, 16–18
    Tocqueville on, 17–18
    transition to egalitarian system, 22
    U.S. avoidance of, 34–37
Arkansas
    civil rights movement, 194
    Ku Klux Klan, 145
Articles of Confederation, 70, 71
Ascriptive class society, 17–18
Australian ballot, 122

Baker, Newton D., 257
Baker v. Carr, 205
Banfield, Edward, 283
Bank of the United States, 30, 66, 90
    established, 65
    vetoed, 90
Beard, Charles A., 201
Beer, Samuel H., 25, 71, 156, 203
Belgium, immigrant quota, 147
Bell, Daniel, 257–258
Bell, John, 107
Benton, Thomas Hart, 73
Bessemer steel process, 113
Big business, growth of, 113–114
Bigler, William, 157
Bingham, Hiram, 219
Birth rate, 61
Blackhurst, James, 223
Blacksmiths Union, 124
Blaine, James G., 159–160, 218
Boeing Aircraft Corporation, 265
Borah, William E., 201
Boston, Mass
    ethnocultural voter identification (1916–1932),
        165
    population, 112
Bradley, John P., 210
Brandegee, Frank, 219
Breckinridge, John, 107
Brinkley, David, 260
Bristow, Joseph, 218
Brookhardt, Smith, 218
Brooks, Preston S., 105
Brown, John, 105
Brown v. Board of Education of Topeka, 139,
        194, 216
Bryan, William Jennings, 119–120, 123, 171,
        172, 218, 296
    campaign of 1896, 160–161
    Cross of Gold speech, 122
    failure as a reformer, 154–155
    nominations of, 151
Bryanite movement, 131, 171
Buchanan, James, 104, 106
Bundy, McGeorge, 289
Burnham, James, 275
Burnquist, J. A. A., 220–221
Business
    as new political class, 114–118
    reaction to New Deal, 187–190
    Republican party and, 151
    Roosevelt (Franklin D.) and, 187–190
    vertical integration, 113

Calhoun, John C., 72, 89
California
    admission to Union, 105
    Ku Klux Klan, 145
Canada, electoral system, 47
Capitalism, 59, 73, 91, 122, 126, 127, 188
    Rural Republic, 61
    See also Business; Economy
Capper, Arthur, 218
Carey, George, 203
Carnegie, Andrew, 115, 118
Carnegie Foundation, 278, 289
Caucus system, 83, 84
Census of 1870, 108

Chafee, John, 292
Change, party response to, 53, 305–311
Chiang Kai-shek, 202
Chicago, Illinois
    ethnocultural voter identification (1916–1932),
        165
    population, 112
China, 15
    communism, 27, 202
    modernization of, 44–45
Christian Democratic Party (Italy), 42, 43
Civil rights movement, 193–196, 214
    Democratic party plank (1948), 215–216
    sit-ins, 194
    southern strategy, 194
Civil War, 4, 38, 67, 71, 90, 108, 112, 124, 132,
        150, 157, 172, 295
Class and status, 267–275
    conflict, 268–274
        black vs. white, 269–271
        increasing saliency, 268–269
        student, 271–274
    established, disestablished, and nonestab-
        lished, 274–275
    meaning of, 267–268
Clay, Henry, 60, 72, 84, 99, 105
Clayton Antitrust Act, 180
Cleveland, Grover, 151, 152, 160, 169
    nominations of, 152
Cleveland Union Club, 118
Clinton, De Witt, 93
Coalition politics
    conservative, 50
    Democratic party, 212–214
    electoral strength, 229–233
    social group composition (1926–1970), 235–
        240
    See also New Deal
Colt, LeBaron, 219
Communications industry, development of, 132
Communism, 21, 27, 42, 202
    Soviet Union, 45
Compromise of 1877, 135
Conant, James, 257
Conflict
    affluence and, 254–256
    American party system, 34–45
        cultural discontinuity, 37–39
        geographic variations, 45
        social change, 44–45
        system confidence, 39–44
    economic (Rural Republic), 62–66
    ethnic, 140–147
        parties and, 158–166
        Rural Republic, 74–79
    slavery, 103–108
Congress of Industrial Organizations (CIO),
        185, 191–192
    formed, 191
    merger with AFL, 192
Connecticut
    election of 1816, 83
    Federalist electoral votes, 96
Conservatives
    in the Industrial State, 203–207
    meaning of, 203–204
    coalition politics, 50
    Democratic party, 212–214
Conservative party (Great Britain), 48
Constituency organization, 81–82
Constitutional Unionist party, 107
Coolidge, Calvin, 142
Cotton gin, invention of, 67
Cotton production (1790–1859), 67
Coughlin, Father Charles, 206
Couzens, James, 218
Craft unions, 124
Crawford, William, 83, 84
Cronkite, Walter, 260
Czechoslovakia, immigrant quota, 147

Daly, Gerald P., 78
Davis, James J., 142
Davis, John W., 162
De Gaulle, Charles, 70
Debs, Eugene V., 149, 206
Declaration of Independence, 19, 92

Delaware
  election of *1816*, 83
  Federalist party, 95, 96
Democratic party
  Conservative coalition, 212–214
  1840 platform, 92–93
  electoral competition (1790–1860), 95–99
  Emergent Society, 281–311
    age groups, 301–303
    majority and, 303–305
    middle class (old and new), 281–289
    new ethnic frontier, 289–290
    Protestant-Catholic divide, 291–293
    social change and response, 305–311
    and the South, 293–301
  factionalism (1920s), 162
  foreign affairs (1926–1970), 224–228
  formation of, 36
  House seats (1830–1860), 97–98
  Index of Loyalty, 212, 213
  industrial nation-building, 151–152
  interests (1830s–40s), 30
  intra-party division (1930s–40s), 210–218
    nativism, 158
    in the 1920s, 207–208
    partisan conflict (1930s), 208–209, 210
    party identification, 232–233
    race relations (1865–1925), 157–158
    split over slavery, 106
    struggle between Whigs and, 88–93
      economic policies, 89–90
      electoral competition, 95–99
      evenness of competition, 99–100
      Roman Catholic Church, 91–92, 93
    two-thirds rule, 104
  See also American party system
Democratic-Republican party, *see* Republicans,
    Jeffersonian
Depression of *1868*, 120
Depression of *1929*, 4, 64, 110, 125, 130, 133,
    169, 179, 180, 189, 190, 199, 206, 241, 247,
    298
  beginning of, 181
  class politics, 268
  per capita income, 185
  population, 112
Developing nations, borrowing of, 37
Dewey, Thomas, 299
Dillon, C. Douglas, 52, 289
Direct primaries, 153
District of Columbia, 105
Dolliver, Jonathan Prentiss, 218
Douglas, Stephen A., 104, 106–107
Dred Scott case, 105
Dubinsky, David, 191
Dulles, John Foster, 52

Easterlin, Richard A., 131
Economy
  demands on egalitarian society, 39
  employment distribution (1860–1930), 111
  growth of, 40
    industrial, 110–114
  Industrial State, 187–205
  productive capacity (1899–1913), 112–113
  Rural Republic, 60–68
    agriculture, 60–62
    boundaries of conflict, 62–66
    regional differences, 66–68
    vertical integration, 113
Edison, Thomas Alva, 257
Education
  college population, 272
  government expenditures, 249
  1875–1927, 133
  party identification and, 238
  Rural Republic, 61–62, 68
  school enrollment (1870–1969), 248
  student status conflict, 271–274
  and voter participation (1840–1900), 168–169
Egalitarianism, 16, 18, 20–27
  economic demands on, 39
  meaning of, 20–27
  race relations and, 195–196
  Rural Republic, 57–60
  Tocqueville on, 60
  transition from aristocracy to, 22
  variety of party in, 24–27

without revolution, 34–37
  working out of, 57–60
Eighteenth Amendment, 145
Eightieth Congress, 214
Eighty-sixth Congress, 214, 215, 227
Eisenhower, Dwight D., 223, 224, 229, 296,
    299
Elections
  popular vote
    1824–1860, 96–97
    1832–1852, 97, 98
    1868–1928, 167, 170, 174
    1932–1968, 230
  presidential vote
    Democratic percentage, 236
    by region, 107, 235
    Republican percentage, 175, 176
    in the South (1960–1968), 297
  1796, 58
  1800, 58, 85
  1816, 83
  1824, 83, 84, 96–97
  1828, 84, 97, 98
  1832, 84, 85, 90, 99, 228, 229
  1836, 84, 85, 99
  1840, 58, 85, 90–91, 97
  1848, 93, 97, 104
  1852, 93, 104, 105
  1856, 93, 104, 106
  1860, 106, 107
  1872, 229
  1876, 135, 157, 160, 169
  1880, 160, 169
  1884, 152, 160, 169
  1888, 152, 160, 169
  1892, 149, 152, 160, 169, 173
  1896, 119, 151, 160–161, 171, 172, 177, 296
  1900, 151
  1904, 117, 229
  1908, 151
  1912, 169, 170, 180, 206
  1916, 169, 171
  1920, 228, 229
  1924, 149, 161–162, 177, 229
  1928, 156, 206, 207–208, 228, 229, 297–298,
      299
  1932, 52, 172, 180, 187, 206, 207, 208, 209,
      228, 229
  1936, 180, 206, 229
  1940, 206, 221, 224, 228, 229
  1944, 52, 206, 224
  1948, 52, 206, 211, 221, 299
  1952, 221, 229
  1956, 229
  1960, 52, 297
  1964, 195, 221, 229, 281, 296, 297, 300
  1968, 211, 228, 251–253, 288, 290, 296, 297,
      300
  voter turnout, 52, 96, 166–169
Electoral College, 46, 206
Electoral competition
  1790–1860, 93–103
    race, conflict and, 103–108
    Republicans *vs*. Federalists, 93–95
    source of evenness, 99–100
    state party systems, 100–102
    in subpresidential elections, 102–103
    Whigs *vs*. Democrats, 95–99
  1865–1928, 166–177
    patterns, 169–177
    patterns in competition, 169–177
    patterns in voter turnout, 166–169
  1926–1970, 228–240
    nationalization of politics, 233–235
    party coalition strength, 229–233
    social composition of coalitions, 235–240
Electoral system, 46–49
Embargo Act of *1807*, 61
Emergent Society, 243–311
  affluence, 243–256
    condition of, 244–247
    patterns in conflict, 254–256
    political implications, 247–248
    technology and, 256–267
    transformation of interests, 248–254
  class and status, 267–275
    black *vs*. white, 269–271

established, disestablished, and nonestablished, 274–275
  student, 271–274
new political class, 275–281
  commonalities, 277–278
  influence, 278–281
party system, 281–311
  the majority, 303–305
  matter of generations, 301–303
  middle class, 281–289
  new ethnic frontier, 289–290
  Protestant-Catholic divide, 291–293
  social change and response, 305–311
  and the South, 293–301
technological society, 256–267
  public *vs.* private distinction, 263–267
  science as ideology, 262–263
  social problems, 258–262
Emerson, Ralph Waldo, 197
Employment
  agriculture, 279, 281
  decline, 110
  1800–1860, 62
  1860, 111
  economic distribution (1860–1930), 111
  labor force (1900–1968), 279–280
  manufacturing (1850), 66
  wage earnings, 125–126
England, *see* Great Britain
Ethnic conflicts, 140–147
  parties and, 158–166
  Rural Republic, 74–79
Everett, Edward, 89

Factions (party), defined, 80
Fair Deal, 218, 242
Family income (1947–1968), 245, 246
Farewell Address (Washington), 79
Farmer-Labor party, 220, 221
Farmers' Alliance, 121, 220
Federal Power Commission, 180
Federal Reserve System, 180
Federal Trade Commission, 180
Federalism, 49
Federalist, The, 80
Federalists, 25, 81, 82, 84, 291
  beginning of, 81
  decline of, 94–95
  electoral competition (1790–1860), 93–95
  factions, 87–88
  end of, 83
  formation of, 36
  position in political agenda, 86–88
  struggle between Republicans and, 84, 86–88
Fifteenth Amendment, 135, 194
Fifth French Republic, 46
Fillmore, Millard, 92, 106
Flacks, Richard, 256, 273
Ford, Henry, 118
France
  commercial retaliation against (1807–1809), 61
  Communist party, 48
  department administrative units, 47–48
  egalitarian revolution, 23
  Fifth Republic, 46
  Fourth Republic, 47–48
  middle class, 34–35
  Radical Socialist party, 29
Frazier, Lynn, 218
Free Soil party, 104
Freedmen's Bureau, 135
Frelinghuysen, Theodore, 92
Frémont, John Charles, 106
French Revolution, 35
Frickey, Edwin, 112

Galbraith, John Kenneth, 243, 244–245, 248, 249, 250, 256, 258, 265, 266, 276, 277
General Electric Company, 278
General Managers Association of Railroads, 125
General Motors Corporation, 190
Georgia
  cotton culture, 67
  populism, 137
  Republican strength (1797–1817), 96
  Whig strength, 101

Germany
  emigration, 78
  1790–1860, 75, 76
  1860–1929, 141
  immigrant quota, 146
  pride in political institutions, 41
Gersh, Harry, 283
Ghent, Treaty of, 86
Gladstone, Herbert John, 49
Goldwater, Barry, 221–222, 281, 292, 304
  convention vote, 222–223
  southern vote, 300
Goodman, Paul, 83
Grangers, 121
Great Britain
  ascriptive class society, 17–18
  anti-machinery riots, 64
  commercial retaliation against, (1807–1809), 61
  Conservative party, 48
  egalitarian system, 23, 24–25
  electoral system, 47
  emigration, 140
  1790–1860, 75, 76
  1860–1929, 141
  executive department, 50
  immigrant quota, 146
  Labour party, 25, 26, 48
  lend-lease, 199
  Liberal party, 25, 48–49
  per capita output, 39
  pride in political institutions, 41
  suffrage, 24, 25
  two-party system, 48–49
Great Society, 186
Greenbackers, 121, 131
Gross National Product (GNP), 61
  in *1865,* 113
  in *1890,* 113
  in *1929,* 113

Hale, Frederick, 219
Hamilton, Alexander, 36, 58, 63, 74, 79, 80
  nationalism of, 70
Hampton, Wade, 136
Hanna, Mark, 118
Harding, Warren G., 142
Harper's Ferry raid, 105
Harrison, Benjamin, 28
Harrison, William Henry, 58, 85
Hartford Convention, 86
Hat Finishers Union, 124
Hayes, Rutherford B., 135
Hays, Samuel P., 149, 154
Helvetius, Claude Adrian, 19–20
Hicks, Louise Day, 290
Hitler, Adolf, 199
Hoover, Herbert, 156, 187, 298
Howell, Robert, 218
Humphrey, Hubert H., 216, 230, 300
Hungary, immigrant quota, 147
Huntley, Chet, 260

Ickes, Harold, 187
Idaho, 175
Illinois, 66
  ethnocultural voter identification, 164, 165
Immigration
  by country (1860–1929), 141
  first restrictions, 146
  and "Melting Pot" politics, 140–147
  political cultures and, 38
  quotas, 146–147
  1790–1860, 75–79
  1900–1921, 140
  political cultures and, 38
  Roman Catholic, 75, 77
Immigration Act of *1921,* 163
Immigration Act of *1924,* 163
Income
  distribution (1929–1947), 184
  party identification and, 238, 240, 285
  per capita (1860–1920), 131
Independent party (Greenbackers), 121, 131
Independent Treasury bill, 90
Index of Loyalty, 211–214
India, 15

Indiana, 66
  ethnic-religious voter identification, 164
  Ku Klux Klan, 145
  Republican strength (1797–1817), 96
Industrial Revolution, 63
  agriculture and, 60–62
Industrial State (1926–1970), 180–242
  economic power, 187–205
  entrepreneurial middle class, 187–190
  growth of, 132–134
  humanization of industrialism, 183–186
  labor, 190–193
  Negroes, 193–196
  party system (1926–1970), 205–242
    electoral competition, 228–240
    foreign affairs, 224–228
    the parties in, 240–242
    positions in the agenda, 207–208
    structural overview, 205–207
  political power, 187–205
  politics in, 203–205
  power and technology, 196–202
  scale, interdependence, and managerial state,
      180–183
  social power, 187–205
  society and political agenda, 180–186
Industrializing Nation (1865–1925), 109–179
  businessmen as political class, 114–118
  ethnic heterogeneity politics, 134
  growth and society of scale, 132–134
  liberalism, 127
  melting pot politics, 140–147
  party system, 147–179
    electoral competition, 166–179
    nation-building and, 150–152
    the parties in, 177–179
    positions in the agenda, 150–166
    race relations, 157–166
    society and political agenda, 109–147
    structural overview, 147–150
    urban based reform, 152–157
  per capita expenditures (1850–1928), 133–
      134
  per capita income (1860–1920), 131
  politics of rapid growth, 109–110
  race politics, 135–140, 157–166
  reactions to, 120–130
    agrarian, 120–124
    urban middle class, 127–130
    urban working class, 124–127
  sectional politics, 130–132
  shaping of, 110–114
  society and political agenda, 109–147
  supportive culture, 118–120
  urban reactions to, 124–130
Interest groups, 24
International Economic Association Confer-
    ence, 110
Interstate Commerce Commission, 180
Ireland
  emigration, 78
    1790–1860, 75, 76
    1860–1929, 141
  immigrant quota, 146
Isolationism, 196–197, 225–226
  ethnic groups and, 200
  legislation (1933–1941), 226
Italy
  emigration
    1790–1859, 76
    1860–1929, 141
  immigrant quota, 147
  Left Socialist party, 42
  pride in political institutions, 41
  unification of, 37–38
Iversen, Gudmund R., 173

Jackson, Andrew, 31, 60, 66, 70, 72, 74, 84,
    85, 89, 151, 154, 172, 189
  bank veto, 90
  election of 1828, 97, 98–99
Jefferson, Thomas, 19, 36, 58, 63, 68, 70, 73,
    79, 80, 92, 93, 120, 151, 154, 172, 189,
    196
  southern popularity, 66–67
Jeffersonian Republicans, see Republicans, Jef-
    fersonian

Jensen, Richard, 164
Jews
  hostility toward (1902), 142–143
  immigration, 142
  party identification, 238–239
Jim Crow system, 135–140
  end of, 195
  in industrial state, 193–196
  populists and, 137–139
  southern conservatives and, 136, 137
  unconstitutionality, 194
Johnson, Andrew, 135
Johnson, Hiram, 201
Johnson, Lyndon B., 292, 300
Jones, Thomas, 136

Kansas, 105
Kendall, Wilmoore, 203
Kennedy, John F., 217, 311
Kennedy, Robert F., 292, 311
Kentucky, 85
  Republican strength (1797–1817), 96
Kernan, Francis, 142
Keyes, Henry, 219
King, Rufus, 83
Knights of Labor, 124
  membership, 125
Know-Nothing party, 78, 92, 93, 105, 106
Korean War, 202, 229
Ku Klux Klan, 135, 143, 161, 162
  founded, 145
Kuznets, Simon, 110

La Follette, Philip, 220
La Follette, Robert, Sr., 150, 201, 218, 220
La Follette, Robert, Jr., 201, 220
Labor, 190–193
Labor-Management Relations Act, 192, 214
Labour party (Great Britain), 25, 26, 48
Ladd, Edwin, 218
Ladies' Garment Workers Union, 191
Land ownership, colonial, 35
Lane, Robert, 41, 246–247
League of Nations, 198, 227
Left-Socialist party (Italy), 42
Lemke, William, 206
Lend-lease, 199
Leo XIII, Pope, 143
Lewis, John L., 191
Liberal party (Great Britain), 25, 48–49
Liberalism, 36, 58, 189, 201
  in the Industrial State, 203–207
  Industrializing Nation, 127
  meaning of, 203–204
  New Deal, 123
  political culture and, 35–36
  Rural Republic, 63
  traditional enemies of, 58–59
Lincoln, Abraham, 238
Lindsay, John V., 31, 290
Localism, politics of, 68–70
Lochner v. New York, 116, 117
Locke, John, 19
Long, Huey, 206
Los Angeles, California, 112
Louis XIV, King, 70
Louis XV, King, 21
Louis XVI, King, 21
Louisiana
  Republican strength (1797–1817), 96
  Whig strength, 101
Louisiana Purchase, 89
Lowi, Theodore, 264, 305–306

McAdoo, William Gibbs, 161–162
McCarthy, Eugene, 31, 292
McCarthy, Joseph R., 220
McCarthyism, 202
McClosky, Herbert, 9
MacGregor, James, 189
McKinley, William, 119, 160–161, 169, 172
McKitrick, Eric L., 157
McNamara, Robert S., 289
Maddox, Lester, 31
Madison, James, 73, 80
Maine, 70, 99

admission to Union, 103
Managerial State, 180–183
  components, 181–182
Marshall Plan, 202, 225
Marx, Karl, 254
Maryland
  Federalist strength, 95
  Republican strength (1797–1817), 96
Massachusetts, 85
  election of 1816, 83
  ethnocultural voter identification (1916–1932), 165
  Federalist votes, 96
  Hartford Convention, 86
Medicare, 210
Meier, Hugo, 64
Melting Pot politics, 140–147
Metcalf, Jesse Houghton, 219
Metropolitanization, 112
Mexican-Americans, 77
Mexico, 41
Michigan, open primary, 29
Middle Class
  industrialization and, 127–130
  party identification, 283–289
Military expenditures (1847–1894), 197
Mills, C. Wright, 265–266, 267, 276
Minnesota, open primary, 29
Mississippi, 70
  civil rights movement, 194
  cotton culture, 67
Missouri, 66
  admission to Union, 103
Missouri Compromise of 1820, 103, 104
Mitchell, John, 288–289
Modernization, 44–45
Monroe, James, 83, 84
Montana, 175
  open primary, 29
Moses, George, 219
Munger, Frank, 223

Napoleonic wars, 67, 196
National Association for the Advancement of Colored People (NAACP), 193
National Association of Manufacturers, 162
National Farmers Alliances, 121, 220
National Labor Relations Act, 181, 188, 192
National Labor Union, 124
National Republicans, see Whig party
Nationalism, 26, 70
Nationalization, political (1926–1970), 233–235
Nation-building, 189
  appeal of, 70–72
  industrial, 150–152, 184, 192
Nativism, 78–79, 92, 145
  anti-Catholic movements, 143–144
  and Democrats, 158
  GOP and, 158
  populism, 123
  and Whigs, 92
  See also American Republican party
Nebraska, 104, 124
Nebraska Act, 105, 106
Negroes, 43, 77, 128, 132, 140, 168, 251, 303
  citizenship, 134
  civil rights movement, 193–196
  disenfranchisement of, 138, 139, 193
  in Industrial State, 193–196
  Jim Crow system, 135–140
  lynched (1882–1936), 193
  migration to North, 195
  New Deal and, 193
  party identification, 238–239
  population, 75, 195, 296
  Reconstruction period, 135
  Republican party and, 238
  slave population (1850), 75
  status conflict, 269–271
  suffrage, 136, 194
  See also Slavery
Netherlands, immigrant quota, 147
Neutrality, 200
Neutrality Act of 1937, 198
New Deal, 53, 156, 184, 201, 205, 209, 218, 221, 224, 242, 289, 291, 303
  business reaction to, 187–190

liberalism, 123
Negroes and, 193
Republican acceptance of, 210
New Freedom, 129
New Frontier, 218
New Hampshire, 99, 101, 102
  Federalist votes, 96
New Jersey, 175
  Republican strength (1797–1817), 96
New Nationalism, 156, 189–190, 242
New Orleans, Battle of, 84, 86
New York, 175
  American Republican party, 78, 92–93, 160
  constituency organization, 81–82
  Irish hostility toward Jews, 142–143
  labor health law, 116
  population, 112
  Republican strength (1797–1817), 96
  Whig party, 30, 90
Neilsen ratings, 260
Nineteenth Amendment, 149, 167
Nixon, Richard M., 230, 288, 290, 300, 304
Non-Intercourse Act of 1809, 61
Nonpartisan League, 220, 221
Norbeck, Peter, 218
Norris, George W., 201, 218
North Atlantic Treaty Organization (NATO), 202
North Carolina
  civil rights movement, 194
  Republican strength (1797–1817), 96
  Whig strength, 101
North Dakota, 175
Northwest Ordinance of 1787, 105
Nullification, doctrine of, 71, 86
Nye, Gerald P., 200, 201
Nye Committee, 200–201

Ohio, 66, 145
  Ku Klux Klan, 145
  Republican strength (1797–1817), 96
Oklahoma, 145
Olney, Richard, 125
Open Hearth steel process, 113
Open primary system, 29–30
Ordinance of Nullification (South Carolina), 71–72
Oregon, 145

Panic of 1837, 90, 150
Paper money controversy, 120–121, 122
Party identification, 237, 283–289
  by age groups, 302
  city whites and Negroes, 290
  class differences, 239
  income and, 238, 240, 285
  education, 238
  middle class, 283–289
  minority groups, 239
  Protestants and Catholics (1952–1968), 294
  by region (1956 and 1968), 306–307
  in the South, 301
Party Unity Score, 211
Pearl Harbor, bombing of, 201–202
Peckham, Rufus W., 116, 117
Pennsylvania
  constituency organization, 81–82
  Republican strength (1797–1817), 96
Per capita income, 39–40
  Depression of 1929, 185
  1932–1968, 185
Philadelphia, Pennsylvania, 112
  riots of 1844, 79
Pierce, Franklin, 104, 105
Plantation system, 67–68
Poland, immigrant quota, 147
Political agenda
  as organizing principle, 1–2
  1790–1860, 57–79, 85–93
  1865–1925, 150–166
  1926–1970s, 180–186, 207–228
  and social change, 2–3
Political culture
  avoidance of sharp discontinuities, 37–39
  defined, 34
  immigration and, 38

liberalism and, 35–36
North-South division, 38
South, 67–68
Political parties
advent of, 15–27
in egalitarian societies, 24–27
extra-parliamentary movements, 26
linkage, 24
nationalist movements and, 26
worldwide extent of, 15–16
See also American party system; *names of political parties*
Poll tax, 138
Pollution, 260, 261
Pomper, Gerald, 170
Population
college student, 272
1790–1860, 68–69
1870–1920, 132
metropolitanization of, 112
Negro, 75, 195, 296
redistribution of, 110, 112
slave (1850), 75
urbanization of, 112
Populist movement, 120–124, 129, 131, 144, 161, 171
agriculture and, 120–124
nativism, 123
platform of *1892*, 121–122, 152
in the South, 137–139
Poverty, 244
in the 1930s, 186
in the 1960s, 186
Primary elections, 29
runoffs, 47
Primogeniture, 35
Procaccino, Mario, 290
Progressive movement, 124, 128–130, 147, 148, 180
development of, 128–130
reforms, 152–157
Progressive party, 129, 149, 150, 153, 206
Progressive party (Wisconsin), 220
Prohibition, 145
Prohibition party, 149
Proportional representation, 47–48
Protestant ethic, 119
Public School Society, 79
Puerto Ricans, 77
Pullman, George, 117–118
Pullman Strike of *1894*, 117–118, 125

Race relations
egalitarianism and, 195–196
1790–1860, 103–108
1865–1925, 135–140, 157–166
Industrializing Nation, 135–140
Rural Republic, 103–108
Radical Reconstruction, 135
Radical Socialists (France), 29
Railroads, 132
development of, 113, 115, 117
Reapportionment, 205
Reconstruction, 132, 139, 157, 174
end of, 135, 136, 137, 158
Rees, Albert, 125
Reform Act of 1832 (Great Britain), 25
Reformist movements, 123
Regionalism
economic differences (Rural Republic), 66–68
geographic variations, 45
industrialization and, 119–120
one-party system, 38
in subpresidential elections (Rural Republic), 102–103
Registration, 231–232
Republican Association of Bucks County (Pennsylvania), 81
Republican party, 27, 29
acceptance of the New Deal, 210
Emergent Society, 281–311
age groups, 301–303
majority and, 303–305
middle class (old and new), 281–289
new ethnic frontier, 289–290
Protestant-Catholic divide, 291–293

social change and response, 305–311
and the South, 293–301
foreign affairs (1926–1970), 224–228
industrial nation-building and, 150–152, 155–156
intra-party divisions (1930s–40s), 218–224
nativism and, 158
Negroes and, 238
in the 1920s, 207–208
nominating convention roll calls (1940–1964), 222–223
partisan conflict (1930s), 208–209, 210
as party of business, 151
party identification, 232–233
race relations (1865–1925), 157–158
slavery and, 105–106, 150
split (1908–1912), 153, 174
suburban vote, 282
Republicans, Jeffersonian, 81, 82, 84
Congressional caucus of (1816), 83
electoral vote (by region, 1797–1817), 95
factions, 87–88
formation of, 36
House seats (1794–1822), 94
electoral competition (1790–1860), 93–95
position in political agenda, 86–88
struggle between Federalists, 84, 86–88
electoral competition, 93–95
Rhode Island, 96
Ripon, Wisconsin, 105
Rivers, L. Mendel, 31
Rockefeller, John D., 114, 118, 124
Roman Catholic Church
bigotry toward, 78, 79
ethnic cleavage (1865–1925), 158–166
immigration, 75, 77
parochial schools, 79
parties and (1960s), 291–293
party identification, 238–239
political agenda (1840s), 91–92, 93
Protestant antagonism, 92, 143–145, 159
Roosevelt, Franklin D., 74, 123, 130, 156, 157, 180, 181–182, 185, 198, 203, 209, 214, 221, 236, 298, 305
New Deal, 187–190
"quarantine the aggressor" speech, 199
Roosevelt, Theodore, 123, 129, 149, 150, 156, 180, 189
Republican vote (1912), 170
urban reforms, 153
Root, Elihu, 52, 199
Rorvik, David M., 259
Ross, Arthur M., 186, 244
Runoff elections, 47
Rural Republic, 57–108, 151, 188
agricultural society, 60–62
before bigness, 72–74
boundaries of economic conflict, 62–66
claims of nation-building, 70–72
ethnicity, 74–79
frontier, 66
industry, 61, 72–73
localized society, 68–70
party system (1790–1860), 79–108
Democrats and Whigs, 88–93
electoral competition, 93–103
Federalists and Republicans, 86–88
positions in the agenda, 85–93
race, conflict and, 103–108
structural overview, 79–85
per capita expenditures, 73, 74
regional economic differences, 66–68
society and political agenda, 57–79
working out of egalitarianism, 57–60
Rusk, Dean, 289

Sartori, Giovanni, 276–277
Scandinavia
emigration
1790–1859, 76
1860–1929, 141
immigrant quotas, 147
Schattschneider, E. E., 50, 171, 234
Schnore, Leo, 112
Science
government expenditures, 249
in technological society, 262–263
Secession, 86

Sectionalism, 98–99, 234–235
    election of *1860*, 107
    industrialization and, 130–132
Security and Exchange Commission (SEC), 181
Segregation, beginning of, 139
Senators, direct election of, 148, 153
Seventeenth Amendment, 147–148
Sherman Antitrust Act, 180
Short, William, 80
Singer Sewing Machine Company, 113
Slave trade, 105
Slavery, 66, 67, 79, 102–103, 128, 157, 158
    controversy (Rural Republic), 103–108
    population (1850), 75
    Republican opposition to, 150
Smith, Alfred E., 156, 161–162, 291, 297
    nomination of, 207
    southern vote, 298
Smith, Frank E., 217, 227–228
Smith, Gerald L. K., 206
Smith v. Allwright, 194, 205
Spanish-American War, 128
Social change
    parties and, 44–45, 305–311
    political agenda and, 2–3
Social Democratic party (U.S.), 126
Social Democratic party (West Germany), 26
Social Security Act, 181–182, 188, 210, 214
    House vote on, 209
Socialism, 149
    trade unions, 26
    weakness of, 126–127
Socialist Labor party (U.S.), 126
Socialist party (U.S.), 126, 206
Sociopolitical periods, concept of, 2–3
South Carolina, 60, 70, 136
    Ordinance of Nullification, 71–72
    Republican strength, (1797–1817), 96
South Dakota, 175
Stalin, Joseph, 26
Standard Oil Company, 113, 124
State party system, 28–29
    Rural Republic, 100–102
    competitiveness, 101
States' rights, 72, 88, 104, 154, 207
    in localized society, 69–70
States' Rights Democratic party, 206, 216, 299
Status politics (1970s), 267–275
Steel industry, development of, 113–114
Steelworkers Organizing Committee, 191
Stevenson, Adlai E., 229
Stimson, Henry, 52
Stokes, Carl, 31
Stokes, Donald E., 173
Stonecutters Union, 124
Students
    campus demonstrations, 254, 255–256
    college population, 272
    radicalism, 261
    status conflict, 271–274
Students for a Democratic Society (SDS), 254
Suffrage
    Great Britain, 24, 25
    Negro, 136
    property qualification for, 59, 85
    universal manhood, 24, 85
    white male, 59
    women, 148
Sumner, Charles, 105
Supportive culture, 118–120
Survey Research Center (University of Michigan), 229, 232, 233, 237, 239, 240, 303, 308
Swift Company, 113
System confidence, extent of, 39–44

Taft, Robert A., 221, 282
    convention vote, 222–223
Taft, William Howard, 153, 180
    Republican vote (1912), 170
Taft-Hartley Act, 192, 214
Tariffs, 117, 150
    agriculture and, 115
    nineteenth-century, 64
    reductions, 115
    Supreme Court and, 115, 116

Taylor, John, 88
Technological society
    affluence and, 256–267
    boredom, 261
    environmental pollution, 260, 261
    interdependence, 262
    new political class, 275–281
    old age and, 261–262
    public *vs.* private distinction, 263–267
    science as ideology, 262–263
    social problems, 258–262
Technology
    innovations in, 111
    power and, 196–202
Tennessee, 106
    Republican strength (1797–1817), 96
    Whig strength, 101
Texas, 145
Third-party movements, 149, 206–207, 211, 219–220
    "wasted vote" charge, 46
Thomas, Norman, 206
Thompson, Frank, 214
Thurmond, J. Strom, 31, 206, 211, 216, 296, 299
Tilden, Samuel J., 157
Tocqueville, Alexis de, 15, 19, 20, 21, 63
    on aristocracy, 17–18
    on democracy, 35
    on egalitarianism, 60
Totalitarianism, 21, 26–27, 119
Townsend, Dr. Francis E., 206
Trade Union Congress, 26
Transportation, development of, 132
Truman, Harry S., 214, 215, 216, 227, 296, 299
Two-party system
    break-up (1850s), 38
    deterioration of, 82–83
    emergence of, 84–85
    Great Britain, 48–49
    House vote (1872–1928), 173
    See also Democratic party; Republican party
Two-thirds rule (Democratic party), 104

Underwood-Simmons Act, 115
Union party, 206
Union of Soviet Socialist Republics (U.S.S.R.), 15
    communism, 26
    egalitarianism, 21–22, 23
    flow of power, 26–27
    industrial development, 119
    modernization, 44–45
    Russian emigration, 76, 141
    Russian immigrant quota, 147
Unions
    development of, 124–126
    economic power of, 190–193
    membership (1900–1968), 190, 191
        decline in, 249–250
    political position of, 250–251
    See also names of unions
United Auto Workers, 190
United Nations, 202, 217, 225
United States Constitution, 92, 116
    American political system and, 45–53
        electoral system, 46–49
        federalism, 49
        one-man executive, 46
        response to change, 53
        separation of president and Congress, 49–53
    in Convention, 103
    ratification of, 71
    slavery compromise, 103
United States Department of Health, Education, and Welfare, 278
United States Steel Corporation, 113, 190–191
United States Supreme Court, 194
    Dred Scott case, 105
    reapportionment, 205
    tariffs and, 115, 116
University of Pennsylvania, 278
Urbanization
    beginning of, 112
    industrialization and
        middle class, 127–130

working class, 124–127
reforms (after 1900), 152–157
Utah, open primary, 29

Van Buren, Martin, 28, 31, 58, 84–85, 104
  bank proposal, 90
  reputation of, 63
Venezuela, 15
Vermont, 101, 102
  Republican strength (1797–1817), 96
Vietnam war, 202
Vinson Naval Expansion Act, 199
Virginia
  Federalist strength, 95
  Republican strength (1797–1817), 96
Voting rights laws, 205

Wagner Act, 181, 188, 192
Wallace, George, 207, 251–253, 281, 304
  southern vote, 300
Wallace, Henry A., 206
War of 1812, 65, 86, 196
Warner, W. Lloyd, 267
Washington, George, 60, 80, 81, 175
  Farewell Address, 79
Watson, Tom, 137, 138, 139
Weaver, James B., 150
Webster, Daniel, 59, 85, 89
Weed, Thurlow, 106
Wheeler, Burton K., 201
Whig party, 28, 29, 78, 84, 85, 90, 104, 106,
  149, 291

Baltimore convention (1831), 60
businessmen support (1840s), 30
campaign of 1840, 90–91
  end of, 105, 106
  nativist groups and, 92
  struggle between Democrats and, 88–93
    economic policies, 89–90
    electoral competition, 95–99
    evenness of competition, 99–100
    Roman Catholic Church, 91–92, 93
White, Hugh Lawson, 85
White, Theodore, 140
White, William Allen, 127, 129
Whitney, Eli, 67
Whitten, Jamie, 217
Willkie, Wendell, 224
Wilson, Woodrow, 49, 115, 123, 129, 153, 165,
  169, 227, 257
Wisconsin
  open primary, 29
  Progressives, 220
Women, suffrage, 148
World War I, 130, 133, 198, 200, 257
World War II, 185, 194, 201, 225, 227, 242
  beginning of, 201–202
  end of, 202
Wyoming, 175

Yorty, Samuel, 290
Yugoslavia, 147
  immigrant quota, 147